College Accounting

College Accounting

Third Edition 1-15

Douglas J. McQuaig

Wenatchee Valley College

Houghton Mifflin Company   Boston

Dallas   Geneva, Illinois   Hopewell, New Jersey   Palo Alto

**This text and its related materials
are dedicated to the students who
will use them.**

Library of Congress Catalog Card No.: 84-81966

ISBN: 0-395-36472-8

ABCDEFGHIJ-RM-8987654

Contents

Preface

College Accounting provides students with a sound basic knowledge of accounting concepts and procedures, always taking into consideration the widely varying objectives students have. It offers:

- Vocational preparation for students entering the job market in accounting.
- A practical background in accounting for students embarking on other careers, such as clerical, secretarial, technical, sales, and managerial positions.
- Preparation and background for students planning more advanced studies in accounting.

Being a "chalk-in-hand" classroom teacher, I see the need for teachable accounting books, logically organized, liberally illustrated, and written in language that students can understand. In every way, I have endeavored to satisfy this need. In revising the text and its related materials, I have not departed from my original approach. However, since I am actively teaching the course, the material is continually reviewed and updated to reflect the latest developments and terminology affecting basic accounting. The accounting principles described are those endorsed by the Financial Accounting Standards Board and its predecessor, the Accounting Principles Board.

The fundamentals of accounting are presented in a practical, easy-to-understand manner. I believe in teaching by example. Consequently, each concept is well illustrated with specific business documents and report forms. An appropriate amount of repetition establishes fundamental concepts clearly in the minds of the students and enables them to develop confidence in handling more complex material. Each chapter relates new topics to the examples, concepts, and procedures presented in previous chapters. Even with computer-assisted accounting, entries for transactions must still be formulated, and the text will prepare students to make this transition.

College Accounting, Chapters 1–15, is designed primarily for use in a short course. Chapters 1–10 cover the full accounting cycle for a service business, including payroll forms and reports. Chapters 11–15 cover the full accounting cycle for a merchandising business. Despite the brevity of a one-quarter or semester course, a number of instructors want to give their students a brief exposure to certain topics on an optional basis. In response to their requests, the following appendices have been added:

- **Appendix A: Methods of Depreciation** (after Chapter 5) Briefly describes methods of depreciation, including the Accelerated Cost Recovery System.
- **Appendix B: Computers and Accounting** (after Chapter 6) Surveys computer hardware, software, and accounting applications.
- **Appendix C: Financial Statement Analysis** (after Chapter 15) Briefly describes percentages and ratios used to interpret information in financial statements.

Chapter Organization

- **Learning Objectives** Objectives state precisely what the students should be able to do when they complete the chapter. Each objective is also printed in the margin beside the relevant text discussion.
- **Examples** Each description of a concept is followed by an example.
- **Glossary** In addition to defining terms as they are introduced in the body of a chapter, the text presents the definitions again in the glossary at the end of the chapter.
- **Questions** Seven discussion questions, based on the main points, are included at the end of each chapter.
- **Classroom Exercises** For practice in applying concepts, eight exercises are provided with each chapter.
- **Problems** Each chapter contains four A problems and four B problems. The A and B problems are parallel in content and level of difficulty. They are arranged in order of difficulty, with Problems 1A and 1B in each chapter being the simplest and the last problem in each series being the most comprehensive.

Special Features

- **Extended Example** NuWay Cleaners, a fictional company, is used throughout Chapters 1–6 to illustrate accounting concepts.
- **Accounting Cycle Review Problem** This mini–practice set, following Chapter 6, involves the full accounting cycle for a fictional company called The Gamerama.
- **Representative T Accounts and Transactions** Simple charts organize this information for Chapters 1–6, 7–10, and 11–15.
- **Chapter 7: Accounting for Professional Enterprises** This is an optional chapter emphasizing the combined journal. (If the chapter is not used, an alternative set of achievement tests is available that omits the combined journal.)

Supplementary Learning Aids

- **Working Papers** Contain self-study review questions, an extended demonstration problem and solution for each chapter (new to this edition), forms for A and B problems and for the Accounting Cycle Review Problem, and answers to the self-study review questions. The Working Papers also include a Review of Business Mathematics and a list of check figures.
- **After Chapter 6** Sounds Abound, a computer practice set for one month in the life of a sole proprietorship service business. It requires only two hours of computer time or may be done manually.
- **Also after Chapter 6** A computer job simulation for a General Ledger Clerk at Lawson's Supply Center. Five computer job simulations are offered for use with *College Accounting*, Third Edition. All offer detailed and realistic training in specific accounting tasks.
- **After Chapter 10** Three practice sets are available. Each covers the basic accounting cycle, cash management, and payroll for one month in the life of a sole proprietorship service business. All three are published in a business papers format for the sake of realism.
  - Skate-O-Rama permits instructors to choose either a combined journal or a general journal.
  - C. W. Hale, M.D., has medical forms and business papers. A combined journal is used.
  - M. T. Chandler, Attorney at Law, has legal forms and business papers. A combined journal is used.
- **Also after Chapter 10** A computer job simulation for Payroll Clerk at Lawson's Supply Center.
- **After Chapter 11** A computer job simulation for Accounts Receivable Clerk at Lawson's Supply Center.
- **After Chapter 12** A computer job simulation for Accounts Payable Clerk at Lawson's Supply Center.
- **After Chapter 13** A computer job simulation for Cash Clerk at Lawson's Supply Center.
- **After Chapter 15** Sinclair Electronics, a practice set featuring business papers and special journals. It covers a one-month accounting cycle for a merchandising firm.
- **Also after Chapter 15** Denton Appliance and Air Conditioning, a computer practice set for a merchandising firm. Students first complete the set fully by hand, using a general journal; they then key the entries into the computer.
- **Also after Chapter 15** Cook's Solar Energy Systems, a computer practice set for one month in the life of a sole proprietorship merchandising firm.

Instructional Aids

- **Instructor's Manual** Includes teaching suggestions for each chapter as well as solutions to questions and exercises. Solutions to all A and B problems are filled in on replicas of the Working Papers.
- **Transparencies** Provide transparencies for solutions to all exercises and all A and B problems. Several teaching transparencies are also provided (new to this edition and supplementary to the figures in the text).
- **Test Bank** New to this edition. Includes objective questions (true-false and multiple-choice) for each group of chapters (Chapters 1–6, 7–10, and 11–15). Also provides final examinations in two versions (covering Chapters 1–10 and Chapters 1–15). These are printed in a format suitable for copying and distributing to classes.
- **Achievement Tests** Preprinted tests ready for class use. Each test covers two or three chapters in the text. Series A, which covers Chapters 1–15, provides 32 copies of each test. Series B is an alternative set of tests covering the same material.
- **Computer Test Bank** This is a computerized version of the objective questions in the Test Bank. We can provide software for your use or a printed test based on your selections from the Test Bank.

Acknowledgments

Again, I would sincerely like to thank the editorial staff of Houghton Mifflin for their continuous support. I am still deeply appreciative of the assistance given to me during the preparation of the first edition of this text by Professors Hobart Adams, University of Akron, and Joseph Goodman, Chicago State University. The cooperation of my colleagues, Professors Audrey Chan-Nui, Geneva Knutson, and John Wisen, has been most helpful. Especially, I want to thank my many students at Wenatchee Valley College for their observations and my former students Esther Loranger and Elizabeth Frack for their diligent proofreading of the text.

During the writing of the third edition, I visited many users of the text throughout the country. Their constructive suggestions are reflected in the changes that have been made. Unfortunately, space does not permit mention of all those who have contributed to this volume. Some of those, however, who have been supportive and have influenced my efforts are:

Joseph Adamo, Cazenovia College
Stanley Augustine, Santa Rosa Junior College
Harry Baggett, Diablo Valley College
Pat Bille, Highline Community College

Linda Block, Babson College
Kenneth Brown, University of Houston
Carmela C. Caputo, Empire State College
Clairmont P. Carter, University of Lowell
John Chestnutt, Allan Hancock Joint Community College
Trudy Chiaravalli, Lansing Community College
Howard West Clark, Polk Community College
Edward Coda, Leeward Community College
Lyle Couse, Chemeketa Community College
Martha J. Curry, Huston-Tillotson College
Leonard Delury, Portland Community College
Fred Fitz-Randolph, American Business Institute, New York
Mary Foster, Illinois Central College
William French, Albuquerque Vocational and Technical College
Stuart Fukushige, Leeward Community College
A. Steven Graham, Vincennes University
Marie Gressel, Santa Barbara City College
Barbara Hall, Wabash Valley College
Robert Hellmer, Milwaukee Area Technical College
Thomas Hilgeman, Meramec Community College
Donald L. Holloway, Long Beach City College
James Howe, Oakland Community College
Eugene Janner, Blinn College
Van Johnson, Midland College
Edward H. Julius, California Lutheran College
Andre E. Kelton, American Business Institute, New York
Donna L. Randall Lacey, Bunker Hill Community College
Elliott S. Levy, Bentley College
Lorraine Lombardi, Katherine Gibbs School, Boston
Loren Long, Elgin Community College
Joyce Loudder, Houston Community College
Donald MacGilvra, Shoreline Community College
Libby Miller, Columbus Technical Institute
V. Eva Molnar, Riverside Community College District
Robert Nash, Henry Ford Community College
M. Salah Negm, Prince George's Community College
Dolores Osborne, Central Washington University
Frank Patterman, Shoreline Community College
Vincent Pelletier, College of DuPage
Bernard Piwkiewica, Laney Community College
William Rodgers, Saint Paul's College, Concordia, Missouri
Frances Rubicek, Kalamazoo Valley Community College
Paul T. Ryan, Jackson State Community College
Viola Sauer-Singer, American Business Institute, New York
Lee H. Schlorff, Bentley College

Steve Schmidt, Butte College
Nelda Shelton, Tarrant County Junior College
Sharon Smith, Texas Southmost College
Mary Steffens, Crafton Hills College
Harold Steinhauser, Rock Valley Community College
Joseph Stella, New Hampshire College
Tom Vannaman, Midland College
William G. Vendemia, Youngstown State University
Russell Vermillion, Prince George's Community College
Florence G. Waldman, Kilgore College
Robert Weaver, Malcolm X College
Stan Weikert, College of the Canyons
Penny Westerfeld, North Harris County College
Maxine Wilson, Los Angeles City College
Theresa Wood, North Harris County College

As always, I would like to thank my family for their understanding and cooperation. Without their support, this book would never have balanced. Pertinent suggestions for updating the material were given by my daughter, Judith Britton, C.P.A., of Price Waterhouse; my son-in-law, Christopher Britton, C.P.A., of Touche Ross; and my son, John McQuaig, C.P.A., of McQuaig and Associates.

Douglas J. McQuaig

1 Analyzing Business Transactions: Asset, Liability, and Owner's Equity Accounts

Learning Objectives

After you have completed this chapter, you will be able to do the following:

1. Define accounting.

2. Record a group of business transactions, in columnar form, involving changes in assets, liabilities, and owner's equity.

3. Prepare a balance sheet.

Accounting is often called the language of business, because when confronted with events of a business nature, all people in society—owners, managers, creditors, employees, attorneys, engineers, and so forth—must use accounting terms and concepts in order to describe these events. Examples of accounting terms are *net, gross, yield, valuation, accrued, deferred*—the list could go on and on. So it is logical that anyone entering the business world should know enough of the "language" to communicate with others and to understand their communications.

The meanings of some terms used in accounting differ from the meanings of the same words used in a nonbusiness situation. If you have studied a foreign language, you undoubtedly found that as you became more familiar with the language, you also became better acquainted with the country in which it is spoken, as well as with the customs of the people. Similarly, as you acquire a knowledge of accounting, you will gain an understanding of the way businesses operate and the reasoning involved in the making of business decisions. Even if you are not involved directly in accounting activities, most assuredly you will need to be sufficiently acquainted with the "language" to be able to understand the meaning of accounting information, how it is compiled, how it can be used, and what its limitations are.

DEFINITION OF ACCOUNTING

Accounting is the process of analyzing, classifying, recording, summarizing, and interpreting business transactions in financial or monetary terms. A business **transaction** is an event that has a direct effect on the operation of the economic unit and can be expressed in terms of money. Examples of business transactions are buying or selling goods, renting a building, paying employees, buying insurance, or any other activity of a business nature.

Objective 1
Define
accounting.

The accountant is the person who keeps the financial history of an economic unit in written form. The term **economic unit** includes not only business enterprises, but also nonprofit entities, such as government bodies, churches, clubs, and fraternal organizations. All these require some type of accounting records. The primary purpose of accounting is to provide the financial information needed for the efficient operation of the economic unit and to make the information available in usable forms to the interested parties, such as owners, members, taxpayers, creditors, and so on.

Accountants follow rules in carrying out the various phases of the accounting process. In the United States, these rules or guidelines have been determined by an independent body called the Financial Accounting Standards Board (FASB) and its predecessors. The Financial Accounting

Standards Board is composed of seven highly skilled accountants who are experienced in various areas of accounting.

FIELDS IN WHICH ACCOUNTING IS NEEDED

A knowledge of accounting is most valuable in the following three fields:

- **Bookkeeping and accounting** Those who plan to enter the field as a vocation naturally need training in accounting.
- **Business management** Those aspiring to managerial positions must be able to understand financial reports, evaluate operations, and make logical decisions.
- **Personal recordkeeping** Every person—even one who does not plan to be an accountant or a business manager—benefits from a study of accounting, because such a study enables one to keep better records, understand financial reports, engage in financial planning and budgeting, invest savings, and prepare necessary tax returns.

Bookkeeping and Accounting

Considerable confusion exists over the distinction between bookkeeping and accounting. Actually the two are closely related, and there is no universally accepted line of separation. Generally, bookkeeping involves the systematic recording of business transactions in financial terms. Accounting is carried on at a higher level or degree than bookkeeping is. An accountant sets up the system by which business transactions are to be recorded by a bookkeeper. An accountant may supervise the work of the bookkeeper and prepare financial statements and tax reports. Although the work of the bookkeeper is more routine, it is hard to draw a line where the bookkeeper's work ends and the accountant's begins. The bookkeeper must understand the entire accounting system, exercise judgment in recording financial details, and organize and report the appropriate information.

Career Opportunities in Accounting

When it comes to career opportunities, accounting is commonly divided into three main fields, listed here in the order of number of positions available.

- **Private accounting** Most people who are accountants work for private business firms. The growing importance of accounting often provides opportunities for advancement into managerial positions, such as office managers, data processing supervisors, systems analysts, internal auditors, and controllers.
- **Governmental and institutional accounting** Local, state, and federal government bodies employ vast numbers of people in accounting jobs, not only for recordkeeping but also for auditing private businesses and individuals whose dealings are subject to government regulation. Many accountants in the federal government work as internal revenue agents, investigators, bank examiners, and the like. At all levels of government, there are traditional accounting positions.
- **Public accounting** Certified public accountants (or CPAs) are independent professionals, comparable to doctors and lawyers, who offer accounting services to clients for a fee. There are approximately 275,000 CPAs and more than 700,000 noncertified public accountants in the United States today. Accounting is easily the fastest growing of all the professions; it is expanding, in fact, at twice the rate the economy is expanding. Factors responsible for the growth of professional accounting include the increasing size and complexity of business corporations, the broadening of income taxes and other forms of taxation, and the increase in government regulation of business activities.

The Lay Person's Need for Accounting

Anyone who aspires to a position of leadership in business or government needs a knowledge of accounting. Managers and supervisors often have to keep financial records, understand accounting data contained in reports and budgets, and express future plans in financial terms. A study of accounting gives a person the necessary background, as well as an understanding of an organization's scope, functions, and policies. People who have managerial jobs must be aware of how accounting information can be developed for use as a tool in the decision-making process, and they should also be acquainted with the recordkeeping and management functions of accounting.

ASSETS AND OWNER'S EQUITY

Assets are properties or things of value owned by an economic unit or business entity, such as cash, equipment, buildings, and land. Always remember that a **business entity** is considered to be separate and distinct from the persons who supply the assets it uses. Property acquired by the business is an asset of the business. The owner is separate from the business and, in fact, has claims upon it. If no money is owed against the assets, then the owner's right would be equal to the value of the assets. The owner's right or claim is expressed by the word **equity,** or *investment.* You often see these terms in the classified-advertising section of a newspaper, where a person wants to sell the ownership right to a property, such as a house. Other terms that may be used include **capital,** *net worth,* or *proprietorship.*

Assets	=	**Owner's Equity**
Items or property of value owned by the business		Owner's right or investment in the business

Suppose that the total value of the assets is $10,000, and the business entity does not owe any amount against the assets. Then,

Assets	=	Owner's Equity
$10,000 =		$10,000

Or suppose that the assets consist of a truck that costs $8,000; the owner has invested $2,000 for the truck, and the business entity has borrowed the remainder from the bank, which is the **creditor** (one to whom money is owed). This can be shown as follows:

Assets	=	Liabilities	+	Owner's Equity
Items owned		Amount owed to creditors		Owner's investment
$8,000	=	$6,000	+	$2,000

We have now introduced a new classification, **liabilities,** which represents debts and includes the amounts that the business entity owes its creditors, or the amount by which it is liable to its creditors. The debts may originate because the business bought goods or services on a credit basis, borrowed money, or otherwise created an obligation to pay. The creditors' claims to the assets have priority over the claims of the owner.

An equation expressing the relationship of these elements is called the **fundamental accounting equation.** We'll be dealing with this equation constantly from now on. If we know two parts of this equation, we can determine the third. Let us look at some examples.

Ms. Smith has $9,000 invested in her advertising agency, and the agency owes creditors $3,000; that is, the agency has liabilities of $3,000. Then,

Assets	=	Liabilities	+	Owner's Equity
?	=	$3,000	+	$9,000

We can find the amount of the business's assets by adding the liabilities and the owner's equity:

$ 3,000 Liabilities
+9,000 Owner's Equity
$12,000 Assets

The completed equation now reads

Assets = Liabilities + Owner's Equity
$12,000 = $3,000   + $9,000

Or take Mr. Jones, who raises mushrooms to sell to canners. His business has assets of $20,000, and it owes creditors $4,000; that is, it has liabilities of $4,000. Then,

Assets = Liabilities + Owner's Equity
$20,000 = $4,000   +   ?

We find the owner's equity by subtracting the liabilities from the assets:

$20,000 Assets
−4,000 Liabilities
$16,000 Owner's Equity

The equation now reads

Assets = Liabilities + Owner's Equity
$20,000 = $4,000   + $16,000

Mr. Anderson, who has an insurance agency, has assets of $18,000; and his investment (his equity) amounts to $12,000. Then,

Assets = Liabilities + Owner's Equity
$18,000 =   ?   + $12,000

In order to find the firm's total liabilities, we subtract the equity from the assets:

$18,000 Assets
−12,000 Owner's Equity
$ 6,000 Liabilities

The completed equation reads

Assets	=	Liabilities	+	Owner's Equity
$18,000	=	$6,000	+	$12,000

Recording Business Transactions

Objective 2

Record a group of business transactions, in columnar form, involving changes in assets, liabilities, and owner's equity.

To repeat: Business transactions are events that have a direct effect on the operations of an economic unit or enterprise and are expressed in terms of money. Each business transaction must be recorded in the accounting records. As one records business transactions, one has to change the amounts listed under the headings Assets, Liabilities, and Owner's Equity. However, **the total of one side of the fundamental accounting equation should always equal the total of the other side.** The subdivisions under these three main headings, as we shall see, are called **accounts.**

Let us now look at a group of business transactions. Although these transactions illustrate a service type of business, they would pertain to a professional enterprise as well. In these transactions, let's assume that Alan Stevenson establishes his own business and calls it NuWay Cleaners.

Transaction (a)   Stevenson invests $32,000 cash in his new business. This means that he deposits $32,000 in the bank in a new separate account entitled NuWay Cleaners. This separate bank account will help Stevenson keep his business investment separate from his personal funds. The Cash account consists of bank deposits and money on hand. The business now has $32,000 more in cash than before, and Stevenson's investment has also increased. The account, denoted by the owner's name followed by the word *Capital,* records the amount of the owner's investment, or equity, in the business. The effect of this transaction on the fundamental accounting equation is as follows:

	Assets	=	Liabilities	+	Owner's Equity
	Items owned		Amounts owed to creditors		Owner's investment
	Cash	=			Alan Stevenson, Capital
(a)	+32,000	=			+32,000

Transaction (b)   Alan Stevenson's first task is to get his cleaning shop ready for business, and to do that he will need the proper equipment. Accordingly, NuWay Cleaners buys $18,000 worth of equipment for cash. It is important to note that at this point Stevenson has not invested any new money; he simply exchanged part of the business's cash for equipment. Because equipment is a new type of property for the firm, a new account, called Equipment, is created. Equipment is included under assets. As a result of this transaction, the accounting equation is changed as follows.

	Assets		=	Liabilities	+	Owner's Equity
	Items owned			Amounts owed to creditors		Owner's investment
	Cash	+ Equipment	=			Alan Stevenson, Capital
Initial investment	32,000		=			32,000
(b)	−18,000 +	18,000				
New balances	14,000 +	18,000	=			32,000
		32,000				32,000

Transaction (c)   NuWay Cleaners buys $4,000 worth of equipment on credit from Sanchez Equipment Company.

The Equipment account shows an increase because the business owns $4,000 worth of additional equipment. There is also an increase in liabilities, because the business now owes $4,000. The liabilities account called Accounts Payable is used for short-term liabilities or charge accounts, usually due within thirty days. There is now a total of $36,000 on each side of the equals sign. Because NuWay Cleaners owes money to Sanchez Equipment Company, Sanchez Equipment is called NuWay's creditor.

	Assets		=	Liabilities	+	Owner's Equity
	Items owned			Amounts owed to creditors		Owner's investment
	Cash	+ Equipment	=	Accounts Payable	+	Alan Stevenson, Capital
Previous balances	14,000 +	18,000	=			32,000
(c)		+4,000		+4,000		
New balances	14,000 +	22,000	=	4,000	+	32,000
		36,000			36,000	

Observe that the recording of each transaction must yield an equation that is in balance. For example, transaction **(c)** resulted in a $4,000 increase to both sides of the equation, and transaction **(b)** resulted in a minus $18,000 and a plus $18,000 *on the same side,* with nothing recorded on the other side. It does not matter whether you change one side or both sides. The important point is that whenever a transaction is properly recorded, the accounting equation remains in balance.

Transaction (d)   NuWay Cleaners pays $1,000 to Sanchez Equipment Company, to be applied against the firm's liability of $4,000.

In analyzing this payment, we recognize that cash is being reduced. At the same time, the firm *owes* less than before, so it should be recorded as a reduction in liabilities.

	Assets	=	Liabilities	+	Owner's Equity
	Items owned		Amounts owed to creditors		Owner's investment
	Cash + Equipment =		Accounts Payable	+	Alan Stevenson, Capital
Previous balances	14,000 + 22,000 =		4,000	+	32,000
(d)	−1,000		−1,000		
New balances	13,000 + 22,000 =		3,000	+	32,000
	35,000			35,000	

Transaction (e)   NuWay Cleaners buys cleaning fluids on credit from Troy Supply Company for $400. Cleaning fluids are listed under Supplies instead of Equipment because a cleaning business uses up cleaning fluids in a relatively short period of time—as a matter of fact, in one or a few cleaning jobs. Equipment, on the other hand, normally lasts a number of years.

	Assets	=	Liabilities	+	Owner's Equity
	Items owned		Amounts owed to creditors		Owner's investment
	Cash + Equip. + Supp. =		Accounts Payable	+	Alan Stevenson, Capital
Previous balances	13,000 + 22,000		3,000	+	32,000
(e)	+ 400		+400		
New balances	13,000 + 22,000 + 400 =		3,400	+	32,000
	35,400			35,400	

Accounting, as we said before, is the process of analyzing, classifying, recording, summarizing, and interpreting business transactions in financial or monetary terms. In relating these elements to the transactions of NuWay Cleaners, we made an analysis to decide which accounts were involved and then determined whether a transaction resulted in an increase or a decrease in those accounts. Then we recorded the transaction. After each transaction, the equation should still be in balance; the totals of both sides should always be equal. This example serves as an introduction to **double-entry accounting.** We have demonstrated that each transaction must be recorded in at least two accounts and that the equation must always remain in balance.

Summary of Transactions

Let us now summarize the business transactions of NuWay Cleaners in columnar form, identifying each transaction by a letter of the alphabet. To test your understanding of the recording procedure, describe the nature of the transactions that have taken place.

	Assets			= Liabilities +	Owner's Equity
	Cash	+ Equip.	+ Supp.	Accounts Payable	Alan Stevenson, Capital
Transaction (a)	+32,000			=	+32,000
Transaction (b)	−18,000	+ 18,000			
Balance	14,000	+ 18,000		=	32,000
Transaction (c)		+ 4,000		+4,000	
Balance	14,000	+ 22,000		= 4,000 +	32,000
Transaction (d)	−1,000			−1,000	
Balance	13,000	+ 22,000		= 3,000 +	32,000
Transaction (e)			+ 400	+400	
Balance	13,000	+ 22,000	+ 400	= 3,400 +	32,000
		35,400			35,400

The following observations apply to all types of business transactions:

1. Every transaction is recorded in terms of increases and/or decreases in two or more accounts.
2. One side of the equation is always equal to the other side of the equation.

THE BALANCE SHEET

Objective 3

Prepare a balance sheet.

Earlier we listed *summarizing* as one of the five basic tasks of the accounting process. To accomplish this task, accountants use financial statements. One of these financial statements, the **balance sheet,** summarizes the balances of the assets, liabilities, and owner's equity accounts on a given date (usually at the end of a month or year). The balance sheet shows the financial position of the company and is sometimes referred to as a *statement of financial position.* Financial position is shown by a list of the values of the assets or property, offset by the liabilities or amounts owed to creditors, and the owner's equity or financial interest. **Financial position,** as used in this accounting concept, means the same thing we would mean if we were to speak of the financial position of a person. A statement of financial position is a listing of what a business owns, as well as a listing of the claims of its creditors. The difference between the total amount owned and total amount owed is the owner's equity or net worth.

Perhaps you might have noticed, in the back pages of a newspaper, the balance sheets of commercial banks and savings and loan associations. The law requires them to publish their balance sheets in daily newspapers at certain times of the year. The purpose of these financial statements is to show the financial positions of these institutions; the total of the assets listed must equal the total claims of the depositors plus the owners' equity.

In the next chapter the fundamental accounting equation will be expanded to include revenue and expense elements. For the moment, however, we may refer to the equation as the *balance sheet equation* because only the three elements that appear on the balance sheet—assets, liabilities, and owner's equity—appear in the equation. And instead of presenting the equation in horizontal form as

Assets = Liabilities + Owner's Equity,

we can now present the same balances in the vertical form in which they appear in the balance sheet below:

Assets
=
Liabilities
+
Owner's Equity

After NuWay Cleaners records its initial transactions, the balance sheet as of June 15 would look like Figure 1-1.

Figure 1-1

NuWay Cleaners
Balance Sheet
June 15, 19–

Assets		
Cash	$13 0 0 0	00
Supplies	4 0 0	00
Equipment	22 0 0 0	00
Total Assets	$35 4 0 0	00
Liabilities		
Accounts Payable	$ 3 4 0 0	00
Owner's Equity		
Alan Stevenson, Capital	32 0 0 0	00
Total Liabilities and Owner's Equity	$35 4 0 0	00

Let's note some details about balance sheets:

1. The three-line heading consists of the name of the firm, the title of the financial statement, and the date of the financial statement. The heading is centered at the top of the page.
2. The headings for the major classifications of accounts (Assets, Liabilities, Owner's Equity) are all centered. The classifications are separated by the space of one line.
3. Dollar signs are placed only at the head of each column and with each total.
4. Single lines (drawn with a ruler) are used to show that figures above are being added or subtracted. Lines should be drawn across the entire column.
5. Double lines are used under the totals in a column.

You should know that balance sheets are presented in one of two forms, the report form or the account form. In the **report form,** assets are placed on top (upper part of the page), and liabilities and owner's equity are placed below (lower part of the page). In the account form, assets are placed on the left side of the page, and liabilities and owner's equity are placed on the right side of the page. The report form will be used throughout this text.

GLOSSARY

Accounting The process of analyzing, classifying, recording, summarizing, and interpreting business transactions in financial or monetary terms.

Accounts Subdivisions under the main headings of Assets, Liabilities, and Owner's Equity.

Assets Cash, properties, and other things of value owned.

Balance sheet A financial statement showing the financial position of a firm or other economic unit at a given point in time, such as June 30 or December 31.

Business entity A business enterprise, separate and distinct from the persons who supply the assets it uses. Property acquired by a business is an asset of the business. The owner is separate from the business and occupies the status of a claimant of the business.

Capital The owner's investment, or equity, in an enterprise.

Creditor One to whom money is owed.

Double-entry accounting The system by which each business transaction is recorded in at least two accounts and the accounting equation is kept in balance.

Economic units Business enterprises; also nonprofit entities such as government bodies, churches, clubs, and fraternal organizations.

Equity The value of a right to or financial interest in an asset or group of assets.

Financial position The resources or assets owned by an economic unit at a point in time, offset by the claims against those resources; shown by a balance sheet.

Fundamental accounting equation An equation expressing the relationship of assets, liabilities, and owner's equity.

Liabilities Debts, or amounts, owed to creditors.

Report form The form of the balance sheet in which assets are placed at the top and the liabilities and owner's equity are placed below.

Transaction An event affecting an economic entity that can be expressed in terms of money and that must be recorded in the accounting records.

QUESTIONS, EXERCISES, AND PROBLEMS

Discussion Questions

1. What do we mean by owner's equity?
2. What is the fundamental accounting equation? Why should the total amount on one side of the equation always equal the total amount on the other side of the equation?
3. Give five examples of assets.
4. What effect will the purchase of supplies on account have on the fundamental accounting equation?
5. What is a business transaction? Give three examples of business transactions.
6. What does a double ruling across an amount column indicate?
7. What are the three sections of the body of a balance sheet?

Exercises

Exercise 1-1 Complete the following equations.

a. Assets of $24,000 = Liabilities of $4,200 + Owner's Equity of $_____
b. Assets of $_____ = Liabilities of $16,000 + Owner's Equity of $31,000
c. Assets of $32,000 − Owner's Equity of $15,000 = Liabilities of $_____

Exercise 1-2 Determine the following values:

a. The amount of the liabilities of a business having $49,463 of assets and in which the owner has a $33,900 equity.
b. The equity of the owner of an automobile that cost $8,700 who owes $3,900 on an installment loan payable to the bank.
c. The amount of the assets of a business having $6,170 in liabilities, in which the owner has a $21,000 equity.

Exercise 1-3 Lois Parker, a real estate broker, owns office equipment amounting to $9,600; a car, which is used for business purposes only, valued at $8,150; and other property that is used in her business amounting to $4,600. She owes business creditors a total of $1,720. What is the value of Parker's equity?

Exercise 1-4   Describe the transactions recorded in the following equation.

	Assets		=	Liabilities	+	Owner's Equity
	Cash	+ Equipment		Accounts Payable		L. Parker, Capital
(a)	+9,450		=			+9,450
(b)		+2,400		+2,400		
Bal.	9,450 +	2,400	=	2,400	+	9,450
(c)	−1,700	+1,700				
Bal.	7,750 +	4,100	=	2,400	+	9,450
(d)	−800	+3,300		+2,500		
Bal.	6,950 +	7,400	=	4,900	+	9,450

Exercise 1-5   Dr. L. C. Jason is a chiropractor. As of April 30, he owned the following property that related to his professional practice: Cash, $960; Supplies, $350; Professional Equipment, $19,500; Office Equipment, $4,260. On the same date, he owed the following business creditors: Weston Supply Company, $1,740; Barton Equipment Sales, $950. Compute the following amounts in the accounting equation.

Assets_____ = Liabilities_____ + Owner's Equity_____

Exercise 1-6   Describe a business transaction that will do the following:

a. Increase an asset and increase a liability.
b. Increase an asset and decrease an asset.
c. Decrease an asset and decrease a liability.
d. Increase an asset and increase owner's equity.

Exercise 1-7   Dr. B. A. Stacy is a dentist. Describe the transactions that have been completed involving the asset, liability, and owner's equity accounts.

	Assets				=	Liabilities +	Owner's Equity
	Cash +	Prepaid + Insurance	Dental + Equipment	Office Furniture and Equipment	=	Accounts Payable	B. A. Stacy, Capital
Bal.	1,964 +	280 +	19,628 +	4,620	=	8,016 +	18,476
(a)	+1,200						+1,200
Bal.	3,164 +	280 +	19,628 +	4,620	=	8,016 +	19,676
(b)	−742					−742	
Bal.	2,422 +	280 +	19,628 +	4,620	=	7,274 +	19,676
(c)			+326			+326	
Bal.	2,422 +	280 +	19,954 +	4,620	=	7,600 +	19,676
(d)	−750		+1,850			+1,100	
Bal.	1,672 +	280 +	21,804 +	4,620	=	8,700 +	19,676

Exercise 1-8 Using the ending balances from Exercise 1-7, prepare a balance sheet, dated as of December 31 of this year. Use notebook paper.

Problem Set A

Problem 1-1A Townhouse Cleaners has just been established by the owner, Jean Moreland. It engages in the following transactions:

a. Moreland deposited $12,800 in the First State Bank in the name of the business.
b. Bought cleaning supplies for cash, $560.
c. Bought equipment for the business on account from Lundborg Company, $7,200.
d. Moreland invested an additional $3,200 in cash.
e. Paid Lundborg Company $1,600 as part payment on account.
f. Bought additional equipment for the business for cash, $1,420.

Instructions

1. Record the transactions in columnar form, using plus and minus signs, and show the balances after each transaction.
2. Prove that the total of one side of the equation equals the total of the other side of the equation.

Problem 1-2A R. C. Baker owns the Baker Real Estate Agency. On September 30 Baker's books show the following balances in assets, liabilities, and owner's equity accounts.

Cash	$1,200	Building	$36,000
Supplies	435	Land	9,000
Office Equipment	4,680	Accounts Payable	8,670
Office Furniture	5,400	R. C. Baker, Capital	48,045

Instructions

Prepare a balance sheet as of September 30 of this year.

Problem 1-3A The Clean-Rite Car Wash has just been established by the owner, J. C. Lloyd. The following transactions affect the asset, liability, and owner's equity accounts.

a. Lloyd deposited $18,200 in cash in the Illinois State Bank in the name of the business.
b. Bought equipment for use in the business for cash, $12,620.
c. Bought supplies consisting of brushes and soap on account from Camus Company, $685.
d. Paid cash for additional cleaning supplies for use in the business, $96.
e. Lloyd invested in the business his personal equipment having a value of $720.
f. Paid Camus Company as part payment on account, $120.
g. Bought additional equipment for use in the business on account from Jacobs Company, $1,400.

Instructions

1. Record the transactions in columnar form, using plus and minus signs, and show the balances after each transaction.
2. Prove that the total on one side of the equation equals the total on the other side of the equation.

Problem 1-4A   The Dallas Chiropractic Clinic is owned by F. L. Leedy. On August 31 the following accounts are listed in random order.

Professional Equipment	$18,760	Supplies	$ 721
Cash	2,356	Office Equipment	2,424
F. L. Leedy, Capital	23,336	Accounts Payable	925

Instructions

Prepare a balance sheet as of August 31 of this year.

Problem Set B

Problem 1-1B   Frome Appliance Repair has just been established by the owner, C. R. Frome, and engages in the following transactions:

a. Frome deposited $14,500 in the Nashua State Bank in the name of the business.
b. Bought equipment for use in the business for cash, $2,600.
c. Paid cash for supplies for use in the business, $720.
d. Bought additional equipment for the business on account from Downey Company, $7,280.
e. Invested an additional $1,860 in cash.
f. Paid Downey Company as part payment on account, $1,650.

Instructions

1. Record the transactions in columnar form, using plus and minus signs, and show the balance after each transaction.
2. Prove that the total on one side of the equation equals the total on the other side of the equation.

Problem 1-2B   A. R. Bergman owns the Bergman Advertising Agency. Bergman's books show the following balances in assets, liabilities, and owner's equity accounts as of August 31.

Cash	$1,440	Building	$42,000
Supplies	465	Land	12,000
Office Equipment	7,020	Accounts Payable	3,255
Office Furniture	6,300	A. R. Bergman, Capital	65,970

Instructions

Prepare a balance sheet as of August 31 of this year.

Problem 1-3B The Safety Insurance Agency has just been established by the owner, R. A. Baxter. The following transactions affect the asset, liability, and owner's equity accounts.

a. Baxter deposited $12,560 in cash in the California State Bank in the name of the business.
b. Bought equipment for use in the business for cash, $5,845.
c. Bought office supplies consisting of stationery and business forms on account from Excell Printers, $486.
d. Baxter invested in the business her own personal office equipment, having a value of $1,420.
e. Paid cash for additional office supplies for use in the business, $126.
f. Paid Excell Printers (creditors) $145 as part payment on account.
g. Bought additional equipment for use in the business on account from Brooks Company, $1,528.

Instructions

1. Record the transactions in columnar form, using plus and minus signs, and show the balances after each transaction.
2. Prove that the total on one side of the equation equals the total on the other side of the equation.

Problem 1-4B Down-Town Barber Shop is owned by R. P. Gower. On October 31, the following accounts are listed in random order.

Supplies	$783	Professional Equipment	$ 6,849
Cash	461	R. P. Gower, Capital	10,131
Accounts Payable	127	Furniture and Fixtures	2,165

Instructions

Prepare a balance sheet as of October 31 of this year.

2 Analyzing Business Transactions: Revenue and Expense Accounts

Learning Objectives

After you have completed this chapter, you will be able to do the following:

1. Record a group of business transactions in columnar form, involving all five elements of the fundamental accounting equation.

2. Present an income statement.

3. Present a statement of owner's equity.

In Chapter 1, we analyzed and recorded a number of transactions in asset, liability, and owner's equity accounts and did so in a way that was consistent with the definition of accounting. In this chapter we shall introduce the remaining two classifications of accounts: revenues and expenses. We shall record business transactions involving revenue and expense accounts in the same type of columnar arrangement we used in Chapter 1. Again let us stress that, after each transaction has been recorded, the total of the balances of the accounts on one side of the equals sign should equal the total of the balances of the accounts on the other side of the equals sign. We shall continue to use transactions of NuWay Cleaners as examples.

REVENUE AND EXPENSE ACCOUNTS

Revenues are the amounts of assets that a business or other economic unit gains as a result of its operations. For example, revenues represent earnings (inflows) of cash, or other assets, derived from fees earned for the performing of services, sales involving the exchange of goods, rent income for providing the use of property, and interest income for the lending of money. Revenues are *not* only in the form of cash; they may also consist of credit-card receipts or charge accounts maintained for customers.

    Expenses are the amounts of assets that a business or other economic unit uses up as a result of its operations. For example, expenses represent payouts (outflows) of cash, or other assets, for services received, such as wages expense for labor performed, rent expense for the use of property, interest expense for the use of money, and supplies expense for supplies used. When payment is to be made at a later time, an increase in an expense will result in an increase in a liability.

    Revenues and expenses directly affect owner's equity. If a business earns revenue, there is an increase in owner's equity. If a business incurs or pays expenses, there is a decrease in owner's equity. So, we place revenue and expenses under the "umbrella" of owner's equity.

Recording Business Transactions

Soon after the opening of NuWay Cleaners, the first customers arrive, beginning a flow of revenue for the business. Let us now itemize further transactions of NuWay Cleaners for the first month of operations.

Transaction (f) NuWay Cleaners receives cash revenue for the first week, $600. As we said, revenue has the effect of increasing the owner's

Objective 1

Record a group of business transactions in columnar form, involving all five elements of the fundamental accounting equation.

equity; however, it is better to keep the revenue separate from the capital account until you have prepared the financial statements. As a result of this transaction, the accounting equation is affected as follows (PB stands for previous balance, and NB stands for new balance):

	Assets			=	Liabilities +		Owner's Equity	
	Cash +	Equipment +	Supplies		Accounts Payable		Alan Stevenson, Capital	+ Revenue
PB	13,000 +	22,000 +	400	=	3,400	+	32,000	
(f)	+600							+600
NB	13,600 +	22,000 +	400	=	3,400	+	32,000	+ 600
		36,000					36,000	

Transaction (g)   Shortly after opening the business, NuWay Cleaners pays the month's rent of $400. Rent is payment for a service—the privilege of occupying a building. Because this service will be used up in one month or less, we record the amount as an expense. If the payment covered a period longer than one month, we would record the amount under Prepaid Rent, which is an asset account.

Expenses have the effect of decreasing the owner's equity. Later, we will consider revenues and expenses as separate elements in the fundamental accounting equation. At that time, through the medium of the financial statements, they will be connected with owner's equity. For now, however, we will list them under the heading Owner's Equity.

	Assets			=	Liabilities +		Owner's Equity		
	Cash +	Equipment +	Supplies		Accounts Payable		Alan Stevenson, Capital	+ Revenue	− Expenses
PB	13,600 +	22,000 +	400	=	3,400	+	32,000	+ 600	
(g)	−400								+400 (Rent)
NB	13,200 +	22,000 +	400	=	3,400	+	32,000	+ 600	− 400
		35,600					35,600		

Transaction (h)   NuWay Cleaners pays $240 in wages to employees for June 1 through June 10. This additional expense of $240 is added to the previous balance of $400, resulting in a total deduction of $640, since the incurring of expense has the result of reducing the owner's equity. Now the equation looks like this:

	Assets			= Liabilities +	Owner's Equity		
	Cash +	Equipment +	Supplies	Accounts Payable	Alan Stevenson, Capital	+ Revenue	− Expenses
PB	13,200 +	22,000 +	400 =	3,400 +	32,000 +	600 −	400
(h)	−240						+240 (Wages)
NB	12,960 +	22,000 +	400 =	3,400 +	32,000 +	600 −	640
		35,360			35,360		

Transaction (i) NuWay Cleaners pays $320 for a two-year liability insurance policy. As it expires, the insurance will become an expense. However, because it is paid in advance for a period longer than one month, it has value and is therefore recorded as an asset. At the end of the year or financial period, an adjustment will have to be made, taking out the expired portion (that is, the coverage that has been used up) and recording it as an expense. In most cases accountants initially record expenses that are paid for more than one month in advance as assets.

	Assets				= Liabilities +	Owner's Equity		
	Cash +	Equip. +	Supp. +	Ppd. Ins.	Accounts Payable	Alan Stevenson, Capital	+ Revenue	− Expenses
PB	12,960 +	22,000 +	400		= 3,400 +	32,000 +	600 −	640
(i)	−320			+320				
NB	12,640 +	22,000 +	400 +	320 =	3,400 +	32,000 +	600 −	640
		35,360				35,360		

Transaction (j) NuWay Cleaners receives cash revenue for the second week, $760.

	Assets				= Liabilities +	Owner's Equity		
	Cash +	Equip. +	Supp. +	Ppd. Ins.	Accounts Payable	Alan Stevenson, Capital	+ Revenue	− Expenses
PB	12,640 +	22,000 +	400 +	320 =	3,400 +	32,000 +	600 −	640
(j)	+760						+760	
NB	13,400 +	22,000 +	400 +	320 =	3,400 +	32,000 +	1,360 −	640
		36,120				36,120		

Observe that each time a transaction is recorded, the total amount on one side of the equation *remains equal* to the total amount on the other side. As proof of this equality, look at the following computation.

	Total		Total
Cash	$13,400	Accounts Payable	$ 3,400
Equipment	22,000	Alan Stevenson, Capital	32,000
Supplies	400	Revenue	1,360
Prepaid Insurance	320		$36,760
	$36,120	Expenses	−640
			$36,120

Let us now continue with the transactions.

Transaction (k)   NuWay Cleaners receives a bill from the Daily News for newspaper advertising, $180. NuWay has simply received the bill for advertising; it has not paid any cash. However, an expense has been incurred, and the firm owes $180 more than it did before, so this transaction must be recorded.

	Assets				= Liabilities +		Owner's Equity		
	Cash +	Equip. +	Supp. +	Ppd. Ins.	Accounts Payable	+	Alan Stevenson, Capital	+ Revenue −	Expenses
PB	13,400 +	22,000 +	400 +	320 =	3,400	+	32,000	+ 1,360 −	640
(k)					+180				+180
									(Advertising)
NB	13,400 +	22,000 +	400 +	320 =	3,580	+	32,000	+ 1,360 −	820
		36,120					36,120		

Transaction (l)   NuWay Cleaners pays $1,800 to Sanchez Equipment Company, its creditor (the party to whom it owes money), as part payment on account.

	Assets				= Liabilities +		Owner's Equity		
	Cash +	Equip. +	Supp. +	Ppd. Ins.	Accounts Payable	+	Alan Stevenson, Capital	+ Revenue −	Expenses
PB	13,400 +	22,000 +	400 +	320 =	3,580	+	32,000	+ 1,360 −	820
(l)	−1,800				−1,800				
NB	11,600 +	22,000 +	400 +	320 =	1,780	+	32,000	+ 1,360 −	820
		34,320					34,320		

Transaction (m)   NuWay Cleaners receives and pays bill for utilities, $220. Because the bill had not been previously recorded as a liability, the accounting equation is affected as follows:

	Assets				= Liabilities +		Owner's Equity			
	Cash	+ Equip.	+ Supp.	+ Ppd. Ins.	Accounts Payable	+	Alan Stevenson, Capital	+ Revenue	−	Expenses
PB (m)	11,600 −220	+ 22,000	+ 400	+ 320 =	1,780	+	32,000	+ 1,360	−	820 +220 (Utilities)
NB	11,380	+ 22,000	+ 400	+ 320 =	1,780	+	32,000	+ 1,360	−	1,040
		34,100					34,100			

Transaction (n)   Now NuWay Cleaners pays $180 to the Daily News for advertising. Recall that it had previously recorded this bill as a liability. The equation is shown below.

	Assets				= Liabilities +		Owner's Equity			
	Cash	+ Equip.	+ Supp.	+ Ppd. Ins.	Accounts Payable	+	Alan Stevenson, Capital	+ Revenue	−	Expenses
PB (n)	11,380 −180	+ 22,000	+ 400	+ 320 =	1,780 −180	+	32,000	+ 1,360	−	1,040
NB	11,200	+ 22,000	+ 400	+ 320 =	1,600	+	32,000	+ 1,360	−	1,040
		33,920					33,920			

Transaction (o)   NuWay Cleaners receives cash revenue for the third week, $830.

	Assets				= Liabilities +		Owner's Equity			
	Cash	+ Equip.	+ Supp.	+ Ppd. Ins.	Accounts Payable	+	Alan Stevenson, Capital	+ Revenue	−	Expenses
PB (o)	11,200 +830	+ 22,000	+ 400	+ 320 =	1,600	+	32,000	+ 1,360 +830	−	1,040
NB	12,030	+ 22,000	+ 400	+ 320 =	1,600	+	32,000	+ 2,190	−	1,040
		34,750					34,750			

Transaction (p)   NuWay Cleaners signs a contract with A-1 Rental to clean their for-hire formal clothes on a credit basis and cleans ten dress suits. NuWay bills A-1 Rental for services performed, $80.

A firm uses the **Accounts Receivable** account to record the amounts owed by charge customers. These receivable accounts represent credit, usually extended for thirty days. Since A-1 Rental owes NuWay Cleaners $80 more than before the transaction took place, it seems logical to add $80 to Accounts Receivable. Revenue is earned when the service is performed, and hence the corresponding increase in revenue. When A-1 pays the $80 bill in cash, NuWay records this as an increase in Cash and a decrease in Accounts Receivable. It does not have to make an entry for the revenue account, as that has already been done.

	Assets					= Liabilities +		Owner's Equity		
	Cash	+ Equip.	+ Supp.	+ Ppd. Ins.	+ Accts. Rec.	Accounts Payable	+	Alan Stevenson, Capital	+ Revenue	− Expenses
PB (p)	12,030	+ 22,000	+ 400	+ 320	+80	= 1,600	+	32,000	+ 2,190 +80	− 1,040
NB	12,030	+ 22,000	+ 400	+ 320	+ 80	= 1,600	+	32,000	+ 2,270	− 1,040
		34,830						34,830		

Transaction (q)   NuWay Cleaners pays wages of employees, $390, for June 11 through June 24.

	Assets					= Liabilities +		Owner's Equity		
	Cash	+ Equip.	+ Supp.	+ Ppd. Ins.	+ Accts. Rec.	Accounts Payable	+	Alan Stevenson, Capital	+ Revenue	− Expenses
PB (q)	12,030 −390	+ 22,000	+ 400	+ 320	+ 80	= 1,600	+	32,000	+ 2,270	− 1,040 +390 (Wages)
NB	11,640	+ 22,000	+ 400	+ 320	+ 80	= 1,600	+	32,000	+ 2,270	− 1,430
		34,440						34,440		

Transaction (r)   NuWay Cleaners buys additional equipment for $940 from Sanchez Equipment Company, paying $140 down, with the remaining $800 on account. Because buying an item on account is the same as buying it on credit, both expressions, *on account* and *on credit*, are used to describe such transactions.

	Assets					= Liabilities +		Owner's Equity		
	Cash	+ Equip.	+ Supp.	+ Ppd. Ins.	+ Accts. Rec.	Accounts Payable	+	Alan Stevenson, Capital	+ Revenue	− Expenses
PB (r)	11,640 −140	+ 22,000 +940	+ 400	+ 320	+ 80	= 1,600 +800	+	32,000	+ 2,270	− 1,430
NB	11,500	+ 22,940	+ 400	+ 320	+ 80	= 2,400	+	32,000	+ 2,270	− 1,430
		35,240						35,240		

Again, because the equipment will last a long time, NuWay lists this $940 as an increase in the assets.

Transaction (s)   NuWay Cleaners receives revenue from cash customers for the rest of the month, $960.

	Assets					= Liabilities +	Owner's Equity		
	Cash	+ Equip.	+ Supp.	+ Ppd. Ins.	+ Accts. Rec.	Accounts Payable	Alan Stevenson, Capital	+ Revenue	− Expenses
PB (s)	11,500 +960	+ 22,940	+ 400	+ 320	+ 80	= 2,400	+ 32,000	+ 2,270 +960	− 1,430
NB	12,460	+ 22,940	+ 400	+ 320	+ 80	= 2,400	+ 32,000	+ 3,230	− 1,430
			36,200				36,200		

Transaction (t)   NuWay Cleaners receives $60 from A-1 Rental to apply on the amount previously billed. A-1 Rental now owes NuWay Cleaners less than before, so NuWay deducts the $60 from Accounts Receivable. It previously recorded this amount as revenue, so the equation looks like the one shown below.

	Assets					= Liabilities +	Owner's Equity		
	Cash	+ Equip.	+ Supp.	+ Ppd. Ins.	+ Accts. Rec.	Accounts Payable	Alan Stevenson, Capital	+ Revenue	− Expenses
PB (t)	12,460 +60	+ 22,940	+ 400	+ 320	+ 80 −60	= 2,400	+ 32,000	+ 3,230	− 1,430
NB	12,520	+ 22,940	+ 400	+ 320	+ 20	= 2,400	+ 32,000	+ 3,230	− 1,430
			36,200				36,200		

Transaction (u)   At the end of the month, Stevenson withdraws $1,000 in çash from the business for his personal living costs. One may consider a **withdrawal** to be the opposite of an investment in cash by the owner.

	Assets					= Liabilities +	Owner's Equity		
	Cash	+ Equip.	+ Supp.	+ Ppd. Ins.	+ Accts. Rec.	Accounts Payable	Alan Stevenson, Capital	+ Revenue	− Expenses
PB (u)	12,520 −1,000	+ 22,940	+ 400	+ 320	+ 20	= 2,400	+ 32,000 −1,000 (Drawing)	+ 3,230	− 1,430
NB	11,520	+ 22,940	+ 400	+ 320	+ 20	= 2,400	+ 31,000	+ 3,230	− 1,430
			35,200				35,200		

Because the owner is taking cash out of the business, there is a decrease in Cash. The withdrawal also decreases Capital, because Stevenson has now reduced his equity. One does not consider a withdrawal as a business expense, since money is not paid to anyone outside the business for services performed or for materials received that would benefit the business.

Summary of Transactions

We have summarized the business transactions of NuWay Cleaners in Figure 2-1, identifying the transactions by letter. To test your understanding of the recording procedure, describe the nature of the transactions that have taken place.

Figure 2-1

	Cash	+ Equip.	+ Supp.	+ Ppd. Ins.	+ Accts. Rec.	= Accounts Payable	+ Alan Stevenson, Capital	+ Revenue	− Expenses
	Assets					**= Liabilities +**	**Owner's Equity**		
Bal.	13,000	+ 22,000	+ 400			= 3,400	+ 32,000		
(f)	+ 600							+ 600	
Bal.	13,600	+ 22,000	+ 400			= 3,400	+ 32,000	+ 600	
(g)	−400								+ 400 (Rent)
Bal.	13,200	+ 22,000	+ 400			= 3,400	+ 32,000	+ 600	− 400
(h)	−240								+ 240 (Wages)
Bal.	12,960	+ 22,000	+ 400			= 3,400	+ 32,000	+ 600	− 640
(i)	−320			+ 320					
Bal.	12,640	+ 22,000	+ 400	+ 320		= 3,400	+ 32,000	+ 600	− 640
(j)	+ 760							+ 760	
Bal.	13,400	+ 22,000	+ 400	+ 320		= 3,400	+ 32,000	+ 1,360	− 640
(k)						+ 180			+ 180 (Advertising)
Bal.	13,400	+ 22,000	+ 400	+ 320		= 3,580	+ 32,000	+ 1,360	− 820
(l)	−1,800					−1,800			
Bal.	11,600	+ 22,000	+ 400	+ 320		= 1,780	+ 32,000	+ 1,360	− 820
(m)	−220								+ 220 (Utilities)
Bal.	11,380	+ 22,000	+ 400	+ 320		= 1,780	+ 32,000	+ 1,360	− 1,040
(n)	−180					−180			

(continued)

	Assets					= Liabilities +	Owner's Equity		
	Cash	+ Equip.	+ Supp.	+ Ppd. Ins.	+ Accts. Rec.	= Accounts Payable	+ Alan Stevenson, Capital	+ Revenue	− Expenses
Bal.	11,200	+ 22,000	+ 400	+	320	= 1,600	+ 32,000	+ 1,360	− 1,040
(o)	+ 830							+ 830	
Bal.	12,030	+ 22,000	+ 400	+	320	= 1,600	+ 32,000	+ 2,190	− 1,040
(p)					+ 80			+80	
Bal.	12,030	+ 22,000	+ 400	+	320 +	80 = 1,600	+ 32,000	+ 2,270	− 1,040
(q)	−390								+390 (Wages)
Bal.	11,640	+ 22,000	+ 400	+	320 +	80 = 1,600	+ 32,000	+ 2,270	− 1,430
(r)	−140	+940				+800			
Bal.	11,500	+ 22,940	+ 400	+	320 +	80 = 2,400	+ 32,000	+ 2,270	− 1,430
(s)	+960							+960	
Bal.	12,460	+ 22,940	+ 400	+	320 +	80 = 2,400	+ 32,000	+ 3,230	− 1,430
(t)	+60					−60			
Bal.	12,520	+ 22,940	+ 400	+	320 +	20 = 2,400	+ 32,000	+ 3,230	− 1,430
(u)	−1,000						−1,000 (Drawing)		
Bal.	11,520	+ 22,940	+ 400	+	320 +	20 = 2,400	+ 31,000	+ 3,230	− 1,430

	Total			Total
Cash	$11,520	Accounts Payable		$ 2,400
Equipment	22,940	Alan Stevenson, Capital		31,000
Supplies	400	Revenue		3,230
Prepaid Insurance	320			$36,630
Accounts Receivable	20	Expenses		−1,430
	$35,200			$35,200

MAJOR FINANCIAL STATEMENTS

A financial statement is a report prepared by accountants for managers and others both inside and outside the economic unit. In Chapter 1, we discussed the balance sheet. We will now consider the income statement and the statement of owner's equity.

The Income Statement

The **income statement** shows total revenue minus total expenses, which yields the net income, or profit. This income statement pictures the results of the business transactions involving revenue and expense accounts over a period of time. In other words, it shows how the business has

Objective 2

Present an income statement.

performed or fared over a period of time, usually a month or year. Other terms that are identical with the name *income statement* are *statement of income and expenses* or *profit and loss statement.* If the total revenue is less than the expenses, the result is a net loss.

The income statement in Figure 2-2 shows the results of the first month of operations of NuWay Cleaners. (It should be noted that the net income figure presented here represents net income before adjustments. We shall discuss adjustments in Chapter 5.)

Note that as in all financial statements, the heading requires three lines:

1. Name of company (or owner, if there is no company name).
2. Title of the financial statement (in this case, income statement).
3. Period of time covered by the financial statement or its date.

Figure 2-2

NuWay Cleaners
Income Statement
For month ended June 30, 19–

Revenue:			
Income from Services			$ 3 2 3 0 00
Expenses:			
Wages Expense	$ 6 3 0 00		
Rent Expense	4 0 0 00		
Utilities Expense	2 2 0 00		
Advertising Expense	1 8 0 00		
Total Expenses		1 4 3 0 00	
Net Income		$ 1 8 0 0 00	

For convenience, the individual expense amounts are recorded in the first amount column. In this way, the total expenses ($1,430) may be subtracted directly from the total revenue ($3,230).

The income statement covers a period of time, whereas the balance sheet has only one date: the end of the financial period. The revenue for June, less the expenses for June, shows the results of operations—a net income of $1,800. To the accountant, the term **net income** means "clear" income, or profit after all expenses have been deducted. Expenses are usually listed in the same order as in the chart of accounts, which is the official list of all the accounts in which transactions are recorded. Some accountants, however, prefer to list expenses in declining order (the largest amount first, followed by the next largest, etc.). In this arrangement, if Miscellaneous Expense is present, it is placed last regardless of the amount. This procedure will be followed in the examples in this text if no chart of accounts is given.

The Statement of Owner's Equity

We said that revenue and expenses are connected with owner's equity through the medium of the financial statements. Let us now demonstrate this by a **statement of owner's equity,** shown in Figure 2-3, which the accountant prepares after he or she has determined the net income in the income statement. The statement of owner's equity shows how—and why—the owner's equity, or capital, account has changed over the financial period.

Objective 3

Present a statement of owner's equity.

Figure 2-3

NuWay Cleaners
Statement of Owner's Equity
For month ended June 30, 19–

Alan Stevenson, Capital, June 1, 19–				$32 0 0 0 00
Net Income for June	$1 8 0 0 00			
Less Withdrawals for June	1 0 0 0 00			
Increase in Capital				8 0 0 00
Alan Stevenson, Capital, June 30, 19–				$32 8 0 0 00

The Balance Sheet

After preparing the statement of owner's equity, we prepare a balance sheet (shown in Figure 2-4). In it we record the ending capital that we determined when we prepared the statement of owner's equity.

Figure 2-4

NuWay Cleaners
Balance Sheet
June 30, 19–

Assets		
Cash		$11 5 2 0 00
Accounts Receivable		2 0 00
Supplies		4 0 0 00
Prepaid Insurance		3 2 0 00
Equipment		22 9 4 0 00
Total Assets		$35 2 0 0 00
Liabilities		
Accounts Payable		$ 2 4 0 0 00
Owner's Equity		
Alan Stevenson, Capital		32 8 0 0 00
Total Liabilities and Owner's Equity		$35 2 0 0 00

This balance sheet is only tentative because adjustments have not been recorded (see Chapter 5).

Income Statement Involving More Than One Revenue Account

When a business firm or other economic unit has more than one distinct source of revenue, separate revenue accounts are set up for each source. See, for example, the income statement of The Ninth Avenue Theater presented in Figure 2-5.

Figure 2-5

The Ninth Avenue Theater
Income Statement
For month ended September 30, 19–

Revenue:									
Admissions Income	$6	9	6	8	00				
Concessions Income	1	7	4	3	00				
Total Revenue						$8	7	1	1	00
Expenses:									
Film Rental Expense	$3	3	2	5	00				
Wages Expense	1	3	5	3	00				
Advertising Expense		9	2	5	00				
Utilities Expense		3	1	6	00				
Taxes Expense		2	2	1	00				
Miscellaneous Expense		1	4	5	00				
Total Expenses						6	2	8	5	00
Net Income						$2	4	2	6	00

Statement of Owner's Equity Involving an Additional Investment and a Net Loss

Any additional investment by the owner during the period covered by the financial statements should be shown in the statement of owner's equity, since such a statement should show what has affected the Capital account from the *beginning* until the *end* of the period covered by the financial statements. For example, assume the following for the C. E. Davis Company, which has a net income:

Balance of C. E. Davis, Capital, on April 1 $86,000
Additional investment by C. E. Davis on April 12   9,000
Net income for the month (from income statement)   1,500
Total withdrawals for the month   1,200

The statement of owner's equity in Figure 2-6 shows this information.

Figure 2-6

C. E. Davis Company
Statement of Owner's Equity
For month ended April 30, 19–

C. E. Davis, Capital, April 1, 19–			$86 0 0 0 00
Additional Investment, April 12, 19–			9 0 0 0 00
Total Investment			$95 0 0 0 00
Net Income for April	$1 5 0 0 00		
Less Withdrawals for April	1 2 0 0 00		
Increase in Capital			3 0 0 00
C. E. Davis, Capital, April 30, 19–			$95 3 0 0 00

As another example, assume the following for the H. L. Spangler Company, which has a net loss:

H. L. Spangler, Capital, on Oct. 1 $70,000
Additional investment by H. L. Spangler on Oct. 25   6,000
Net loss for the month (from income statement)   250
Total withdrawals for the month   420

Again, the statement of owner's equity in Figure 2-7 shows this information.

Figure 2-7

H. L. Spangler Company
Statement of Owner's Equity
For month ended October 31, 19–

H. L. Spangler, Capital, October 1, 19–			$70 0 0 0 00
Additional Investment, October 25, 19–			6 0 0 0 00
Total Investment			$76 0 0 0 00
Less: Net Loss for October	$ 2 5 0 00		
Withdrawals for October	4 2 0 00		
Decrease in Capital			6 7 0 00
H. L. Spangler, Capital, October 31, 19–			$75 3 3 0 00

IMPORTANCE OF FINANCIAL STATEMENTS

The owners or managers of a business look on their financial statements as a coach looks on the scoreboard and team statistics, as showing the results of the present game as well as the team's standing. The income statement shows the results of operations for the current month or year. It condenses the results of operations into one figure, either net income or net loss. The income statement is prepared first so that the net income can be recorded in the statement of owner's equity, which comes next. It shows why—and how—the owner's investment has changed. The ending capital in the statement of owner's equity is used in the balance sheet, which shows the present standing or financial position of the business. All these relationships are shown in Figure 2-8.

The owner or manager can use the figures on the financial statements to plan future operations. Owners and managers are not the only ones interested in financial statements. Creditors, prospective investors, and government agencies are also interested in the profitability and financial standing of the business. Financial statements are the way in which one takes the pulse of the business. They are extremely important.

Figure 2-8

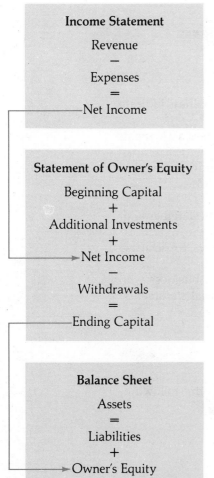

Income Statement

Revenue

−

Expenses

=

Net Income

Statement of Owner's Equity

Beginning Capital
+
Additional Investments
+
Net Income

−

Withdrawals

=

Ending Capital

Balance Sheet

Assets

=

Liabilities
+
Owner's Equity

GLOSSARY

Accounts Receivable Charge accounts or receivable accounts maintained for customers, representing credit usually extended for thirty-day periods.

Expenses The amounts of assets that a business or other economic unit uses up as a result of its operations; the cost of services or goods acquired or consumed in the operation of the business or economic unit.

Income statement A financial statement showing the results of business transactions over a period of time: total revenue minus total expenses.

Net income Total revenue minus total expenses over a period of time.

Revenues The amounts of assets that a business or other economic unit gains as a result of its operations; the total price charged for services rendered or goods sold during a period of time; may be in the form of cash or receivables.

Statement of owner's equity A financial statement showing how—and why—the owner's equity, or capital, account has changed over the financial period.

Withdrawal The taking of cash or goods out of a business by the owner for his or her own personal use. (This is also referred to as a *drawing*.) One treats a withdrawal as a temporary decrease in the owner's equity, since one anticipates that it will be offset by net income.

QUESTIONS, EXERCISES, AND PROBLEMS

Discussion Questions

1. Define the term *expense*. Does every payment of cash by a business indicate that an expense has been incurred?
2. What titles might you select to describe the kinds of expenses a TV repair shop would incur in its operations?
3. What happens to the elements in the fundamental accounting equation when a sale of services is made on a charge-account basis?
4. What does an income statement show?
5. What is the difference between the headings required for statements of owner's equity and the headings required for balance sheets?
6. Name two ways to increase owner's equity and two ways to decrease owner's equity.
7. Suggest some groups other than the owner or owners of a business who would be interested in data contained in the firm's financial statements. What is the specific interest of each group?

Exercises

Exercise 2-1 Describe a business transaction that will do the following:

a. Decrease a liability and decrease an asset.
b. Increase an asset and increase a revenue.

c. Decrease an asset and increase an expense.
d. Increase a liability and increase an expense.

Exercise 2-2   Using the following data, determine the total owner's equity.

Equipment	$ 8,000	Accounts Payable	$1,200
Cash	2,000	Accounts Receivable	1,600
Building	60,000	Supplies	400
Land	10,000		

Exercise 2-3   Describe the transactions recorded in the following equation.

	Assets			=	Liabilities +		Owner's Equity		
	Cash	+ Accounts Receivable	+ Equipment		Accounts Payable	+	C. P. Lee, Capital	+ Revenue	− Expenses
(a)	+12,000		+ 4,000	=		+	16,000		
(b)	−900								+900
Bal.	11,100		4,000	=		+	16,000		− 900
(c)		+ 2,100						+ 2,100	
Bal.	11,100 +	2,100	+ 4,000	=		+	16,000 +	2,100	− 900
(d)	−3,000		+12,000		+9,000				
Bal.	8,100 +	2,100	+ 16,000	=	9,000	+	16,000 +	2,100	900
(e)	−1,600						−1,600 (Drawing)		
Bal.	6,500 +	2,100	+ 16,000	=	9,000	+	14,400 +	2,100	− 900

Exercise 2-4   From the following balances, in the elements of the fundamental accounting equation, determine the amount of the ending owner's equity.

Assets	$64,000
Liabilities	20,000
Owner's Equity (beginning)	32,000
Revenue	48,000
Expenses	36,000

Exercise 2-5   A. M. Woods is an attorney. Describe the transactions that have been completed.

	Assets				=	Liabilities +		Owner's Equity		
	Cash	+ Accts. Rec.	+ Supp.	+ Equip.		Accounts Payable	+	A. M. Woods, Capital	+ Revenue	− Expenses
Bal.	1,620 +	810 +	819	+ 7,493	=	2,416	+	8,326		
(a)	+360	−360								
Bal.	1,980 +	450 +	819	+ 7,493	=	2,416	+	8,326		
(b)	−418									+418 (Rent)

	Assets				= Liabilities +	Owner's Equity		
	Cash +	Accts. Rec. +	Supp. +	Equip.	Accounts Payable	A. M. Woods, Capital	+ Revenue	− Expenses
Bal.	1,562 +	450 +	819 +	7,493 =	2,416 +	8,326		− 418
(c)	+2,730						+2,730	
Bal.	4,292 +	450 +	819 +	7,493 =	2,416 +	8,326	+ 2,730	− 418
(d)	−300				−300			
Bal.	3,992 +	450 +	819 +	7,493 =	2,116 +	8,326	+ 2,730	− 418
(e)	−410							+410 (Wages)
Bal.	3,582 +	450 +	819 +	7,493 =	2,116 +	8,326	+ 2,730	− 828
(f)	−1,200					−1,200 (Drawing)		
Bal.	2,382 +	450 +	819 +	7,493 =	2,116 +	7,126	+ 2,730	− 828
(g)	−875				−875			
Bal.	1,507 +	450 +	819 +	7,493 =	1,241 +	7,126	+ 2,730	− 828

Exercise 2-6 From Exercise 2-5, present an income statement for the month ending September 30.

Exercise 2-7 From Exercises 2-5 and 2-6, present a statement of owner's equity and a balance sheet.

Exercise 2-8 On January 1, L. P. Romano's equity in his business, Romano's Excavating, was $56,000. On May 22, Romano made an additional investment of $4,000. The firm's net income for the year was $23,500. Romano's total withdrawals amounted to $18,000. Prepare a statement of owner's equity for the year ended December 31.

Problem Set A

Problem 2-1A In June of this year, Lewis Scott established a business under the name Scott Realty. The account headings are presented below. Transactions completed during the month follow.

Assets		= Liabilities +	Owner's Equity		
Cash + Supplies + Equipment		Accounts Payable	Lewis Scott, Capital	+ Revenue	− Expenses

a. Deposited $9,000 in a bank account entitled Scott Realty.
b. Paid office rent for the month, $500.
c. Bought supplies consisting of stationery, folders, and stamps for cash, $252.
d. Bought office equipment consisting of desks, chairs, filing cabinets, and other furniture on account from Simcoe Company, $5,400.
e. Received bill for advertising, $360.

f. Paid $800 to Simcoe Company on amount owed on purchase of office equipment recorded previously.
g. Earned sales commissions, receiving cash, $2,820.
h. Received and paid bill for utilities, $136.
i. Paid bill for advertising recorded previously, $360.
j. Paid automobile expenses, $230.
k. Scott withdrew cash for personal use, $970.

Instructions

1. Record the transactions and the balance after each transaction.
2. Prepare an income statement and a statement of owner's equity for June and a balance sheet as of June 30.

Problem 2-2A A. L. Stone, CPA, opened her public accounting practice on September 1. The account headings are presented below. Transactions completed during the month follow.

Assets	= Liabilities +	Owner's Equity
Cash + Supp. + Ppd. + Library + Equip. Ins.	Accounts Payable	A. L. + Revenue − Expenses Stone, Capital

a. Deposited $14,000 in a bank account in the name of the business, A. L. Stone, CPA.
b. Bought office equipment on account from Jacobs Company, $9,800.
c. Invested a professional library costing $3,800. (Increase the account for Library and the account of A. L. Stone, Capital, and include in the statement of owner's equity as Additional Investment, as shown on page 32.)
d. Paid office rent for the month, $640.
e. Bought office supplies for cash, $590.
f. Paid the premium for a two-year insurance policy on the equipment and the library, $124.
g. Received professional fees for services rendered, $1,640.
h. Received and paid bill for telephone service, $152.
i. Paid salary of part-time receptionist, $640.
j. Paid automobile expense, $192.
k. Received professional fees for services rendered, $1,480.
l. Paid Jacobs Company on amount owed on the purchase of office equipment, $1,000.
m. Stone withdrew cash for personal use, $1,450.

Instructions

1. Record the transactions and the balances after each transaction.
2. Prepare an income statement and a statement of owner's equity for September and a balance sheet as of September 30.

Problem 2-3A Evans Engineering Consultants hires an accountant, who determines the following account balances, listed in random order, as of November 30.

Cash	$3,528	D. L. Evans, Drawing	$2,400
Wages Expense	2,800	Accounts Receivable	1,442
Professional Fees	7,834	Accounts Payable	2,848
Equipment	7,948	Supplies	232
Rent Expense	1,500	Miscellaneous Expense	220
D. L. Evans, Capital,		Advertising Expense	252
Nov. 1	9,640		

Instructions

Prepare an income statement and a statement of owner's equity for November and a balance sheet as of November 30.

Problem 2-4A   C. P. Moore started the Moore Delivery Service on October 1 of this year. The account headings are presented below. During October, Moore completed the following transactions.

Assets						= Liabilities +	Owner's Equity		
Cash +	Accts. Rec.	+ Supp. +	Ppd. Ins.	+ Delivery Equip.	+ Office Equip.	Accounts Payable	C. P. Moore, Capital	+ Revenue	− Expenses

a.   Invested cash in the business, $4,000.
b.   Bought delivery equipment from Acme Motors for $7,500, paying $800 in cash with the remainder due in thirty days.
c.   Bought office equipment on account from Dietz and Company, $1,200.
d.   Paid rent for the month, $300.
e.   Paid cash for insurance on delivery equipment for the year, $384.
f.   Cash receipts for the first half of the month from cash customers, $1,850.
g.   Bought supplies for cash, $182.
h.   Billed customers for services on account, $296.
i.   Paid cash for utilities, $64.
j.   Received bill for gas and oil used during the current month, $276.
k.   Receipts for the remainder of the month from cash customers, $1,720.
l.   Moore withdrew cash for personal use, $760.
m.   Paid drivers' commissions, $966. (This is an expense.)

Instructions

1.   Record the transactions and the balance after each transaction.
2.   Prepare an income statement and a statement of owner's equity for October and a balance sheet as of October 31.

Problem Set B

Problem 2-1B   On April 1 of this year, Edward Savage, D.D.S., established an office for the practice of dentistry. The account headings are presented below. Transactions completed during the month follow.

	Assets	= Liabilities +		Owner's Equity	
Cash + Supp. +	Dental + Office Equip. Equip.	Accounts Payable	Edward Savage, Capital	+ Revenue	− Expenses

a. Deposited $9,000 in a bank account entitled Edward Savage, D.D.S.
b. Paid office rent for the month, $570.
c. Bought dental supplies for cash, $1,110.
d. Bought dental equipment consisting of a chair, drills, x-ray equipment, and instruments on account from Peerless Dental Supply, $14,700.
e. Bought a desk and chairs for the reception room from Wagner Office Equipment, for $3,600, paying $600 in cash and the remainder on account.
f. Received cash for professional fees earned, $1,365.
g. Received and paid bill for utilities, $147.
h. Paid Peerless Dental Supply on amount owed on dental equipment recorded previously, $900.
i. Paid salary of assistant, $800.
j. Earned professional fees, receiving $2,142 cash.
k. Savage withdrew cash for personal use, $1,140.

Instructions

1. Record the transactions and the balance after each transaction.
2. Prepare an income statement and a statement of owner's equity for April and a balance sheet as of April 30.

Problem 2-2B   G. N. Little, a photographer, opened a studio for her professional practice on July 1. The account headings are presented below. Transactions completed during the month follow.

	Assets	= Liabilities +		Owner's Equity	
Cash + Supp. +	Ppd. + Photographic Ins. Equip.	Accounts Payable	G. N. Little, Capital	+ Revenue	− Expenses

a. Deposited $13,125 in a bank account in the name of the business, Little Photographic Studio.
b. Bought photographic equipment on account from Precision Equipment, $6,930.
c. Invested personal photographic equipment, $5,040. (Increase the account for Photographic Equipment, and include in the statement of owner's equity as Additional Investment as shown on page 32.)
d. Paid office rent for the month, $525.
e. Bought photographic supplies for cash, $789.
f. Paid premium for a two-year insurance policy on photographic equipment, $108.
g. Received $878 as professional fees for services rendered.
h. Paid salary of part-time assistant, $500.
i. Received and paid bill for telephone service, $58.
j. Paid Precision Equipment on amount owed on the purchase of photographic equipment, $410.
k. Received $1,479 as professional fees for services rendered.
l. Paid for minor repairs to photographic equipment (Repair Expense), $54.
m. Little withdrew cash for personal use, $900.

Instructions

1. Record the transactions and the balances after each transaction.
2. Prepare an income statement and a statement of owner's equity for July and a balance sheet as of July 31.

Problem 2-3B An accountant determines the following balances, listed in random order, for Lambert Auto Repair as of September 30 of this year.

Cash	$ 3,436	Rent Expense	$ 780
Advertising Expense	630	Accounts Receivable	5,746
Income from Services	10,032	D. C. Lambert, Capital,	
Wages Expense	6,414	Sept. 1	37,638
Equipment	30,328	D. C. Lambert, Drawing	1,500
Accounts Payable	2,700	Miscellaneous Expense	308
		Supplies	1,228

Instructions

Prepare an income statement and a statement of owner's equity for September and a balance sheet as of September 30.

Problem 2-4B On May 1 of this year, C. W. Ennis started the Ennis Advertising Agency. The account headings are presented below. During May, Ennis completed these transactions.

Assets	= Liabilities +	Owner's Equity
Cash + Accts. + Supp. + Ppd. + Car + Office Rec. Ins. Equip.	Accounts Payable	C. W. + Revenue − Expenses Ennis, Capital

a. Invested cash in the business, $11,280.
b. Bought a car for use in the business from Merino Motors for $8,160, paying $1,200 in cash with the balance due in thirty days.
c. Bought office equipment on account from Wallingford Company, $2,210.
d. Paid rent for the month, $430.
e. Cash receipts for the first half of the month from cash customers, $1,840.
f. Paid cash for property and liability insurance on car for the year, $352.
g. Bought office supplies for cash, $148.
h. Received and paid heating bill, $46.
i. Received bill for gas and oil used during the current month from Finch Oil Company for the company car, $91.
j. Billed customers for services performed on account, $374.
k. Receipts for the remainder of the month from cash customers, $2,126.
l. Paid salary of commercial artist, $1,180.
m. Ennis withdrew cash for personal use, $1,850.

Instructions

1. Record the transactions and the balance after each transaction.
2. Prepare an income statement and a statement of owner's equity for May and a balance sheet as of May 31.

3 Recording Business Transactions in Ledger Account Form; The Trial Balance

Learning Objectives

After you have completed this chapter, you will be able to do the following:

1. Record a group of business transactions for a service business directly in T accounts involving changes in assets, liabilities, owner's equity, revenue, and expense accounts.

2. Determine balances of T accounts having entries recorded on both sides of the accounts.

3. Present the fundamental accounting equation with the T account forms, the plus and minus signs, and the debit and credit sides labeled.

4. Prepare a trial balance.

Up to now we have discussed the fundamental accounting equation in two places. In Chapter 1 we described it as *Assets = Liabilities + Owner's Equity.* In Chapter 2 we introduced two more accounts (Revenues and Expenses) and then described the equation as *Assets = Liabilities + Owner's Equity + Revenue − Expenses.* With the last two accounts, the fundamental accounting equation was brought up to its full complement of five account classifications. There are only five; so, as far as you go in accounting—whether you are dealing with a small one-owner business or a large corporation—there will be only these five major classifications of accounts. These classifications relate to the principal financial statements as follows:

Assets = Liabilities + Owner's Equity + Revenue − Expenses

Balance Sheet	Statement of Owner's Equity	Income Statement
Assets	Beginning Capital	Revenue
=	+	−
Liabilities	Net Income	Expenses
+	−	=
Owner's Equity	Withdrawals	Net Income
	=	
	Ending Capital	

In this chapter we shall record in T account form the same transactions we used in Chapters 1 and 2, and we shall prove the equality of both sides of the fundamental accounting equation. We'll do this by means of a trial balance, which we'll talk about soon.

THE T ACCOUNT FORM

In Chapters 1 and 2, we recorded business transactions in a columnar arrangement. For example, the Cash account column in the books of NuWay Cleaners is shown at the top of the next page. As an introduction to the recording of transactions, this arrangement has two advantages.

1. In the process of analyzing the transaction, you recognize the need to determine *which* accounts are involved. Next, you must decide whether the transaction results in an increase or a decrease in each of these accounts.
2. You further realize that after each transaction has been recorded, the balance of each account, when combined with the balances of other accounts, proves the equality of the two sides of the fundamental accounting equation.

Cash Account Column

Transaction	(a)	32,000	Balance		12,640	Balance		11,640
Transaction	(b)	−18,000	Transaction	(j)	+760	Transaction	(r)	−140
Balance		14,000	Balance		13,400	Balance		11,500
Transaction	(d)	−1,000	Transaction	(l)	−1,800	Transaction	(s)	+960
Balance		13,000	Balance		11,600	Balance		12,460
Transaction	(f)	+600	Transaction	(m)	−220	Transaction	(t)	+60
Balance		13,600	Balance		11,380	Balance		12,520
Transaction	(g)	−400	Transaction	(n)	−180	Transaction	(u)	−1,000
Balance		13,200	Balance		11,200	Balance		11,520
Transaction	(h)	−240	Transaction	(o)	+830			
Balance		12,960	Balance		12,030			
Transaction	(i)	−320	Transaction	(q)	−390			
Balance		12,640	Balance		11,640			

The **T account form** (that is, an account shaped like the letter T) is the traditional form. It is also known as a ledger account, because the records of *all* the accounts are kept in the **ledger.** The ledger may be as simple as a loose-leaf binder or as complex as a whole filing system.

The T form, developed for convenience as a space-saving device, is divided into two sides: one side to record increases in the account and the other to record decreases. Let us now record in T account form those transactions just listed for NuWay Cleaners that affect the Cash account.

Cash

	+			−	
(a)	32,000		(b)	18,000
(f)	600		(d)	1,000
(j)	760		(g)	400
(o)	830		(h)	240
(s)	960		(i)	320
(t)	60		(l)	1,800
	35,210		(m)	220
			(n)	180
			(q)	390
			(r)	140
			(u)	1,000

Footings → 23,690

Balance → **11,520**

After we record a group of transactions in an account, we add both sides and record the totals in small pencil-written figures called **footings.** Next, we subtract one footing from the other to determine the balance of the account. For the account shown above, the balance would be $11,520 ($35,210 − $23,690).

We now record the balance on the side of the account having the larger footing, which, with a few minor exceptions, is the plus (+) side. The plus side of an account is the side that represents the **normal balance** of the account. The normal balance may, however, fall on either the left or the right side of an account.

Each classification of accounts uses a consistent placement of the plus and minus signs. For example, the T accounts for *all* assets are

+	−
Left	Right

In Chapter 2 we placed revenue and expenses under the "umbrella" of owner's equity. Revenue increases owner's equity, and expenses decrease owner's equity. In T account form, it looks like this:

Owner's Equity

−	+
Left	Right

Expenses		**Revenue**	
+	−	−	+
Left	Right	Left	Right

Also, in Chapter 2, using the five classifications of accounts, we stated the fundamental accounting equation like this:

Assets = Liabilities + $\underbrace{\text{Owner's Equity}}_{\text{Capital + Revenue − Expenses}}$

Because revenue and expenses appear separately in the income statement, we'll stretch out the equation to include them as separate headings, like this:

Assets = Liabilities + Owner's Equity + Revenue − Expenses

We can now restate the equation with the T forms and plus and minus signs for each account classification.

Assets		=	**Liabilities**		+	**Owner's Equity**		+	**Revenue**		−	**Expenses**	
+	−		−	+		−	+		−	+		+	−
Left	Right		Left	Right		Left	Right		Left	Right		Left	Right

Revenue has been treated as an addition to owner's equity, so the placement of the plus and minus signs is the same as in owner's equity. On the other hand, expenses have been treated as deductions from owner's equity, so the placement of the plus and minus signs is reversed. We shall use this form of the fundamental accounting equation throughout the remainder of the text.

Your accounting background up to this point has taught you to analyze business transactions in order to determine which accounts are involved and to recognize that the amounts should be recorded as either an increase or a decrease in the accounts. Now, the recording process becomes a simple matter of knowing which side of the T accounts should be used to record increases and which side to record decreases. **Generally speaking, you will not be using the minus side of the revenue and expense accounts, since transactions involving revenue and expense accounts usually result in increases in these accounts.**

RECORDING TRANSACTIONS IN T ACCOUNT FORM

Objective 1

Record a group of business transactions for a service business directly in T accounts.

Our task now is to learn how to record business transactions in the T account form. To facilitate this transition, let's use the transactions of NuWay Cleaners again; we are familiar with them and can readily recognize the increases or decreases in the accounts involved.

There are only five classifications of accounts. These classifications are embodied in the fundamental accounting equation.

Assets		=	Liabilities		+	Owner's Equity		+	Revenue		−	Expenses	
+	−		−	+		−	+		−	+		+	−
Left	Right		Left	Right		Left	Right		Left	Right		Left	Right

The fundamental accounting equation with T accounts for NuWay Cleaners is presented below. We have given specific account titles for revenue and expense accounts, as it is necessary to list each account separately in the income statement. The order of Supplies, Prepaid Insurance, and Equipment has been changed, so that the presentation will be consistent with the account number sequence shown in Chapter 4.

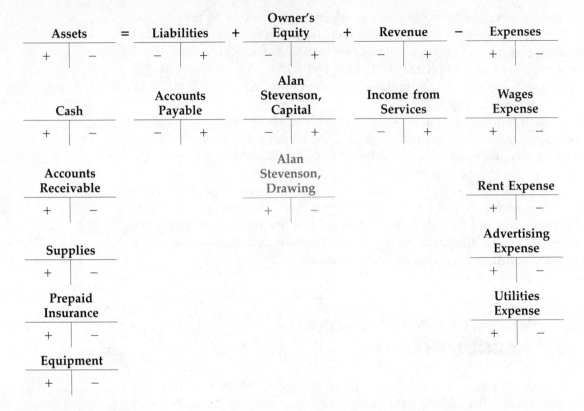

To stress the Drawing account, which can cause some confusion, we have printed it in color. One might think of the relationship between Drawing and Capital like this: Amounts put into the business are recorded as increases, and amounts taken out of the business are recorded as decreases.

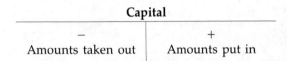

We would, however, like to reserve the minus side of Capital for permanent withdrawals, were the owner to reduce the size of the business permanently. As we said in Chapter 2, amounts taken out for the owner's personal use may be considered to be temporary. Because the owner plans to replenish these amounts from the net income earned by the firm, it is much more convenient to use a separate account to record these withdrawals. Any temporary withdrawals will be listed on the plus side of Drawing. This concept can be illustrated by showing the Drawing T account under the umbrella of the Capital account.

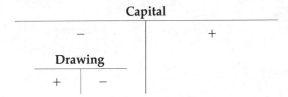

Capital	
−	+

Drawing	
+	−

Drawing is placed under the heading of owner's equity, because it appears in the statement of owner's equity. As you will recall, in the statement of owner's equity, we list beginning capital, plus net income, minus withdrawals. When we want to treat one account as a deduction from another, we reverse the plus and minus signs.

Transaction (a)   Alan Stevenson invests $32,000 cash in his new business. This transaction results in an increase in Cash and an increase in the Capital account, affecting the T accounts shown below.

Assets		=	Liabilities		+	Owner's Equity		+	Revenue		−	Expenses	
+	−		−	+		−	+		−	+		+	−

Cash			Alan Stevenson, Capital	
+	−		−	+
(a) 32,000				(a) 32,000

Transaction (b)   NuWay Cleaners buys $18,000 worth of equipment, paying cash. This transaction results in an increase in Equipment and a decrease in Cash.

Assets		=	Liabilities		+	Owner's Equity		+	Revenue		−	Expenses	
+	−		−	+		−	+		−	+		+	−

Cash	
+	−
	(b) 18,000

Equipment	
+	−
(b) 18,000	

Transaction (c)   NuWay Cleaners buys equipment on credit from Sanchez Equipment Company, $4,000. This transaction results in an increase in both Equipment and Accounts Payable and is shown in T accounts as follows:

Assets	=	Liabilities	+	Owner's Equity	+	Revenue	−	Expenses
+ | −		− | +		− | +		− | +		+ | −

Equipment		Accounts Payable	
+	−	−	+
(c) 4,000			(c) 4,000

Transaction (d) NuWay Cleaners pays $1,000 to be applied against the firm's liability of $4,000. This transaction results in a decrease in Cash and a decrease in Accounts Payable.

Assets	=	Liabilities	+	Owner's Equity	+	Revenue	−	Expenses
+ | −		− | +		− | +		− | +		+ | −

Cash		Accounts Payable	
+	−	−	+
	(d) 1,000	(d) 1,000	

Transaction (e) NuWay Cleaners buys cleaning fluids for $400 on credit from Troy Supply Company. This transaction results in an increase in Supplies and an increase in Accounts Payable.

Assets	=	Liabilities	+	Owner's Equity	+	Revenue	−	Expenses
+ | −		− | +		− | +		− | +		+ | −

Supplies		Accounts Payable	
+	−	−	+
(e) 400			(e) 400

Objective 2

Determine balances of T accounts having entries recorded on both sides of the accounts.

Here is a restatement of the accounts after recording **a** through **e**. To test your understanding of the process, trace through the recording of each transaction and describe the nature of the transaction. Footings, or totals—remember always to write them in pencil—are included as a means of determining the balances of the accounts. The balances are inserted in the accounts on the side having the largest total.

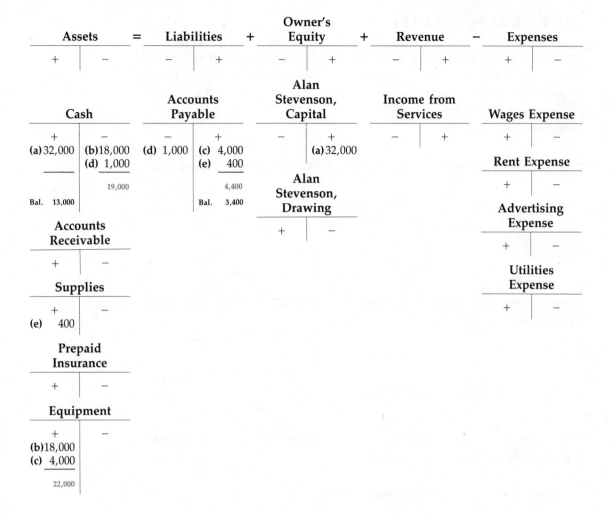

At this point let us pause to determine the equality of the two sides of the equation by listing the balances of the accounts.

Account Name	Accounts with Normal Balances on the Left Side Assets Expenses	Accounts with Normal Balances on the Right Side Liabilities Owner's Equity Revenue
Cash	$13,000	
Supplies	400	
Equipment	22,000	
Accounts Payable		$ 3,400
Alan Stevenson, Capital		32,000
	$35,400	$35,400

LEFT EQUALS RIGHT

In recording each transaction, the amount recorded on the left side of one T account, or accounts, must equal the amount recorded on the right side of another T account, or accounts. This is *double-entry accounting*. To emphasize this point, let us review the recording of the transactions for NuWay Cleaners.

Transaction (a) Stevenson invests $32,000 cash in his new business.

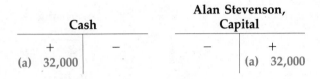

Cash		Alan Stevenson, Capital	
+	−	−	+
(a) 32,000			(a) 32,000

Transaction (b) NuWay Cleaners buys $18,000 worth of equipment, paying cash.

Cash		Equipment	
+	−	+	−
	(b) 18,000	(b) 18,000	

Transaction (c) NuWay Cleaners buys equipment on credit from Sanchez Equipment Company, $4,000.

Equipment		Accounts Payable	
+	−	−	+
(c) 4,000			(c) 4,000

We observe from the foregoing that transactions are recorded in various combinations of pluses and minuses in the accounts. However, the important point to remember is that **the amount recorded on the left side of one T account, or accounts, must equal the amount recorded on the right side of another T account, or accounts.**

Transaction (d) NuWay Cleaners pays $1,000 to be applied against the firm's liability of $4,000. (Left side of Accounts Payable and right side of Cash.)

Cash		Accounts Payable	
+	−	−	+
	(d) 1,000	(d) 1,000	

Transaction (e) NuWay Cleaners buys cleaning fluids on credit from Troy Supply Company, $400. (Left side of Supplies and right side of Accounts Payable.)

Supplies			Accounts Payable		
+		−	−		+
(e) 400				(e)	400

Transaction (f) NuWay Cleaners receives $600 cash revenue for the first week. We write $600 on the plus, or left, side of Cash and $600 on the plus, or right, side of Income from Services. In other words, the firm has more cash than before, so we record $600 in the Cash account on the plus side (which happens to be the left side). Also, we recognize that there is an increase in income from services, so we record $600 in Income from Services on the plus side (which happens to be the right side).

Assets	=	Liabilities	+	Owner's Equity	+	Revenue	−	Expenses
+ | −		− | +		− | +		− | +		+ | −

Cash		Income from Services
+ | −		− | +
(f) 600		(f) 600

Transaction (g) NuWay Cleaners pays $400 for one month's rent on its shop. We write $400 on the plus, or left, side of Rent Expense. From the point of view of a running record of the Rent Expense account, there is an increase in this account. We also write $400 on the minus, or right, side of Cash.

Assets	=	Liabilities	+	Owner's Equity	+	Revenue	−	Expenses
+ | −		− | +		− | +		− | +		+ | −

Cash		Rent Expense
+ | −		+ | −
(g) 400		(g) 400

Transaction (h) NuWay Cleaners pays wages to employees, $240. We write $240 on the plus, or left, side of Wages Expense and $240 on the minus, or right, side of Cash.

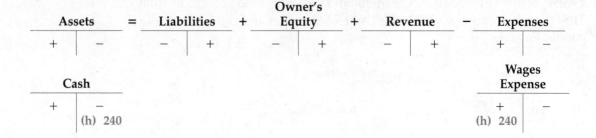

Assets		=	Liabilities		+	Owner's Equity		+	Revenue		−	Expenses	
+	−		−	+		−	+		−	+		+	−

Cash				Wages Expense	
+	−			+	−
(h) 240				(h) 240	

DEBIT AND CREDIT SIDES

In accounting, the *left side* of a T account is called the **debit** side; the *right side* is called the **credit** side. To repeat the fundamental accounting equation with the T's as shown here:

Assets		=	Liabilities		+	Owner's Equity		+	Revenue		−	Expenses	
+	−		−	+		−	+		−	+		+	−
Left	Right		Left	Right		Left	Right		Left	Right		Left	Right
Debit	Credit		Debit	Credit		Debit	Credit		Debit	Credit		Debit	Credit

Objective 3

Present the fundamental accounting equation with the T account forms, the plus and minus signs, and the debit and credit sides labeled.

Note that the left side is always the debit side, regardless of whether it represents the plus or minus side of an account. One may use the word *debit* as a verb. If we debit Wages Expense for $240, for example, this means that we write $240 on the left side of Wages Expense. If the other half of the entry results in a credit to Cash for $240, this means that we write $240 on the right side of Cash.

Rules of Debit and Credit

When we use T accounts to study the fundamental accounting equation, we can make the following observation.

Debits Signify		Credits Signify	
Increases in	{ Assets { Expenses	Decreases in	{ Assets { Expenses
Decreases in	{ Liabilities { Owner's Equity { Revenue	Increases in	{ Liabilities { Owner's Equity { Revenue

Previously we said that when one records each business transaction, the amount placed on the left side of one account (or accounts) must equal the amount placed on the right side of another account (or accounts). Let us now state this rule in terms of debits and credits. **The amount placed** on the debit side of one account, or accounts, must equal the amount placed on the credit side of another account, or accounts.

In your own personal experience, you may have heard the terms *debit* and *credit* used. So, as an aside, let's talk about these terms. First, keep in mind that the debit side is always the left side of any account and the credit side is always the right side of any account. Here's an example: You deposit $50 in a bank savings account. Every firm keeps its books from its own point of view. From the bank's point of view, the bank now has $50 more in cash, but it also owes you $50 more than before. As you know, you have the right to withdraw $50 at any time. In other words, the bank is liable to you (Deposits Payable account). The bank records the transaction like this:

Assets		=	Liabilities		+	Owner's Equity		+	Revenue		−	Expenses	
+	−		−	+		−	+		−	+		+	−
Debit	Credit		Debit	Credit		Debit	Credit		Debit	Credit		Debit	Credit

Cash		Deposits Payable	
+	−	−	+
50			50

Note that the bank increased its liability by recording $50 on the plus, or credit, side of Deposits Payable. So, when you deposit $50 in the bank, the bank *credits* your account. Conversely, if you withdraw $50 from the bank, the bank *debits* your account.

Now let's return to the transactions of NuWay Cleaners.

Transaction (i) NuWay Cleaners pays $320 for a two-year insurance policy. We write $320 on the plus, or debit, side of Prepaid Insurance and $320 on the minus, or credit, side of Cash.

Assets		=	Liabilities		+	Owner's Equity		+	Revenue		−	Expenses	
+	−		−	+		−	+		−	+		+	−
Debit	Credit		Debit	Credit		Debit	Credit		Debit	Credit		Debit	Credit

Cash	
+	−
	(i) 320

Prepaid Insurance	
+	−
(i) 320	

Transaction (j) NuWay Cleaners receives cash revenue for the second week, $760. We write $760 on the plus, or debit, side of Cash and $760 on the plus, or credit, side of Income from Services.

Assets		=	Liabilities		+	Owner's Equity		+	Revenue		−	Expenses	
+	−		−	+		−	+		−	+		+	−
Debit	Credit		Debit	Credit		Debit	Credit		Debit	Credit		Debit	Credit

Cash			Income from Services	
+	−		−	+
(j) 760				(j) 760

Transaction (k) NuWay Cleaners receives a bill for newspaper advertising, $180. We write $180 on the plus, or debit, side of Advertising Expense and $180 on the plus, or credit, side of Accounts Payable.

Assets		=	Liabilities		+	Owner's Equity		+	Revenue		−	Expenses	
+	−		−	+		−	+		−	+		+	−
Debit	Credit		Debit	Credit		Debit	Credit		Debit	Credit		Debit	Credit

Accounts Payable			Advertising Expense	
−	+		+	−
	(k) 180		(k) 180	

Transaction (l) NuWay Cleaners pays $1,800 to creditors as part payment on account. We write $1,800 on the minus, or debit, side of Accounts Payable and $1,800 on the minus, or credit, side of Cash.

Assets		=	Liabilities		+	Owner's Equity		+	Revenue		−	Expenses	
+	−		−	+		−	+		−	+		+	−
Debit	Credit		Debit	Credit		Debit	Credit		Debit	Credit		Debit	Credit

Cash		Accounts Payable	
+	−	−	+
	(l) 1,800	(l) 1,800	

In order to help you determine how to record debits and credits in the foregoing transactions, we have continually repeated the fundamental accounting equation:

Assets	=	Liabilities	+	Owner's Equity	+	Revenue	−	Expenses
+ ∣ −		− ∣ +		− ∣ +		− ∣ +		+ ∣ −
Debit ∣ Credit		Debit ∣ Credit		Debit ∣ Credit		Debit ∣ Credit		Debit ∣ Credit

Let us again stress the steps in the analytical phase of accounting:

1. Decide which accounts are involved.
2. Determine whether there is an increase or a decrease in the accounts.
3. Formulate the entry as a debit to one account (or accounts) and a credit to another account (or accounts).

For the last step, you must be able to visualize this last equation. It is so useful that you ought to engrave it in your mind. For example, in the analysis of transaction **e,** you decide that Accounts Payable is involved; then you mentally classify Accounts Payable as a liability account. You should be able to picture in your mind the T account for Liabilities, with the minus sign on the debit side and the plus sign on the credit side. There is a decrease in Accounts Payable, so the entry should be recorded on the debit side. Without a doubt, this is the most important concept that you will ever learn in accounting. Memorize the fundamental accounting equation and placement of the plus and minus signs in the T accounts. Memorize as well the accounts that are exceptions, such as the Drawing account. It will make everything that follows much, much easier.

Now let's get back to the transactions of NuWay Cleaners.

Transaction (m)   NuWay Cleaners receives and pays bill for utilities, $220. We write $220 on the plus, or debit, side of Utilities Expense and $220 on the minus, or credit, side of Cash.

Assets	=	Liabilities	+	Owner's Equity	+	Revenue	−	Expenses
+ ∣ −		− ∣ +		− ∣ +		− ∣ +		+ ∣ −

Cash								Utilities Expense
+ ∣ −								+ ∣ −
∣ (m) 220								(m) 220 ∣

Transaction (n)   NuWay Cleaners pays $180 to a newspaper for advertising. (This bill has previously been recorded.) We write $180 on the minus, or debit, side of Accounts Payable and $180 on the minus, or credit, side of Cash.

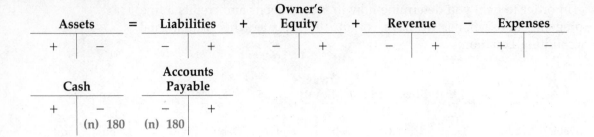

Assets	=	Liabilities	+	Owner's Equity	+	Revenue	−	Expenses
+ | −		− | +		− | +		− | +		+ | −

Cash		Accounts Payable
+ | −		− | +
(n) 180		(n) 180

Transaction (o) NuWay Cleaners receives cash revenue for the third week, $830. We write $830 on the plus, or debit, side of Cash and $830 on the plus, or credit, side of Income from Services.

Assets	=	Liabilities	+	Owner's Equity	+	Revenue	−	Expenses
+ | −		− | +		− | +		− | +		+ | −

Cash						Income from Services
+ | −						− | +
(o) 830						(o) 830

Transaction (p) NuWay Cleaners signs a contract with A-1 Rental to clean their for-hire rental clothes on a credit basis. When NuWay bills A-1 Rental $80 for services performed, we write $80 on the plus, or debit, side of Accounts Receivable and $80 on the plus, or credit, side of Income from Services.

Assets	=	Liabilities	+	Owner's Equity	+	Revenue	−	Expenses
+ | −		− | +		− | +		− | +		+ | −

Accounts Receivable						Income from Services
+ | −						− | +
(p) 80						(p) 80

Transaction (q) NuWay Cleaners pays wages of employees, $390. We write $390 on the plus, or debit, side of Wages Expense and $390 on the minus, or credit, side of Cash.

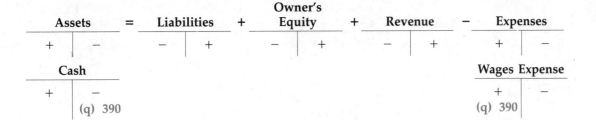

Assets	=	Liabilities	+	Owner's Equity	+	Revenue	−	Expenses
+ −		− +		− +		− +		+ −

Cash								Wages Expense
+ −								+ −
(q) 390								(q) 390

Transaction (r) NuWay Cleaners buys additional equipment from Sanchez Equipment Company, $940, paying $140 down with the remaining $800 on account. We write $940 on the plus, or debit, side of Equipment. We write $140 on the minus, or credit, side of Cash and $800 on the plus, or credit, side of Accounts Payable. When a transaction is recorded using two or more debits and/or two or more credits, it is called a **compound entry.**

Assets	=	Liabilities	+	Owner's Equity	+	Revenue	−	Expenses
+ −		− +		− +		− +		+ −

Cash		Accounts Payable
+ −		− +
(r) 140		(r) 800

Equipment
+   −
(r) 940

Transaction (s) NuWay Cleaners receives revenue from cash customers for the remainder of the month, $960. We write $960 on the plus, or debit, side of Cash and $960 on the plus, or credit, side of Income from Services.

Assets	=	Liabilities	+	Owner's Equity	+	Revenue	−	Expenses
+ −		− +		− +		− +		+ −

Cash						Income from Services
+ −						− +
(s) 960						(s) 960

Transaction (t) NuWay Cleaners receives $60 from A-1 Rental to apply on the amount previously billed. We write $60 on the plus, or debit, side of Cash and $60 on the minus, or credit, side of Accounts Receivable.

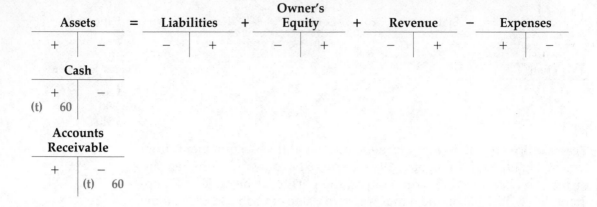

Assets	=	Liabilities	+	Owner's Equity	+	Revenue	−	Expenses
+ −		− +		− +		− +		+ −

Cash

+	−
(t) 60	

Accounts Receivable

+	−
	(t) 60

Transaction (u)   At the end of the month Stevenson withdraws from the business $1,000 in cash for his personal use. We write $1,000 on the minus, or credit, side of Cash and $1,000 on the plus, or debit, side of Alan Stevenson, Drawing. Because the account, Alan Stevenson, Drawing, is used to record personal withdrawals by the owner, it should be recorded on the plus, or debit, side of this account.

Assets	=	Liabilities	+	Owner's Equity	+	Revenue	−	Expenses
+ −		− +		− +		− +		+ −

Cash

Alan Stevenson, Drawing

+	−		+	−
	(u) 1,000		(u) 1,000	

Summary of Transactions

The T accounts that follow show the transactions as they are ordinarily recorded. Footings are shown in color. Note that, in recording expenses, one places the entries only on the plus, or debit, side. Also, in recording revenues, one places the entries on the plus, or credit, side.

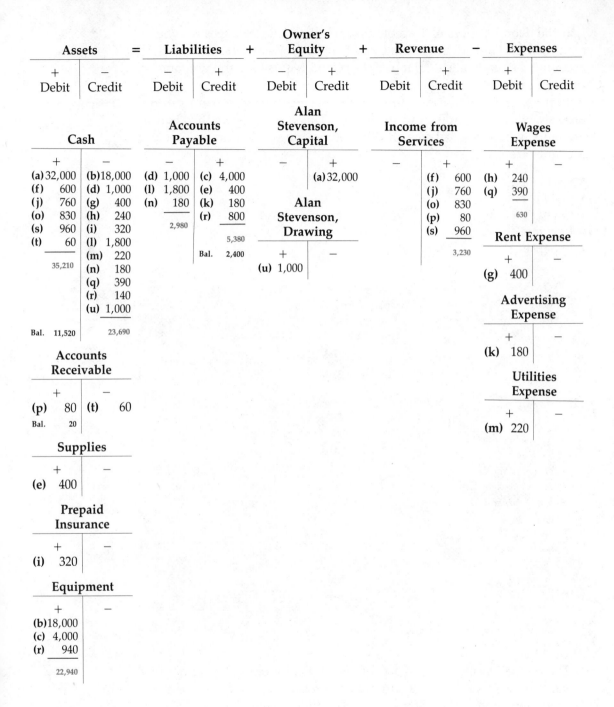

THE TRIAL BALANCE

You can now prepare a **trial balance** by simply recording the balances of the T accounts. This is not considered to be a financial statement, but, as the name implies, it is in essence a trial run by the accountant to prove that the debit balances of T accounts equal the credit balances of other T accounts. This is evidence of the equality of both sides of the fundamental accounting equation. The trial balance is a prerequisite to the preparation of financial statements.

In preparing a trial balance, record the balances of the accounts in the order in which they appear in the ledger. This order follows the chart of accounts, where first balance sheet accounts and then income statement accounts are listed:

Objective 4

Prepare a trial balance.

- Assets
- Liabilities
- Owner's Equity
- Revenue
- Expenses

NuWay Cleaners
Trial Balance
June 30, 19–

ACCOUNT NAME	DEBIT	CREDIT
Cash	11 5 2 0 00	
Accounts Receivable	2 0 00	
Supplies	4 0 0 00	
Prepaid Insurance	3 2 0 00	
Equipment	22 9 4 0 00	
Accounts Payable		2 4 0 0 00
Alan Stevenson, Capital		32 0 0 0 00
Alan Stevenson, Drawing	1 0 0 0 00	
Income from Services		3 2 3 0 00
Wages Expense	6 3 0 00	
Rent Expense	4 0 0 00	
Advertising Expense	1 8 0 00	
Utilities Expense	2 2 0 00	
	37 6 3 0 00	37 6 3 0 00

The normal balance of each account is on its plus side. Remember that when there is more than one entry in an account, we record the totals in footings and subtract one footing from the other to determine the balance. Record this balance on the side of the account having the larger footing. (Here we record the Drawing account balance in the debit column, because it has a debit balance. We don't deduct Drawing from the Capital account at the time that we prepare the trial balance.) The following table indicates where each of the account balances would normally be shown in a trial balance.

| Account Titles | Trial Balance | |
	Left or Debit Balances	Right or Credit Balances
	Assets	
		Liabilities
		Owner's Equity
	Drawing	
		Revenue
	Expenses	
Totals	XXXX XX	XXXX XX

Errors Exposed by the Trial Balance

If the debit and credit columns are not equal, then it is evident that we have made an error. Possible causes of errors include the following:

- Recording only half an entry, such as a debit without a corresponding credit, or vice versa.
- Recording both halves of the entry on the same side, such as two debits, rather than a debit and a credit.
- Recording one or more amounts incorrectly.
- Making errors in arithmetic, such as errors in adding the trial balance columns or in finding the balances of the ledger accounts.

Procedure for Locating Errors

Suppose that you are in a business situation in which you have recorded transactions for a month in the account books, and the accounts do not balance. To save yourself time, you need to have a definite procedure for tracking down the errors. The best method is to do everything in reverse, as follows:

- Re-add the trial balance columns.
- Check the transferring of the figures from the ledger accounts to the trial balance.
- Verify the footings and balances of the ledger accounts.

As an added precaution, form the habit of verifying all addition and subtraction as you go along. You can thus correct many mistakes *before* making a trial balance.

When the trial balance totals do not balance, the difference might indicate you forgot to record half of an entry in the accounts. For example, if the difference in the trial balance totals is $20, you may have recorded $20 on the debit side of one account without recording $20 on the credit side of another account. Another possibility is to divide the difference by two; this may provide a clue that you accidentally posted half an entry twice. For example, if the difference in the trial balance is $600, you may have recorded $300 on the debit side of one account and an additional $300 on the debit side of another account. Look for a transaction that involved $300 and then see if you have recorded a debit and a credit. By knowing which transactions to check, you can save a lot of time.

Transpositions and Slides

If the difference is evenly divisible by 9, the discrepancy may be either a **transposition** or a **slide.** A transposition means that the digits have been transposed, or switched around. For example, one transposition of digits in 916 can be written as 619:

$$
\begin{array}{r}
916 \\
-\ 619 \\
\hline
297
\end{array}
\qquad
\begin{array}{r}
33 \\
\overline{9)297}
\end{array}
$$

A slide refers to an error in placing the decimal point, in other words, a slide in the decimal point. For example, $163 could be inadvertently written as $1.63:

$$
\begin{array}{r}
\$163.00 \\
-\ 1.63 \\
\hline
\$161.37
\end{array}
\qquad
\begin{array}{r}
17.93 \\
\overline{9)161.37}
\end{array}
$$

Or the error may be a combination of transposition and slide, such as when $216 is written as $6.21:

$$
\begin{array}{r}
\$216.00 \\
-\ 6.21 \\
\hline
\$209.79
\end{array}
\qquad
\begin{array}{r}
23.31 \\
\overline{9)209.79}
\end{array}
$$

Again, the difference is evenly divisible by 9.

GLOSSARY

Compound entry A transaction that is recorded using two or more debits and/or two or more credits.

Credit The right side of a ledger T account; to credit is to record an amount on the right side of a ledger T account. Credits represent increases in liability, capital, and revenue accounts, and decreases in asset and expense accounts.

Debit The left side of a ledger T account; to debit is to record an amount on the left side of a ledger T account. Debits represent increases in asset and expense accounts, and decreases in liability, capital, and revenue accounts.

Footings The totals of each side of a T account, recorded in pencil.

Ledger A book, a binder, or a file containing all the accounts of an enterprise.

Normal balance The plus side of any T account.

Slide An error in the placement of the decimal point of a number.

T account form A form of ledger account having one side for entries on the debit, or left, side, and one side for entries on the credit, or right, side.

Transposition An error that involves interchanging, or switching around, the digits during the recording of a number.

Trial balance A list of all ledger account balances to prove that the total of all the debit balances equals the total of all the credit balances.

QUESTIONS, EXERCISES, AND PROBLEMS

Discussion Questions

1. Name the five classifications of accounts. Which classifications are identified with the balance sheet? Which classifications are identified with the income statement?
2. Regarding the five classifications of accounts, indicate the normal balance (whether debit or credit) of each account classification.
3. Does the term *debit* always mean increase? Does the term *credit* always mean decrease? Explain.
4. What is the reason for using a separate owner's drawing account?
5. What is a compound entry?
6. Give an example of (a) a transposition and (b) a slide.
7. N. Blacow runs his own grounds maintenance business and keeps his own books. Upon taking a trial balance, Blacow finds the total debits amount to $107,400, and total credits amount to $107,600. What are some possible reasons for the $200 difference between debit and credit totals?

Exercises

Exercise 3-1 Name the account in which each of the following items would be recorded.

a. Premiums paid in advance for two years on a liability insurance policy.
b. Amounts owed to the business by customers.

c. Money on deposit in the business checking account.

d. The value of blank forms used to send out bills to charge customers.

e. Amounts owed to suppliers.

f. D. Aikens's claim against the assets of Aikens's business.

Exercise 3-2 On a sheet of paper set up the fundamental accounting equation with T accounts under each of the five account classifications, noting plus and minus signs on the appropriate sides of each account. Under each of the five classifications, set up T accounts—again with the correct plus and minus signs—for each of the following ledger accounts of the Towncraft Shoe Repair: Cash; Accounts Receivable; Supplies; Equipment; Accounts Payable; Sara Dugan, Capital; Sara Dugan, Drawing; Income from Services; Rent Expense; Telephone Expense; Utilities Expense; Miscellaneous Expense.

Exercise 3-3 James Fulton operates Fulton Carpet Cleaners. The company has the following chart of accounts:

Assets
Cash
Accounts Receivable
Supplies
Prepaid Insurance
Cleaning Equipment
Truck
Office Equipment

Liabilities
Accounts Payable

Owner's Equity
James Fulton, Capital
James Fulton, Drawing

Revenue
Income from Services

Expenses
Wages Expense
Truck Expense
Utilities Expense
Miscellaneous Expense

On a sheet of ordinary notebook paper, record the following transactions directly in pairs of T accounts. (*Example:* Paid telephone bill, $18.)

Utilities Expense		Cash	
+	−	+	−
18			18

a. Paid $440 for liability insurance.

b. Paid $72 for advertising.

c. Fulton withdrew $192 in cash for personal use.

d. Paid creditors on account, $570.

e. Received $882 from charge customers to apply on account.

f. Paid electric bill, $38.

g. Paid gasoline bill for truck, $216.

Exercise 3-4 During the first month of operation, Anderson's Framing Shop recorded the following transactions. Describe transactions **a** through **k**.

Cash			Accounts Payable			C. Anderson, Capital		Income from Services		Rent Expense	

Cash		
(a) 2,600	(c)	63
(k) 840	(e)	320
	(f)	70
	(g)	1,000
	(i)	200
	(j)	71

Accounts Receivable
(h) 795

Framing Supplies
(b) 290

Framing Equipment
(d) 3,800
(g) 1,900

Accounts Payable	
(b) 290	
(g) 900	

C. Anderson, Capital	
	(a) 2,600
	(d) 3,800

C. Anderson, Drawing
(i) 200

Income from Services	
	(h) 795
	(k) 840

Rent Expense
(e) 320

Utilities Expense
(j) 71

Advertising Expense
(c) 63

Miscellaneous Expense
(f) 70

Exercise 3-5 From the accounts in Exercise 4, prepare a trial balance for Anderson's Framing Shop, dated September 30 of this year.

Exercise 3-6 The accounts (all normal balances) of Donna's Beauty Salon as of September 30 of this year are listed in alphabetical order. On a sheet of notebook paper, prepare a trial balance listing the accounts in proper order.

Accounts Payable	$11,400	Insurance Expense	$ 600
Accounts Receivable	16,200	Miscellaneous	
Cash	2,200	Expense	200
Donna Milnor,		Prepaid Insurance	600
Capital	42,200	Rent Expense	4,200
Donna Milnor,		Supplies	6,400
Drawing	1,200	Utilities Expense	2,200
Equipment	40,000	Wages Expense	23,800
Income from Services	44,000		

Exercise 3-7 Answer the following questions by adding the word *debit* or the word *credit*.

a. The Equipment account is increased by entering a _____.
b. The Capital account is increased by entering a _____.
c. The Accounts Receivable account is decreased by entering a _____.
d. The Rent Expense account is increased by entering a _____.
e. The Drawing account is increased by entering a _____.
f. The Accounts Payable account is decreased by entering a _____.

Exercise 3-8 Assume that a trial balance has been prepared and that the total of the debit balances is not equal to the total of the credit balances. On a sheet of paper, note the amount by which the two totals would differ. Identify which column is overstated or understated.

Error	Amount of Difference	Debit or Credit Column Understated or Overstated
Example: A $142 debit to Prepaid Insurance was not posted.	$142	Debit column understated
a. A $47 credit to Cash was not posted.		
b. A $420 debit to Supplies was posted twice.		
c. A $34 debit to Equipment was posted as $340.		
d. A $36 debit to Supplies was posted as a $36 debit to Miscellaneous Expense.		
e. A $91 debit to Accounts Payable was posted twice.		
f. A $48 debit to Accounts Receivable was posted as $84.		

Problem Set A

Problem 3-1A During January of this year, R. L. Ricardo established the Ricardo Autotronics Company. The following asset, liability, and owner's equity accounts are included in the ledger: Cash; Parts and Supplies; Shop Equipment; Store Equipment; Truck; Accounts Payable; R. L. Ricardo, Capital. The following transactions occurred during the month of January.

a. Ricardo invested $16,000 cash in the business.
b. Bought testing equipment for cash, $1,562 (Shop Equipment).
c. Bought repair parts on account from Consolidated Supply, $418; payment is due in 30 days.
d. Bought store fixtures for $924 from Fischer Hardware; payment is due in 30 days.
e. Bought a used service truck for $6,400 from Ludwick Motors, paying $1,500 down; the balance is due in 30 days.
f. Paid $300 on account for the store fixtures in **d**.
g. Ricardo invested his personal tools and testing devices in the business, $1,250.

Instructions

1. Label the account titles under the appropriate headings in the fundamental accounting equation.
2. Correctly place the plus and minus signs under each T account, and label the debit and credit sides of the T account.
3. Record the amounts in the proper positions in the T accounts. Key each entry to the alphabetical symbol identifying each transaction.

Problem 3-2A Dora Shafer established Dora's Fun and Games during October of this year. The accountant prepared the following chart of accounts.

Assets
Cash
Prepaid Insurance
Gaming Equipment
Office Equipment
Neon Sign

Liabilities
Accounts Payable

Owner's Equity
Dora Shafer, Capital
Dora Shafer, Drawing

Revenue
Income from Services

Expenses
Rent Expense
Utilities Expense
Wages Expense
Repair Expense
Miscellaneous Expense

The transactions listed below occurred during the month.

a. Shafer invested $12,200 cash to establish her business.
b. Paid rent for the month, $640.
c. Bought an office desk and filing cabinet for cash, $155.
d. Bought electronic games for use in the business, $10,300; paid $2,300 down, with the balance due in 30 days.
e. Bought a neon sign for $650; paid $200 down, with the balance due in 30 days.
f. Shafer invested her personal electronic games in the business, $740.
g. Received bill for repairs, $52.
h. Received cash for services rendered, $583.
i. Received and paid electric bill, $121.
j. Paid $240 for a two-year liability insurance policy.
k. Paid bill for repairs, billed previously in **g**.
l. Received cash for services rendered, $967.
m. Paid wages to employees, $525.
n. Paid city business license, $27.
o. Shafer withdrew cash for personal use, $325.

Instructions

1. Place the account titles under the appropriate headings in the fundamental accounting equation.
2. Record the plus and minus signs under each T account, and label the debit and credit sides of the T accounts.
3. Record the transactions in the T accounts. Key each entry to the alphabetical symbol identifying each transaction.
4. Foot the T accounts.
5. Prepare a trial balance with a three-line heading, dated October 31.

Problem 3-3A Doris L. Langdon, an attorney, opens a law office. Her accountant recommends the following chart of accounts:

Assets
Cash
Accounts Receivable
Office Equipment
Office Furniture
Law Library

Liabilities
Accounts Payable

Owner's Equity
Doris L. Langdon, Capital
Doris L. Langdon, Drawing

Revenue
Professional Fees

Expenses
Salary Expense
Rent Expense
Utilities Expense
Travel Expense

The following transactions occurred during June of this year.

a. Langdon invested $12,600 cash in her law practice.
b. Bought a set of filing cabinets on account from Cohn Office Supply (Office Equipment), $270.
c. Paid cash for desks, chairs, and carpets, $110.
d. Bought an electric typewriter for $520 from Macon Office Machines, paying $240 down; the balance is due in 30 days.
e. Received and paid telephone bill, $96.
f. Billed clients for legal services performed, $1,580.
g. Langdon invested her personal law books in the firm, $6,700 (additional investment).
h. Paid $156 in expenses for business trip.
i. Received and paid electric bill, $82.
j. Received $660 from clients previously billed (transaction **f**).
k. Paid $140 on the filing cabinets purchased on credit from Cohn Office Supply.
l. Paid office rent for the month, $400.
m. Paid salary of receptionist, $685.
n. Langdon withdrew cash for personal use, $950.

Instructions

1. Correctly place plus and minus signs under each T account. Label the debit and credit sides of the T accounts.
2. Record the transactions in the T accounts. Key each entry to the alphabetical symbol identifying each transaction.
3. Foot the T accounts.
4. Prepare a trial balance as of June 30, 19–.
5. Prepare an income statement for June.
6. Prepare a statement of owner's equity for June.
7. Prepare a balance sheet as of June 30, 19–.

Problem 3-4A On August 1, L. C. Kane opened a coin-operated laundry called Modern Self-Service Laundry. Kane's accountant listed the following accounts for the ledger: Cash; Supplies; Prepaid Insurance; Equipment; Furniture and Fixtures; Accounts Payable; L. C. Kane, Capital; L. C. Kane, Drawing; Laundry Revenue; Wages Expense; Rent Expense; Power Expense; Miscellaneous Expense. During August the following transactions were completed.

a. Kane deposited $18,750 in a bank account in the name of the business.
b. Bought tables and chairs for cash, $246.
c. Paid rent for the month, $475.
d. Bought washers and dryers for $15,600, giving $2,700 cash as a down payment with the remainder due in 30 days.
e. Bought washing supplies on account, $423.
f. Received $1,386 from cash customers for the first half of the month.
g. Paid $153 cash for liability insurance for twelve months.
h. Paid $330 as a partial payment on the equipment purchased in **d**.
i. Received and paid electric bill, $172.
j. Paid $115 on account for the washing supplies acquired in **e**.
k. Received $1,160 from cash customers for the second half of the month.
l. Paid $54 for license and other miscellaneous expenses.
m. Paid wages to employee, $815.
n. Kane withdrew cash for personal use, $720.

Instructions

1. Correctly place the plus and minus signs under each T account. Label the debit and credit sides of the T accounts.
2. Record the transactions in the T accounts. Key each entry to the alphabetical symbol identifying each transaction.
3. Foot the T accounts.
4. Prepare a trial balance as of August 31, 19–.
5. Prepare an income statement for August.
6. Prepare a statement of owner's equity for August.
7. Prepare a balance sheet as of August 31, 19–.

Problem Set B

Problem 3-1B During August of this year, B. L. Chamberlin established the Chamberlin Linen Supply Company. The following asset, liability, and owner's equity accounts are included in the ledger: Cash; Linen Supplies; Laundry Equipment; Office Equipment; Truck; Accounts Payable; B. L. Chamberlin, Capital. During August, the following transactions occurred.

a. Chamberlin invested $15,400 in the business.
b. Bought used washers and dryers for $4,720, paying cash.
c. Bought sheets and pillow cases from Andover Textile Company for cash, $648.
d. Bought towels on account from Restaurant and Hotel Supply Company, $828.

e. Bought a typewriter, desk, and filing cabinet for cash, $516.

f. Bought a used delivery truck for $6,400 from Reliable Used Cars, paying $800 down; the balance is due in 30 days.

g. Paid $200 on account to Restaurant and Hotel Supply Company.

Instructions

1. Label the accounts and put each under the appropriate heading in the fundamental accounting equation.
2. Correctly place plus and minus signs under each T account and label the debit and credit sides of the T accounts.
3. Record the amounts in the proper positions in the T accounts. Key each entry to the alphabetical symbol identifying each transaction.

Problem 3-2B L. P. Rodriguez established the Supra Game Room during November of this year. The accountant prepared the following chart of accounts.

Assets
Cash
Prepaid Insurance
Gaming Equipment
Office Equipment
Neon Sign

Liabilities
Accounts Payable

Owner's Equity
L. P. Rodriguez, Capital
L. P. Rodriguez, Drawing

Revenue
Income from Services

Expenses
Rent Expense
Utilities Expense
Wages Expense
Repair Expense
Miscellaneous Expense

The transactions listed below occurred during the month.

a. Rodriguez invested $12,400 cash to establish his business.
b. Bought an office desk and filing cabinet for cash, $195.
c. Bought electronic games for use in the business, $8,400, paying $1,400 down; the balance is due in 30 days.
d. Paid rent for the month, $525.
e. Received cash for services rendered, $496.
f. Bought a neon sign for $868, with $200 as a down payment; the balance is due in 30 days.
g. Received bill for repairs, $321.
h. Paid $316 for a two-year liability insurance policy.
i. Received and paid electric bill, $116.
j. Paid bill for repairs, billed previously in **g**.
k. Received cash for services rendered, $915.
l. Paid wages to employee, $520.
m. Rodriguez invested his personal electronic games in the business, $1,425.
n. Rodriguez withdrew cash for personal use, $325.
o. Paid city business license, $32.

Instructions

1. Place the account titles under the appropriate headings in the fundamental accounting equation.
2. Correctly place the plus and minus signs under each T account and label the debit and credit sides of the accounts.
3. Record the transactions in the T accounts. Key each entry to the alphabetical symbol identifying each transaction.
4. Foot the T accounts.
5. Prepare a trial balance, with a three-line heading, dated November 30.

Problem 3-3B Sylvia A. Koski, an attorney, opens an office for the practice of law. Her accountant recommends the following chart of accounts.

Assets
Cash
Accounts Receivable
Office Equipment
Office Furniture
Law Library

Liabilities
Accounts Payable

Owner's Equity
Sylvia A. Koski, Capital
Sylvia A. Koski, Drawing

Revenue
Professional Fees

Expenses
Salary Expense
Rent Expense
Utilities Expense
Travel Expense

The following transactions occurred during May of this year.

a. Koski invested $9,800 cash in her law practice.
b. Bought a typewriter for $415 from Smithwick Office Machines, paying $250 down; the balance is due in 30 days.
c. Koski invested her personal law books in the firm, $8,430 (additional investment).
d. Bought desks, chairs, and carpets, paying cash, $1,426.
e. Bought a set of filing cabinets on account from Lewis Office Supply (Office Equipment), $312.
f. Received and paid telephone bill, $86.
g. Billed clients for legal services performed, $1,242.
h. Received and paid electric bill for heat and lights, $82.
i. Paid expenses for business trip, $126.
j. Bought bookcases on account from Lewis Office Supply (Office Furniture), $416.
k. Billed clients for additional legal fees, $1,575.
l. Paid office rent for the month, $425.
m. Paid salary of receptionist, $680.
n. Koski withdrew cash for her personal use, $840.

Instructions

1. Correctly place plus and minus signs under each T account, and label the debit and credit sides of the T accounts.
2. Record the transactions in the T accounts. Key each entry to the alphabetical symbol identifying each transaction.

3. Foot the T accounts.
4. Prepare a trial balance as of May 31, 19–.
5. Prepare an income statement for May.
6. Prepare a statement of owner's equity for May.
7. Prepare a balance sheet as of May 31, 19–.

Problem 3-4B   On June 1, A. F. Dukes opened a coin-operated laundry under the name Speedy Self-Service Laundry. Dukes's accountant listed the following accounts for the ledger: Cash; Supplies; Prepaid Insurance; Equipment; Furniture and Fixtures; Accounts Payable; A. F. Dukes, Capital; A. F. Dukes, Drawing; Laundry Revenue; Wages Expense; Rent Expense; Power Expense; Miscellaneous Expense. During June the following transactions were completed.

a. Dukes deposited $15,550 in a bank account in the name of the business.
b. Bought chairs and tables for cash, $232.
c. Bought laundry detergent on account from Oakland Supply Company, $294.
d. Paid rent for the month, $540.
e. Bought washing machines and dryers from Starr Equipment Company, $14,400; paid $2,400 down, with the remainder due in 30 days.
f. Received $1,230 from cash customers for the first half of the month.
g. Paid $210 cash for liability insurance for 12 months.
h. Paid $240 as a partial payment on the equipment purchased from Starr Equipment Company.
i. Received and paid electric bill, $159.
j. Received $1,473 from cash customers for the second half of the month.
k. Paid $36 for license and other miscellaneous expenses.
l. Paid wages to employee, $600.
m. Dukes withdrew cash for his personal use, $575.
n. Paid $225 on account for the washing supplies acquired in **c**.

Instructions

1. Correctly place the plus and minus signs under each T account and label the debit and credit sides of the T accounts.
2. Record the transactions in the T accounts. Key each entry to the alphabetical symbol identifying each transaction.
3. Foot the T accounts.
4. Prepare a trial balance as of June 30, 19–.
5. Prepare an income statement for June.
6. Prepare a statement of owner's equity for June.
7. Prepare a balance sheet as of June 30, 19–.

4 The General Journal and Posting

Learning Objectives

After you have completed this chapter, you will be able to do the following:

1. Record a group of transactions pertaining to a service-type enterprise in a two-column general journal.

2. Post entries from a two-column general journal to general ledger accounts.

In Chapter 3 we recorded business transactions as debits and credits to T accounts. This enabled you to visualize the accounts and tell which should be debited and which should be credited.

The initial steps in the accounting process are:

1. Record business transactions in a journal.
2. Post to T accounts in the ledger.
3. Foot the T accounts and determine the balances.
4. Prepare a trial balance.

Up to this time we have covered steps 2, 3, and 4. In our previous presentation, we introduced T accounts because, in the process of formulating debits and credits for business transactions, one has to think in terms of T accounts. Now we need to backtrack slightly in order to take up step 1, recording business transactions in a journal. In this chapter we shall present the general journal and the posting procedure.

THE GENERAL JOURNAL

We have seen that an accountant must keep a written record of each transaction. One could record the transactions directly in T accounts; however, one would list only part of the transaction in each T account. A **journal** is a book in which a person makes the original record of a business transaction. The journal serves the function of recording both the debits and credits of the entire transaction. This journal is like a diary for the business, in which one records in day-by-day order all the events involving financial affairs. A journal is called a *book of original entry.* In other words, a transaction is always recorded in the journal first and then recorded in the T accounts. The process of recording in the journal is called **journalizing.** One obtains information about transactions from business papers, such as checks, invoices, receipts, letters, and memos. These **source documents** furnish proof that a transaction has taken place, so we should identify them in the journal entry whenever possible. Later on we shall introduce a variety of special journals. However, the basic form of journal is the two-column general journal. The term *two-column* refers to the two money columns used for debit and credit amounts.

As an example of journalizing business transactions, let's use the transactions for NuWay Cleaners listed in Chapter 3. Each page of the journal is numbered in consecutive order. This is the first page, so we write a 1 in the space for the page number. Also, we must write the date of transaction. Now let's get on with the first entry.

Transaction (a)   June 1: Alan Stevenson deposited $32,000 in a bank account in the name of NuWay Cleaners.

Objective 1

We write the year and month in the left part of the date column. We don't have to repeat the year and month until we start a new page, or until the year or month changes. (Our illustrations, however, may repeat the month simply to eliminate confusion.) We write the day in the right part of the date column, and repeat it for each journal entry.

Record a group of transactions pertaining to a service-type enterprise in a two-column general journal.

	DATE		DESCRIPTION	POST. REF.	DEBIT	CREDIT	
1	19— Jun.	1					1
2							2

GENERAL JOURNAL   PAGE __1__

Since we are familiar with the accounts, the next step is to decide which accounts should be debited and which credited. We do this by first figuring out which accounts are involved and whether they are increased or decreased. We then visualize the accounts mentally with their respective plus and minus sides.

Cash is involved in our example. Cash is considered to be an asset because it falls within the definition of "things owned." Cash is increased, so we debit Cash.

Cash

+	−
Debit	Credit
32,000	

Alan Stevenson, Capital is involved; this is an owner's equity account because it represents the owner's investment. Alan Stevenson, Capital is increased, so we credit Alan Stevenson, Capital.

Alan Stevenson, Capital

−	+
Debit	Credit
	32,000

As we said earlier, you perform this process mentally. If the transaction is more complicated, then use scratch paper, drawing the T accounts. Using T accounts is the accountant's way of drawing a picture of the transaction. This is why we stressed the fundamental accounting equation, with the T accounts and plus and minus signs, so heavily in Chapter 3. You are most definitely urged to get in the T-account habit.

Always record the debit part of the entry first. Enter the account title—in this case, Cash—in the description column. Record the amount—$32,000—in the debit amount column.

	DATE		DESCRIPTION	POST. REF.	DEBIT	CREDIT	
1	19– Jun.	1	Cash		32 0 0 0 00		1
2							2

Next, record the credit part of the entry. Enter the account title—in this case, Alan Stevenson, Capital—on the line below the debit, in the Description column, indented about one-half inch. Do not abbreviate account titles, and do not extend them into the Posting Reference column. On the same line, write the amount in the credit column.

	DATE		DESCRIPTION	POST. REF.	DEBIT	CREDIT	
1	19– Jun.	1	Cash		32 0 0 0 00		1
2			Alan Stevenson, Capital			32 0 0 0 00	2
3							3

You should now give a brief explanation, in which you may refer to business papers, such as check numbers or invoice numbers; you may also list names of charge customers or creditors, or terms of payment. Enter the explanation below the credit entry, indented an additional one-half inch.

	DATE		DESCRIPTION	POST. REF.	DEBIT	CREDIT	
1	19– Jun.	1	Cash		32 0 0 0 00		1
2			Alan Stevenson, Capital			32 0 0 0 00	2
3			Original investment by Stevenson				3
4			in NuWay Cleaners.				4
5							5

In order for an entry in the general journal to be complete, it must contain (1) a debit entry, (2) a credit entry, and (3) an explanation. To anyone thoroughly familiar with the accounts, the explanation may seem to be quite obvious or redundant. This will take care of itself later; but in the meantime, let us record the explanation as a required, integral part of the entry.

Transaction (b) June 2: NuWay Cleaners buys $18,000 worth of equipment, for cash.

Decide which accounts are involved. Next classify them under the five possible classifications. Visualize the plus and minus signs under the classifications. Now decide whether the accounts are increased or decreased. When you use T accounts to analyze the transaction, the results are as follows:

Equipment		Cash	
+	−	+	−
Debit	Credit	Debit	Credit
18,000			18,000

Now journalize this analysis below the first transaction. For the sake of appearance, leave one blank line between transactions. Record the day of the month in the date column. Remember, you don't have to record the month and year again until the month or year changes or you use a new journal page.

	DATE		DESCRIPTION	POST. REF.	DEBIT	CREDIT	
	GENERAL JOURNAL					PAGE __1__	
1	19– Jun.	1	Cash		32 0 0 0 00		1
2			Alan Stevenson, Capital			32 0 0 0 00	2
3			Original investment by Stevenson				3
4			in NuWay Cleaners.				4
5							5
6		2	Equipment		18 0 0 0 00		6
7			Cash			18 0 0 0 00	7
8			Bought equipment for cash.				8
9							9

Transaction (c) On June 2 NuWay Cleaners buys $4,000 worth of equipment on account from Sanchez Equipment Company. In order to get organized, think of the T accounts first.

Equipment		Accounts Payable	
+	−	−	+
Debit	Credit	Debit	Credit
4,000			4,000

Skip a line in the journal and record the day of the month and then the entry. In journalizing a transaction involving Accounts Payable, always state the name of the creditor. Similarly, in journalizing a transaction involving Accounts Receivable, always state the name of the charge customer as is done in the example on page 80.

GENERAL JOURNAL   PAGE __1__

	DATE	DESCRIPTION	POST. REF.	DEBIT	CREDIT	
10	2	Equipment		4 0 0 0 00		10
11		Accounts Payable			4 0 0 0 00	11
12		Bought equipment on account				12
13		from Sanchez Equipment				13
14		Company.				14
15						15

Transaction (d) On June 4, NuWay Cleaners pays $1,000 to be applied against the firm's liability of $4,000. Mentally picture the T accounts like this.

Cash		Accounts Payable	
+	−	−	+
Debit	Credit	Debit	Credit
	1,000	1,000	

Cash is an easy account to recognize. So, in every transaction, ask yourself, "Is Cash involved?" If Cash is involved, determine whether it is coming in or going out. In this case we see that cash is going out, so we record it on the minus side. We now have a credit to Cash and half of the entry. Next, we recognize that Accounts Payable is involved. We ask ourselves, "Do we owe more or less as a result of this transaction?" The answer is "less," so we record it on the minus, or debit, side of the account.

GENERAL JOURNAL   PAGE __1__

	DATE	DESCRIPTION	POST. REF.	DEBIT	CREDIT	
16	4	Accounts Payable		1 0 0 0 00		16
17		Cash			1 0 0 0 00	17
18		Paid Sanchez Equipment				18
19		Company on account.				19
20						20

Now let's list the transactions for June for NuWay Cleaners with the date of each transaction. The journal entries are illustrated on the following pages in Figures 4-1, 4-2, and 4-3.

Jun. 1 Stevenson invests $32,000 cash in his new business.
2 Buys $18,000 worth of equipment for cash.
2 Buys $4,000 worth of equipment on credit from Sanchez Equipment Company.

Figure 4-1

GENERAL JOURNAL

PAGE 1

	DATE		DESCRIPTION	POST. REF.	DEBIT	CREDIT	
1	19– Jun.	1	Cash		32 0 0 0 00		1
2			Alan Stevenson, Capital			32 0 0 0 00	2
3			Original investment by Stevenson				3
4			in NuWay Cleaners.				4
5							5
6		2	Equipment		18 0 0 0 00		6
7			Cash			18 0 0 0 00	7
8			Bought equipment for cash.				8
9							9
10		2	Equipment		4 0 0 0 00		10
11			Accounts Payable			4 0 0 0 00	11
12			Bought equipment on account				12
13			from Sanchez Equipment				13
14			Company.				14
15							15
16		4	Accounts Payable		1 0 0 0 00		16
17			Cash			1 0 0 0 00	17
18			Paid Sanchez Equipment				18
19			Company on account.				19
20							20
21		4	Supplies		4 0 0 00		21
22			Accounts Payable			4 0 0 00	22
23			Bought cleaning fluids on account				23
24			from Troy Supply Company.				24
25							25
26		7	Cash		6 0 0 00		26
27			Income from Services			6 0 0 00	27
28			For week ended June 7.				28
29							29
30		8	Rent Expense		4 0 0 00		30
31			Cash			4 0 0 00	31
32			For month ended June 30.				32
33							33
34		10	Wages Expense		2 4 0 00		34
35			Cash			2 4 0 00	35
36			Paid wages, June 1 to June 10.				36
37							37

Jun. 4 Pays $1,000 to Sanchez Equipment Company, to be applied against the firm's liability of $4,000.

4 Buys cleaning fluids on credit from Troy Supply Company, $400.

7 Cash revenue received for first week, $600.

8 Pays rent for the month, $400.

10 Pays wages to employees, $240, June 1 through June 10.

Figure 4-2

GENERAL JOURNAL

PAGE __2__

	DATE		DESCRIPTION	POST. REF.	DEBIT	CREDIT	
1	19– Jun.	10	Prepaid Insurance		3 2 0 00		1
2			Cash			3 2 0 00	2
3			Premium for two-year liability				3
4			insurance.				4
5							5
6		14	Cash		7 6 0 00		6
7			Income from Services			7 6 0 00	7
8			For week ended June 14.				8
9							9
10		14	Advertising Expense		1 8 0 00		10
11			Accounts Payable			1 8 0 00	11
12			Received bill for advertising				12
13			from Daily News.				13
14							14
15		15	Accounts Payable		1 8 0 0 00		15
16			Cash			1 8 0 0 00	16
17			Paid Sanchez Equipment				17
18			Company on account.				18
19							19
20		15	Utilities Expense		2 2 0 00		20
21			Cash			2 2 0 00	21
22			Paid bill for utilities.				22
23							23
24		15	Accounts Payable		1 8 0 00		24
25			Cash			1 8 0 00	25
26			Paid Daily News for advertising.				26
27							27
28		21	Cash		8 3 0 00		28
29			Income from Services			8 3 0 00	29
30			For week ended June 21.				30
31							31
32		23	Accounts Receivable		8 0 00		32
33			Income from Services			8 0 00	33
34			A-1 Rental, for services rendered.				34
35							35

Jun. 10 Pays for a two-year liability insurance policy, $320.
     14 Cash revenue received for second week, $760.
     14 Receives bill for newspaper advertising, from the *Daily News*, $180.
     15 Pays $1,800 to Sanchez Equipment Company as part payment on account.
     15 Receives and pays bill for utilities, $220.
     15 Pays the *Daily News* for advertising, $180. (This bill has previously been recorded.)
     21 Cash revenue received for third week, $830.
     23 NuWay Cleaners enters into a contract with A-1 Rental to clean their for-hire formal garments on a credit basis. Bills A-1 Rental for services performed, $80.
     24 Pays wages of employees, $390, June 11 through June 24.

Figure 4-3

GENERAL JOURNAL   PAGE ___3___

	DATE		DESCRIPTION	POST. REF.	DEBIT	CREDIT	
1	19– Jun.	24	Wages Expense		3 9 0 00		1
2			Cash			3 9 0 00	2
3			Paid wages, June 11 to June 24.				3
4							4
5		26	Equipment		9 4 0 00		5
6			Cash			1 4 0 00	6
7			Accounts Payable			8 0 0 00	7
8			Bought equipment on account				8
9			from Sanchez Equipment				9
10			Company.				10
11							11
12		30	Cash		9 6 0 00		12
13			Income from Services			9 6 0 00	13
14			For remainder of June, ended				14
15			June 30.				15
16							16
17		30	Cash		6 0 00		17
18			Accounts Receivable			6 0 00	18
19			A-1 Rental, to apply on account.				19
20							20
21		30	Alan Stevenson, Drawing		1 0 0 0 00		21
22			Cash			1 0 0 0 00	22
23			Withdrawal for personal use.				23
24							24

Jun. 26 Buys additional equipment on account, $940 from Sanchez Equipment Company, paying $140 down with the remaining $800 on account.

   30 Cash revenue received for the remainder of the month, $960.

   30 Receives $60 from A-1 Rental to apply on amount previously billed.

   30 Stevenson withdraws cash for personal use, $1,000.

POSTING TO THE GENERAL LEDGER

From this example, you can see that the journal is indeed the *book of original entry.* Each transaction must first be recorded in the journal in its entirety. Ledger accounts give us a cumulative record of the transactions recorded in each individual account. The general ledger is simply a book that contains all the accounts. The book used for the ledger is usually a loose-leaf binder, so that one can add or remove leaves. The process of transferring figures from the journal to the ledger accounts is called **posting.**

Objective 2

Post entries from a two-column general journal to general ledger accounts.

The Chart of Accounts

One arranges the accounts in the ledger according to the chart of accounts. The **chart of accounts** is the official list of accounts in which transactions may be recorded. Assets are listed first, liabilities second, owner's equity third, revenue fourth, and expenses fifth. The chart of accounts for NuWay Cleaners is as follows.

Chart of Accounts

Assets (100–199)
111 Cash
112 Accounts Receivable
113 Supplies
114 Prepaid Insurance
121 Equipment

Liabilities (200–299)
211 Accounts Payable

Owner's Equity (300–399)
311 Alan Stevenson, Capital
312 Alan Stevenson, Drawing

Revenue (400–499)
411 Income from Services

Expenses (500–599)
511 Wages Expense
512 Rent Expense
513 Advertising Expense
514 Utilities Expense

Notice that the arrangement consists of the balance sheet accounts followed by the income statement accounts. The numbers preceding the account titles are the **account numbers.** Accounts in the ledger are kept by numbers rather than by pages because it's hard to tell in advance how many pages to reserve for a particular account. When you use the number system, you can add sheets quite readily. The digits in the account numbers also indicate *classifications* of accounts: For most companies, assets start with 1, liabilities with 2, owner's equity with 3, revenue with 4, and expenses with 5. The second and third digits indicate the positions of the individual accounts within their respective classifications.

The Ledger Account Form

We have been looking at accounts in the simple T form primarily because T accounts illustrate situations so well. The debit and credit sides are readily apparent. As we have said, accountants usually use the T form to solve problems because it's such a good way to visualize accounts. However, the T form is awkward when you are trying to determine the balance of an account. One must add both columns and subtract the smaller total from the larger. To overcome this disadvantage, accountants generally use the four-column account form with balance columns. Let's look at the Cash account of NuWay Cleaners in four-column form (Figure 4-4) and in T form. Temporarily, the Posting Reference column is left blank. The meaning and use of this column is described in the discussion of the posting process that follows.

Figure 4-4

GENERAL LEDGER

ACCOUNT *Cash*   ACCOUNT NO. *111*

DATE		ITEM	POST. REF.	DEBIT	CREDIT	BALANCE DEBIT	CREDIT
19– Jun.	1			32 0 0 0 00		32 0 0 0 00	
	2				18 0 0 0 00	14 0 0 0 00	
	4				1 0 0 0 00	13 0 0 0 00	
	7			6 0 0 00		13 6 0 0 00	
	8				4 0 0 00	13 2 0 0 00	
	10				2 4 0 00	12 9 6 0 00	
	10				3 2 0 00	12 6 4 0 00	
	14			7 6 0 00		13 4 0 0 00	
	15				1 8 0 0 00	11 6 0 0 00	
	15				2 2 0 00	11 3 8 0 00	
	15				1 8 0 00	11 2 0 0 00	
	21			8 3 0 00		12 0 3 0 00	
	24				3 9 0 00	11 6 4 0 00	
	26				1 4 0 00	11 5 0 0 00	
	30			9 6 0 00		12 4 6 0 00	
	30			6 0 00		12 5 2 0 00	
	30				1 0 0 0 00	11 5 2 0 00	

Cash

	+		−
(a)	32,000	(b)	18,000
(f)	600	(d)	1,000
(j)	760	(g)	400
(o)	830	(h)	240
(s)	960	(i)	320
(t)	60	(l)	1,800
	35,210	(m)	220
		(n)	180
		(q)	390
		(r)	140
		(u)	1,000
			23,690
Bal.	**11,520**		

The Posting Process

In the posting process, you must transfer the following information from the journal to the ledger accounts: the *date of the transaction*, the *debit and credit amounts*, and the *page number* of the journal. Post each account separately, using the following steps. Post the debit part of the entry first.

1. Write the date of transaction.
2. Write the amount of transaction and the new balance.
3. Write the page number of the journal in the Posting Reference column of the ledger account. (This is a **cross-reference**.)
4. Record the ledger account number in the Posting Reference column of the journal. (This is also a cross-reference.)

The transactions for NuWay Cleaners are illustrated in Figure 4-5. Let's look first at the debit part of the entry.

Next we post the credit part of the entry, as shown in Figure 4-6.

Entering the account number in the Posting Reference column of the journal should be the last step. It acts as a verification of the three preceding steps.

The accountant usually uses the Item column only at the end of a financial period. The words that may appear in this column are *balance*, *closing*, *adjusting*, and *reversing*. We'll introduce these terms later.

Follow the four steps in the recording of the second transaction, shown in Figure 4-7.

Figure 4-5

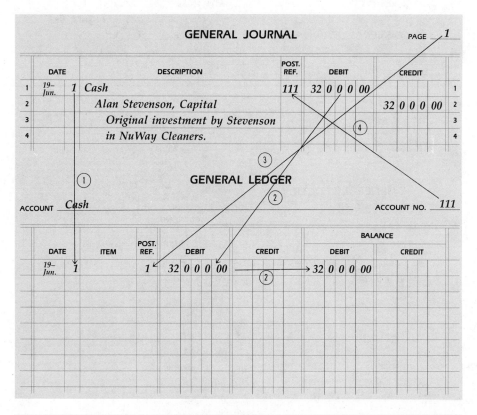

Figure 4-6

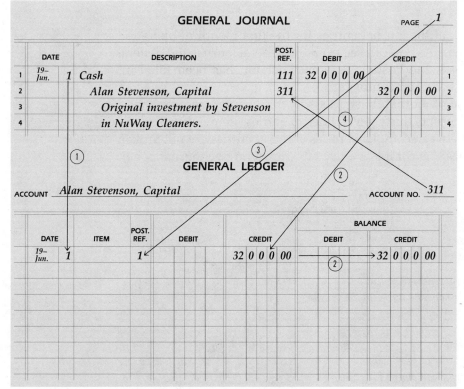

THE GENERAL JOURNAL AND POSTING

Figure 4-7

GENERAL JOURNAL   PAGE __1__

	DATE		DESCRIPTION	POST. REF.	DEBIT	CREDIT	
6	19– Jun.	2	Equipment	121	18 0 0 0 00		6
7			Cash	111		18 0 0 0 00	7
8			Bought equipment for cash.				8

GENERAL LEDGER

ACCOUNT _Equipment_   ACCOUNT NO. _121_

DATE		ITEM	POST. REF.	DEBIT	CREDIT	BALANCE DEBIT	BALANCE CREDIT
19– Jun.	2		1	18 0 0 0 00		18 0 0 0 00	

ACCOUNT _Cash_   ACCOUNT NO. _111_

DATE		ITEM	POST. REF.	DEBIT	CREDIT	BALANCE DEBIT	BALANCE CREDIT
19– Jun.	1		1	32 0 0 0 00		32 0 0 0 00	
	2		1		18 0 0 0 00	14 0 0 0 00	

Let us now look at the journal entries for the first month of operation for NuWay Cleaners. As you can see from the general journal and general ledger in Figure 4-8, the Posting Reference column has been filled in, since the posting has been completed.

For the purpose of journal illustrations in this chapter, assume that a full journal page permits thirty-seven lines of entries. Remember that one blank line is left between complete entries and that entries are not broken up (that is, all lines of a complete entry are shown on one journal page).

Figure 4-8

GENERAL JOURNAL   PAGE __1__

	DATE		DESCRIPTION	POST. REF.	DEBIT	CREDIT	
1	19– Jun.	1	Cash	111	32 0 0 0 00		1
2			Alan Stevenson, Capital	311		32 0 0 0 00	2
3			Original investment by Stevenson				3
4			in NuWay Cleaners.				4
5							5
6		2	Equipment	121	18 0 0 0 00		6
7			Cash	111		18 0 0 0 00	7
8			Bought equipment for cash.				8

Figure 4-8
(continued)

	Date	Description	Post. Ref.	Debit	Credit	
9						9
10	2	Equipment	121	4 0 0 0 00		10
11		Accounts Payable	211		4 0 0 0 00	11
12		Bought equipment on account				12
13		from Sanchez Equipment				13
14		Company.				14
15						15
16	4	Accounts Payable	211	1 0 0 0 00		16
17		Cash	111		1 0 0 0 00	17
18		Paid Sanchez Equipment Company				18
19		on account.				19
20						20
21	4	Supplies	113	4 0 0 00		21
22		Accounts Payable	211		4 0 0 00	22
23		Bought cleaning fluids on account				23
24		from Troy Supply Company.				24
25						25
26	7	Cash	111	6 0 0 00		26
27		Income from Services	411		6 0 0 00	27
28		For week ended June 7.				28
29						29
30	8	Rent Expense	512	4 0 0 00		30
31		Cash	111		4 0 0 00	31
32		For month ended June 30.				32
33						33
34	10	Wages Expense	511	2 4 0 00		34
35		Cash	111		2 4 0 00	35
36		Paid wages, June 1 to June 10.				36
37						37

GENERAL JOURNAL

PAGE 2

	DATE		DESCRIPTION	POST. REF.	DEBIT	CREDIT	
1	19– Jun.	10	Prepaid Insurance	114	3 2 0 00		1
2			Cash	111		3 2 0 00	2
3			Premium for two-year liability				3
4			insurance.				4
5							5
6		14	Cash	111	7 6 0 00		6
7			Income from Services	411		7 6 0 00	7
8			For week ended June 14.				8
9							9
10		14	Advertising Expense	513	1 8 0 00		10
11			Accounts Payable	211		1 8 0 00	11
12			Received bill for advertising				12
13			from Daily News.				13
14							14
15		15	Accounts Payable	211	1 8 0 0 00		15
16			Cash	111		1 8 0 0 00	16
17			Paid Sanchez Equipment				17
18			Company on account.				18

Figure 4-8
(continued)

	DATE	DESCRIPTION	POST. REF.	DEBIT	CREDIT	
19						19
20	15	Utilities Expense	514	2 2 0 00		20
21		Cash	111		2 2 0 00	21
22		Paid bill for utilities.				22
23						23
24	15	Accounts Payable	211	1 8 0 00		24
25		Cash	111		1 8 0 00	25
26		Paid Daily News for advertising.				26
27						27
28	21	Cash	111	8 3 0 00		28
29		Income from Services	411		8 3 0 00	29
30		For week ended June 21.				30
31						31
32	23	Accounts Receivable	112	8 0 00		32
33		Income from Services	411		8 0 00	33
34		A-1 Rental, for services rendered.				34
35						35
36						36
37						37

GENERAL JOURNAL

PAGE __3__

	DATE	DESCRIPTION	POST. REF.	DEBIT	CREDIT	
1	19–Jun. 24	Wages Expense	511	3 9 0 00		1
2		Cash	111		3 9 0 00	2
3		Paid wages, June 11 to June 24.				3
4						4
5	26	Equipment	121	9 4 0 00		5
6		Cash	111		1 4 0 00	6
7		Accounts Payable	211		8 0 0 00	7
8		Bought equipment on account				8
9		from Sanchez Equipment				9
10		Company.				10
11						11
12	30	Cash	111	9 6 0 00		12
13		Income from Services	411		9 6 0 00	13
14		For remainder of June, ended				14
15		June 30.				15
16						16
17	30	Cash	111	6 0 00		17
18		Accounts Receivable	112		6 0 00	18
19		A-1 Rental, to apply on account.				19
20						20
21	30	Alan Stevenson, Drawing	312	1 0 0 0 00		21
22		Cash	111		1 0 0 0 00	22
23		Withdrawal for personal use.				23
24						24

GENERAL LEDGER

Figure 4-8
(continued)

ACCOUNT _Cash_   ACCOUNT NO. _111_

DATE	ITEM	POST. REF.	DEBIT	CREDIT	BALANCE DEBIT	BALANCE CREDIT
19– Jun. 1		1	32 0 0 0 00		32 0 0 0 00	
2		1		18 0 0 0 00	14 0 0 0 00	
4		1		1 0 0 0 00	13 0 0 0 00	
7		1	6 0 0 00		13 6 0 0 00	
8		1		4 0 0 00	13 2 0 0 00	
10		1		2 4 0 00	12 9 6 0 00	
10		2		3 2 0 00	12 6 4 0 00	
14		2	7 6 0 00		13 4 0 0 00	
15		2		1 8 0 0 00	11 6 0 0 00	
15		2		2 2 0 00	11 3 8 0 00	
15		2		1 8 0 00	11 2 0 0 00	
21		2	8 3 0 00		12 0 3 0 00	
24		3		3 9 0 00	11 6 4 0 00	
26		3		1 4 0 00	11 5 0 0 00	
30		3	9 6 0 00		12 4 6 0 00	
30		3	6 0 00		12 5 2 0 00	
30		3		1 0 0 0 00	11 5 2 0 00	

ACCOUNT _Accounts Receivable_   ACCOUNT NO. _112_

DATE	ITEM	POST. REF.	DEBIT	CREDIT	BALANCE DEBIT	BALANCE CREDIT
19– Jun. 23		2	8 0 00		8 0 00	
30		3		6 0 00	2 0 00	

ACCOUNT _Supplies_   ACCOUNT NO. _113_

DATE	ITEM	POST. REF.	DEBIT	CREDIT	BALANCE DEBIT	BALANCE CREDIT
19– Jun. 4		1	4 0 0 00		4 0 0 00	

Figure 4-8
(continued)

ACCOUNT _Prepaid Insurance_   ACCOUNT NO. _114_

DATE		ITEM	POST. REF.	DEBIT	CREDIT	BALANCE DEBIT	BALANCE CREDIT
19– Jun.	10		2	3 2 0 00		3 2 0 00	

ACCOUNT _Equipment_   ACCOUNT NO. _121_

DATE		ITEM	POST. REF.	DEBIT	CREDIT	BALANCE DEBIT	BALANCE CREDIT
19– Jun.	2		1	18 0 0 0 00		18 0 0 0 00	
	2		1	4 0 0 0 00		22 0 0 0 00	
	26		3	9 4 0 00		22 9 4 0 00	

ACCOUNT _Accounts Payable_   ACCOUNT NO. _211_

DATE		ITEM	POST. REF.	DEBIT	CREDIT	BALANCE DEBIT	BALANCE CREDIT
19– Jun.	2		1		4 0 0 0 00		4 0 0 0 00
	4		1	1 0 0 0 00			3 0 0 0 00
	4		1		4 0 0 00		3 4 0 0 00
	14		2		1 8 0 00		3 5 8 0 00
	15		2	1 8 0 0 00			1 7 8 0 00
	15		2	1 8 0 00			1 6 0 0 00
	26		3		8 0 0 00		2 4 0 0 00

ACCOUNT _Alan Stevenson, Capital_   ACCOUNT NO. _311_

DATE		ITEM	POST. REF.	DEBIT	CREDIT	BALANCE DEBIT	BALANCE CREDIT
19– Jun.	1		1		32 0 0 0 00		32 0 0 0 00

ACCOUNT _Alan Stevenson, Drawing_   ACCOUNT NO. _312_

DATE		ITEM	POST. REF.	DEBIT	CREDIT	BALANCE DEBIT	BALANCE CREDIT
19– Jun.	30		3	1 0 0 0 00		1 0 0 0 00	

Figure 4-8
(continued)

ACCOUNT _Income from Services_   ACCOUNT NO. _411_

DATE		ITEM	POST. REF.	DEBIT	CREDIT	BALANCE DEBIT	BALANCE CREDIT
19– Jun.	7		1		6 0 0 00		6 0 0 00
	14		2		7 6 0 00		1 3 6 0 00
	21		2		8 3 0 00		2 1 9 0 00
	23		2		8 0 00		2 2 7 0 00
	30		3		9 6 0 00		3 2 3 0 00

ACCOUNT _Wages Expense_   ACCOUNT NO. _511_

DATE		ITEM	POST. REF.	DEBIT	CREDIT	BALANCE DEBIT	BALANCE CREDIT
19– Jun.	10		1	2 4 0 00		2 4 0 00	
	24		3	3 9 0 00		6 3 0 00	

ACCOUNT _Rent Expense_   ACCOUNT NO. _512_

DATE		ITEM	POST. REF.	DEBIT	CREDIT	BALANCE DEBIT	BALANCE CREDIT
19– Jun.	8		1	4 0 0 00		4 0 0 00	

ACCOUNT _Advertising Expense_   ACCOUNT NO. _513_

DATE		ITEM	POST. REF.	DEBIT	CREDIT	BALANCE DEBIT	BALANCE CREDIT
19– Jun.	14		2	1 8 0 00		1 8 0 00	

ACCOUNT _Utilities Expense_   ACCOUNT NO. _514_

DATE		ITEM	POST. REF.	DEBIT	CREDIT	BALANCE DEBIT	BALANCE CREDIT
19– Jun.	15		2	2 2 0 00		2 2 0 00	

THE GENERAL JOURNAL AND POSTING

A trial balance is presented in Figure 4-9.

Figure 4-9

NuWay Cleaners
Trial Balance
June 30, 19–

ACCOUNT NAME	DEBIT	CREDIT
Cash	11 5 2 0 00	
Accounts Receivable	2 0 00	
Supplies	4 0 0 00	
Prepaid Insurance	3 2 0 00	
Equipment	22 9 4 0 00	
Accounts Payable		2 4 0 0 00
Alan Stevenson, Capital		32 0 0 0 00
Alan Stevenson, Drawing	1 0 0 0 00	
Income from Services		3 2 3 0 00
Wages Expense	6 3 0 00	
Rent Expense	4 0 0 00	
Advertising Expense	1 8 0 00	
Utilities Expense	2 2 0 00	
	37 6 3 0 00	37 6 3 0 00

If the temporary balance of an account happens to be zero, insert long dashes through both the Debit Balance and Credit Balance columns. We'll use the Donegal Company in this example. Their Accounts Receivable ledger account appears below.

ACCOUNT   Accounts Receivable   ACCOUNT NO.   113

DATE	ITEM	POST. REF.	DEBIT	CREDIT	BALANCE DEBIT	BALANCE CREDIT
19– Oct. 7		96	1 4 0 00		1 4 0 00	
19		97	2 3 8 00		3 7 8 00	
21		97		1 4 0 00	2 3 8 00	
29		98		2 3 8 00	—	—
31		98	1 6 2 00		1 6 2 00	

FLOW OF ACCOUNTING INFORMATION

The journal is a chronological record of the business transactions of a firm. The first step in the accounting process is recording the transactions in the journal. Each journal entry should be based on some material evidence that a transaction has occurred, such as a sales invoice, a receipt, or a check. The second step in the accounting process is posting to the T accounts in the ledger. This step consists of transferring the amounts to the debit or credit columns of the specified accounts in the ledger, using a cross-reference system. The ledger is the book in which all accounts are kept. Accounts are placed in the ledger according to the account numbers in the chart of accounts. After one has journalized and posted a group of transactions for a period of time, one prepares a trial balance to prove that the totals of the debit balances and of the credit balances of the ledger accounts are equal. Figure 4-10 shows the flow of information in the recording process.

Figure 4-10

TROY SUPPLY COMPANY   No. 4-962
2430 East Second Street
Bartell, LA 70990

Sold By: _203_   Date: _6/4/_

Name: _NuWay Cleaners_

Address: _1628 East Fifth Avenue_

Bartell, LA 70990

Terms: _Net 30 days_

Quantity	Description	Amount	
20 gal.	Cleaning fluid CR 411 @ $20 per gallon	400	00
	Total	400	00

(continued)

Record in the journal

Figure 4-10
(continued)

21	4	Supplies	113	4 0 0 00		21
22		Accounts Payable	211		4 0 0 00	22
23		Bought cleaning fluids on account				23
24		from Troy Supply Company.				24
25						25

Post to the ledger

ACCOUNT __Supplies__   ACCOUNT NO. __113__

						BALANCE	
DATE	ITEM	POST. REF.	DEBIT	CREDIT		DEBIT	CREDIT
19– Jun. 4		1	4 0 0 00			4 0 0 00	

ACCOUNT __Accounts Payable__   ACCOUNT NO. __211__

					BALANCE		
DATE	ITEM	POST. REF.	DEBIT	CREDIT	DEBIT	CREDIT	
19– Jun. 2		1		4 0 0 0 00		4 0 0 0 00	} previous
4		1	1 0 0 0 00			3 0 0 0 00	} postings
4		1		4 0 0 00		3 4 0 0 00	

GLOSSARY

Account numbers The numbers assigned to accounts according to the chart of accounts.

Chart of accounts The official list of the ledger accounts in which the transactions of a business are to be recorded.

Cross-reference The ledger account number in the Posting Reference column of the journal or the journal page number in the Posting Reference column of the ledger account.

Journal The book in which a person originally records business transactions; commonly referred to as a *book of original entry*.

Journalizing The process of recording a business transaction in a journal.

Posting The process of recording accounting entries in ledger accounts, the source of information being a journal.

Source documents Business papers such as checks, invoices, receipts, letters, and memos that furnish proof that a transaction has taken place.

QUESTIONS, EXERCISES, AND PROBLEMS

Discussion Questions

1. What is the sequence of the accounts in the general ledger?
2. Is it necessary to add the columns of a two-column general journal?
3. What is a chart of accounts?
4. In the process of recording transactions in a journal, which is recorded first, the title of the account debited or the title of the account credited?
5. Arrange the following steps in the posting process in proper order: (a) Write the page number of the journal in the Posting Reference column of the ledger account. (b) Write the amount of the transaction. (c) Record the ledger account number in the Posting Reference column of the journal. (d) Write the date of the transaction.
6. What is the difference between a journal and a ledger?
7. What is meant by *cross-reference?*

Exercises

Exercise 4-1 In the two-column general journal below, the capital letters represent parts of a journal entry. On notebook paper, write the numbers 1 through 8. Alongside each number, write the letter that indicates where in the journal the items are recorded.

							GENERAL JOURNAL								PAGE _1_	
DATE			DESCRIPTION			POST. REF.		DEBIT					CREDIT			
G H	I	J				O		M								
		K				P					N					
		L														

1. Ledger account number of account credited
2. Month
3. Explanation
4. Title of account debited
5. Year
6. Day of the month
7. Title of account credited
8. Amount of debit

Exercise 4-2 How would the following entry be posted?

GENERAL JOURNAL

PAGE ___1___

DATE		DESCRIPTION	POST. REF.	DEBIT	CREDIT
19– Sep.	1	Cash		3 6 6 2 00	
		Shop Equipment		2 1 8 4 00	
		R. E. Stanfield, Capital			5 8 4 6 00
		Original investment in			
		Stanfield Auto Repair			

GENERAL LEDGER

ACCOUNT _Cash_

ACCOUNT NO. __111__

DATE	ITEM	POST. REF.	DEBIT	CREDIT	BALANCE DEBIT	BALANCE CREDIT

ACCOUNT _Shop Equipment_

ACCOUNT NO. __121__

DATE	ITEM	POST. REF.	DEBIT	CREDIT	BALANCE DEBIT	BALANCE CREDIT

ACCOUNT _R. E. Stanfield, Capital_

ACCOUNT NO. __311__

DATE	ITEM	POST. REF.	DEBIT	CREDIT	BALANCE DEBIT	BALANCE CREDIT

Exercise 4-3 The accounts of Groening Realty on December 31 of this year are listed below in alphabetical order. Prepare a trial balance, with a three-line heading, and list the accounts in the proper sequence by account classification.

Accounts Payable	$ 2,400	G. C. Groening,	
Accounts Receivable	16,200	Drawing	$14,000
Automobile	4,000	Land	8,000
Building	30,000	Office Equipment	5,200
Cash	7,600	Realty Commissions	38,000
G. C. Groening,		Rent Expense	7,200
Capital	61,400	Salary Expense	9,600

Exercise 4-4 The following transactions of Donner Company occurred during this year. Journalize the transactions in general journal form, including brief explanations.

May 8 Bought equipment for $6,000 from Benton Equipment Company, paying $1,500 down; balance due in 30 days.
 10 Paid wages for the period May 1 through 9, $960.
 14 Billed Specker Company for services performed, $156.

Exercise 4-5 Landon Soft-Water Service completed the following selected transactions. Journalize the transactions in general journal form, including brief explanations.

Jun. 3 Collected $646 from C. Buckley, a charge customer.
 9 Issued a check in full payment of an Account Payable to Lafferty Company, $116.
 15 L. E. Landon (the owner) withdrew cash for personal use, $950.

Exercise 4-6 Which of the following errors would cause unequal totals in a trial balance? Explain why or why not.

a. An accountant recorded a $45 payment for advertising as a debit to Advertising Expense of $54 and a credit to Cash of $45.
b. An accountant recorded a withdrawal of $42 in cash by the owner as a debit to Miscellaneous Expense of $42 and a credit to Cash of $42.
c. An accountant recorded an $83 payment to a creditor by a debit to Accounts Payable of $38 and a credit to Cash of $38.

Exercise 4-7 In reviewing the work of the bookkeeper, the office manager discovered the following errors:

a. A typewriter was purchased for $540, and cash was paid and credited. The debit was posted twice in the asset account; the credit was posted correctly.
b. A debit to the Cash account of $1,420 was posted as $1,240; the credit was posted correctly.
c. Cash collections of $1,250 from customers in payment of their accounts were not posted to the Accounts Receivable account but were posted correctly to the Cash account.
For each error, indicate the effect of the error using the following form:

Error	Is the trial balance out of balance?	If yes, by how much?	Which would be incorrect? Debit total	Credit total
a.				
b.				
c.				

Exercise 4-8   The bookkeeper of Newell Company has prepared the following trial balance.

Newell Company
Trial Balance
June 30, 19–

ACCOUNT NAME	DEBIT	CREDIT
Cash		1 6 0 0 00
Accounts Receivable	2 3 0 0 00	
Supplies	2 0 0 00	
Prepaid Insurance	3 0 0 00	
Equipment	10 0 0 0 00	
Accounts Payable		2 2 0 0 00
D. Brogan, Capital		8 0 0 0 00
D. Brogan, Drawing	2 0 0 0 00	
Income from Services		12 3 0 0 00
Rent Expense	4 0 0 0 00	
Miscellaneous Expense	1 0 0 0 00	
	19 8 0 0 00	24 1 0 0 00

The bookkeeper is quite upset and has asked you to help prepare a corrected trial balance. In examining the firm's journal and ledger, you discover the following:

a. The debits to the Cash account total $4,000, and the credits total $2,400.
b. A $200 payment to a creditor was entered in the journal but was not posted to the Accounts Payable account.
c. The first two digits in the balance of the Accounts Receivable account were transposed in copying the balance from the ledger to the trial balance.

Problem Set A

Problem 4-1A   The chart of accounts of the Roberts Carpet Cleaning Company is given below, followed by the transactions that took place during October.

Assets
111 Cash
112 Accounts Receivable
117 Supplies
121 Equipment
123 Service Truck

Liabilities
211 Accounts Payable

Owner's Equity
311 J. P. Roberts, Capital
312 J. P. Roberts, Drawing

Revenue
411 Cleaning Service Sales

Expenses
511 Wages Expense
512 Service Truck Expense
513 Rent Expense
514 Repair Expense
515 Utilities Expense
516 Miscellaneous Expense

Oct.   1 Bought cleaning supplies on account from Ajax Chemical Company, $94.
1 Billed First National Bank for services rendered, $316.
3 Received and paid telephone bill, $62.
5 Paid rent for the month, $350.
7 Bought vacuum cleaner on account from Lund Hardware, $229.
14 Sold cleaning services for cash, $241.
16 Paid two weeks' wages to employees, $425.
16 Received and paid gasoline and oil bill relating to the service truck, $64.
18 Received and paid bill from Fanning Company for repairs to equipment, $75.
19 J. P. Roberts invested additional cleaning equipment in the business, $327.
24 Billed Anders Property Management for services performed, $498.
25 Paid Lund Hardware $100 to apply on account.
30 Sold services for cash, $942.
31 Paid two weeks' wages to employees, $540.
31 J. P. Roberts withdrew cash for personal use, $850.

Instructions

Record the transactions in a general journal, including a brief explanation for each entry. Number the journal pages 17, 18, and 19.

Problem 4-2A   The journal entries in the *Working Papers* relate to NuWay Cleaners for its second month of operation. The balances of the accounts as of July 1 have been recorded in the accounts in the ledger.

Instructions

1. Post the journal entries to ledger accounts.
2. Prepare a trial balance as of July 31.
3. Prepare an income statement for the two months ended July 31.
4. Prepare a statement of owner's equity for the two months ended July 31.
5. Prepare a balance sheet as of July 31.

Problem 4-3A Jansen Building Security uses the following chart of accounts.

Assets
111 Cash
112 Accounts Receivable
113 Supplies
114 Prepaid Insurance
115 Weapons and Communication Equipment
121 Patrol Cars

Liabilities
211 Accounts Payable

Owner's Equity
311 C. Jansen, Capital
312 C. Jansen, Drawing

Revenue
411 Security Service Revenue

Expenses
511 Salary Expense
512 Rent Expense
513 Gas and Oil Expense
514 Utilities Expense

The following transactions were completed during October.

Oct.   1 Jansen transferred cash from a personal bank account to an account to be used for the business, $16,200.
       1 Jansen invested personal weapons in the business having a fair market value of $742.
       4 Bought communication equipment on account from Seegel Audio, $916.
       4 Paid rent for the month, $245.
       6 Bought a used patrol car for $6,200 from the City of Bristol, paying $3,000 down, with the balance due in 30 days.
       9 Received and paid insurance premium to Norwalk Fidelity Group for bonding employees, $514.
      11 Performed security services for Limpuri Galleries. Billed Limpuri for services rendered, $550.
      15 Received bill from Arrend Printing Company for office stationery, $117.
      18 Billed Sinclair Development Company for services rendered, $986.
      22 Received and paid bill from City Service for gas and oil for patrol car, $48.
      24 Performed security services at a jewelers' convention. Billed Central Gem Association for services rendered, $474.
      27 Paid Seegel Audio $300 to apply on account.
      29 Received $550 from Limpuri Galleries in full payment of account.
      30 Billed Downtown Merchants Association for services rendered, $1,440.
      31 Received and paid telephone bill, $69.
      31 Paid salaries to employees, $2,100.
      31 Jansen withdrew cash for personal use, $1,200.

Instructions

1. Record the transactions in the general journal, giving a brief explanation for each entry.
2. Post the entries to the ledger accounts.
3. Prepare a trial balance dated October 31.

Problem 4-4A   The chart of accounts of C. E. Reece, M.D., is as follows.

Assets
111 Cash
112 Accounts Receivable
113 Supplies
114 Prepaid Insurance
121 Equipment

Liabilities
211 Accounts Payable

Owner's Equity
311 C. E. Reece, Capital
312 C. E. Reece, Drawing

Revenue
411 Professional Fees

Expenses
511 Salary Expense
512 Laboratory Expense
513 Rent Expense
514 Utilities Expense

Dr. Reece completed the following transactions during September.

Sep. 2 Bought laboratory equipment on account from Aston Surgical Supply Company, $717.
  2 Paid office rent for the month, $465.
  3 Received cash on account from patients, $2,720.
  6 Bought bandages and other supplies on account, $59.
  10 Received and paid bill for laboratory analyses, $183.
  12 Paid cash for property insurance policy, $46.
  13 Billed patients on account for professional services rendered, $1,518.
  16 Received cash for professional services, $281. (Patients were not billed previously.)
  17 Part of the laboratory equipment purchased on September 2 was defective; returned equipment and received a reduction in bill, $49.
  23 Received cash for professional services, $285. (Patients were not billed previously.)
  30 Paid salary of nurse, $640.
  30 Received and paid telephone bill for the month, $32.
  30 Billed patients on account for professional services rendered, $1,015.
  30 Dr. Reece withdrew cash for personal use, $1,010.

Instructions

1. Journalize the transactions for September.
2. Post the entries to the ledger accounts. (Because the professional enterprise was in operation previously, the balances have been recorded in the

ledger accounts. A check mark has been placed in the Posting Reference column to represent the various pages of the journal from which the entries were posted.)

3. Prepare a trial balance as of September 30.

Problem Set B

Problem 4-1B The chart of accounts of Murdoch Carpet Cleaners is given below.

Assets
111 Cash
112 Accounts Receivable
117 Supplies
121 Equipment
123 Service Truck

Liabilities
211 Accounts Payable

Owner's Equity
311 R. L. Murdoch, Capital
312 R. L. Murdoch, Drawing

Revenue
411 Cleaning Service Sales

Expenses
511 Wages Expense
512 Service Truck Expense
513 Rent Expense
514 Repair Expense
515 Utilities Expense
516 Miscellaneous Expense

The following transactions took place during September.

Sep.   1 Received and paid telephone bill, $49.
1 Received bill from Jenkins Company for repairs to equipment, $91.
4 Received and paid bill for gasoline and oil used by the service truck, $76.
6 Paid rent for the month, $315.
8 R. L. Murdoch invested additional cleaning equipment in the business, $240.
11 Billed Hotel Randolph for services performed, $298.
15 Paid two weeks' wages to employees, $375.
18 Sold services for cash, $879.
23 Billed Modern Condominiums for services performed, $416.
26 Paid Acme Electrical Supply on account, $224.
28 Bought cleaning supplies from Gerhardt Supply Company on account, $72.
30 Sold services for cash, $785.
30 Paid two weeks' wages to employees, $392.
30 R. L. Murdoch withdrew cash for personal use, $800.

Instructions

Record the transactions in a general journal, including a brief explanation for each entry. Number the journal pages 21 and 22.

Problem 4-2B The journal entries in the *Working Papers* relate to NuWay Cleaners for its second month of operation. The balances of the accounts as of July 1 have been recorded in the accounts in the ledger.

Instructions

1. Post the journal entries to ledger accounts.
2. Prepare a trial balance as of July 31.
3. Prepare an income statement for the two months ended July 31.
4. Prepare a statement of owner's equity for the two months ended July 31.
5. Prepare a balance sheet as of July 31.

Problem 4-3B Modern Building Security had the following transactions during June of this year. The chart of accounts is as follows:

Assets
111 Cash
112 Accounts Receivable
113 Supplies
114 Prepaid Insurance
115 Weapons and Communication Equipment
121 Patrol Cars

Liabilities
211 Accounts Payable

Owner's Equity
311 J. Walsh, Capital
312 J. Walsh, Drawing

Revenue
411 Security Service Revenue

Expenses
511 Salary Expense
512 Rent Expense
513 Gas and Oil Expense
514 Utilities Expense

Jun. 2 Walsh transferred cash from a personal bank account to an account to be used for the business, $12,400.
      3 Paid rent for the month, $225.
      5 Bought a used patrol car for $5,600 from the City of Anders, paying $4,000 down, with the balance due in 30 days.
      6 Walsh invested personal weapons in the business having a present value of $628.
      8 Bought communication equipment on account from Noble Electronics, $724.
     12 Performed security services at a special rock concert. Billed Music Enterprises for services rendered, $662.
     16 Received bill from Perfection Printing for office stationery, $121.
     16 Purchased additional weapons for cash from Kimball Hardware, $295.
     18 Billed Proctor Property Management for services rendered, $1,620.
     19 Paid Noble Electronics $200 to apply on account.
     19 Performed security services at a jewelers' convention. Billed Eastern Jewelers' Association for services rendered, $516.
     22 Received and paid insurance premiums to Regal Fidelity for bonding employees, $317.
     25 Received bill for gas and oil for patrol car from Central Petroleum, $67.
     26 Billed City Merchants Association for services rendered, $1,762.
     28 Received $662 from Music Enterprises in full payment of account.
     30 Paid one month's salary to employees, $2,520.
     30 Walsh withdrew cash for personal use, $1,100.
     30 Received and paid telephone bill, $71.

Instructions

1. Record the transactions in the general journal, giving a brief explanation for each entry.
2. Post the entries to the ledger accounts.
3. Prepare a trial balance dated June 30.

Problem 4-4B The chart of accounts of C. E. Reece, M.D., is as follows.

Assets
111 Cash
112 Accounts Receivable
113 Supplies
114 Prepaid Insurance
121 Equipment

Liabilities
211 Accounts Payable

Owner's Equity
311 C. E. Reece, Capital
312 C. E. Reece, Drawing

Revenue
411 Professional Fees

Expenses
511 Salary Expense
512 Laboratory Expense
513 Rent Expense
514 Utilities Expense

Dr. Reece completed the following transactions during September.

Sep.		
	2	Bought laboratory equipment from Cox Company on account, $620.
	2	Paid office rent for the month, $400.
	3	Bought bandages and other supplies on account, $55.
	5	Received cash on account from patients, $2,600.
	7	Paid cash to creditors on account, $840.
	9	Received and paid bill for laboratory analyses, $175.
	11	Billed patients on account for professional services rendered, $1,420.
	13	Paid cash for property insurance policy for the year, $40.
	15	Part of the laboratory equipment purchased on September 2 was defective. Returned the equipment and received a reduction in bill, $40.
	16	Received cash for professional services, $260.
	29	Paid salary of nurse, $620.
	30	Received and paid telephone bill for the month, $26.
	30	Received and paid electric bill, $85.
	30	Billed patients on account for professional services rendered, $940.
	30	Dr. Reece withdrew $975 in cash for personal use.

Instructions

1. Journalize the transactions for September.
2. Post the entries to the ledger accounts. (Because the professional enterprise was in operation previously, the balances have been recorded in the ledger accounts. A check mark has been placed in the Posting Reference column to represent the various pages of the journal from which the entries were posted.)
3. Prepare a trial balance as of September 30.

5 Adjustments and the Work Sheet

Learning Objectives

After you have completed this chapter, you will be able to do the following:

1. Complete a work sheet for a service-type enterprise, involving adjustments for supplies consumed, expired insurance, depreciation, and accrued wages.

2. Prepare an income statement and a balance sheet for a service-type business directly from the work sheet.

3. Journalize and post the adjusting entries.

Now that you have become familiar with the classifying and recording phase of accounting for a service-type enterprise, let's look at the remaining steps in the accounting procedure.

FISCAL PERIOD

A **fiscal period** is any period of time covering a complete accounting cycle. A **fiscal year** is a fiscal period consisting of twelve consecutive months. It does not have to coincide with the calendar year. If a business has seasonal peaks, it's a good idea to complete the accounting operations at the end of the most active season. At that time the management wants to know the results of the year and where the business stands financially. As an example, the fiscal period of a resort that is operated during the summer months may be from October 1 of one year to September 30 of the next year. Governments, at some levels, have a fiscal period from July 1 of one year to June 30 of the following year. Department stores often use a fiscal period extending from February 1 of one year to January 31 of the next year. For income tax purposes, any period of twelve consecutive months may be selected. However, you have to be consistent and use the same fiscal period from year to year.

THE ACCOUNTING CYCLE

The **accounting cycle** represents the steps that are involved in the accounting process. In Chapter 4 we summarized the first three steps in the accounting cycle. Figure 5-1 shows all of the steps and their placement in this text.

Figure 5-1

Step	Description	Text Placement
1	Record business transactions in a journal.	
2	Post to the accounts in the ledger.	Chapter 4
3	Prepare a trial balance.	
4	Compile adjustment data and record the adjusting entries in the work sheet.	Chapter 5
5	Complete the work sheet.	
6	Complete the financial statements.	Chapters 1, 2
7	Journalize and post adjusting entries.	Chapter 5
8	Journalize and post closing entries.	Chapter 6
9	Prepare a post-closing trial balance.	Chapter 6

First we shall complete the entire accounting cycle for NuWay Cleaners, which is a service type of business. To show you the accounts for a professional enterprise, Chapter 7 will present the transactions of Dr. Rory T. Barker. We'll go through the entire accounting cycle for each of these examples.

This summary has brought you up to date on what we have accomplished thus far and what we hope to do in the future. The chapters that are not listed cover additional topics about the steps in the accounting cycle.

THE WORK SHEET

At the moment we are concerned with the **work sheet.** As we said in listing the steps of the accounting cycle, the work sheet is a prelude to the preparation of financial statements. The work sheet serves as a medium for recording necessary adjustments and for furnishing the account balances for making up the income statement and balance sheet. We described the income statement and balance sheet that we looked at in Chapter 2 as being tentative, in that adjustments had not been recorded at that time. Often accountants refer to the work sheet as *working papers* because the work sheet is the tool accountants use to bring all the accounts up to date. Accountants use pencil to make entries in the work sheet, since it is a working document.

For our purposes, we will use a ten-column work sheet—so called because two amount columns are provided for each of the work sheet's five major sections. We will discuss the function of each of these sections, again basing our discussion on the accounting activities of NuWay Cleaners. But first, we will fill in the heading, which consists of three lines: the name of the company, the title of the working paper, and the inclusive period of the time covered.

NuWay Cleaners
Work Sheet
For month ended June 30, 19–

ACCOUNT NAME	TRIAL BALANCE		ADJUSTMENTS		ADJUSTED TRIAL BALANCE		INCOME STATEMENT		BALANCE SHEET	
	DEBIT	CREDIT	DEBIT	CREDIT	DEBIT	CREDIT	DEBIT	CREDIT	DEBIT	CREDIT

The Columns of the Work Sheet

When you use a work sheet, you do not have to prepare a trial balance on a separate piece of paper because you enter it in the first two columns of the work sheet. As usual, list the accounts as they appear in the chart of accounts. Thus, in abbreviated form, the accounts are listed in the Trial Balance section of the work sheet as follows:

Trial Balance	
Debit	**Credit**
Assets	
	Liabilities
	Owner's Equity
	Revenue
Expenses	

Entries in the Income Statement section, in abbreviated form, look like the following:

Income Statement	
Debit	**Credit**
	Revenue
Expenses	

Revenue accounts have credit balances, so they are recorded in the Income Statement Credit column. Expense accounts have debit balances, so they are recorded in the Income Statement Debit column.

And in abbreviated form, the accounts in the Balance Sheet section are recorded as follows:

Balance Sheet	
Debit	**Credit**
Assets	Liabilities
	Capital (Owner's Equity)
Drawing	

Asset accounts have debit balances, so they are recorded in the Balance Sheet Debit column. Liability accounts have credit balances, so they are recorded in the Balance Sheet Credit column. The Capital account has a credit balance, so it is recorded in the Balance Sheet Credit column. Because the Drawing account (debit balance) is a deduction from Capital, Drawing is recorded in the Balance Sheet Debit column (the opposite column in which Capital is recorded).

The Classifications of Accounts

It is important that you know where the different classifications of accounts go in the various columns. Observe that all five classifications are placed in the Trial Balance and Adjusted Trial Balance columns. Up-to-date balances are taken directly from the Adjusted Trial Balance columns. The revenue and expense accounts go in the Income Statement columns; the assets, liabilities, and owner's equity accounts go in the Balance Sheet columns.

Account Classification	Trial Balance		Adjustments		Adjusted Trial Balance		Income Statement		Balance Sheet	
	Debit	Credit	Debit	Credit	Debit	Credit	Debit	Credit	Debit	Credit
Assets	X				X				X	
Liabilities		X				X				X
Capital		X				X				X
Drawing	X				X				X	
Revenue		X				X		X		
Expenses	X				X		X			

ADJUSTMENTS

Adjustments may be considered *internal transactions*. They have not been recorded in the accounts up to this time because no outside party has been involved. Adjustments are determined after the trial balance has been prepared.

The accounts that require adjusting are few in number and, after one has a limited exposure to accounting, are easy to recognize. They are used by service, merchandising, and all other kinds of businesses. To describe the reasons for—and techniques of handling—adjustments, let's return to NuWay Cleaners. First, let's select the accounts that require adjustments. For the moment, we'll show the adjusting entries by T accounts; later on we'll record them in the work sheet and journalize them.

Supplies   In the trial balance, the Supplies account has a balance of $400. Each time NuWay Cleaners bought supplies, Stevenson wrote the entry as a debit to Supplies and a credit to either Cash or Accounts Payable; so he recorded each purchase of supplies as an increase in the Supplies account.

But we haven't taken into consideration the fact that any business is continually using up supplies in the process of carrying on business operations. For NuWay Cleaners, the items recorded under Supplies consist of cleaning fluids. At the end of the month, obviously some of these supplies have been used. It would be very time consuming to keep a continual record of the exact amount of supplies on hand; so at the end of the month someone takes a physical count of the amount on hand.

When Stevenson takes an inventory on June 30, he finds that there are $320 worth of supplies left. The situation looks like this:

Had	$400	(Recorded under Supplies)
− Have left	− 320	(Determined by taking an inventory)
Used	$ 80	(The amount used is an expense of doing business. This is Supplies Expense.)

To bring the books up to date, Stevenson has to make an **adjusting entry** in NuWay's journal. Let's look at this in the form of T accounts.

(a)

	Supplies			Supplies Expense	
+		−	+		−
Balance	400	Adjusting 80	Adjusting	80	

Drawing T accounts on scratch paper is an excellent way of organizing the adjusting entry. By making this entry, Stevenson has merely taken the amount used out of Supplies and put it into Supplies Expense. The new balance of Supplies, $320, represents the cost of supplies that are on hand and should therefore appear in the balance sheet. The $80 figure in Supplies Expense represents the cost of supplies that have been used and should therefore appear in the income statement.

When supplies are bought and originally recorded as an asset (as we have been doing it):

Amount of adjusting entry = Balance of Supplies account − Amount of supplies remaining

Prepaid Insurance   The $320 balance in Prepaid Insurance stands for the premium paid in advance for a two-year liability insurance policy. One month of the premium has now expired, which amounts to $13.33 (see next page).

$$\frac{\$\ 13.33\ \text{per month}}{24\ \text{months})\$320.00}$$

In the adjustment, Stevenson deducts the expired or used portion from Prepaid Insurance and transfers it to Insurance Expense.

(b)

Prepaid Insurance		Insurance Expense	
+	−	+	−
Balance 320	Adjusting 13.33	Adjusting 13.33	

The new balance of Prepaid Insurance, $306.67 ($320 − $13.33), represents the cost of insurance that is now paid in advance and should therefore appear in the balance sheet. The $13.33 figure in Insurance Expense represents the cost of insurance that has expired and should therefore appear in the income statement.

Depreciation of Equipment   We have followed the policy of recording durable items such as appliances and fixtures under Equipment, because they will last longer than one year. However, since the benefits derived from these assets will eventually be used up, we should systematically apportion their costs over the period of their useful lives. In other words, we write off the cost of the assets as an expense over the estimated useful life of the equipment and call it **depreciation,** because such equipment loses its usefulness. In the case of NuWay Cleaners, the Equipment account has a balance of $22,940. Suppose we estimate that the dry cleaning equipment will have a useful life of six years, with a trade-in value of $2,294 at the end of that time. Then the total depreciation over the estimated useful life of the equipment is $20,646 ($22,940 − $2,294). The calculation of the depreciation for one month is given below.

$$\frac{\$\ 3,441\ \text{per year}}{6\ \text{years})\$20,646\ \text{full depreciation}}$$

$$\frac{\$\ 286.75\ \text{per month}}{12\ \text{months})\$3,441}$$

One always records this as a debit to Depreciation Expense and a credit to Accumulated Depreciation. The adjustment in T account form would appear as follows. Note that both accounts are increased.

(c)

Depreciation Expense		Accumulated Depreciation	
+	−	−	+
Adjusting 286.75			Adjusting 286.75

On the balance sheet, the balance of Accumulated Depreciation is a deduction from the balance of the related asset account as illustrated below on the partial balance sheet for NuWay Cleaners.

NuWay Cleaners
Balance Sheet
June 30, 19–

Assets		
Equipment	$22 9 4 0 00	
Less Accumulated Depreciation	2 8 6 75	$22 6 5 3 25

Accumulated Depreciation is contrary to Equipment, so we call it a **contra account.** To show the accounts under their proper headings, let's look at the fundamental accounting equation. (Brackets indicate that Accumulated Depreciation is a deduction from the Equipment account.)

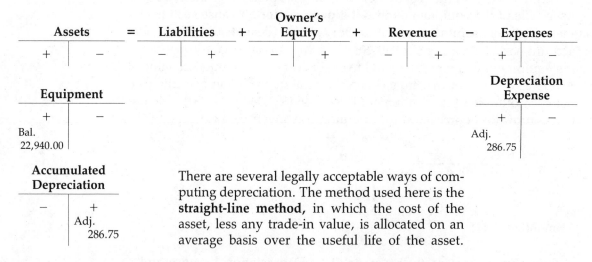

Assets	=	Liabilities	+	Owner's Equity	+	Revenue	–	Expenses
+ –		– +		– +		– +		+ –

Equipment

+   –
Bal.
22,940.00

Depreciation Expense

+   –
Adj.
286.75

Accumulated Depreciation

–   +
Adj.
286.75

There are several legally acceptable ways of computing depreciation. The method used here is the **straight-line method,** in which the cost of the asset, less any trade-in value, is allocated on an average basis over the useful life of the asset.

Accumulated Depreciation, as the title implies, is the total depreciation that the company has taken since the original purchase of the asset. Rather than crediting the Equipment account, NuWay Cleaners keeps track of the total depreciation taken since it first acquired the asset in a separate account. The maximum depreciation it could take would be the cost of the equipment, $22,940, less trade-in value of $2,294. So, for the first year, Accumulated Depreciation will increase at the rate of $286.75 per month, assuming that no additional equipment has been purchased.

CHAPTER 5

For example, at the end of the second month, Accumulated Depreciation will amount to $573.50 ($286.75 + $286.75). The **book value** of an asset is the cost of the asset minus the accumulated depreciation.

Wages Expense The end of the fiscal period and the end of the employees' payroll period rarely fall on the same day. A diagram of the situation looks like this.

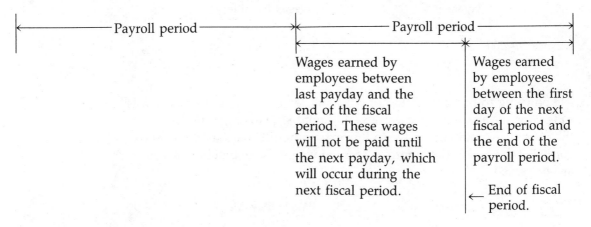

As an example, assume that a firm pays its employees a total of $400 per day and that payday falls on Friday throughout the year. When the employees pick up their paychecks on Friday, at the end of the work day, the amount of the checks includes their wages for that day as well as for the preceding four days. The employees work a five-day week. And suppose that the last day of the fiscal period falls on Wednesday, December 31. We can diagram this as shown in the following illustration.

								End of Fiscal Year	
				Dec. 26	Dec. 29	Dec. 30	Dec. 31	Jan. 1	Jan. 2
Mon	Tue	Wed	Thur	Fri	Mon	Tue	Wed	Thur	Fri
400	400	400	400	400	400	400	400	400	400
		Payroll period				Payroll period			
				Payday $2,000					Payday $2,000

December						
S	M	T	W	T	F	S
	1	2	3	4	⑤	6
7	8	9	10	11	⑫	13
14	15	16	17	18	⑲	20
21	22	23	24	25	㉖	27
28	29	30	31			

—Paydays

In order to have the Wages Expense account reflect an accurate balance for the fiscal period, you should add $1,200 for the cost of labor between the last payday, December 26, and the end of the year, December 31 (for December 29, $400; for December 30, $400; for December 31, $400). Because the $1,200 is owed to the employees at December 31, you should also add $1,200 to Wages Payable, a liabilities account.

Wages Expense			Wages Payable	
+	−		−	+
Balance 104,000				Adjusting 1,200
Adjusting 1,200				

Returning to our illustration of NuWay Cleaners: The last payday was June 24. NuWay Cleaners owes an additional $100 in wages at the end of the month. Accountants refer to this extra amount that has not been recorded at the end of the month as **accrued wages.** Note that both accounts are increased.

Wages Expense			Wages Payable	
+	−		−	+
Balance 630				Adjusting 100
Adjusting 100				

Placement of Accounts in the Work Sheet   First we have to enter the adjustments in the work sheet. But before doing so, let's digress briefly to discuss the Drawing and Accumulated Depreciation accounts, as well as net income, and their effect on the work sheet.

The Drawing account looks like this:

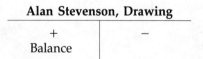

Drawing is a deduction from capital and is shown in the column opposite the normal balance of the Capital account.

The Accumulated Depreciation account looks like this:

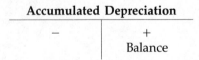

Accumulated depreciation is a deduction from the respective asset account; and, as we have said, it is shown in the column opposite the normal balance of the asset account.

Net income (or net loss) is the difference between revenue and expenses. It is used to balance off the Income Statement columns; and, since revenue is normally larger than expenses, the balancing-off amount must be added to the expense side. Net income (or net loss) is also used to balance off the Balance Sheet columns. As in the statement of owner's equity, one adds net income to the owner's equity. The following illustration shows these relationships in diagram form:

Account Name	Trial Balance		Adjustments		Adjusted Trial Balance		Income Statement		Balance Sheet	
	Debit	Credit	Debit	Credit	Debit	Credit	Debit	Credit	Debit	Credit
	A + E + Draw.	L + Cap. + R + Accum. Depr.			A + E + Draw.	L + Cap. + R + Accum. Depr.	E	R	A + Draw.	L + Cap. + Accum. Depr.
Net Income							NI			NI

On the other hand, if expenses are larger than revenue, the result is a net loss. One must add net loss to the revenue side to balance off the Income Statement columns. Also, because one deducts a net loss from the owner's equity, one includes net loss in the debit side of the Balance Sheet columns, thereby balancing off these columns. To show this, let's look at the Income Statement and Balance Sheet columns diagrammed here.

	Income Statement		Balance Sheet	
	Debit	Credit	Debit	Credit
	E	R	A + Draw.	L + Cap. + Accum. Depr.
Net Loss		NL	NL	

Summary of Adjustments by T Accounts

To test your understanding, describe why the following adjustments are necessary. The answers are shown below the accounts.

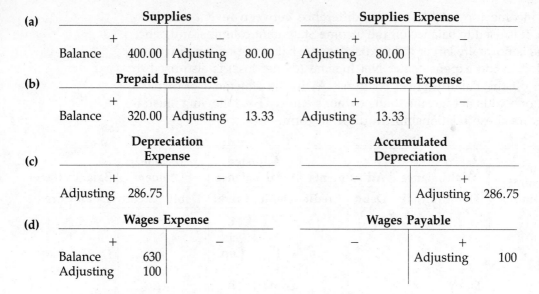

(a)

Supplies					Supplies Expense			
+		−			+		−	
Balance	400.00	Adjusting	80.00		Adjusting	80.00		

(b)

Prepaid Insurance					Insurance Expense			
+		−			+		−	
Balance	320.00	Adjusting	13.33		Adjusting	13.33		

(c)

Depreciation Expense					Accumulated Depreciation			
+		−			−		+	
Adjusting	286.75						Adjusting	286.75

(d)

Wages Expense					Wages Payable			
+		−			−		+	
Balance	630						Adjusting	100
Adjusting	100							

a. To record the cost of supplies used during June
b. To record the insurance expired during June
c. To record the depreciation for the month of June
d. To record accrued wages owed at the end of June

Recording the Adjustments in the Work Sheet

In the examples above, we used T accounts to explain how to handle adjustments. T accounts, as you are aware, represent a reliable method of organizing any type of accounting entry. Now it is time to record adjustments in the work sheet. To help you remember which classifications of accounts appear in each column of the work sheet, we will label the columns by letter, for example, *A* for assets and *L* for liabilities.

After completing the trial balance in the first two columns of the work sheet, enter the adjustments directly in the Adjustments columns.

Adjustments Columns of the Work Sheet

When we enter the adjustments, we identify them as **(a), (b), (c),** and **(d)** to indicate the relationships between the debit and credit sides of the individual adjusting entries, as shown in Figure 5-2.

Note that Supplies Expense, Insurance Expense, Depreciation Expense, and Wages Payable did not appear in the trial balance because there were no balances in the accounts to record. So we wrote them below

NuWay Cleaners
Work Sheet
For month ended June 30, 19–

	ACCOUNT NAME	TRIAL BALANCE DEBIT (A + E + Draw.)	TRIAL BALANCE CREDIT (L + C + R + Accum. Deprec.)	ADJUSTMENTS DEBIT	ADJUSTMENTS CREDIT	
1	Cash	11 5 2 0 00				1
2	Accounts Receivable	2 0 00				2
3	Supplies	4 0 0 00			(a) 8 0 00	3
4	Prepaid Insurance	3 2 0 00			(b) 1 3 33	4
5	Equipment	22 9 4 0 00				5
6	Accounts Payable		2 4 0 0 00			6
7	Alan Stevenson, Capital		32 0 0 0 00			7
8	Alan Stevenson, Drawing	1 0 0 0 00				8
9	Income from Services		3 2 3 0 00			9
10	Wages Expense	6 3 0 00		(d) 1 0 0 00		10
11	Rent Expense	4 0 0 00				11
12	Advertising Expense	1 8 0 00				12
13	Utilities Expense	2 2 0 00				13
14		37 6 3 0 00	37 6 3 0 00			14
15	Supplies Expense			(a) 8 0 00		15
16	Insurance Expense			(b) 1 3 33		16
17	Depreciation Expense			(c) 2 8 6 75		17
18	Accumulated Depreciation				(c) 2 8 6 75	18
19	Wages Payable				(d) 1 0 0 00	19
20				4 8 0 08	4 8 0 08	20

Figure 5-2

the Trial Balance totals. Some people consider them to be new accounts, because they were never used during the fiscal period. But observe that they all have one thing in common: *They are all increased.* In other words, you bring a new account into existence in order to increase it; definitely not to decrease it. This hint can help you formulate any adjusting entry correctly.

Steps in the Completion of the Work Sheet

Before proceeding to the completion of the work sheet, let us list the recommended steps to follow.

1. Complete the Trial Balance columns—making sure both columns are equal. In the Account Name column above the trial balance totals, we list only the accounts having balances, as in the trial balances in Chap-

ters 3 and 4. However, as an alternative, many accountants list all the accounts in the ledger.

2. Complete the Adjustments columns—labeling each adjustment as (a), (b), (c), and so on, and making sure both columns are equal.
3. Complete the Adjusted Trial Balance columns—carrying across any balance from the Trial Balance columns plus or minus any amounts appearing in the Adjustments columns. Make sure both columns are equal.
4. Complete the Income Statement and Balance Sheet columns—distributing each amount from the Adjusted Trial Balance columns, according to the account classification, to either the Income Statement or the Balance Sheet columns, but never to more than one column. For example, Accounts Payable is a liability, and liabilities are recorded in the Balance Sheet Credit column only.

NuWay Cleaners
Work Sheet
For month ended June 30, 1

	ACCOUNT NAME	TRIAL BALANCE		ADJUSTMENTS	
		DEBIT A + E + Draw.	CREDIT L + C + R + Accum. Deprec.	DEBIT	CREDIT
1	Cash	11 5 2 0 00			
2	Accounts Receivable	2 0 00			
3	Supplies	4 0 0 00			(a) 8 0
4	Prepaid Insurance	3 2 0 00			(b) 1 3
5	Equipment	22 9 4 0 00			
6	Accounts Payable		2 4 0 0 00		
7	Alan Stevenson, Capital		32 0 0 0 00		
8	Alan Stevenson, Drawing	1 0 0 0 00			
9	Income from Services		3 2 3 0 00		
10	Wages Expense	6 3 0 00		(d) 1 0 0 00	
11	Rent Expense	4 0 0 00			
12	Advertising Expense	1 8 0 00			
13	Utilities Expense	2 2 0 00			
14		37 6 3 0 00	37 6 3 0 00		
15	Supplies Expense			(a) 8 0 00	
16	Insurance Expense		Step 1	(b) 1 3 33	
17	Depreciation Expense			(c) 2 8 6 75	
18	Accumulated Depreciation				(c) 2 8 6
19	Wages Payable				(d) 1 0 0
20				4 8 0 08	4 8 0
21					
22				Step 2	
23					

5. Add the Income Statement Debit and Credit columns and find the difference between the two columns. (The difference represents the net income or net loss.) Use the amount of the net income or net loss to balance off the two columns.
6. Add the Balance Sheet Debit and Credit columns and insert the amount of the net income or net loss to balance off the two columns.

Now we include the Adjusted Trial Balance columns, as shown in Figure 5-3, bringing the balances of the accounts that were adjusted up to date.

After the Adjusted Trial Balance columns are completed, we go through the mental process of classifying the accounts so that we know where to place the classifications in the various columns; and we enter each account balance in the appropriate column. We now carry forward

Figure 5-3

ADJUSTED TRIAL BALANCE		INCOME STATEMENT		BALANCE SHEET		
DEBIT	CREDIT	DEBIT	CREDIT	DEBIT	CREDIT	
+ E Draw.	L + C + R + Accum. Deprec.	E	R	A + Draw.	L + C + Accum. Deprec.	
2 0 00						1
2 0 00						2
2 0 00						3
0 6 67						4
4 0 00						5
	2 4 0 0 00					6
	32 0 0 0 00					7
0 0 00						8
	3 2 3 0 00					9
3 0 00						10
0 0 00						11
8 0 00						12
2 0 00						13
						14
8 0 00						15
1 3 33						16
8 6 75						17
	2 8 6 75					18
	1 0 0 00					19
1 6 75	38 0 1 6 75					20
						21
Step 3						22
						23

ACCOUNT NAME	TRIAL BALANCE		ADJUSTMENTS	
	DEBIT $A + E + Draw.$	CREDIT $L + C + R + Accum. Deprec.$	DEBIT	CREDIT
1 *Cash*	11 5 2 0 00			
2 *Accounts Receivable*	2 0 00			
3 *Supplies*	4 0 0 00			(a) 8 (
4 *Prepaid Insurance*	3 2 0 00			(b) 1 3
5 *Equipment*	22 9 4 0 00			
6 *Accounts Payable*		2 4 0 0 00		
7 *Alan Stevenson, Capital*		32 0 0 0 00		
8 *Alan Stevenson, Drawing*	1 0 0 0 00			
9 *Income from Services*		3 2 3 0 00		
10 *Wages Expense*	6 3 0 00		(d) 1 0 0 00	
11 *Rent Expense*	4 0 0 00			
12 *Advertising Expense*	1 8 0 00			
13 *Utilities Expense*	2 2 0 00			
14	37 6 3 0 00	37 6 3 0 00		
15 *Supplies Expense*			(a) 8 0 00	
16 *Insurance Expense*		Step 1	(b) 1 3 33	
17 *Depreciation Expense*			(c) 2 8 6 75	
18 *Accumulated Depreciation*				(c) 2 8 (
19 *Wages Payable*				(d) 1 0 (
20			4 8 0 08	4 8 (
21 *Net Income*				
22			Step 2	
23				
24				
25				
26				
27				
28				
29				
30				

the amounts in the Adjusted Trial Balance columns to the remaining four columns, recording each amount in only one column. Net income or net loss is recorded in both the Income Statement column and the Balance Sheet column to balance off the columns. The completed work sheet is shown in Figure 5-4.

Accountants refer to accounts such as Supplies and Prepaid Insurance, as they appear in the trial balance, as **mixed accounts**—accounts with

	ADJUSTED TRIAL BALANCE		INCOME STATEMENT		BALANCE SHEET		
	EBIT (+ E Draw.)	CREDIT (L + C + R + Accum. Deprec.)	DEBIT (E)	CREDIT (R)	DEBIT (A + Draw.)	CREDIT (L + C + Accum. Deprec.)	
1	2 0 00				11 5 2 0 00		
2	2 0 00				2 0 00		
3	2 0 00				3 2 0 00		
4	0 6 67				3 0 6 67		
5	4 0 00				22 9 4 0 00		
6		2 4 0 0 00				2 4 0 0 00	
7		32 0 0 0 00				32 0 0 0 00	
8	0 0 00				1 0 0 0 00		
9		3 2 3 0 00		3 2 3 0 00			
10	3 0 00		7 3 0 00				
11	0 0 00		4 0 0 00				
12	8 0 00		1 8 0 00				
13	2 0 00		2 2 0 00				
14							
15	8 0 00		8 0 00				
16	1 3 33		1 3 33				
17	8 6 75		2 8 6 75				
18		2 8 6 75				2 8 6 75	
19		1 0 0 00				1 0 0 00	
20	1 6 75	38 0 1 6 75	1 9 1 0 08	3 2 3 0 00	36 1 0 6 67	34 7 8 6 75	
21			1 3 1 9 92			1 3 1 9 92	
22	Step 3		3 2 3 0 00	3 2 3 0 00	36 1 0 6 67	36 1 0 6 67	
23							
24			Steps 4, 5, 6				
25							

Figure 5-4

balances that are partly income statement amounts and partly balance sheet amounts. For example, Supplies is recorded as $400 in the Trial Balance, but after adjustment this is apportioned as $80 in Supplies Expense in the Income Statement columns and $320 in Supplies in the Balance Sheet columns. Similarly, Prepaid Insurance is recorded as $320 in the trial balance, but is apportioned as $13.33 in Insurance Expense in the Income Statement columns and as $306.67 in Prepaid Insurance in the

Balance Sheet columns. In other words, portions of these accounts are recorded in each section.

After the first fiscal period, Accumulated Depreciation will always have a balance until the related asset is sold or disposed of. Consequently, it will be listed in the Trial Balance columns immediately below the appropriate asset (Equipment, in this case).

Sometimes it may be necessary to continue the work sheet on another page. Using a different company as an example, follow this procedure:

(First Page)		
Account Name	**Trial Balance**	**Adjustments**
Depreciation Expense		(c)220 50
Totals carried forward		962 50 126 50

(Second Page)				
	Trial Balance		**Adjustments**	
Account Name	**Debit**	**Credit**	**Debit**	**Credit**
Totals brought forward			962 50	126 50
Accumulated Depreciation				(c)220 50

COMPLETION OF THE FINANCIAL STATEMENTS

We now prepare the income statement, the statement of owner's equity, and the balance sheet, taking the figures directly from the work sheet. These statements are shown in Figure 5-5.

Note that one records Accumulated Depreciation in the asset section of the balance sheet as a direct deduction from Equipment. As we have said, accountants refer to it as a *contra account*, because it is contrary to its companion account. The difference, $22,653.25, is called the *book value*, because it represents the cost of the assets after Accumulated Depreciation has been deducted.

ADJUSTING ENTRIES

In order to change the balance of an account, you need a journal entry as evidence of the change. Up to this time, we have been listing adjustments in the Adjustments columns of the work sheet only. Since the work sheet

Objective 2

Prepare an income statement and a balance sheet for a service-type business directly from the work sheet.

Objective 3

Journalize and post the adjusting entries.

Figure 5-5

NuWay Cleaners
Income Statement
For month ended June 30, 19–

Revenue:									
Income from Services						$3	2	3	0	00
Expenses:									
Wages Expense	$	7	3	0	00				
Rent Expense		4	0	0	00				
Utilities Expense		2	2	0	00				
Depreciation Expense		2	8	6	75				
Advertising Expense		1	8	0	00				
Supplies Expense			8	0	00				
Insurance Expense			1	3	33				
Total Expenses						1	9	1	0	08
Net Income						$1	3	1	9	92

NuWay Cleaners
Statement of Owner's Equity
For month ended June 30, 19–

Alan Stevenson, Capital, June 1, 19–						$32	0	0	0	00
Net Income for month of June	$1	3	1	9	92				
Less Withdrawals for month of June	1	0	0	0	00				
Increase in Capital							3	1	9	92
Alan Stevenson, Capital, June 30, 19–						$32	3	1	9	92

Figure 5-5
(continued)

NuWay Cleaners
Balance Sheet
June 30, 19–

Assets								
Cash						$11 5 2 0 00
Accounts Receivable						2 0 00
Supplies						3 2 0 00
Prepaid Insurance						3 0 6 67
Equipment	$22 9 4 0 00					
Less Accumulated Depreciation	2 8 6 75			22 6 5 3 25
Total Assets						$34 8 1 9 92
Liabilities						
Accounts Payable	$ 2 4 0 0 00				
Wages Payable	1 0 0 00				
Total Liabilities						$ 2 5 0 0 00
Owner's Equity						
Alan Stevenson, Capital						32 3 1 9 92
Total Liabilities and Owner's Equity						$34 8 1 9 92

Figure 5-6

GENERAL JOURNAL PAGE ___4___

DATE		DESCRIPTION	POST. REF.	DEBIT	CREDIT
		Adjusting Entries			
19– Jun.	30	Supplies Expense		8 0 00	
		Supplies			8 0 00
	30	Insurance Expense		1 3 33	
		Prepaid Insurance			1 3 33
	30	Depreciation Expense		2 8 6 75	
		Accumulated Depreciation			2 8 6 75
	30	Wages Expense		1 0 0 00	
		Wages Payable			1 0 0 00

does not constitute a journal, we must journalize the entries. You can take the information for these entries directly from the Adjustments columns of the work sheet, debiting and crediting exactly the same accounts.

In the Description column of the general journal, write "Adjusting Entries" before you begin making these entries. This does away with the need to write explanations for each entry. The adjusting entries for NuWay Cleaners are shown in Figure 5-6.

When you post the adjusting entries to the ledger accounts, write the word "Adjusting" in the Item column of the ledger account. For example, the adjusting entry for Supplies is posted as shown below.

GENERAL LEDGER

ACCOUNT _Supplies_   ACCOUNT NO. _113_

DATE		ITEM	POST. REF.	DEBIT	CREDIT	BALANCE DEBIT	BALANCE CREDIT
19— Jun.	4		1	4 0 0 00		4 0 0 00	
	30	Adjusting	4		8 0 00	3 2 0 00	

ACCOUNT _Supplies Expense_   ACCOUNT NO. _515_

DATE		ITEM	POST. REF.	DEBIT	CREDIT	BALANCE DEBIT	BALANCE CREDIT
19— Jun.	30	Adjusting	4	8 0 00		8 0 00	

Businesses with More Than One Revenue Account and More Than One Accumulated Depreciation Account

NuWay Cleaners's only revenue account is Income from Services. However, a business may have several distinct sources of revenue. For example, City Veterinary Clinic has two revenue accounts, Professional Fees and Boarding Fees. Figure 5-7 illustrates the placement of these accounts in the income statement.

Figure 5-7

City Veterinary Clinic
Income Statement
For year ended December 31, 19–

Revenue:			
Professional Fees	$ 111 7 2 0 00		
Boarding Fees	22 0 8 0 00		
Total Revenue		$ 133 8 0 0 00	
Expenses:			
Salaries Expense	$ 84 0 0 0 00		
Depreciation Expense, Building	6 4 8 0 00		
Depreciation Expense, Furniture			
and Equipment	3 8 4 0 00		
Supplies Expense	3 7 2 0 00		
Prepaid Insurance	7 2 0 00		
Miscellaneous Expense	2 1 6 0 00		
Total Expenses		100 9 2 0 00	
Net Income		$ 32 8 8 0 00	

In the example of NuWay Cleaners, Equipment is the only type of asset that is subject to depreciation, so the related accounts are simply titled Depreciation Expense and Accumulated Depreciation. On the other hand, if NuWay Cleaners buys a building that is also subject to depreciation, NuWay would have to separate the depreciation taken on the equipment from the depreciation taken on the building. As a result, separate related accounts would be set up for each type of asset: Depreciation Expense, Equipment and Accumulated Depreciation, Equipment; Depreciation Expense, Building and Accumulated Depreciation, Building.

To illustrate the placement of these accounts in a balance sheet, let's use another example. Standard Travel Agency has the balance sheet shown in Figure 5-8.

Land supposedly will last forever; consequently, land is not depreciated. Separate adjustments would already have been recorded in the work sheet for depreciation of office equipment and building.

GLOSSARY

Accounting cycle The steps in the accounting process that are completed during the fiscal period.

Accrued wages The amount of unpaid wages owed to employees for the time between the last payday and the end of the fiscal period.

Adjusting entry An entry to help bring the books up to date at the end of the fiscal period.

Figure 5-8

Standard Travel Agency
Balance Sheet
September 30, 19–

Assets														
Cash									$	6	2	4	0	00
Supplies											2	0	0	00
Office Equipment	$	4	6	0	0	00								
Less Accumulated Depreciation		2	2	0	0	00				2	4	0	0	00
Building	$26	7	0	0	00									
Less Accumulated Depreciation		1	4	0	0	00			25	3	0	0	00	
Land										4	4	0	0	00
Total Assets									$38	5	4	0	00	
Liabilities														
Accounts Payable									$	2	8	0	0	00
Owner's Equity														
Stanley C. Clay, Capital									35	7	4	0	00	
Total Liabilities and Owner's Equity									$38	5	4	0	00	

Adjustments Internal transactions that bring ledger accounts up to date, as a planned part of the accounting procedure. They are first recorded in the Adjustments columns of the work sheet.

Book value The cost of an asset minus the accumulated depreciation.

Contra account An account that is contrary to, or a deduction from, another account; for example, Accumulated Depreciation entered as a deduction from Equipment.

Depreciation An expense, based on the expectation that an asset will gradually decline in usefulness due to time, wear and tear, or obsolescence; the cost of the asset is therefore spread out over its estimated useful life. A part of depreciation expense is apportioned to each fiscal period.

Fiscal period or year The period of time covered by the entire accounting cycle, generally consisting of twelve consecutive months.

Mixed accounts The balances of certain accounts that appear in the trial balance that are partly income statement amounts and partly balance sheet amounts—for example, Prepaid Insurance and Supplies.

Straight-line method A means of calculating depreciation by taking the cost of an asset, less any trade-in value, and allocating this amount, on an average basis, over the useful life of the asset.

Work sheet A chart for recording necessary adjustments and for furnishing the account balances for making up the income statement and balance sheet.

QUESTIONS, EXERCISES, AND PROBLEMS

Discussion Questions

1. If it is agreed that there is a need to make adjusting entries at the end of a fiscal period, does this mean that errors were made in the accounts during the period? Explain.
2. Why is it necessary to journalize adjusting entries?
3. What is meant by a mixed account? Give an example.
4. What is a contra account? Give an example.
5. What is the nature of the balance in the prepaid insurance account at the end of the fiscal period (a) before the adjusting entry? (b) after the adjusting entry?
6. In which column of a work sheet (Income Statement columns or Balance Sheet columns) would the adjusted balances of the following accounts appear?
   a. Depreciation Expense
   b. Prepaid Insurance
   c. Wages Payable
   d. Income from Services
   e. Insurance Expense
   f. Supplies
   g. Accumulated Depreciation
   h. C. D. Jones, Drawing
7. At the end of the fiscal period, the usual adjusting entry to record supplies used was unintentionally omitted. What is the effect of the omission on (a) the amount of net income for the period? (b) the balance sheet as of the end of the fiscal period?

Exercises

Exercise 5-1   Using a form similar to the one shown, list the following classifications of accounts in all the columns in which they appear in the work sheet, with the exception of the Adjustments columns: Liabilities, Capital, Expenses, Accumulated Depreciation, Revenue, Net Income, Drawing. (*Example:* Assets)

Trial Balance		Adjustments		Adjusted Trial Balance		Income Statement		Balance Sheet	
Debit	Credit	Debit	Credit	Debit	Credit	Debit	Credit	Debit	Credit
Assets				Assets				Assets	

Exercise 5-2   From the following ledger accounts, journalize adjusting entries (a) through (d).

Supplies		Depreciation Expense		Accumulated Depreciation		Prepaid Insurance	
916	(a) 510	(b) 728			1,960	640	(c) 418
					(b) 728		

Wages Payable	Taxes Expense	Prepaid Taxes	Wages Expense
(d) 420	(e) 406	523 | (e) 406	4,296
			(d) 420

Insurance Expense	Supplies Expense
(c) 418	(a) 510

Exercise 5-3 Journalize the necessary adjusting entries at June 30, the close of the current fiscal year, based on the following data.

a. The Prepaid Insurance account before adjustments on June 30 has a balance of $1,260. You now figure out that $820 worth of the insurance has expired during the year.

b. The Supplies account before adjustments on June 30 has a balance of $872. By taking a physical inventory, you now determine that the amount of supplies on hand is worth $260.

c. The last payday was June 27. From June 28 to 30, $590 of wages accrue.

Exercise 5-4 From the ledger accounts for Supplies, determine the missing figures.

a.
Supplies	
Balance 310	Used 728
Bought 916	
End. Inv. ____	

b.
Supplies	
Balance ____	Used 114
Bought 260	
End. Inv. 210	

c.
Supplies	
Balance 148	Used ____
Bought 480	
End. Inv. 160	

d.
Supplies	
Balance 670	Used 820
Bought ____	
End. Inv. 711	

Exercise 5-5 Journalize the year-end adjusting entry for each of the following.

a. Depreciation on equipment was estimated at $3,460 for the year.

b. The payment of the $360 insurance premium for three years in advance was originally recorded as Prepaid Insurance. One year of the policy has now expired.

c. The Supplies account had a balance of $116 on January 1, the beginning of the year; $340 worth of supplies were bought during the year; a year-end inventory shows that $180 worth are still on hand.

d. Two employees earn a total of $200 per day for a five-day week beginning on Monday and ending on Friday. They were paid for the workweek ending December 28. They worked on Monday, December 31.

Exercise 5-6 If the required adjusting entries for Exercise 5 were not made at the end of the year, what would be the cumulative effect of the omissions on net income?

Exercise 5-7 Presented below is a partial work sheet in which the Trial Balance and Income Statement columns have been completed. All amounts are in dollars. Check the adjustments and then journalize the adjusting entries. Why is the Wages Payable line left blank here?

Account Name	Trial Balance		Income Statement	
	Debit	Credit	Debit	Credit
Cash	500			
Accounts Receivable	2,000			
Supplies	800			
Prepaid Insurance	600			
Building	50,000			
Accumulated Depreciation		16,000		
Accounts Payable		700		
L. Bryan, Capital		35,200		
L. Bryan, Drawing	1,000			
Income from Services		4,000		4,000
Wages Expense	900		1,100	
Miscellaneous Expense	100		100	
	55,900	55,900		
Insurance Expense			100	
Supplies Expense			300	
Depreciation Expense			1,200	
Wages Payable				
			2,800	4,000
Net Income			1,200	
			4,000	4,000

Exercise 5-8 Record the adjusting entry in each of the following situations.

a.

Supplies			Supplies Expense	
+		−	+	−
Bal.	260			
Purchases	490			

Ending inventory, $135.

b.

Supplies			Supplies Expense	
+		−	+	−
Bal.	400			
Purchases	920			

Supplies used, $840.

Problem Set A

Problem 5-1A Here is the trial balance for the A. C. Jones Insurance Agency as of March 31, after it has completed its first month of operations.

A. C. Jones Insurance Agency
Trial Balance
March 31, 19–

ACCOUNT NAME	DEBIT	CREDIT
Cash	2 7 3 2 00	
Accounts Receivable	1 0 8 7 00	
Prepaid Insurance	2 8 6 00	
Office Equipment	2 9 6 4 00	
Automobile	3 2 0 0 00	
A. C. Jones, Capital		9 9 2 2 00
A. C. Jones, Drawing	4 2 0 00	
Commissions Earned		1 3 3 5 00
Rent Expense	2 6 0 00	
Advertising Expense	1 4 4 00	
Travel Expense	9 8 00	
Utility Expense	1 6 00	
Telephone Expense	3 2 00	
Miscellaneous Expense	1 8 00	
	11 2 5 7 00	11 2 5 7 00

Instructions

1. Record the trial balance in the Trial Balance columns of the work sheet.
2. Record the letters standing for the account classifications at the top of each column of the work sheet (as shown in Figure 5-2).
3. Complete the work sheet. (Data for the adjustments: depreciation expense of office equipment, $26; depreciation expense of automobile, $63; expired insurance, $21.)

Problem 5-2A The *Working Papers* present the completed work sheet for N. L. Smith, Attorney at Law, for Smith's law practice for August.

Instructions

1. Prepare an income statement.
2. Prepare a statement of owner's equity.
3. Prepare a balance sheet.
4. Journalize the adjusting entries.

Problem 5-3A The trial balance of Supreme Hair Salon as of December 31, the end of the current fiscal year, and data needed for year-end adjustments are shown on the next page.

Supreme Hair Salon
Trial Balance
December 31, 19–

ACCOUNT NAME	DEBIT	CREDIT
Cash	1 4 7 1 00	
Beauty Supplies	1 9 8 0 00	
Prepaid Insurance	4 8 4 00	
Shop Equipment	28 1 8 0 00	
Accumulated Depreciation, Shop Equipment		18 1 3 5 00
Accounts Payable		4 9 2 00
C. Everett, Capital		17 5 4 8 00
C. Everett, Drawing	7 3 0 0 00	
Income from Services		17 6 2 0 00
Wages Expense	11 6 5 8 00	
Rent Expense	1 8 0 0 00	
Utilities Expense	4 8 6 00	
Telephone Expense	1 2 0 00	
Miscellaneous Expense	3 1 6 00	
	53 7 9 5 00	53 7 9 5 00

Data for the adjustments are as follows:

a. Inventory of beauty supplies at December 31, $826.
b. Wages accrued at December 31, $126.
c. The amount in Prepaid Insurance represents twenty-four months' premium paid on July 1 of the current year. Six months' insurance has now expired.
d. Depreciation of shop equipment for the year is $4,030.

Instructions

1. Complete the work sheet.
2. Journalize the adjusting entries.

Problem 5-4A   The trial balance for Donovan Miniature Golf at September 30, the end of the current fiscal year, is on the next page. Data for year-end adjustments are as follows:

a. Inventory of supplies at September 30, $146.
b. Insurance expired during the year, $184.
c. Depreciation of field equipment during the year, $3,860.
d. Depreciation of lighting fixtures during the year, $416.
e. Wages accrued at September 30, $288.

Donovan Miniature Golf
Trial Balance
September 30, 19–

ACCOUNT NAME	DEBIT	CREDIT
Cash	1 9 6 2 00	
Supplies	5 1 9 00	
Prepaid Insurance	4 7 6 00	
Golf Clubs	5 1 5 00	
Field Equipment	19 7 6 0 00	
Accumulated Depreciation, Field Equipment		6 4 6 6 00
Lighting Fixtures	1 8 7 8 00	
Accumulated Depreciation, Lighting Fixtures		4 2 0 00
Accounts Payable		3 2 1 00
Contracts Payable		9 6 0 00
J. C. Donovan, Capital		10 1 8 1 00
J. C. Donovan, Drawing	4 8 7 8 00	
Golf Fees Income		20 6 6 7 00
Concession Income		9 2 3 00
Wages Expense	6 8 2 0 00	
Repair Expense	1 9 8 6 00	
Advertising Expense	4 8 9 00	
Utilities Expense	3 6 4 00	
Miscellaneous Expense	2 9 1 00	
	39 9 3 8 00	39 9 3 8 00

Instructions

1. Complete the work sheet.
2. Journalize the adjusting entries.
3. Prepare an income statement and a statement of owner's equity for the year and a balance sheet as of September 30.

Problem Set B

Problem 5-1B   The trial balance of the C. R. Lind Company, as of November 30, after the company has completed the first month of operations, is on the next page.

Instructions

1. Record the trial balance in the Trial Balance columns of the work sheet.
2. Record the letters standing for the account classifications at the top of each column of the work sheet (as shown in Figure 5-2).
3. Complete the work sheet. (Data for the adjustments: depreciation expense of office equipment, $96; accrued salaries, $108.)

C. R. Lind Company
Trial Balance
November 30, 19–

ACCOUNT NAME	DEBIT	CREDIT
Cash	4 1 1 6 00	
Accounts Receivable	5 6 2 1 00	
Office Equipment	3 1 1 0 00	
Accounts Payable		6 5 4 00
C. R. Lind, Capital		11 3 0 8 00
C. R. Lind, Drawing	1 2 0 0 00	
Commissions Earned		3 0 7 2 00
Salary Expense	6 5 0 00	
Rent Expense	2 1 0 00	
Advertising Expense	8 5 00	
Utilities Expense	2 5 00	
Miscellaneous Expense	1 7 00	
	15 0 3 4 00	15 0 3 4 00

Problem 5-2B The *Working Papers* present the completed work sheet for N. L. Smith, Attorney at Law, for Smith's law practice for August.

Instructions

1. Prepare an income statement.
2. Prepare a statement of owner's equity.
3. Prepare a balance sheet.
4. Journalize the adjusting entries.

Problem 5-3B The trial balance of Collier Launderette as of December 31, the end of the current fiscal year, is shown on the next page. The data needed for year-end adjustments are shown below.

Data for the adjustments are as follows:

a. Inventory of supplies at December 31, $382.
b. The amount in Prepaid Insurance represents twenty-four months' premium paid January 2 of the current year. Twelve months' insurance has now expired.
c. Depreciation of furniture and equipment for the year is $6,000.
d. Wages accrued at December 31, $220.

Instructions

1. Complete the work sheet.
2. Journalize the adjusting entries.

Collier Launderette
Trial Balance
December 31, 19–

ACCOUNT NAME	DEBIT	CREDIT
Cash	2 3 9 2 00	
Laundry Supplies	2 8 4 1 00	
Prepaid Insurance	6 2 6 00	
Furniture and Equipment	25 6 0 0 00	
Accumulated Depreciation, Furniture and Equipment		14 1 6 0 00
Accounts Payable		4 1 9 00
J. L. Collier, Capital		18 2 7 6 00
J. L. Collier, Drawing	8 6 4 0 00	
Income from Services		23 5 4 8 00
Wages Expense	10 6 4 0 00	
Rent Expense	3 6 0 0 00	
Utilities Expense	1 2 7 1 00	
Advertising Expense	4 1 8 00	
Miscellaneous Expense	3 7 5 00	
	56 4 0 3 00	56 4 0 3 00

Problem 5-4B   Shown on page 136 is the trial balance of Recreation Lanes, a bowling alley, as of June 30, the end of the current fiscal year. Data for the year-end adjustments are given below.

a. Inventory of supplies at June 30, $272.
b. Insurance expired during the year, $418.
c. Depreciation of bowling equipment during the year, $14,000.
d. Depreciation of furniture and fixtures during the year, $1,610.
e. Depreciation of building during the year, $2,700.
f. Wages accrued at June 30, $384.

Instructions

1. Complete the work sheet.
2. Journalize the adjusting entries.
3. Prepare an income statement and a statement of owner's equity for the year and a balance sheet as of June 30.

ACCOUNT NAME	DEBIT	CREDIT
Cash	2 9 8 4 00	
Supplies	8 6 2 00	
Prepaid Insurance	6 2 0 00	
Bowling Equipment	90 4 6 0 00	
Accumulated Depreciation, Bowling Equipment		47 2 0 0 00
Furniture and Fixtures	8 4 0 0 00	
Accumulated Depreciation, Furniture and Fixtures		4 1 6 0 00
Building	70 5 0 0 00	
Accumulated Depreciation, Building		20 0 0 0 00
Land	8 0 0 0 00	
Accounts Payable		3 8 2 0 00
Mortgage Payable		42 0 0 0 00
E. L. Boulding, Capital		42 3 3 8 00
E. L. Boulding, Drawing	12 5 0 0 00	
Bowling Fees Income		47 6 6 4 00
Concession Income		5 8 2 0 00
Wages Expense	10 6 0 0 00	
Advertising Expense	3 8 2 0 00	
Repair Expense	2 1 7 0 00	
Utilities Expense	1 5 7 0 00	
Miscellaneous Expense	5 1 6 00	
	213 0 0 2 00	213 0 0 2 00

APPENDIX A

Methods of Depreciation

Depreciation methods will all be calculated using the same example. At the beginning of a year, a delivery truck was bought at a cost of $10,000. The truck is estimated to have a useful life of five years and a trade-in value of $2,500 at the end of the five-year period.

Assets Acquired Before January 1, 1981

For assets bought before January 1, 1981, a business has a choice of depreciation methods, both for general financial reporting and for tax purposes. Three of these methods will be presented here: straight line, sum of the years' digits, and double declining balance.

For assets acquired after 1980, the business may still select any of these methods for general financial reporting so long as it uses just one method consistently for each asset. But it must use a different method for tax purposes; we will discuss that method later in the appendix. Now, let's turn to the three standard methods of depreciation.

Straight-Line Method

$$\text{Yearly depreciation} = \frac{\text{Cost of asset} - \text{Trade-in value}}{\text{Years of life}} = \frac{\$10,000 - \$2,500}{5 \text{ years}} = \$1,500 \text{ per year}$$

Year	Depreciation for the Year	Accumulated Depreciation	Book Value (Cost Less Accumulated Depreciation)
1	$7,500 ÷ 5 years = $1,500	$1,500	$10,000 − $1,500 = $8,500
2	$7,500 ÷ 5 years = $1,500	$1,500 + $1,500 = $3,000	$10,000 − $3,000 = $7,000
3	$7,500 ÷ 5 years = $1,500	$3,000 + $1,500 = $4,500	$10,000 − $4,500 = $5,500
4	$7,500 ÷ 5 years = $1,500	$4,500 + $1,500 = $6,000	$10,000 − $6,000 = $4,000
5	$7,500 ÷ 5 years = $1,500	$6,000 + $1,500 = $7,500	$10,000 − $7,500 = $2,500
	$7,500		

Sum-of-the-Years'-Digits Method   Add the number of years and use the sum as the denominator of the fractions. As numerators in the fractions, use the years in reverse order.

$$1 + 2 + 3 + 4 + 5 = 15$$

$$\frac{5}{15} + \frac{4}{15} + \frac{3}{15} + \frac{2}{15} + \frac{1}{15} = \frac{15}{15}$$

Year	Depreciation for the Year	Accumulated Depreciation	Book Value (Cost Less Accumulated Depreciation)
1	$7,500 × $\frac{5}{15}$ = $2,500	$2,500	$10,000 − $2,500 = $7,500
2	$7,500 × $\frac{4}{15}$ = $2,000	$2,500 + $2,000 = $4,500	$10,000 − $4,500 = $5,500
3	$7,500 × $\frac{3}{15}$ = $1,500	$4,500 + $1,500 = $6,000	$10,000 − $6,000 = $4,000
4	$7,500 × $\frac{2}{15}$ = $1,000	$6,000 + $1,000 = $7,000	$10,000 − $7,000 = $3,000
5	$7,500 × $\frac{1}{15}$ = $500	$7,000 + $500 = $7,500	$10,000 − $7,500 = $2,500
15	$\frac{15}{15}$ $7,500		

Double-Declining-Balance Method   With a life of five years, the straight-line rate is $\frac{1}{5}$. Twice, or double, the straight-line rate is $\frac{2}{5}$ ($\frac{1}{5}$ × 2). The trade-in value is not counted until the end of the schedule. Multiply *book value* at beginning of year by twice the straight-line rate.

Year	Depreciation for the Year	Accumulated Depreciation	Book Value (Cost Less Accumulated Depreciation)
1	$10,000 × $\frac{2}{5}$ = $4,000	$4,000	$10,000 − $4,000 = $6,000
2	$6,000 × $\frac{2}{5}$ = $2,400	$4,000 + $2,400 = $6,400	$10,000 − $6,400 = $3,600
3	$3,600 − $2,500 = $1,100	$6,400 + $1,100 = $7,500	$10,000 − $7,500 = $2,500
4	0	$7,500	$10,000 − $7,500 = $2,500
5	0	$7,500	$10,000 − $7,500 = $2,500
	$7,500		

In the third year, if we calculate depreciation as $3,600 × ⅖, the amount equals $1,440. In this case, the book value would amount to $2,160 ($3,600 − $1,440), which is less than the $2,500 set as the trade-in value. Because the book value cannot be less than the established trade-in value of $2,500, the maximum depreciation that can be taken in Year 3 is $1,100 ($3,600 − $1,100 = $2,500).

In this case, after the end of the third year, no more depreciation may be taken. In other words, the truck has been fully depreciated for income-tax purposes before the end of its estimated useful life.

Assets Acquired After December 31, 1980

For assets bought after 1980, a business must use the Accelerated Cost Recovery System (ACRS) for tax purposes. Property is divided into four categories: three-year, such as automobiles and light trucks; five-year, such as other machinery and equipment; fifteen-year, for certain buildings; and eighteen-year, for other buildings. Under the ACRS method, trade-in value is ignored. Percentage tables have been established; however, Congress may change the percentages from time to time.

Our light truck qualifies as three-year property. The established rates are: first year, 25 percent; second year, 38 percent; third year, 37 percent.

Year	Depreciation for the Year	Accumulated Depreciation	Book Value (Cost Less Accumulated Depreciation)
1	$10,000 × .25 = $2,500	$2,500	$10,000 − $ 2,500 = $7,500
2	$10,000 × .38 = $3,800	$2,500 + $3,800 = $ 6,300	$10,000 − $ 6,300 = $3,700
3	$10,000 × .37 = $3,700	$6,300 + $3,700 = $10,000	$10,000 − $10,000 = 0

In preparing financial reports for its own use, a company may calculate depreciation using any of the methods described in this appendix. However, for tax purposes, a company must use ACRS for assets acquired after December 31, 1980.

Problems

Problem A-1   A delivery van was bought for $7,200 before January 1, 1981. The estimated life of the van is four years. The trade-in value at the end of four years is estimated to be $800. Prepare a schedule of depreciation for the four-year period using the straight-line method.

Problem A-2   Using the information in Problem A-1, prepare a schedule of depreciation using the sum-of-the-years'-digits method.

Problem A-3   Assume the van was purchased after January 1, 1981. Using the information in Problem A-1, prepare a schedule of depreciation under ACRS.

6 Closing Entries and the Post-Closing Trial Balance

Learning Objectives

After you have completed this chapter, you will be able to do the following:

1. Journalize and post closing entries for a service-type enterprise.

2. Prepare a post-closing trial balance for any type of enterprise.

After you have prepared the financial statements from the work sheet and journalized and posted the adjusting entries, the remaining steps of the accounting cycle consist of (1) journalizing and posting the closing entries, and (2) preparing a post-closing trial balance.

This chapter explains the functions of and procedures for accomplishing these final steps in the accounting cycle.

INTERIM STATEMENTS

Interim statements consist of the financial statements that are prepared during the fiscal year for periods of *less* than twelve months. For example, a business may prepare the income statement, the statement of owner's equity, and the balance sheet *monthly*. These statements provide up-to-date information about the results and status of operations. Suppose a company has a fiscal period extending from January 1 of one year through December 31 of the same year; it might have the following interim statements.

Jan. 1	**Jan. 31**	**Feb. 28**	**Mar. 31**	**Apr. 30**
	Income statement for month ended Jan. 31	Income statement for month ended Feb. 28	Income statement for month ended Mar. 31	Income statement for month ended Apr. 30
Beginning of fiscal period		Balance sheet dated Jan. 31	Balance sheet dated Feb. 28	Balance sheet dated Mar. 31	Balance sheet dated Apr. 30

Income statement for 2 months ended Feb. 28

Income statement for 3 months ended Mar. 31

Income statement for 4 months ended Apr. 30

In this case, the company would prepare statements of owner's equity for the same periods as the income statements.

The work sheet and the financial statements would be completed at each of the interim dates. However, the accountant would perform the remaining steps—journalizing the adjusting and closing entries and pre- paring the post-closing trial balance—only at the end of the fiscal year. As an example and to gain practice, however, let's assume that a fiscal year, with the closing entries and post-closing trial balance, consists of only one month. We need to make this assumption so that we can thoroughly cover the material. The entire accounting cycle is presented graphically in Figure 6-1.

CLOSING ENTRIES

So that you will understand the reason for the closing entries, let us first repeat the fundamental accounting equation:

Assets = Liabilities + Owner's Equity + Revenue − Expenses

We know that the income statement, as stated in the third line of its heading, covers a definite period of time. It consists of revenue minus expenses for this period of time only. So, when this period is over, we should start from zero for the next period. In other words, we wipe the slate clean, so that we can start all over again next period.

Purposes of Closing Entries

This brings us to the *purpose* of the closing entries, which is to close off the revenue and expense accounts. We do this because their balances apply to only one fiscal period. As stated before, with the coming of the next fiscal period, we want to start from scratch, recording brand-new revenue and expenses. Accountants also refer to this as *clearing the accounts.* For income tax purposes, this is certainly understandable. No one wants to pay in- come tax more than once on the same income, and the Internal Revenue Service frowns on counting an expense more than once. So now we have this:

$$\text{(closed)} \quad \text{(closed)}$$
Assets = Liabilities + Owner's Equity + ~~Revenue~~ − ~~Expenses~~

The assets, liabilities, and owner's equity accounts remain open. The balance sheet, with its one date in the heading, merely gives the present balances of these accounts. The accountant carries them over to the next fiscal period.

During the accounting period

Source Document
Check, invoice, receipt, cash register tape, etc.

Analyze
Transactions

Journalize
Transactions

post to

Ledger

Trial Balance
Assets
Liabilities
Owner's Equity
Capital
Drawing
Revenue
Expenses

At the end of the accounting period

Worksheet

Trial Balance	Adjustments	Adjusted Trial Balance	Income Statement	Balance Sheet
Assets	Prepaid expenses		Revenue	Assets
Liabilities	Depreciation		Expenses	Liabilities
Owner's Equity	Accrued expenses			Capital
Capital				Drawing
Drawing				
Revenue				
Expenses				

Income Statement
Revenue
− Expenses
= Net Income
(or Net Loss)

Statement of Owner's Equity
Beginning Capital
+ Investments (if any)
+ Net Income (− Net Loss)
− Withdrawals
= Ending Capital

Balance Sheet
Assets
= Liabilities
+ Ending Capital

Journalize
adjusting entries

post to

Ledger

Journalize
closing entries

post to

Ledger

Post-closing Trial Balance
Assets
Liabilities
Capital

End of Cycle

Normal closing entries

1. Revenue
   Income Summary

2. Income Summary
   Expense
   Expense
   Expense

3. Income Summary*
   Capital

4. Capital
   Drawing

*Assuming a net income. If there is a net loss, the entry would be:

3. Capital
   Income Summary

Figure 6-1 The accounting cycle

Procedure for Closing

Objective 1

Journalize and post closing entries for a service-type enterprise.

The procedure for closing is simply to balance off the account, in other words, to make the balance *equal to zero.* This meets our objective, which is to start from zero in the next fiscal period. Let's illustrate this first with T accounts. Suppose an account happens to have a debit balance; then, to make the balance equal zero, we *credit* the account. We write *closing* in the Item column of the ledger account.

Debit		Credit	
Balance	960	Closing	960

To take another example, suppose an account happens to have a credit balance; then, to make the balance equal to zero, we *debit* the account.

Debit		Credit	
Closing	1,200	Balance	1,200

Every entry must have both a debit and a credit. So, in order to record the other half of the closing entry, we bring into existence **Income Summary.** Thus, there are four steps in the closing procedure:

1. Close the revenue accounts into Income Summary.
2. Close the expense accounts into Income Summary.
3. Close the Income Summary account into the Capital account.
4. Close the Drawing account into the Capital account.

To illustrate by making the entries directly in T accounts, we again fall back on the accounts of our friendly neighborhood business, NuWay Cleaners. For the purpose of the illustration, assume that NuWay Cleaners's fiscal period consists of one month. We now have the following revenue and expense accounts.

Income from Services			Utilities Expense		
−	+		+	−	
	Balance	3,230	Balance 220.00		

Wages Expense			Supplies Expense		
+	−		+	−	
Balance 730.00			Balance 80.00		

Rent Expense			Insurance Expense		
+	−		+	−	
Balance 400.00			Balance 13.33		

Advertising Expense	Depreciation Expense
+	−	+	−
Balance 180.00		Balance 286.75	

Step 1   Close the revenue account, or accounts, into Income Summary. In order to make the balance of Income from Services equal to zero, we *balance it off*, or debit it, in the amount of $3,230. Because we need an offsetting credit, we credit Income Summary for the same amount.

Income from Services	Income Summary
−	+		
Closing 3,230.00	Balance 3,230.00		3,230.00

In essence, the balance of Income from Services is transferred to Income Summary. Now let's look at the journal entry for this step.

GENERAL JOURNAL   PAGE   4

DATE	DESCRIPTION	POST. REF.	DEBIT	CREDIT
	Closing Entries			
30	*Income from Services*		3 2 3 0 00	
	Income Summary			3 2 3 0 00

Writing *Closing Entries* in the Description column eliminates the need to write explanations for all the closing entries.

Step 2   Close the expense accounts into Income Summary. In order to make the balances of the expense accounts equal to zero, we need to balance them off, or credit them. Again the T accounts are a basis for formulating the journal entry. In essence, the balances of the expense accounts are transferred to Income Summary, as shown in Figure 6-2.

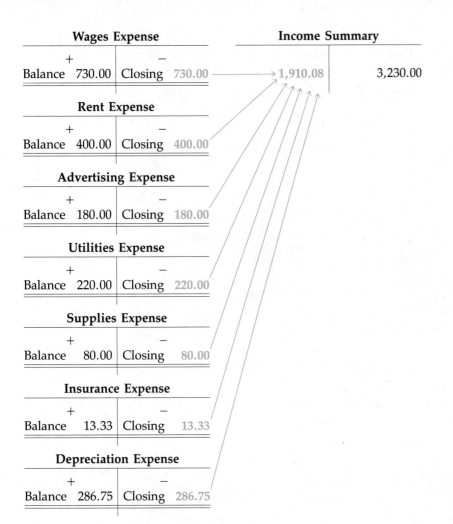

Figure 6-2

The journal entries for step 2 are shown in Figure 6-3 (next page).

Step 3 Recall that we created Income Summary so that we could have a debit and credit with each closing entry. Now that it has done its job, we close it out. We use the same procedure as before, in that we make the balance equal to zero, or balance off the account. In essence, we transfer, or close, the balance of the Income Summary account into the Capital account, as shown in the T accounts and in Figure 6-4 (next page).

	Income Summary		Alan Stevenson, Capital	
			−	+
	1,910.08	3,230.00		Balance	32,000.00
Closing	1,319.92			(Net Inc.)	1,319.92

Figure 6-3

DATE	DESCRIPTION	POST. REF.	DEBIT	CREDIT
	GENERAL JOURNAL			PAGE __4__
	Closing Entries			
30	*Income from Services*		3 2 3 0 00	
	Income Summary			3 2 3 0 00
30	*Income Summary*		1 9 1 0 08	
	Wages Expense			7 3 0 00
	Rent Expense			4 0 0 00
	Advertising Expense			1 8 0 00
	Utilities Expense			2 2 0 00
	Supplies Expense			8 0 00
	Insurance Expense			1 3 33
	Depreciation Expense			2 8 6 75

Income Summary is always closed into the Capital account by the amount of the net income or the net loss. Comparing net income or net loss with the closing entry for Income Summary can serve as a check point or verification for you.

Figure 6-4

DATE	DESCRIPTION	POST. REF.	DEBIT	CREDIT
	GENERAL JOURNAL			PAGE __4__
	Closing Entries			
30	*Income from Services*		3 2 3 0 00	
	Income Summary			3 2 3 0 00
30	*Income Summary*		1 9 1 0 08	
	Wages Expense			7 3 0 00
	Rent Expense			4 0 0 00
	Advertising Expense			1 8 0 00
	Utilities Expense			2 2 0 00
	Supplies Expense			8 0 00
	Insurance Expense			1 3 33
	Depreciation Expense			2 8 6 75
30	*Income Summary*		1 3 1 9 92	
	Alan Stevenson, Capital			1 3 1 9 92

Net income is added or credited to the Capital account because in the statement of owner's equity, as we have seen, net income is treated as an addition. Net loss, on the other hand, should be subtracted from or debited to the Capital account because net loss is treated as a deduction in the statement of owner's equity. Here's how one would close Income Summary for J. Doe Company, which had a net loss.

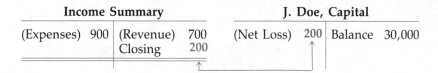

Income Summary				J. Doe, Capital		
(Expenses) 900	(Revenue)	700		(Net Loss) 200	Balance	30,000
	Closing	200				

For a situation involving a net loss of $200, the entry to close Income Summary into the Capital account would look like this.

GENERAL JOURNAL					PAGE 3		
DATE	DESCRIPTION	POST. REF.	DEBIT		CREDIT		
	Closing Entries						
31	*J. Doe, Capital*		2 0 0 00				
	Income Summary				2 0 0 00		

Step 4 Let us return to the example of NuWay Cleaners. The Drawing account applies to only one fiscal period, so it too must be closed. You may recall from Chapter 2 that Drawing is not an expense because no money is paid to anyone outside the business. And because Drawing is not an expense, it cannot affect net income or net loss. It appears in the statement of owner's equity as a deduction from the Capital account, and so it is closed directly into the Capital account. So we balance off the Drawing account, or make the balance of it equal to zero. The balance of Drawing is transferred to the Capital account.

Alan Stevenson, Drawing				Alan Stevenson, Capital		
+		−		−	+	
Balance 1,000.00	Closing	1,000.00		1,000	Balance	32,000.00
					(Net Inc.)	1,319.92

The four journal entries in the closing procedure are illustrated in Figure 6-5.

Figure 6-5

GENERAL JOURNAL				PAGE 4	
DATE	DESCRIPTION	POST. REF.	DEBIT	CREDIT	

	Closing Entries				
30	Income from Services		3 2 3 0 00		
	Income Summary			3 2 3 0 00	
30	Income Summary		1 9 1 0 08		
	Wages Expense			7 3 0 00	
	Rent Expense			4 0 0 00	
	Advertising Expense			1 8 0 00	
	Utilities Expense			2 2 0 00	
	Supplies Expense			8 0 00	
	Insurance Expense			1 3 33	
	Depreciation Expense			2 8 6 75	
30	Income Summary		1 3 1 9 92		
	Alan Stevenson, Capital			1 3 1 9 92	
30	Alan Stevenson, Capital		1 0 0 0 00		
	Alan Stevenson, Drawing			1 0 0 0 00	

These closing entries show that NuWay Cleaners has net income of $1,319.92, the owner has withdrawn $1,000 for personal expenses, and $319.92 has been retained or plowed back into the business, thereby increasing capital.

Closing Entries Taken Directly from the Work Sheet

One can gather the information for the closing entries either directly from the ledger accounts or from the work sheet. Since the Income Statement columns of the work sheet consist entirely of revenues and expenses, one can pick up the figures for the closing entries from these columns. Figure 6-6 shows a partial work sheet for NuWay Cleaners.

You may formulate the closing entries by simply balancing off all the figures that appear in the Income Statement columns. For example, in the Income Statement column, there is a credit for $3,230; so we debit that account for $3,230 and credit Income Summary for $3,230.

There are debits for $730, $400, $180, $220, $80, $13.33, and $286.75. So now we *credit* these accounts for the same amounts, and we debit Income Summary for their total.

		TRIAL BALANCE		ADJUSTED TRIAL BALANCE		INCOME STATEMENT		
	ACCOUNT NAME	DEBIT	CREDIT	DEBIT	CREDIT	DEBIT	CREDIT	
1	Cash	11 5 2 0 00						1
2	Accounts							2
3	Receivable	2 0 00						3
4	Supplies	4 0 0 00			(a) 8 0 00			4
5	Prepaid Insurance	3 2 0 00			(b) 1 3 33			5
6	Equipment	22 9 4 0 00						6
7	Accounts Payable		2 4 0 0 00					7
8	Alan Stevenson,							8
9	Capital		32 0 0 0 00					9
10	Alan Stevenson,							10
11	Drawing	1 0 0 0 00						11
12	Income from							12
13	Services		3 2 3 0 00				3 2 3 0 00	13
14	Wages Expense	6 3 0 00		(d) 1 0 0 00		7 3 0 00		14
15	Rent Expense	4 0 0 00				4 0 0 00		15
16	Advertising							16
17	Expense	1 8 0 00				1 8 0 00		17
18	Utilities Expense	2 2 0 00				2 2 0 00		18
19		37 6 3 0 00	37 6 3 0 00					19
20	Supplies Expense			(a) 8 0 00		8 0 00		20
21	Insurance Expense			(b) 1 3 33		1 3 33		21
22	Depreciation							22
23	Expense			(c) 2 8 6 75		2 8 6 75		23
24	Accumulated							24
25	Depreciation				(c) 2 8 6 75			25
26	Wages Payable				(d) 1 0 0 00			26
27				4 8 0 08	4 8 0 08	1 9 1 0 08	3 2 3 0 00	27
28	Net Income					1 3 1 9 92		28
29						3 2 3 0 00	3 2 3 0 00	29
30								30

Figure 6-6

Next, as usual, we close Income Summary into Capital, by using the net income figure already shown on the work sheet.

We would of course have to pick up the last entry from the Balance Sheet columns to close Drawing.

Collectively, we call the accounts that are closed **temporary-equity accounts,** or nominal accounts. In this context they are temporary in that the balances apply to one fiscal period only. A **closing entry** is simply an entry made at the end of a fiscal period in order to make the balance of a temporary-equity account equal to zero. In the last analysis, temporary-equity accounts are closed into the Capital account.

We indicate that the accounts are closed by writing the word *Closing* in the Item column of the ledger, and by extending a line through both the debit and credit balance columns.

Posting the Closing Entries

After we have posted the closing entries, the Capital, Drawing, Income Summary, revenue, and expense accounts of NuWay Cleaners appear as follows.

GENERAL LEDGER

ACCOUNT _Alan Stevenson, Capital_   ACCOUNT NO. _311_

DATE		ITEM	POST. REF.	DEBIT	CREDIT	BALANCE DEBIT	BALANCE CREDIT
19– Jun.	1		1		32 0 0 0 00		32 0 0 0 00
	30		4		1 3 1 9 92		33 3 1 9 92
	30		4	1 0 0 0 00			32 3 1 9 92

ACCOUNT _Alan Stevenson, Drawing_   ACCOUNT NO. _312_

DATE		ITEM	POST. REF.	DEBIT	CREDIT	BALANCE DEBIT	BALANCE CREDIT
19– Jun.	30		4	1 0 0 0 00		1 0 0 0 00	
	30	Closing	4		1 0 0 0 00		

ACCOUNT _Income Summary_   ACCOUNT NO. _313_

DATE		ITEM	POST. REF.	DEBIT	CREDIT	BALANCE DEBIT	BALANCE CREDIT
19– Jun.	30		4		3 2 3 0 00		3 2 3 0 00
	30		4	1 9 1 0 08			1 3 1 9 92
	30	Closing	4	1 3 1 9 92			

GENERAL LEDGER

ACCOUNT *Income from Services*   ACCOUNT NO. *411*

DATE		ITEM	POST. REF.	DEBIT	CREDIT	BALANCE DEBIT	BALANCE CREDIT
19– Jun.	7		1		6 0 0 00		6 0 0 00
	14		2		7 6 0 00		1 3 6 0 00
	21		2		8 3 0 00		2 1 9 0 00
	23		3		8 0 00		2 2 7 0 00
	30		3		9 6 0 00		3 2 3 0 00
	30	Closing	4	3 2 3 0 00			

ACCOUNT *Wages Expense*   ACCOUNT NO. *511*

DATE		ITEM	POST. REF.	DEBIT	CREDIT	BALANCE DEBIT	BALANCE CREDIT
19– Jun.	10		2	2 4 0 00		2 4 0 00	
	24		3	3 9 0 00		6 3 0 00	
	30	Adjusting	4	1 0 0 00		7 3 0 00	
	30	Closing	4		7 3 0 00		

ACCOUNT *Rent Expense*   ACCOUNT NO. *512*

DATE		ITEM	POST. REF.	DEBIT	CREDIT	BALANCE DEBIT	BALANCE CREDIT
19– Jun.	8		1	4 0 0 00		4 0 0 00	
	30	Closing	4		4 0 0 00		

ACCOUNT *Advertising Expense*   ACCOUNT NO. *513*

DATE		ITEM	POST. REF.	DEBIT	CREDIT	BALANCE DEBIT	BALANCE CREDIT
19– Jun.	14		2	1 8 0 00		1 8 0 00	
	30	Closing	4		1 8 0 00		

GENERAL LEDGER

ACCOUNT __Utilities Expense__   ACCOUNT NO. __514__

DATE		ITEM	POST. REF.	DEBIT	CREDIT	BALANCE DEBIT	BALANCE CREDIT
19– Jun.	15		2	2 2 0 00		2 2 0 00	
	30	Closing	4		2 2 0 00		

ACCOUNT __Supplies Expense__   ACCOUNT NO. __515__

DATE		ITEM	POST. REF.	DEBIT	CREDIT	BALANCE DEBIT	BALANCE CREDIT
19– Jun.	30	Adjusting	4	8 0 00		8 0 00	
	30	Closing	4		8 0 00		

ACCOUNT __Insurance Expense__   ACCOUNT NO. __516__

DATE		ITEM	POST. REF.	DEBIT	CREDIT	BALANCE DEBIT	BALANCE CREDIT
19– Jun.	30	Adjusting	4	1 3 33		1 3 33	
	30	Closing	4		1 3 33		

ACCOUNT __Depreciation Expense__   ACCOUNT NO. __517__

DATE		ITEM	POST. REF.	DEBIT	CREDIT	BALANCE DEBIT	BALANCE CREDIT
19– Jun.	30	Adjusting	4	2 8 6 75		2 8 6 75	
	30	Closing	4		2 8 6 75		

Figure 6-7

NuWay Cleaners
Post-Closing Trial Balance
June 30, 19–

ACCOUNT NAME	DEBIT	CREDIT
Cash	11 5 2 0 00	
Accounts Receivable	2 0 00	
Supplies	3 2 0 00	
Prepaid Insurance	3 0 6 67	
Equipment	22 9 4 0 00	
Accumulated Depreciation		2 8 6 75
Accounts Payable		2 4 0 0 00
Wages Payable		1 0 0 00
Alan Stevenson, Capital		32 3 1 9 92
	35 1 0 6 67	35 1 0 6 67

THE POST-CLOSING TRIAL BALANCE

After posting the closing entries and before going on to the next fiscal period, one should verify the balances of the accounts that remain open. To do so, make up a **post-closing trial balance,** using the final-balance figures from the ledger accounts. This represents a last-ditch effort to make absolutely sure that the debit balances equal the credit balances.

The accounts listed in the post-closing trial balance (assets, liabilities, owner's equity, balance sheet accounts) are called **real accounts** or **permanent accounts.** (See Figure 6-7.) The accountant carries forward the balances of real accounts from one fiscal period to another.

Contrast this to the handling of temporary-equity accounts, which, as you have seen, are closed at the end of each fiscal period.

Objective 2

Prepare a post-closing trial balance for any type of enterprise.

GLOSSARY

Closing entry An entry made at the end of a fiscal period to make the balance of a temporary-equity account equal to zero. This is also referred to as *clearing the accounts.*

Income Summary An account brought into existence in order to have a debit and credit with each closing entry.

Interim statements Financial statements prepared during the fiscal year, covering a period of time less than the entire twelve months.

Post-closing trial balance The listing of the final balances of the real accounts at the end of the fiscal period.

Real accounts Assets, liabilities, and the Capital account in owner's equity, having balances that are carried forward from one fiscal period to another. Also known as *permanent accounts.*

Temporary-equity accounts Accounts that apply to only one fiscal period and that are closed at the end of that fiscal period, such as revenue, expense, Income Summary, and Drawing accounts. This category may also be described as all accounts except assets, liabilities, and the Capital account. Also known as *nominal accounts*.

QUESTIONS, EXERCISES, AND PROBLEMS

Discussion Questions

1. For the first two months of the year, what interim statements would you suggest for a restaurant that operates on a fiscal year of January 1 through December 31?
2. Explain the functions served by the Income Summary account?
3. What is the difference between a real account and a temporary-equity account?
4. What is the closing entry required for a firm that made a profit for the fiscal period? What entry is required for a firm that had a loss for the fiscal period?
5. Name the four steps in the closing procedure.
6. What is the purpose of the post-closing trial balance?
7. What accounts appear in the post-closing trial balance?

Exercises

Exercise 6-1 As of December 31, the end of the current year, the ledger of the Harmon Company contained the following account balances: Cash, $4,000; Equipment, $24,000; Accounts Payable, $3,000; L. H. Harmon, Capital, $28,000; L. H. Harmon, Drawing, $20,000; Income from Services, $62,000; Concession Income, $2,000; Salary Expense, $36,000; Taxes Expense, $4,000; Depreciation Expense, Equipment, $6,000; Miscellaneous Expense, $1,000. All the accounts have normal balances. Journalize the closing entries.

Exercise 6-2 Complete the posting of the closing entry for this account.

GENERAL LEDGER

ACCOUNT __Commissions Earned__   ACCOUNT NO. __411__

DATE		ITEM	POST. REF.	DEBIT	CREDIT	BALANCE	
						DEBIT	CREDIT
19– Mar.	31		56		16 4 0 0 00		16 4 0 0 00
Jun.	30		71		18 4 6 0 00		34 8 6 0 00
Sep.	30		84		19 7 2 0 00		54 5 8 0 00
Dec.	31		96		13 1 7 0 00		67 7 5 0 00
	31		97	67 7 5 0 00			

Exercise 6-3 The Income Statement columns of the work sheet of M. R. Zeller Company for the fiscal year ended April 30 contain the following.

	ACCOUNT NAME	INCOME STATEMENT		BALANCE SHEET		
		DEBIT	CREDIT	DEBIT	CREDIT	
1						1
2	Income from Services		52 0 0 0 00			2
3	Salary Expense	26 0 0 0 00				3
4	Rent Expense	4 8 0 0 00				4
5	Supplies Expense	1 2 0 0 00				5
6	Miscellaneous Expense	1 0 0 0 00				6
7						7

The Balance Sheet columns of the work sheet contain the following.

	ACCOUNT NAME	INCOME STATEMENT		BALANCE SHEET		
		DEBIT	CREDIT	DEBIT	CREDIT	
1						1
2	M. R. Zeller, Capital				80 0 0 0 00	2
3	M. R. Zeller, Drawing			17 0 0 0 00		3
4						4

Record the four closing entries.

Exercise 6-4 The Income Summary ledger account is as follows.

Income Summary

8,700	10,200

1. Total revenue is _____.
2. Total expenses are _____.
3. Net income is _____.

Exercise 6-5 After all revenues and expenses have been closed at the end of the fiscal period, Income Summary has a debit of $29,000 and a credit of $27,000. On the same date, A. C. Marker, Drawing, has a debit balance of $6,000, and A. C. Marker, Capital, has a credit balance of $46,000. On a sheet of paper, record the journal entries necessary to complete the closing of the accounts. What is the new balance of A. C. Marker, Capital?

Exercise 6-6 From the following ledger accounts, journalize the adjusting entries and closing entries that have been posted to the accounts.

Accumulated Depreciation			Prepaid Insurance			Depreciation Expense		
		1,900	360	(b)	120	(a)	500	(2)	500
	(a)	500	90					

Insurance Expense			Income from Services			Wages Expense		
(b)	120	(2)	120	(1)	3,500	300		800	(2)	1,670
						2,900		800	
						300	(c)	70	

Wages Payable		Miscellaneous Expense			Income Summary		
(c)	70	160	(2)	160	(2)	2,450	(1)	3,500

Exercise 6-7 The ledger accounts of D. L. Minor Company are as follows. Prepare a statement of owner's equity.

Income Summary				D. L. Minor, Capital			
Dec. 31	60,000	Dec. 31	90,000	Dec. 31	24,000	Jan. 1 Bal.	67,000
Dec. 31 Closing	30,000					Dec. 31	30,000

D. L. Minor, Drawing	
Mar. 31	6,000
Oct. 30	9,000
Nov. 30	9,000

Exercise 6-8 Financial information for three different one-owner businesses is shown below. Fill in the missing figures. (Assume no additional investments were made during the year.)

	a	b	c
Net income (loss) for the year	$ 75,000	$?	$(12,000)
Owner's equity at beginning of year	?	105,000	45,000
Owner's equity at end of year	142,000	102,000	30,000
Withdrawals by owner during year	12,000	9,000	?

Problem Set A

Problem 6-1A The partial work sheet for Precision Termite Control for the fiscal year ending December 31 of this year is presented on the next page.

Instructions

Journalize the closing entries with the four steps in order.

	ACCOUNT NAME	TRIAL BALANCE		INCOME STATEMENT		
		DEBIT	CREDIT	DEBIT	CREDIT	
1	Cash	2 963 00				1
2	Accounts					2
3	Receivable	1 781 00				3
4	Supplies	887 00				4
5	Equipment	4 914 00				5
6	Accumulated					6
7	Depreciation,					7
8	Equipment		3 298 00			8
9	Truck	3 584 00				9
10	Accumulated					10
11	Depreciation,					11
12	Truck		2 780 00			12
13	Accounts Payable		826 00			13
14	N. B. Petrie, Capital		3 899 00			14
15	N. B. Petrie,					15
16	Drawing	10 400 00				16
17	Service Income		25 716 00		25 716 00	17
18	Wages Expense	7 420 00		7 420 00		18
19	Rent Expense	2 400 00		2 400 00		19
20	Truck Operating					20
21	Expense	1 930 00		1 930 00		21
22	Telephone Expense	240 00		240 00		22
23		36 519 00	36 519 00			23
24	Supplies Expense			232 00		24
25	Depreciation					25
26	Expense,					26
27	Equipment			312 00		27
28	Depreciation					28
29	Expense, Truck			440 00		29
30				12 974 00	25 716 00	30
31	Net Income			12 742 00		31
32				25 716 00	25 716 00	32

Problem 6-2A After the adjusting entries have been posted, the ledger of S. T. Dixon, consulting engineer, contains the following account balances as of March 31.

Cash	$14,166	Income Summary	$ 0
Office Supplies	1,413	Professional Fees	15,189
Furniture and Fixtures	8,637	Salary Expense	6,780
Accumulated Depreciation,		Rent Expense	1,050
Furniture and Fixtures	5,523	Telephone Expense	156
Accounts Payable	2,823	Office Supplies Expense	360
Salaries Payable	120	Depreciation Expense,	
S. T. Dixon, Capital	13,200	Furniture and Fixtures	228
S. T. Dixon, Drawing	3,240	Miscellaneous Expense	825

Instructions

Journalize the closing entries with the four steps in order.

Problem 6-3A The trial balance section of the work sheet for Clean-Sweep Chimney Service as of December 31, the end of the current fiscal year, is as follows.

ACCOUNT NAME	TRIAL BALANCE DEBIT	TRIAL BALANCE CREDIT
Cash	1 2 9 8 00	
Accounts Receivable	2 1 1 0 00	
Cleaning Supplies	4 2 6 00	
Cleaning Equipment	3 8 6 4 00	
Accumulated Depreciation, Cleaning Equipment		1 9 3 2 00
Truck	2 9 8 0 00	
Accumulated Depreciation, Truck		2 1 2 0 00
Accounts Payable		8 7 2 00
R. A. Fallon, Capital		1 8 3 9 00
R. A. Fallon, Drawing	10 8 0 0 00	
Service Income		24 8 4 0 00
Wages Expense	8 6 4 0 00	
Advertising Expense	2 6 2 00	
Truck Operating Expense	4 2 4 00	
Utilities Expense	3 1 9 00	
Miscellaneous Expense	4 8 0 00	
	31 6 0 3 00	31 6 0 3 00

Data for the adjustments are as follows.

a. Accrued wages, $116.
b. Inventory of cleaning supplies, $304.
c. Depreciation of cleaning equipment, $120.
d. Depreciation of truck, $296.

Instructions

1. Complete the work sheet.
2. Prepare an income statement.
3. Prepare a statement of owner's equity.
4. Prepare a balance sheet.
5. Journalize the closing entries, with the four steps in order.

Problem 6-4A The completed work sheet for Twinning Employment Agency is presented in the *Working Papers*.

Instructions

1. Journalize and post the adjusting entries.
2. Journalize and post the closing entries.
3. Prepare a post-closing trial balance.

Problem Set B

Problem 6-1B   The partial work sheet for Jarris Tree-Spraying Service for the fiscal year ending December 31 of this year is presented below.

	ACCOUNT NAME	TRIAL BALANCE DEBIT	TRIAL BALANCE CREDIT	INCOME STATEMENT DEBIT	INCOME STATEMENT CREDIT	
1	Cash	3 4 0 0 00				1
2	Accounts					2
3	Receivable	1 8 0 0 00				3
4	Supplies	9 1 0 00				4
5	Equipment	4 2 2 0 00				5
6	Accumulated					6
7	Depreciation,					7
8	Equipment		2 6 0 0 00			8
9	Truck	3 1 9 0 00				9
10	Accumulated					10
11	Depreciation,					11
12	Truck		1 4 7 2 00			12
13	Accounts Payable		6 4 0 00			13
14	T. Jarris, Capital		7 5 9 8 00			14
15	T. Jarris, Drawing	9 6 0 0 00				15
16	Service Income		23 6 7 0 00		23 6 7 0 00	16
17	Wages Expense	8 4 2 0 00		8 4 2 0 00		17
18	Rent Expense	2 4 0 0 00		2 4 0 0 00		18
19	Truck Operating					19
20	Expense	1 8 6 0 00		1 8 6 0 00		20
21	Telephone Expense	1 8 0 00		1 8 0 00		21
22		35 9 8 0 00	35 9 8 0 00			22
23	Supplies Expense			2 2 7 00		23
24	Depreciation					24
25	Expense,					25
26	Equipment			3 2 6 00		26
27	Depreciation					27
28	Expense, Truck			4 8 2 00		28
29				13 8 9 5 00	23 6 7 0 00	29
30	Net Income			9 7 7 5 00		30
31				23 6 7 0 00	23 6 7 0 00	31
32						32

Instructions

Journalize the closing entries with the four steps in order.

Problem 6-2B After the adjusting entries have been posted, the ledger of N. L. Francis, marriage counselor, contains the following account balances as of May 31.

Cash	$10,911	Income Summary	$ 0
Office Supplies	570	Income from Professional	
Furniture and Fixtures	4,758	Fees	11,460
Accumulated Depreciation,		Salary Expense	5,064
Furniture and Fixtures	3,252	Rent Expense	624
Accounts Payable	2,559	Telephone Expense	72
Salaries Payable	492	Office Supplies Expense	1,263
N. L. Francis, Capital	9,747	Depreciation Expense,	
N. L. Francis, Drawing	3,600	Furniture and Fixtures	648

Instructions

Journalize the closing entries with the four steps in order.

Problem 6-3B The trial balance section of the work sheet for the Super Janitorial Service as of December 31, the end of the current fiscal year, is as follows.

	TRIAL BALANCE	
ACCOUNT NAME	DEBIT	CREDIT
Cash	1 6 8 3 00	
Accounts Receivable	1 7 9 0 00	
Cleaning Supplies	2 4 3 00	
Cleaning Equipment	2 9 7 0 00	
Accumulated Depreciation, Cleaning Equipment		1 8 6 0 00
Truck	3 1 7 5 00	
Accumulated Depreciation, Truck		1 4 2 5 00
Accounts Payable		6 2 7 00
S. A. Maki, Capital		3 3 3 2 00
S. A. Maki, Drawing	9 6 0 0 00	
Service Income		19 6 4 1 00
Wages Expense	6 4 2 0 00	
Advertising Expense	2 6 4 00	
Truck Operating Expense	4 1 5 00	
Utilities Expense	3 2 5 00	
	26 8 8 5 00	26 8 8 5 00

Data for the adjustments are as follows.

a. Accrued wages, $128.
b. Inventory of cleaning supplies, $120.
c. Depreciation of cleaning equipment, $225.
d. Depreciation of truck, $340.

Instructions

1. Complete the work sheet.
2. Prepare an income statement.
3. Prepare a statement of owner's equity.
4. Prepare a balance sheet.
5. Journalize the closing entries with the four steps in order.

Problem 6-4B The completed work sheet for Twinning Employment Agency is presented in the *Working Papers.*

Instructions

1. Journalize and post the adjusting entries.
2. Journalize and post the closing entries.
3. Prepare a post-closing trial balance.

APPENDIX B

Computers and Accounting

Businesses, governments, and nonprofit organizations use computers to improve their efficiency and reduce the cost of doing business. Computers can provide more timely and accurate management information, which enhances efficiency, as well as improving customer relations.

Large business organizations began to use computers in the 1950s. Since that time, the size and cost of computers have been gradually reduced. Today medium-sized and small business firms enjoy the benefits of computer use. Only a brief overview is presented in this appendix, but it is vitally important that people going into business become acquainted with computers.

Types of Computers

Mainframe Computers Computers may be divided into three categories by size: mainframe computers (large), minicomputers (medium), and microcomputers (small). Large economic units, such as petroleum and airline companies, research laboratories, banks, universities, and government agencies, invest several million dollars in mainframe computers. These computers are able to process 100 million operations per second.

Many other organizations also use mainframe computers. Typical examples include a stock exchange that executes customer buy and sell orders from locations throughout the country; travel agents, who verify space availability as well as departure and arrival times; the Internal Revenue Service, which matches taxable income with tax returns; and police organizations that check criminal records and traffic violations.

Minicomputers   Minicomputers are compact, powerful machines used in business, education, and government. The cost begins at about $25,000. By using remote terminals or keyboards, these computers can link branch offices to an organization's main office. Or they may be used entirely in one location. Minicomputers are used to monitor patients in health-care facilities, handle the record keeping of car rental agencies, and make hotel reservations. Libraries and insurance companies are likely to use minicomputers.

Microcomputers   Microcomputers have changed both business and personal information management. As their cost has fallen to under $5,000, they have become increasingly popular. Small businesses use these computers for accounting applications such as accounts receivable and payable, payroll records, and inventory records. Many businesses use microcomputers for data management, text editing, creation and updating of membership or mailing lists, and maintenance of personnel files. Today many tax preparers rely on microcomputers. New applications are unveiled regularly as schools, businesses, public institutions, and individuals acquire these machines.

Definitions

Data are facts, concepts, or instructions that can be communicated, interpreted, or processed. *Data processing* consists of recording, coding, sorting, calculating, summarizing, communicating, storing, retrieving, and arranging information in a usable form—with or without the aid of a computer. Data processing converts raw data into usable information. A *system* is a series of procedures designed to do a specific task. A *computer* is an electronic machine that processes data quickly.

Parts of a Computer

Computers consist of three major segments—input, central processing, and output. *Input devices* give instructions and data to the computer system. *Input mediums* may include disks, magnetic or punched card readers, magnetic tapes, paper tape readers, optical scanners, magnetic ink readers, audio units, numeric pads, and alphabetic keyboards.

The second part of a computer is the *Central Processing Unit* (CPU). It has a *control unit* that interprets instructions from a program, an *arithmetic-logic unit* that performs calculations and executes the actual instructions, and a *memory section*. The Read Only Memory (ROM) unit stores programs built into the computer by the manufacturer. The Random Access Memory (RAM) allows the computer to receive information and store it efficiently. Memory is measured in kilobytes. One kilobyte stores 1,024 characters. The word *kilobyte,* for example, has eight characters.

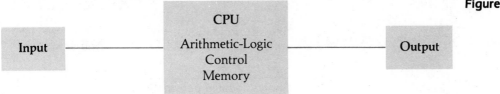

The third part of a computer is an *output device,* which may provide permanent or temporary storage of the results of the data processed. It may be a disk, printer, card punch, magnetic tape unit, paper tape unit, or a visual display unit (screen). A disk system is very flexible. The disk looks like a phonograph record with a cover, and the computer can select data quickly from different sections of the disk's surface. A tape system, on the other hand, must run in sequence, like a tape recorder. Only a fraction of a second is needed for the computer to search a disk, but it could take several minutes to locate a specific section on a tape. Today both "floppy disk" and hard disk systems are available. Hard disks provide more storage and faster processing times, but their high cost makes them inappropriate for many small users.

Hardware and Software

Hardware includes the physical machines or display screens and printer. *Software* consists of specific *programs* that provide a set of instructions for the CPU to follow to perform a particular job. Software also contains instructions for the computer operator on how to use the program. Separate programs are needed for different applications, such as the general ledger, accounts payable, accounts receivable, inventory, and payroll. *User friendly software* helps a person follow the program by indicating what choices can be made at a specific point. Well-designed software helps eliminate operator mistakes by anticipating possible errors and by building in controls that prevent those errors. It can also include internal controls to prevent fraud.

Some companies purchase accounting programs, which can cost as much as 25 percent of the price of the hardware. A good list of available accounting software programs can be found in the most recent updates of DataPro Research Corporation's reports on software (available at many college and university libraries). Other companies hire programmers to custom design programs for their special needs. Still other companies buy data-processing services, such as the handling of accounts receivable or payroll, from banks or specialized data-processing companies.

Computer Personnel

A systems analyst precisely describes every logical step needed in a new computer program by creating a flow chart or graphic presentation of the process to be performed. Analysts consider such matters as source documents, the personnel needed to enter data into the computer, the type of calculations to be performed and their sequence, the ways in which one pro-

Screen

Shows information keyed in, such as debits and credits for a transaction.

Shows updated information, such as account balances after new amounts have been entered.

Keyboard

Requests processing, such as posting amounts to accounts.

CPU sends processed information to screen, such as debits and credits for a transaction and account balances updated.

Central Processing Unit (CPU)

Arithmetic-Logic
Control
Memory

CPU saves processed information for permanent storage, such as account balances.

CPU retrieves processed information from storage for further processing, such as making account balances ready for another entry.

Permanent Storage for Programs and Data

Magnetic tape
Punch card
Big disk
Diskette

Printer

Presents processed data in final form, such as a print-out of a trial balance.

gram should relate to others, the kinds of reports that will be needed, and other potential applications of the program.

A programmer may either adapt an existing program or create a new program that will tell the computer how to read, record, and store information. Programs are written in languages that the computers understand. Two languages frequently used for business applications are COBOL and BASIC. Common Business Oriented Language (COBOL) is a high-level language developed for business data processing applications. The Beginner's All-Purpose Symbolic Instruction Code (BASIC) is used for programming in personal as well as business computing. Each brand of computer has its own adaptation of BASIC.

An accounting computer operator enters data from source documents and may also be responsible for selecting the correct data file, entering correct raw information for calculations, creating various records, and printing the necessary forms and reports. Business transactions are recorded in the computer in terms of debits and credits to specific accounts, much as hand-written entries are.

Implementation

As mentioned earlier, some firms send their work to a *service bureau*. This arrangement provides many of the benefits of computer use without the problems or expense of computer ownership. Sometimes a firm sends its source documents to the service bureau, where the data are entered for the customer. This is called *batch processing*. In other cases, terminals may be hooked up in the firm's own office, thereby allowing the firm's employees to enter transactions. This is known as *on-line processing*.

Other companies purchase their own *in-house* computers. Smaller companies often buy microcomputers or minicomputers.

Introducing Computers to a Company   A firm may elect to begin with only one phase of the accounting cycle. In many cases the phase selected is accounts receivable; it is often followed by accounts payable, payroll, inventory control, and general ledger. As the complete accounting cycle becomes involved, special reports may be generated to enhance management decision-making.

Whether a firm starts with one portion of the accounting cycle or implements the complete cycle, it should use a dual system, manual and computer, until all the "bugs" have been worked out.

Back-up System   If a firm has its own computer system, it is imperative that a back-up system be maintained. Many microprocessor systems rely on disks, and disks are easily damaged or erased. To prevent fraud, as well as to have a record available, a duplicate disk should be made daily and stored in a safe place. This procedure allows information to be stored in two different places at the same time, limiting the potential damage of natural disasters, fire, theft, malicious destruction of company property, or simple human error.

Advantages

There are many advantages to using computerized accounting procedures. For instance, computerizing Accounts Receivable may help to ensure that prompt, accurate, and legible statements are sent to customers. This procedure results in faster collections.

Computerizing Accounts Payable helps the business take advantage of cash discounts. Computerized inventories allow firms to upgrade purchasing and delivery systems. In addition, a computer can make up-to-date financial reports available at any time.

Other advantages include faster, more accurate computations and the automatic updating of balances, which eliminate possible transposition and footing errors. Sales analysis of the activity of individual salespeople is a valuable tool for evaluating the efforts of the sales force. *Spreadsheets,* or "what if" programs, are also commonly used in businesses. The spreadsheet considers what would happen if certain amounts or figures were changed. For example, a firm can see what is likely to happen if it changes its mark-up on merchandise, adjusts the size of the inventory, adds or deletes a product line, or leases facilities instead of buying them. Spreadsheets are particularly valuable for analyzing changes in interest rates and various repayment schedules.

The microcomputer has given all sizes and types of business organizations access to computerized accounting systems. As computers become used more widely, accounting records are likely to become more standardized. Software programs will evolve that allow each type of business to have its own accounting system. Organizations will no longer need to adapt programs designed for another type of business.

Disadvantages

The computer only does what it is told to do. Accurate data will not be available unless information from the source documents is entered into the computer correctly. It is important to select software that will encourage accuracy. The software should have controls built in that will ensure the input of correct data and that will protect against fraud and theft. In general, compatible software and hardware must be teamed with accounting personnel who are comfortable working with computers. The machine is no better than the people who use it.

Summary

The computer operator inputs data from source documents. Someone who understands the accounting cycle must formulate the debits and credits of the transactions and adjustments to be keyed into the computer. The computer will post, prepare a trial balance, provide a work sheet, and prepare financial statements and certain schedules such as those for accounts receivable and accounts payable.

Management uses data-based systems for making decisions. It recognizes that effective decisions must be based on reliable data. Accurate financial data that can be quickly obtained are essential to business success. Basic accounting concepts, with or without the aid of computers, will always be the foundation for accurate financial records and reports.

REVIEW OF T ACCOUNT PLACEMENT AND REPRESENTATIVE TRANSACTIONS CHAPTERS 1 THROUGH 6

Review of T Account Placement

The following display sums up the placement of T accounts covered in Chapters 3 through 6 in relation to the fundamental accounting equation.

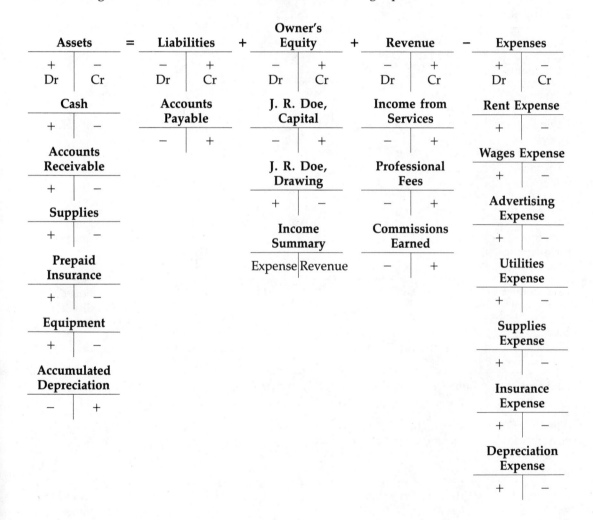

Review of Representative Transactions

The following table summarizes the recording of the various transactions described in Chapters 1 through 6. It also summarizes the classification of the accounts involved.

Transaction	Accounts Involved	Class.	Increase or Decrease	Therefore Debit or Credit	Financial Statement
Owner invested cash in business	Cash J. R. Doe, Capital	A OE	I I	Debit Credit	Bal. Sheet Bal. Sheet
Bought equipment for cash	Equipment Cash	A A	I D	Debit Credit	Bal. Sheet Bal. Sheet
Bought supplies on account	Supplies Accounts Payable	A L	I I	Debit Credit	Bal. Sheet Bal. Sheet
Bought equipment paying a down payment with the remainder on account	Equipment Cash Accounts Payable	A A L	I D I	Debit Credit Credit	Bal. Sheet Bal. Sheet Bal. Sheet
Paid premium for insurance policy	Prepaid Insurance Cash	A A	I D	Debit Credit	Bal. Sheet Bal. Sheet
Paid creditor on account	Accounts Payable Cash	L A	D D	Debit Credit	Bal. Sheet Bal. Sheet
Sold services for cash	Cash Income from Services	A R	I I	Debit Credit	Bal. Sheet Inc. State.
Paid rent for month	Rent Expense Cash	E A	I D	Debit Credit	Inc. State. Bal. Sheet
Billed customers for services performed	Accounts Receivable Income from Services	A R	I I	Debit Credit	Bal. Sheet Inc. State.
Owner withdrew cash for personal use	J. R. Doe, Drawing Cash	OE A	I D	Debit Credit	State. of O. E. Bal. Sheet

Transaction	Accounts Involved	Class.	Increase or Decrease	Therefore Debit or Credit	Financial Statement
Received cash from charge customers to apply on account	Cash Accounts Receivable	A A	I D	Debit Credit	Bal. Sheet Bal. Sheet
Paid wages to employees	Wages Expense Cash	E A	I D	Debit Credit	Inc. State. Bal. Sheet
Adjusting entry for supplies used	Supplies Expense Supplies	E A	I D	Debit Credit	Inc. State. Bal. Sheet
Adjusting entry for insurance expired	Insurance Expense Prepaid Insurance	E A	I D	Debit Credit	Inc. State. Bal. Sheet

Adjusting entry for depreciation of assets	Depreciation Expense
	  Accumulated
	    Depreciation
		E
		A
			I
			I
				Debit
				Credit
					Inc. State.
					Bal. Sheet

Adjusting entry for accrued wages	Wages Expense Wages Payable	E L	I I	Debit Credit	Inc. State. Bal. Sheet
Closing entry for revenue accounts	Revenue accounts Income Summary	R OE	D —	Debit Credit	Inc. State. —
Closing entry for expense accounts	Income Summary Expense accounts	OE E	— D	Debit Credit	— Inc. State.
Closing entry for Income Summary account (Net Income)	Income Summary J. R. Doe, Capital	OE OE	— I	Debit Credit	— Bal. Sheet
Closing entry for Drawing account	J. R. Doe, Capital J. R. Doe, Drawing	OE OE	D D	Debit Credit	Bal. Sheet State. of O. E.

Accounting Cycle Review Problem

This problem is designed to get you to review and apply the knowledge that you have acquired in the preceding chapters. In accounting, the ultimate test is being able to handle data in real-life situations. This problem will give you valuable experience.

Chart of Accounts

Assets
111 Cash
112 Accounts Receivable
114 Prepaid Insurance
121 Electronic Games
122 Accumulated Depreciation, Electronic Games
123 Furniture and Fixtures
124 Accumulated Depreciation, Furniture and Fixtures
127 Building
128 Accumulated Depreciation, Building
129 Land

Liabilities
211 Accounts Payable
212 Wages Payable
221 Mortgage Payable

Owner's Equity
311 R. C. Belko, Capital
312 R. C. Belko, Drawing
313 Income Summary

Revenue
411 Income from Services
412 Concession Income

Expenses
511 Equipment Rental Expense
512 Wages Expense
513 Advertising Expense
514 Utilities Expense
515 Interest Expense
516 Insurance Expense
517 Depreciation Expense, Electronic Games
518 Depreciation Expense, Furniture and Fixtures
519 Depreciation Expense, Building
522 Miscellaneous Expense

You are to record transactions in a two-column general journal. To get in a little more practice, assume that the fiscal period is one month. You will then be able to complete all the steps in the accounting cycle.

When you are analyzing the transactions, think them through by mentally visualizing the T accounts or by writing them down on scratch paper. In the case of unfamiliar types of transactions, specific instructions for recording them are included. However, go ahead and reason them out for yourself as well. Check off each transaction as it is recorded.

The following transactions were completed during June of this year.

Jun.　1 Belko deposited $41,600 in a bank account for the purpose of buying The Gamerama, a business offering the use of electronic games to the public.

　　　2 Bought The Gamerama in its entirety for a total price of $106,650. The assets include games, $10,400; furniture and fixtures, $4,250; building, $72,000; land, $20,000. Paid $32,200 down, and signed a mortgage note for the remainder. (Debit the assets and credit Cash and the liability.)

　　　3 Received and paid bill for newspaper advertising, $74.

　　　3 Received and paid bill for property and liability insurance for the coming year, $518.

　　　3 Bought additional games from Royer Electronics for $3,260, paying $1,600 down, with the remainder due in 30 days.

　　　3 Signed a contract for leasing out space for vending machines. The rental income is to be 10 percent of sales, with the estimated total payable in advance. Received cash payment for June, $90. (Debit Cash and credit Concession Income.)

　　　3 Received bill from Pronto Printing for promotional handouts, $184.

　　　3 Signed a contract for leasing games from Vue Fine Amusement Company and paid rental fee for June, $316.

　　　3 Paid cash for miscellaneous expenses, $46.22.

　　　8 Received $1,316.25 in cash as income for the use of games.

　　　9 Bought stools on account from Smithwick Furniture Company, $418.

　　15 Paid wages to employees for the period ending June 14, $2,100.

　　16 Paid the bill for promotional handouts already recorded on June 3.

　　16 Belko withdrew cash for personal use, $526.

　　16 Bought additional games on account from Peterson Electronic, $427; payment due in 30 days.

　　16 Received $1,521.50 in cash as income for the use of games.

　　19 Paid cash for miscellaneous expenses, $21.32.

　　20 Paid cash to Royer Electronics as part payment on account, $240.

　　22 Received $2,541 in cash as income for the use of games.

　　23 Returned one game to Royer Electronics purchased on June 3 and received full credit (a reduction in the outstanding bill), $226.

　　24 Received and paid telephone bill, $42.

　　29 Paid wages for period June 15 through 28, $2,326.

　　30 Paid cash to Smithwick Furniture Company to apply on account, $209.

　　30 Received and paid electric bill, $216.

　　30 Paid cash as an installment payment on the mortgage, $940. Of this amount, $340 represents a reduction in the principal, and the remainder is interest. (Debit Mortgage Payable, debit Interest Expense, and credit Cash.)

　　30 Received and paid water bill, $21.

Jun.   30 Bought additional games from Moyer Company for $2,426, paying $226 down, with the remainder due in 30 days.

   30 Received $2,316 in cash as income for the use of games.

   30 Belko withdrew cash for personal use, $578.

   30 Sales for vending machines for the month amounted to $1,160. (Ten percent of $1,160 equals $116. Since you have already recorded $90 as concession income, list the additional $26 revenue from the vending machine operator.)

Instructions

1. Journalize the transactions, starting on page 1 of the general journal.
2. Post the transactions to the ledger accounts.
3. Prepare a trial balance in the first two columns of the work sheet.
4. Complete the work sheet. Data for the adjustments are as follows:
    a. Insurance expired during the month, $43.
    b. Depreciation of electronic games for the month, $402.
    c. Depreciation of furniture and fixtures for the month, $81.50.
    d. Depreciation of building for the month, $300.
    e. Wages accrued at June 30, $348.
5. Prepare the income statement.
6. Prepare the statement of owner's equity.
7. Prepare the balance sheet.
8. Journalize adjusting entries.
9. Post adjusting entries to the ledger accounts.
10. Journalize closing entries.
11. Post closing entries to the ledger accounts.
12. Prepare a post-closing trial balance.

7 Accounting for Professional Enterprises: The Combined Journal (optional)

Learning Objectives

After you have completed this chapter, you will be able to do the following:

1. Define the following methods of accounting: accrual basis, cash-receipts-and-disbursements basis, modified cash basis.

2. Record transactions for both a professional and a service-type enterprise in a combined journal.

3. Complete the entire accounting cycle for a professional enterprise.

Professional Enterprises include the practice of medicine, dentistry, law, architecture, engineering, optometry, and so forth. Your knowledge of accounting procedures can be readily applied to professional enterprises. Generally, the accounting records for professional enterprises are kept on a modified cash basis. Let us digress briefly to define the three bases of accounting currently in use and officially recognized.

ACCRUAL BASIS VERSUS CASH BASIS OF ACCOUNTING

Objective 1

Define the following methods of accounting: accrual basis, cash-receipts-and-disbursements basis, modified cash basis.

Up to this time we have been dealing with the **accrual basis** of accounting, and therefore we shall look at it first in this section. **When we use the accrual basis, we record revenue when it is earned and expenses when they are incurred.** In this way, revenue and expenses are matched up with the appropriate fiscal period. For example, the books of NuWay Cleaners were recorded on the accrual basis; as proof, let us recall two transactions that we first looked at in Chapter 3.

Transaction (k)   Received the bill for newspaper advertising, $180. The expense was recorded before it was paid in cash. The expense is matched up with the fiscal period in which it was incurred.

Advertising Expense	Accounts Payable
(k) 180	(k) 180

Transaction (p)   Entered into a contract with A-1 Rental to clean their for-hire garments on a credit basis. Billed A-1 Rental for services performed, $80.

Accounts Receivable	Income from Services
(p) 80	(p) 80

The revenue was recorded before it was received in cash. The revenue is matched up with the fiscal period in which it was earned. Incidentally, accountants feel strongly that the accrual basis gives the most realistic picture of the revenue and expense accounts and hence the net income. (Net income equals total revenue minus total expenses.) We shall depart from the accrual basis temporarily because we are now concerned with professional enterprises and their accounting records. As we said, the books of professional firms are often kept on a modified cash basis.

The *cash basis* is used primarily for convenience and simplicity. As a practical matter, the cash basis is divided into two types: the cash-receipts-and-disbursements basis and the modified cash basis.

Cash-Receipts-and-Disbursements Basis

The term *disbursements* refers to cash payments. A firm that uses the **cash-receipts-and-disbursements basis** records revenue only when it is received in cash and expenses when they are paid in cash. The only type of business that could use this basis is a firm having practically no equipment. Consequently, no adjusting entries need be made. Actually, the cash-receipts-and-disbursements basis is used by most individuals in filing their personal income tax returns. Revenue in the form of salaries, wages, dividends, and so on is recorded in the year in which it is received. Likewise, expenditures—to be counted as employee business expenses or personal deductions—are recorded in the year they are paid.

Modified Cash Basis

Professional enterprises are not alone in using a modified cash basis; many small business firms use it as well. It is also suitable for accounting for income from rental units. In Internal Revenue Service publications, the **modified cash basis** is referred to as the *hybrid method.* It is similar to the cash-receipts-and-disbursements basis in that revenue is recorded only when received in cash, and expenses are ordinarily recorded only when paid in cash. However, exceptions are made for expenditures on items with an economic life of more than one year and on some prepaid items. Examples would be supplies, insurance, and equipment. Costs of these items must be spread out over their useful lives, and so adjusting entries are made for supplies used, insurance expired, and depreciation of equipment. There is no need to make further adjusting entries, such as an adjustment for accrued salaries or other adjustments that we shall introduce later.

EXAMPLE: RECORDS OF A DENTIST

To understand the accounting system used for a professional enterprise, let us look at the records of Dr. Rory T. Barker, a dentist. The basic records used in his office are the appointment record and the patient's ledger record. The chart of accounts for the office is shown on the top of the following page.

Chart of Accounts

Assets
111 Cash
112 X-ray Supplies
113 Dental Supplies
114 Office Supplies
115 Prepaid Insurance
121 Dental Equipment
122 Accumulated Depreciation, Dental Equipment
123 Office Furniture and Equipment
124 Accumulated Depreciation, Office Furniture and Equipment

Liabilities
211 Notes Payable

Owner's Equity
311 R. T. Barker, Capital
312 R. T. Barker, Drawing
313 Income Summary

Revenue
411 Professional Fees

Expenses
511 Dental Instruments Expense
512 Laundry and Cleaning Expense
513 Office Salary Expense
514 Laboratory Expense
515 Dental Supplies Expense
516 Rent Expense
517 Depreciation Expense, Dental Equipment
518 Depreciation Expense, Office Furniture and Equipment
519 X-ray Supplies Expense
520 Office Supplies Expense
521 Insurance Expense
522 Telephone Expense
523 Utilities Expense
524 Repairs and Maintenance Expense
525 Miscellaneous Expense

Appointment Record

The dentist's receptionist keeps a daily appointment record, showing the time of appointment and the name of each patient and gives a copy of the appointment record to the dentist the day before the scheduled appointments. Dr. Barker's appointment record is shown in Figure 7-1.

Patient's Ledger Record

The receptionist also maintains a patient's ledger record card for each patient. One side of this card shows a daily record of the services performed, amount of any cost estimate given, plan of payment, information regarding collections, and the like. A card is shown in Figure 7-2.

The other side of the card contains a diagram of the patient's teeth and a space for personal information about the patient.

After Dr. Barker has completed the work, he (or an assistant) describes the services performed and writes the amount of the fees in the debit column. The card is returned to the receptionist, who records the services rendered and the fees charged on the appointment record.

Figure 7-1

APPOINTMENT RECORD

DATE ___12/1___

HOUR	PATIENT	SERVICE RENDERED	FEES	RECEIPTS
8 00	Donald Rankin			
15	Patricia Fischer			
30				
45	Cecil Hansen			
9 00				
15				
30				
45	Donna Heller			
10 00	C. F. Elliott			
15				
30				
45	Ralph Simons			
11 00	Peter Smithson			
15				
30				
45				
1 00	Donald C. Kraft			
15				
30	N. C. Byers			
45				
2 00	Mrs. N. D. Silversmith			
15				
30	John F. Piper			
45	Nolan F. Sanderson			
3 00				
15	Nancy Stacy			
30				
45	C. D. Harper			
4 00	Ardis Newell			
15				
30				
45				
5 00				
15				

When a patient sends in a payment, the receptionist records the amount on the appointment record on the day the payment was received and on the patient's ledger record in the credit column. Remember that the fees charged are not recorded in the Professional Fees account until they are received in cash. The record showing the amounts patients owe is much like Accounts Receivable, except that these amounts are not offi-

Figure 7-2

Elliott, C. F.   365-2619

1629 S. W. Arbor St.

Denver

DATE		SERVICE RENDERED	TIME	DEBIT			CREDIT			BALANCE			
Jun.	15	#31—M.O.D. (4)	10:00	4	0	00				4	0	00	
Jul.	4	Ck.					4	0	00	—			
	16	#27—D.O. (Amal.)	9:15	3	3	00				3	3	00	
Aug.	5	Ck.					3	3	00	—			
Sep.	24	#25—P.J.C.	10:00	1 8	8	00				1 8	8	00	
Oct.	6	Ck.					7	5	00	1 1	3	00	
	18	#24—D. (Porc.)	9:00	3	0	00				1 4	3	00	
Nov.	3	Ck.					7	5	00	6	8	00	
	9	#18—full gold crown	10:00	1 5	0	00				2	1 8	00	
Dec.	1	B.W. X-rays (6)		4	2	00				2	6 0	00	
		Impression upper 7/1		3 6	8	00				6	2 8	00	
	1	C.S.					9	0	00	5	3 8	00	

PLAN OF SERVICE	PLAN OF PAYMENT	COLLECTION EFFORTS
1–2 surf. ⎫ amalgam	30-day basis	
2–3 surf. ⎬ 1 full gold crown	or $75 per	
1–1 surf. ⎭ 1 ceramic crown	month	
2 anterior porcelain		

ESTIMATE IF ANY		
$273 upper denture (6 appt.)	$90 per month	

cially recorded in the books. As with Accounts Receivable, debits mean increases in the amounts owed by patients and credits mean decreases in the amounts owed by patients. The balance columns show the final amounts owed by patients at the time of the latest entry.

The services to be performed may require a number of appointments. Some patients may make partial payments each time they have appointments. Others may pay the entire amount at—or after—the last appointment. Patients' bills are compiled directly from the ledger cards. The dentist or receptionist keeps a constant watch on the patients' ledger records to determine which accounts are past due and to take the necessary steps to speed up collections. The statement shown in Figure 7-3 was mailed to a patient at the end of the month.

Figure 7-3

Rory T. Barker, D.D.S.
1620 South Canton Place
Denver, Colorado 80226

STATEMENT

C. F. ELLIOTT
1629 S.W. ARBOR STREET
DENVER, CO 80232

Date	Professional Service	Charges	Payments	Balance
6/15	#31-MOD (4)	40.00		40.00
7/4	Ck		40.00	—
7/16	#27-DO (Amal.)	33.00		33.00
8/5	Ck		33.00	—
9/24	#25-PJC	188.00		188.00
10/6	Ck		75.00	113.00
10/18	#24-D (Porc.)	30.00		143.00
11/3	Ck		75.00	68.00
11/9	#18-full gold crown	150.00		218.00
12/1	B. W. X-rays (6)	42.00		260.00
	Impression upper	368.00		628.00
12/1	CS		90.00	538.00

Pay last amount in Balance column. ▲

Receipt of Payments from Patients

Depending on the size of the office, the person who receives payments may be the receptionist or the cashier in the accounting office. Whoever receives them issues a written receipt for all incoming cash, filled out in duplicate, sending the first copy to the patient and filing the second copy as evidence of the transaction. Receipts should be prenumbered, so that they can all be accounted for. The payment is recorded in the Receipts column of the appointment record.

The form in Figure 7-4 is a typical appointment record for a day, showing services rendered, fees (recorded by the dentist on the patients' ledger records), and payments received (recorded by the receptionist). The receptionist deposits $608 in the bank.

Figure 7-4

APPOINTMENT RECORD

DATE ___12/1___

HOUR	PATIENT	SERVICE RENDERED	FEES		RECEIPTS	
8 00	Donald Rankin	Extraction	22	00		
15	Patricia Fischer	Three amalgam fillings				
30		D.O. (3)	68	00	16	00
45	Cecil Hansen	Gold inlay filling	97	00		
9 00						
15						
30						
45	Donna Heller	Amalgam filling D.O.	18	00		
10 00	C. F. Elliott	Denture—full upper	410	00	90	00
15		(6 appointments)				
30						
45	Ralph Simons	Prophylaxis	24	00	24	00
11 00	Peter Smithson	Endodontia treatment	120	00	15	00
15						
30						
45						
1 00	Donald C. Kraft	Amalgam filling M.O.D.	27	00	22	00
15						
30	N. C. Byers	Porcelain jacket crown	173	00		
45						
2 00	Mrs. N. D. Silversmith	Extraction	26	00		
15						
30	John F. Piper	Amalgam filling 1 surf.	12	00		
45	Nolan F. Sanderson	Prophylaxis and full-				
3 00		mouth X-ray (14)	27	00		
15	Nancy Stacy	Fixed bridge 3 units	540	00	60	00
30		(Gold) (5 appointments)				
45	C. D. Harper	Prophylaxis & bitewing				
4 00		X-rays	30	00		
15	Ardis Newell	Periodontal treatment	62	00		
30						
45						
5 00						
15						
	Ronald T. McCaw				60	00
	Helen Bower				55	00
	Eugene Sampson				72	00
	Sidney Weeks				27	00
	C. D. Sanderson				100	00
	Roger Lindsay				27	00
	Gilbert Rae				40	00
			1,656	00	608	00

Summary of Procedures

1. Patients request appointments.
2. Receptionist records appointments on appointment record: date, time, and name of patient.
3. Receptionist furnishes dentist with appointment record for the day, plus the patients' ledger records.
4. Dentist performs services and records on each patient's ledger card descriptions of the services performed and lists the fees to be charged in the Debit column.
5. Receptionist accepts payments from patients both in the office and through the mail and records receipt of payments in the Receipts column of the appointment record.
6. At the end of the day, receptionist deposits in the bank any cash received.
7. Receptionist lists the description of services and the amount charged on the appointment record.
8. Receptionist records the payments received from patients on the patients' ledger cards in the Credit column. The source is the appointment record.
9. The receptionist compiles monthly statements directly from the patients' ledger records.

This procedure may vary, depending on the size of the office staff. It could be further shortened by describing the services rendered only once. For the sake of security or internal control, if the size of the office staff is sufficiently large, the function of accepting and depositing money should be separated from the function of recording payments.

Here is a list of Dr. Barker's transactions for December, the last month of the fiscal period. To save time and space, cash receipts are recorded on a weekly basis.

Dec. 1 Paid rent for the month, $1,000.
      1 Paid telephone bill, $32.
      1 Paid electric bill, $66.
      3 Issued check to First-Rate Printing for patient statement forms, $132.
      5 Bought short-term supply of drills for cash from Murdoch Dental Supply, $254.
      5 Total cash received from patients during the week, $5,524.
      8 Paid bill for repair of typewriter to Greeley Office Supply, $58.
      9 Barker withdrew cash for personal use, $400.
    11 Paid Reliable Building Maintenance Company for janitorial service, $120.

Figure 7-5

19– Dec.	1	Rent Expense		1	0	0	0	00						
		Cash								1	0	0	0	00
		Rent for December.												
	1	Telephone Expense				3	2	00						
		Cash										3	2	00
		Telephone bill for November.												
	1	Utilities Expense				6	6	00						
		Cash										6	6	00
		Electric bill for November.												
	3	Office Supplies			1	3	2	00						
		Cash									1	3	2	00
		First-Rate Printing for												
		statement forms.												
	5	Dental Instruments Expense			2	5	4	00						
		Cash									2	5	4	00
		Murdoch Dental Supply for												
		drills.												
	5	Cash		5	5	2	4	00						
		Professional Fees								5	5	2	4	00
		For period December 1 through 5.												
	8	Repairs and Maintenance Expense				5	8	00						
		Cash										5	8	00
		Greeley Office Supply,												
		typewriter.												
	9	R. T. Barker, Drawing			4	0	0	00						
		Cash									4	0	0	00
		For personal use.												
	11	Laundry and Cleaning Expense			1	2	0	00						
		Cash									1	2	0	00
		Reliable Building Maintenance												
		Company.												

Because you are now used to a general journal, we'll record these transactions first in this form (Figure 7-5). However, our objective is to introduce the combined journal; so we will record the same transactions, as well as the rest of the month's transactions, in a combined journal.

Dec. 12 Total cash received from patients during the week, $1,842.

16 Paid Pender Dental Supply for miscellaneous dental supplies, $432.

16 Paid salaries of dental assistant and receptionist, $980.

19 Bought new dental chair from Murdoch Dental Supply, $1,234; $434 down, the balance to be paid in eight monthly payments of $100 each.

19 Total cash received from patients during the week, $620.

22 Barker withdrew $520 for personal use.

23 Paid bill for laboratory expense to Nollen Dental Laboratory, $296.

23 Paid Pender Dental Supply $320 as a contract payment on dental equipment purchased in October.

27 Total cash received from patients during the week, $392.

29 Barker wrote check to garage for repairing his car, $128 (to be recorded as Drawing).

31 Paid Murdoch Dental Supply for miscellaneous dental supplies, $192.

31 Paid salaries of dental assistant and receptionist, $980.

31 Barker withdrew $780 for personal use.

31 Paid $54 to Jersey Publishers Service for magazines for the office.

31 Paid Clement Linen Supply for laundry service, $84.

31 Total cash received from patients up until last day of year, $266.

THE COMBINED JOURNAL

The **combined journal** is designed to make the recording and posting of transactions more efficient. It is used widely by professional and service-type enterprises, where it replaces the general journal. Notice that no explanations are given in the combined journal. Special columns are set up to record accounts that are used frequently by a particular business.

Compare the recording of the first nine transactions in the combined journal in Figure 7-6 with the same transactions portrayed in the general journal in Figure 7-5. For example, in the first transaction (paid rent for the month, $1,000), you determine that the entry is a debit to Rent Expense and a credit to Cash. There is a Cash Credit column, so you list $1,000 in this column; that $1,000 will be posted as a part of the column total. The Sundry columns are used to record any accounts for which there are no special columns. Since there is no Rent Expense Debit column, the $1,000 debit to Rent Expense must be recorded in the Sundry Debit column. Notice, however, that the Sundry column does not tell you where to post $1,000. Therefore, you need to write the title of the account to be posted in the Account Name column. This amount will be posted separately.

Objective 2

Record transactions for both a professional and a service-type enterprise in a combined journal.

	DATE		ACCOUNT NAME	POST. REF.	SUNDRY			DENTAL SUPPLIES	R. T. BARKE DRAWING
					DEBIT		CREDIT	DEBIT	DEBIT
1	19– Dec.	1	Rent Expense	516	1 0 0 0 00				
2		1	Telephone Expense	522	3 2 00				
3		1	Utilities Expense	523	6 6 00				
4		3	Office Supplies	114	1 3 2 00				
5		5	Dental Instruments Expense	511	2 5 4 00				
6		5	Professional Fees	—					
7		8	Repairs and Maintenance						
8			Expense	524	5 8 00				
9		9	R. T. Barker, Drawing	—					4 0 0
10		11	Laundry and Cleaning						
11			Expense	—					
12		12	Professional Fees	—					
13		16	Dental Supplies	—				4 3 2 00	
14		16	Office Salary Expense	—					
15		19	Dental Equipment	121	1 2 3 4 00				
16			Notes Payable	211			8 0 0 00		
17		19	Professional Fees	—					
18		22	R. T. Barker, Drawing	—					5 2 0
19		23	Laboratory Expense	—					
20		23	Notes Payable	211	3 2 0 00				
21		27	Professional Fees	—					
22		29	R. T. Barker, Drawing	—					1 2 8
23		31	Dental Supplies	—				1 9 2 00	
24		31	Office Salary Expense	—					
25		31	R. T. Barker, Drawing	—					7 8 0
26		31	Miscellaneous Expense	—					
27		31	Laundry and Cleaning						
28			Expense	—					
29		31	Professional Fees	—					
30		31			3 0 9 6 00		8 0 0 00	6 2 4 00	1 8 2 8
31					(✓)		(✓)	(1 1 3)	(3 1 2
32									

Figure 7-6

In the entry of December 5 to record professional fees received in cash, special columns are available to handle both the debit to Cash and the credit to Professional Fees. In this case, Professional Fees is entered in the Account Name column purely as a means of filling up the space; some accountants prefer to leave the space blank.

After you have added all columns at the end of the month, prove on scratch paper that the sum of the debit totals equals the sum of the credit totals, as shown in the following example.

PROFESSIONAL FEES CREDIT	LAUNDRY AND CLEANING EXPENSE DEBIT	OFFICE SALARY EXPENSE DEBIT	LABORATORY EXPENSE DEBIT	MISC. EXPENSE DEBIT	CASH DEBIT	CASH CREDIT	
						1000 00	1
						32 00	2
						66 00	3
						132 00	4
						254 00	5
5524 00					5524 00		6
							7
						58 00	8
						400 00	9
							10
	120 00					120 00	11
1842 00					1842 00		12
						432 00	13
		980 00				980 00	14
						434 00	15
							16
620 00					620 00		17
						520 00	18
			296 00			296 00	19
						320 00	20
392 00					392 00		21
						128 00	22
						192 00	23
		980 00				980 00	24
						780 00	25
				54 00		54 00	26
							27
	84 00					84 00	28
266 00					266 00		29
8644 00	204 00	1960 00	296 00	54 00	8644 00	7262 00	30
(11)	(512)	(513)	(514)	(525)	(111)	(111)	31
							32

Column	Debit totals	Credit totals
Sundry	$ 3,096.00	$ 800.00
Dental Supplies	624.00	
R. T. Barker, Drawing	1,828.00	
Professional Fees		8,644.00
Laundry and Cleaning Expense	204.00	
Office Salary Expense	1,960.00	
Laboratory Expense	296.00	
Miscellaneous Expense	54.00	
Cash	8,644.00	7,262.00
	$16,706.00	$16,706.00

Posting from the Combined Journal

The person who is keeping records posts items in the Sundry columns individually, usually daily. After posting the ledger account, the person records the ledger account number in the Posting Reference column of the combined journal. This procedure is similar to posting from a general journal.

Special columns, used only for the debit or credit to specific accounts, are posted as totals. After posting the ledger account, the accountant records the ledger account number in the special column immediately below the total. The account number is placed in parentheses. The total of the Cash debit column in Figure 7-6 may be used as an example. After the Cash account in the general ledger has been debited for $8,644.00, the account number of Cash (111) is placed in parentheses below the total of the Cash debit column in the combined journal. Notice that the accountant puts a check mark in parentheses below the totals of the Sundry columns. The check mark indicates that the amounts have been posted individually and should not be posted again.

A dash in the Posting Reference column indicates that individual amounts in the special columns are being posted as totals. Selected accounts from Dr. Barker's completed general ledger are shown in Figure 7-7. Cash, Dental Supplies, and Rent Expense are used to illustrate the posting process.

Figure 7-7

GENERAL LEDGER

ACCOUNT __Cash__   ACCOUNT NO. __111__

	DATE		ITEM	POST. REF.	DEBIT	CREDIT	BALANCE DEBIT	BALANCE CREDIT	
1	19– Dec.	1	Balance	✓			6 4 0 4 00		1
2		31		12	8 6 4 4 00		15 0 4 8 00		2
3		31		12		7 2 6 2 00	7 7 8 6 00		3

ACCOUNT __Dental Supplies__   ACCOUNT NO. __113__

	DATE		ITEM	POST. REF.	DEBIT	CREDIT	BALANCE DEBIT	BALANCE CREDIT	
1	19– Dec.	1	Balance	✓			4 8 5 6 00		1
2		31		12	6 2 4 00		5 4 8 0 00		2

ACCOUNT __Rent Expense__   ACCOUNT NO. __516__

	DATE		ITEM	POST. REF.	DEBIT	CREDIT	BALANCE DEBIT	BALANCE CREDIT	
1	19– Dec.	1	Balance	✓			11 0 0 0 00		1
2		1		12	1 0 0 0 00		12 0 0 0 00		2

Determining Cash Balance

The cash balance may be determined at any time during the month by taking the beginning balance of cash, adding the total cash debits so far during the month, and subtracting the total cash credits so far during the month. For example, to determine the balance of cash on December 5:

Cash

Dec. 1 Balance 6,404

	COMBINED JOURNAL				PAGE 12
				CASH	
DATE		MISC. EXPENSE	DEBIT	CREDIT	
19– Dec. 1				1 0 0 0 00	
1				3 2 00	
1				6 6 00	
3				1 3 2 00	
5				2 5 4 00	
5			5 5 2 4 00		
			5 5 2 4 00	1 4 8 4 00	

Beginning balance (Dec. 1)	$ 6,404	
Add cash debits	5,524	
Total	$11,928	
Less cash credits	1,484	
Ending balance (Dec. 5)	$10,444	

Work Sheet for a Professional Enterprise

Assume that Dr. Barker's receptionist has posted the journal entries to the ledger accounts and has recorded the trial balance in the first two columns of the work sheet. Dr. Barker uses the modified cash basis of accounting, recording revenue only when he has received it in cash, and recording expenses only when he has paid for them in cash. In addition, when Dr. Barker buys an item that is going to last a number of years, he records this item as an asset and writes it off or depreciates it by making an adjusting

	ACCOUNT NAME	TRIAL BALANCE DEBIT	TRIAL BALANCE CREDIT	ADJUSTMENTS DEBIT	ADJUSTMENTS CREDIT
1	Cash	7 7 8 6 00			
2	X-ray Supplies	2 7 6 2 00			(c)2 1 4 4
3	Dental Supplies	5 4 8 0 00			(d)3 8 6 4
4	Office Supplies	1 3 0 8 00			(e)1 1 1 2
5	Prepaid Insurance	8 4 8 00			(f) 7 2 0
6	Dental Equipment	85 2 3 4 00			
7	Accum. Depr., Dental Equipment		17 2 0 0 00		(a)8 4 0 0
8	Office Furniture and Equipment	7 8 0 0 00			
9	Accum. Depr., Office Furniture & Equipment		4 2 0 0 00		(b)1 5 2 0
10	Notes Payable		7 6 0 0 00		
11	R. T. Barker, Capital		52 5 5 8 00		
12	R. T. Barker, Drawing	33 2 8 0 00			
13	Professional Fees		112 0 2 4 00		
14	Dental Instruments Expense	1 9 8 2 00			
15	Laundry and Cleaning Expense	3 0 2 4 00			
16	Office Salary Expense	23 5 2 0 00			
17	Laboratory Expense	5 8 5 6 00			
18	Rent Expense	12 0 0 0 00			
19	Telephone Expense	4 1 2 00			
20	Utilities Expense	7 7 8 00			
21	Repairs and Maintenance Expense	8 8 8 00			
22	Miscellaneous Expense	6 2 4 00			
23		193 5 8 2 00	193 5 8 2 00		
24	Depreciation Expense, Dental Equipment			(a)8 4 0 0 00	
25	Depreciation Expense, Off. Furn. & Equip.			(b)1 5 2 0 00	
26	X-ray Supplies Expense			(c)2 1 4 4 00	
27	Dental Supplies Expense			(d)3 8 6 4 00	
28	Office Supplies Expense			(e)1 1 1 2 00	
29	Insurance Expense			(f) 7 2 0 00	
30				17 7 6 0 00	17 7 6 0
31	Net Income				
32					
33					

entry each year of its useful life. He also makes adjusting entries for expired insurance, as well as for supplies used.

Data for the adjustments are as follows:

a. Additional depreciation on dental equipment, $8,400.
b. Additional depreciation on office furniture and equipment, $1,520.
c. Inventory of x-ray supplies, $618.
d. Inventory of dental supplies, $1,616.

ADJUSTED TRIAL BALANCE		INCOME STATEMENT		BALANCE SHEET		
DEBIT	CREDIT	DEBIT	CREDIT	DEBIT	CREDIT	
7 8 6 00				7 7 8 6 00		1
6 1 8 00				6 1 8 00		2
6 1 6 00				1 6 1 6 00		3
1 9 6 00				1 9 6 00		4
1 2 8 00				1 2 8 00		5
2 3 4 00				85 2 3 4 00		6
	25 6 0 0 00				25 6 0 0 00	7
8 0 0 00				7 8 0 0 00		8
	5 7 2 0 00				5 7 2 0 00	9
	7 6 0 0 00				7 6 0 0 00	10
	52 5 5 8 00				52 5 5 8 00	11
2 8 0 00				33 2 8 0 00		12
	112 0 2 4 00		112 0 2 4 00			13
9 8 2 00		1 9 8 2 00				14
0 2 4 00		3 0 2 4 00				15
5 2 0 00		23 5 2 0 00				16
8 5 6 00		5 8 5 6 00				17
0 0 0 00		12 0 0 0 00				18
4 1 2 00		4 1 2 00				19
7 7 8 00		7 7 8 00				20
8 8 8 00		8 8 8 00				21
6 2 4 00		6 2 4 00				22
						23
4 0 0 00		8 4 0 0 00				24
5 2 0 00		1 5 2 0 00				25
1 4 4 00		2 1 4 4 00				26
8 6 4 00		3 8 6 4 00				27
1 1 2 00		1 1 1 2 00				28
7 2 0 00		7 2 0 00				29
5 0 2 00	203 5 0 2 00	66 8 4 4 00	112 0 2 4 00	136 6 5 8 00	91 4 7 8 00	30
		45 1 8 0 00			45 1 8 0 00	31
		112 0 2 4 00	112 0 2 4 00	136 6 5 8 00	136 6 5 8 00	32
						33

Figure 7-8

e. Inventory of office supplies, $196.

f. Insurance expired, $720.

With these adjusting entries, the rest of the work sheet can now be completed as shown in Figure 7-8. First the balances of the accounts that were adjusted are brought up to date in the Adjusted Trial Balance columns. Then these amounts are carried forward to the remaining columns.

Financial Statements

From the work sheet, Dr. Barker's accountant prepares the financial statements shown in Figure 7-9. In this case, there was no additional investment made to R. T. Barker, Capital, during the year. However, whenever you are preparing a statement of owner's equity, always look into the capital account to see if any additional investment was recorded.

Figure 7-9

R. T. Barker, D.D.S.
Income Statement
For year ended December 31, 19–

Revenue:		
Professional Fees		$ 112 024 00
Expenses:		
Dental Instruments Expense	$ 1 982 00	
Laundry and Cleaning Expense	3 024 00	
Office Salary Expense	23 520 00	
Laboratory Expense	5 856 00	
Dental Supplies Expense	3 864 00	
Rent Expense	12 000 00	
Depreciation Expense,		
Dental Equipment	8 400 00	
Depreciation Expense,		
Office Furniture and Equipment	1 520 00	
X-ray Supplies Expense	2 144 00	
Office Supplies Expense	1 112 00	
Insurance Expense	720 00	
Telephone Expense	412 00	
Utilities Expense	778 00	
Repairs and Maintenance Expense	888 00	
Miscellaneous Expense	624 00	
Total Expenses		66 844 00
Net Income		$ 45 180 00

R. T. Barker, D.D.S.
Statement of Owner's Equity
For year ended December 31, 19–

R. T. Barker, Capital, Jan. 1, 19–		$52 558 00
Net Income for year	$45 180 00	
Less Withdrawals for year	33 280 00	
Increase in Capital		11 900 00
R. T. Barker, Capital, Dec. 31, 19–		$64 458 00

Figure 7-9
(continued)

R. T. Barker, D.D.S.
Balance Sheet
December 31, 19–

Assets				
Cash			$ 7 7 8 6 00	
X-ray Supplies			6 1 8 00	
Dental Supplies			1 6 1 6 00	
Office Supplies			1 9 6 00	
Prepaid Insurance			1 2 8 00	
Dental Equipment	$85 2 3 4 00			
Less Accumulated Depreciation,				
Dental Equipment	25 6 0 0 00		59 6 3 4 00	
Office Furniture and Equipment	$ 7 8 0 0 00			
Less Accumulated Depreciation,				
Office Furniture and Equipment	5 7 2 0 00		2 0 8 0 00	
Total Assets			$72 0 5 8 00	
Liabilities				
Notes Payable			$ 7 6 0 0 00	
Owner's Equity				
R. T. Barker, Capital			64 4 5 8 00	
Total Liabilities and Owner's Equity			$72 0 5 8 00	

Adjusting and Closing Entries

Dr. Barker (or his receptionist) records the adjusting and closing entries in the Sundry columns of the combined journal. These entries must be posted individually. For example, the adjusting and closing entries are shown in Figure 7-10, two pages of a shortened combined journal (see pages 194 and 195).

There are a number of aspects of the accounting for a professional enterprise which we have not yet considered:

1. Special funds, such as the change fund and the petty cash fund. (We shall discuss these in Chapter 8.)
2. Payroll deductions, such as withholdings for employees' income taxes, Social Security taxes, and other salary deductions. (We shall discuss these in Chapter 9.)
3. Payroll taxes levied on the employer, such as the matching for Social Security, and unemployment taxes. (We shall discuss these in Chapter 10.)

Objective 3

Complete the entire accounting cycle for a professional enterprise.

Figure 7-10

			POST. REF.	SUNDRY											
DATE		ACCOUNT NAME		DEBIT					CREDIT						
		Adjusting Entries													
19– Dec.	31	*Depreciation Expense,*													
		Dental Equipment	517	8	4	0	0	00							
		Accumulated Deprecia-													
		tion, Dental Equipment	122							8	4	0	0	00	
	31	*Depreciation Expense,*													
		Office Furniture and													
		Equipment	518	1	5	2	0	00							
		Accumulated Deprecia-													
		tion, Office Furniture													
		and Equipment	124							1	5	2	0	00	
	31	*X-ray Supplies Expense*	519	2	1	4	4	00							
		X-ray Supplies	112							2	1	4	4	00	
	31	*Dental Supplies*													
		Expense	515	3	8	6	4	00							
		Dental Supplies	113							3	8	6	4	00	
	31	*Office Supplies Expense*	520	1	1	1	2	00							
		Office Supplies	114							1	1	1	2	00	
	31	*Insurance Expense*	521		7	2	0	00							
		Prepaid Insurance	115								7	2	0	00	
	31			17	7	6	0	00	17	7	6	0	00		

COMBINED JOURNAL PAGE 13

ACCOUNTING FOR OTHER PROFESSIONAL ENTERPRISES

Accounting records for other professional enterprises are similar to our dentist's records. Professional people often use the modified cash basis, recording revenue when received in cash and recording expenses when paid in cash. Adjusting entries may be made for supplies used, expired insurance, and depreciation on specialized equipment. Ledger cards for patients or clients are used, although they may be given special titles. Lawyers, for example, call their clients' ledger cards Collection Dockets.

Lawyers have an additional asset account, Advances for Clients, representing amounts they have paid on behalf of their clients. Advances for Clients is a receivable, similar to Accounts Receivable. Lawyers also have an additional liability account, Collections for Clients, representing amounts they receive on behalf of their clients. Collections for Clients is a payable, similar to Accounts Payable. All in all, the same general accounting principles and procedures prevail in all professional enterprises.

COMBINED JOURNAL   PAGE 14

DATE		ACCOUNT NAME	POST. REF.	SUNDRY DEBIT	SUNDRY CREDIT		
		Closing Entries					
19– Dec.	31	Professional Fees	411	112 0 2 4 00			
		Income Summary	313		112 0 2 4 00		
	31	Income Summary	313	66 8 4 4 00			
		Dental Instruments					
		Expense	511		1 9 8 2 00		
		Laundry and Clean-					
		ing Expense	512		3 0 2 4 00		
		Office Salary Expense	513		23 5 2 0 00		
		Laboratory Expense	514		5 8 5 6 00		
		Dental Supplies					
		Expense	515		3 8 6 4 00		
		Rent Expense	516		12 0 0 0 00		
		Depreciation Expense,					
		Dental Equipment	517		8 4 0 0 00		
		Depreciation Expense,					
		Office Furniture					
		and Equipment	518		1 5 2 0 00		
		X-ray Supplies Expense	519		2 1 4 4 00		
		Office Supplies Expense	520		1 1 1 2 00		
		Insurance Expense	521		7 2 0 00		
		Telephone Expense	522		4 1 2 00		
		Utilities Expense	523		7 7 8 00		
		Repairs and Main-					
		tenance Expense	524		8 8 8 00		
		Miscellaneous Expense	525		6 2 4 00		
	31	Income Summary	313	45 1 8 0 00			
		R. T. Barker, Capital	311		45 1 8 0 00		
	31	R. T. Barker, Capital	311	33 2 8 0 00			
		R. T. Barker, Drawing	312		33 2 8 0 00		
	31			257 3 2 8 00	257 3 2 8 00		

DESIGNING A COMBINED JOURNAL

As we have said, the combined journal is widely used in professional offices and service-type business firms. It is interesting to look over the varieties of combined journals that are available at stores that sell office supplies. Some are bound journals, and others are loose-leaf type books. The number of columns may vary from six to twenty, and they are available with or without column headings. Those that have printed column headings represent a "canned" type of combined journal. In other words, these combined journals are set up for a particular kind of business enterprise and describe how to channel routine transactions into the journal. These journals are available for service stations, dry cleaners, doctors' offices, and many other types of businesses.

A person with even a limited knowledge of accounting can keep books as long as the transactions are routine and fall into the established channels. In every business, however, unusual or nonroutine transactions pop up from time to time. You need to have enough knowledge and background to be able to handle them, and you will have to understand the entire accounting system if you are ever going to see *why* transactions are recorded as they are.

Combined journals with blank columns can be customized to meet the specific requirements of a given business. Prior to labeling the columns, one first studies the operations of the business and makes up a chart of accounts. Next one identifies those accounts that are likely to be used frequently in recording typical transactions of the business. Naturally, if these accounts are used over and over again, one needs to set up special columns for them. The combined journal is appropriate for businesses using either the accrual basis or the modified cash basis of accounting.

GLOSSARY

Accrual basis An accounting method by which revenue is recorded when it is earned, regardless of when it is received. Expenses are recorded when they are incurred, regardless of when they are paid.

Cash-receipts-and-disbursements basis An accounting method by which revenue is recorded only when it is received in cash, and expenses, consisting of all expenditures, are recorded only when they are paid in cash.

Combined journal A journal format widely used by professional and service-type businesses in place of a general journal. Designed to make the recording and posting of transactions more efficient.

Modified cash basis An accounting method by which revenue is recorded only when it is received in cash. Expenditures classified as expenses are recorded only when they are paid in cash. Exceptions can be made in cases of expenditures for items having a useful life of more than one year and for certain prepaid items. For example, expenditures for supplies and insurance premiums can be *prorated*, or apportioned over the fiscal periods covered. Expenditures for long-lived items are recorded as assets and later depreciated or written off as an expense during their useful lives.

QUESTIONS, EXERCISES, AND PROBLEMS

Discussion Questions

1. What is meant by the modified cash basis of accounting?
2. In regard to a combined journal, describe the procedure followed in posting amounts in the following columns: Cash Debit, Professional Fees Credit, Sundry Debit, Miscellaneous Expense Debit, Sundry Credit.
3. Where is a check mark (√) used in a combined journal, and what does it indicate?
4. What is the meaning of the numbers that appear in the Posting Reference column of the combined journal?
5. What is the purpose of the dashes that appear in the Posting Reference column of the combined journal?
6. Describe the process of proving the combined journal at the end of the month.
7. You have been asked to set up a combined journal for Jack's Appliance Repair. The business maintains charge accounts for customers and buys parts on account from creditors. The space occupied by the shop is rented on a monthly basis. J. Rowe, the owner, makes withdrawals on a weekly basis. The firm subscribes to a telephone answering service on a monthly basis. There are no employees. What money columns would you suggest?

Exercises

Exercise 7-1   The Champion Insurance Agency uses a combined journal, which has the following columns.

Date	Accounts Payable Debit
Account Name	Accounts Payable Credit
Post. Ref.	Commissions Income Credit
Cash Debit	Salary Expense Debit
Cash Credit	Miscellaneous Expense Debit
Accounts Receivable Debit	Sundry Debit
Accounts Receivable Credit	Sundry Credit

Answer the following.

a. Which money column totals are not posted?
b. How do you record an investment of additional cash in the business by C. T. Champion?
c. How do you determine the balance of Cash at any time during the month?
d. Which columns are used to record the payment of rent for the month?

Exercise 7-2 Journalize the closing entries in the proper sequence for the following ledger accounts.

Professional Fees		Utilities Expense	
	37,640	560	

Salary Expense		Miscellaneous Expense	
16,400		420	

Rent Expense		J. D. Cameron, Drawing	
4,800		14,600	

Supplies Expense		Depreciation Expense	
365		2,980	

Exercise 7-3 On the appointment record for the dentist, the total of the fees column is $624, and the total of the receipts column is $386. The dentist deposits $386 in the bank at the end of the day. Record the journal entry for the deposit.

Exercise 7-4 Record the proper account or classification of accounts in the blank spaces of the partial work sheet shown in this exercise. Number 1 is given as an example. (Omit the Adjustments column.)

1. Assets
2. Expenses
3. Revenue
4. Liabilities
5. Drawing
6. Accumulated Depreciation
7. Capital

Account Name	Trial Balance		Adjustments		Adjusted Trial Balance		Income Statement		Balance Sheet	
	Debit	Credit	Debit	Credit	Debit	Credit	Debit	Credit	Debit	Credit
	1	___			1	___	___	___	1	___
	___	___			___	___			___	___
	___	___			___	___				___

Exercise 7-5 Determine the cash balance after September 6.

Cash

Sep. 1 Balance 941.60

Combined Journal

Date				Cash Dr.		Cash Cr.	
19–							
Sept.	1			600	00		
	3					425	00
	4			172	60		
	4			21	52		
	5					341	58
	6			83	22		

Exercise 7-6 In the following T accounts, record the plus and minus signs and $418 depreciation for the fiscal period.

Depreciation Expense, Equipment	Accumulated Depreciation, Equipment

Exercise 7-7 Record the depreciation in Exercise 7-6 in the following partial work sheet.

Account Name	Trial Balance		Adjustments		Adjusted Trial Balance	
	Debit	Credit	Debit	Credit	Debit	Credit
Equipment	12,000.00					
Accumulated Depreciation, Equipment		4,650.00				
	56,720.00	56,720.00				
Depreciation Expense, Equipment						

Exercise 7-8 Number the steps in the accounting cycle in the proper sequence.

__ Financial statements
__ Trial balance
__ Journalizing adjusting entries
__ Journalizing transactions
__ Journalizing closing entries

__ Completing the work sheet
__ Formulating the data for the adjustments
__ Posting to the ledger accounts
__ Post-closing trial balance

Problem Set A

Problem 7-1A The following chart of accounts is used by L. E. Benson, M.D.

Assets
111 Cash
112 Medical Supplies
113 X-ray Supplies
114 Office Supplies
115 Medical Equipment
116 Accumulated Depreciation, Medical Equipment
117 Office Furniture and Equipment
118 Accumulated Depreciation, Office Furniture and Equipment
119 Automobile
120 Accumulated Depreciation, Automobile

Liabilities
211 Notes Payable

Owner's Equity
311 L. E. Benson, Capital
312 L. E. Benson, Drawing
313 Income Summary

Revenue
411 Professional Fees

Expenses
511 Salaries Expense
512 Rent Expense
513 Equipment Rental Expense
514 Medical Supplies Expense
515 X-ray Supplies Expense
516 Laboratory Expense
517 Laundry and Cleaning Expense
518 Office Supplies Expense
519 Depreciation Expense, Medical Equipment
520 Depreciation Expense, Office Furniture and Equipment
521 Depreciation Expense, Automobile
522 Automobile Expense
523 Insurance Expense
524 Telephone Expense
525 Utilities Expense
526 Miscellaneous Expense

Dr. Benson's records consist of an appointment record book, examination and charge reports, patients' ledger records, a general journal, and a general ledger. The doctor fills out an examination and charge report each time a patient visits. The reports contain a description or listing of the treatments and tests administered and the amount of the charges. The charges are then recorded in the patient's ledger record. Monthly statements based on the patients' ledger records are mailed to patients. Dr. Benson's books are kept on the modified cash basis.

The following transactions took place during September.

Sep.   1 Bought medical supplies for cash from Porter Surgical Supply, $285.
       1 Paid rent for the month to Dolan Realty, $850.
       5 Paid office salaries for the month, $590.

Sep. 6 Received cash from patients during the week, $4,916.

7 Bought an examination table from Malcom Surgical Supply, costing $420, paying $120 in cash and agreeing by contract to pay the balance in three monthly installments of $100 each. (Credit Notes Payable.)

8 Paid telephone bill, $62.

9 Paid Superior Laboratories for laboratory expense, $216 (not previously recorded).

13 Total cash received from patients during the week, $3,114.

16 Paid for x-ray supplies to Modern Supply Company, $129.

16 Dr. Benson withdrew $615 for personal use.

20 Total cash received from patients during the week, $1,222.

23 Bought postage stamps, $60 (Miscellaneous Expense); paid cash.

25 Paid Mike's Service Station for gas and oil, $65.50.

29 Paid United Building Maintenance for janitorial service, $40.

30 Paid nurses' salaries, $1,342.

30 Dr. Benson withdrew $920 for personal use.

30 Paid Peerless Laundry for laundry service through September 30, $61.40 (not previously recorded).

Instructions

1. Journalize these transactions in the combined journal. Record them on page 41 of the journal.
2. Prove the equality of the debit and credit totals on a sheet of scratch paper.

Problem 7-2A The completed work sheet for D. D. Paige, Architect, is presented on the next two pages.

Instructions

Journalize the adjusting and closing entries.

Problem 7-3A Donna C. Perkins, M.D., completed the transactions described below during November of this year. Her chart of accounts is as follows.

Assets
111 Cash
112 Accounts Receivable
113 Supplies
114 Prepaid Insurance
121 Equipment
122 Accumulated Depreciation, Equipment

Liabilities
211 Accounts Payable

Owner's Equity
311 Donna C. Perkins, Capital
312 Donna C. Perkins, Drawing
313 Income Summary

Revenue
411 Professional Fees

Expenses
511 Salary Expense
512 Rent Expense
513 Laboratory Expense
514 Utilities Expense
515 Depreciation Expense
516 Miscellaneous Expense

	ACCOUNT NAME	TRIAL BALANCE		ADJUSTMENTS	
		DEBIT	CREDIT	DEBIT	CREDIT
1	Cash	3 1 7 9 00			
2	Supplies	2 1 7 2 00			(b)1 1 9 3
3	Office Equipment	31 7 1 8 00			
4	Accumulated Depreciation, Office Equipment		9 7 6 0 00		(a)2 9 8 2
5	D. D. Paige, Capital		22 4 9 6 56		
6	D. D. Paige, Drawing	15 7 8 0 00			
7	Professional Fees		46 7 5 8 00		
8	Salary Expense	17 1 6 4 00			
9	Blueprint Expense	2 0 0 8 64			
10	Rent Expense	4 2 0 0 00			
11	Automobile Expense	8 8 6 19			
12	Travel Expense	1 2 9 2 00			
13	Entertainment Expense	4 1 6 53			
14	Miscellaneous Expense	1 9 8 20			
15		79 0 1 4 56	79 0 1 4 56		
16	Depreciation Expense, Office Equipment			(a)2 9 8 2 00	
17	Supplies Expense			(b)1 1 9 3 00	
18				4 1 7 5 00	4 1 7 5
19	Net Income				
20					
21					

Problem 7-3A   (continued)

Nov. 2 Bought laboratory equipment on account, $1,872.

2 Paid office rent for month, $920.

2 Received cash on account from patients, $940: A. C. Cummings, $170; Agnes Denton, $296; Frank Curtis, $384; Simon Russell, $90. (Dr. Perkins is on the accrual basis. Use four lines, recording individual amounts in both the Cash Debit column and the Accounts Receivable Credit column. List each patient's name in the Account Name column.)

4 Received cash for professional services rendered, $284.

6 Received and paid telephone bill for the month, $52.

6 Received and paid electric bill, $164.76.

9 Recorded fees charged to patients on account for professional services rendered, $938: Derek Stevens, $498; Mildred Wendt, $440.

16 Paid salary of nurse, $670.

19 Received cash for professional services, $632.

23 Returned part of equipment purchased on November 2 and received a reduction on the bill, $84.

27 Billed patients on account, $1,280: Emerson Schultz, $720; Mary MacIntyre, $290; David Allen, $270. (Use three lines.)

ADJUSTED TRIAL BALANCE		INCOME STATEMENT		BALANCE SHEET		
DEBIT	CREDIT	DEBIT	CREDIT	DEBIT	CREDIT	
1 7 9 00				3 1 7 9 00		1
9 7 9 00				9 7 9 00		2
7 1 8 00				31 7 1 8 00		3
	12 7 4 2 00				12 7 4 2 00	4
	22 4 9 6 56				22 4 9 6 56	5
7 8 0 00				15 7 8 0 00		6
	46 7 5 8 00		46 7 5 8 00			7
1 6 4 00		17 1 6 4 00				8
0 0 8 64		2 0 0 8 64				9
2 0 0 00		4 2 0 0 00				10
8 8 6 19		8 8 6 19				11
2 9 2 00		1 2 9 2 00				12
4 1 6 53		4 1 6 53				13
9 8 20		1 9 8 20				14
						15
9 8 2 00		2 9 8 2 00				16
1 9 3 00		1 1 9 3 00				17
9 96 56	81 9 9 6 56	30 3 4 0 56	46 7 5 8 00	51 6 5 6 00	35 2 3 8 56	18
		16 4 1 7 44			16 4 1 7 44	19
		46 7 5 8 00	46 7 5 8 00	51 6 5 6 00	51 6 5 6 00	20
						21

Nov.   30 Paid salary of nurse, $670.
   30 Paid salary of receptionist, $840.
   30 Dr. Perkins withdrew cash for personal use, $1,970.

Instructions

1. Record these transactions in the combined journal.
2. On scratch paper, prove the equality of the debit and credit totals.
3. Post to the accounts in the general ledger.
4. Prepare a trial balance.

Problem 7-4A   On September 1 of this year, C. T. Pitts decided to open a moving business serving the local area. Pitts completed the following transactions related to "Pitts the Mover."

Sep.   1 Pitts invested $16,000 cash in the new business.
   2 Bought a used moving van from Chelsea Van and Storage for $12,450, paying $4,000 down with the balance on account.
   2 Placed an advertisement in *The Guardian* and received a bill for $94.
   3 Bought three hand trucks from Sanderson Rent-All for $227, paying cash.

Sep. 4 Paid Steve's Fast Service for gas and oil for moving van, $84.
      6 Paid rent for subletting office space, $85.
      7 Received revenue for the week, $476.
      7 Paid wages to part-time employee, $184.
      9 Paid for city business license, $32.
     12 Paid for telephone answering service for the month, $58.
     14 Bought two piano dollies on account from Sanderson Rent-All for $118.
     14 Received revenue for the week, $588.
     14 Paid wages to part-time employee, $192.
     14 Pitts withdrew $318 for personal use.
     17 Paid Chelsea Van and Storage $800 as part payment on account.
     18 Paid Steve's Fast Service for gas and oil for moving van, $116.
     18 Paid $62 for advertisement in the telephone directory.
     21 Paid utilities for the month, $47.
     21 Received revenue for the week, $646.
     23 Paid wages to part-time employee, $212.
     26 Paid Sanderson Rent-All in full payment of account, $118.
     30 Received revenue for the week, $784.
     30 Received bill from Steve's Fast Service for performing a tune-up on the moving van, $91.
     30 Paid wages of part-time employee, $220.
     30 Pitts withdrew $425 for personal use.

Instructions

1. By reviewing the transactions, formulate a chart of accounts for "Pitts the Mover."
2. Label the appropriate columns in the combined journal.
3. Record the transactions in the combined journal.
4. Prove the equality of debits and credits on scratch paper.

Problem Set B

Problem 7-1B N. B. Carter, M.D., uses the following chart of accounts.

Assets
111 Cash
112 Medical Supplies
113 X-ray Supplies
114 Office Supplies
115 Medical Equipment
116 Accumulated Depreciation, Medical Equipment
117 Office Furniture and Equipment
118 Accumulated Depreciation, Office Furniture and Equipment
119 Automobile
120 Accumulated Depreciation, Automobile

Liabilities
211 Notes Payable

Owner's Equity
311 N. B. Carter, Capital
312 N. B. Carter, Drawing
313 Income Summary

Revenue
411 Professional Fees

Expenses

511 Nurses' Salaries Expense
512 Office Salaries Expense
513 Rent Expense
514 Equipment Rental Expense
515 Medical Supplies Expense
516 X-ray Supplies Expense
517 Laboratory Expense
518 Laundry and Cleaning Expense
519 Office Supplies Expense
520 Depreciation Expense, Medical
   Equipment

521 Depreciation Expense, Office Furniture
   and Equipment
522 Depreciation Expense, Automobile
523 Automobile Expense
524 Insurance Expense
525 Telephone Expense
526 Utilities Expense
527 Miscellaneous Expense

Dr. Carter's records consist of an appointment record book, examination and charge reports, patients' ledger records, a general journal, and a general ledger. The doctor fills out an examination and charge report each time a patient visits. The reports contain a description or listing of the treatments and tests administered and the amount of the charges. The charges are then recorded in the patient's ledger record. Monthly statements based on the patient's ledger record are mailed to the patient. Dr. Carter's books are kept on the modified cash basis.

These transactions took place during April.

Apr.   1 Paid rent for the month to M. B. Faris, $900.
       3 Bought medical supplies for cash from Shinn Surgical Supply, $260.
       4 Paid office salaries for the month, $520.
       6 Received cash from patients during week, $4,160.
      10 Paid telephone bill, $54.
      12 Paid for laboratory expense to Shelton Laboratories, $210.
      13 Total cash received from patients during week, $2,932.
      16 Paid for x-ray supplies to Meier Supply Company, $122.
      17 Dr. Carter withdrew $520 for personal use.
      19 Bought postage stamps, $26 (Miscellaneous Expense); paid cash.
      20 Received cash from patients during week, $1,184.
      23 Paid Roy's Service Station for gas and oil, $62.
      24 Paid Speedy News Service for magazines, $41.
      27 Paid Modern Laundry for laundry service, $56.
      30 Paid nurses' salaries for the month, $1,260.
      30 Dr. Carter withdrew $680 for personal use.
      30 Paid Johnson Janitorial Service, $82.
      30 Received cash from patients (April 21 through 30), $917.

Instructions

1. Journalize these transactions in the combined journal. Record them on page 39 of the journal.
2. Prove the equality of the debit and credit totals on a sheet of scratch paper.

	ACCOUNT NAME	TRIAL BALANCE		ADJUSTMENTS	
		DEBIT	CREDIT	DEBIT	CREDIT
1	Cash	4 2 8 0 00			
2	Supplies	1 4 2 6 00			(b)1 2 1 4
3	Office Equipment	23 7 0 0 00			
4	Accumulated Depreciation, Office Equipment		10 8 7 0 00		(a)3 4 1 0
5	A. L. Brown, Capital		12 5 4 1 00		
6	A. L. Brown, Drawing	16 2 0 0 00			
7	Professional Fees		50 6 8 0 00		
8	Salary Expense	18 7 2 0 00			
9	Blueprint Expense	2 1 7 2 00			
10	Rent Expense	4 2 0 0 00			
11	Automobile Expense	9 2 0 00			
12	Travel Expense	1 4 8 0 00			
13	Entertainment Expense	5 6 4 00			
14	Miscellaneous Expense	4 2 9 00			
15		74 0 9 1 00	74 0 9 1 00		
16	Depreciation Expense, Office Equipment			(a)3 4 1 0 00	
17	Supplies Expense			(b)1 2 1 4 00	
18				4 6 2 4 00	4 6 2 4
19	Net Income				
20					
21					

Problem 7-2B The work sheet for A. L. Brown, Architect, is above.

Instructions

Journalize the adjusting and closing entries.

Problem 7-3B Donna C. Perkins, M.D., uses the following chart of accounts.

Assets
111 Cash
112 Accounts Receivable
113 Supplies
114 Prepaid Insurance
121 Equipment

Liabilities
211 Accounts Payable

Owner's Equity
311 Donna C. Perkins, Capital
312 Donna C. Perkins, Drawing
313 Income Summary

Revenue
411 Professional Fees

Expenses
511 Salary Expense
512 Rent Expense
513 Laboratory Expense
514 Utilities Expense
515 Depreciation Expense
516 Miscellaneous Expense

ADJUSTED TRIAL BALANCE		INCOME STATEMENT		BALANCE SHEET		
DEBIT	CREDIT	DEBIT	CREDIT	DEBIT	CREDIT	
8 0 00				4 2 8 0 00		1
1 2 00				2 1 2 00		2
0 0 00				23 7 0 0 00		3
	14 2 8 0 00				14 2 8 0 00	4
	12 5 4 1 00				12 5 4 1 00	5
0 0 00				16 2 0 0 00		6
	50 6 8 0 00		50 6 8 0 00			7
2 0 00		18 7 2 0 00				8
7 2 00		2 1 7 2 00				9
0 0 00		4 2 0 0 00				10
2 0 00		9 2 0 00				11
8 0 00		1 4 8 0 00				12
6 4 00		5 6 4 00				13
2 9 00		4 2 9 00				14
						15
1 0 00		3 4 1 0 00				16
1 4 00		1 2 1 4 00				17
0 1 00	77 5 0 1 00	33 1 0 9 00	50 6 8 0 00	44 3 9 2 00	26 8 2 1 00	18
		17 5 7 1 00			17 5 7 1 00	19
		50 6 8 0 00	50 6 8 0 00	44 3 9 2 00	44 3 9 2 00	20
						21

These transactions were completed during November of this year.

Nov. 2 Paid office rent for the month, $920.

2 Bought laboratory equipment on account, $1,880.

3 Received cash on account from patients, $940: R. C. Striker, $320; Dennis Horton, $380; Angela Higgins, $240. (Dr. Perkins is on the accrual basis. Use three lines, recording individual amounts in both the Cash Debit column and the Accounts Receivable Credit column. List each patient's name in the Account Name column.)

4 Received cash for professional services rendered, $250.

6 Received and paid telephone bill for the month, $48.

9 Recorded fees charged to patients on account for professional services rendered, $1,090: J. C. Prescott, $520; Arthur Lewis, $570. (Use two lines.)

9 Received and paid electric bill for the month, $170.

16 Paid salary of nurse, $630.

23 Received cash for professional services, $620.

23 Returned part of equipment purchased on November 2 and received a reduction on the bill, $120.

Nov.   27 Billed patients on account for professional services rendered, $740:
            R. L. Graves, $180; C. C. Simon, $320; Charles Marshall, $240.
       30 Paid receptionist's salary for the month, $780.
       30 Paid salary of nurse, $630.
       30 Dr. Perkins withdrew cash for personal use, $1,680.

Instructions

1. Record these transactions in the combined journal.
2. On scratch paper, prove the equality of the debit and credit totals.
3. Post to the accounts in the general ledger.
4. Prepare a trial balance.

Problem 7-4B   On October 1 of this year, R. D. Spargo decided to open a
tree trimming service. Spargo completed the following transactions related to
Spargo's Tree Service.

Oct.   1 Spargo invested cash in the business by depositing $6,000 in the
            bank under the name Spargo's Tree Service.
        1 Paid office rent for the month, $125.
        2 Bought a used truck from Midland Truck and Tractor for $8,200,
            paying $1,500 down, with the balance on account.
        2 Bought a used chipper from Jones Equipment for $2,400, paying
            $1,000 as a down payment and the balance on account.
        3 Received a bill for advertising from the City Chronicle, $72.
        4 Bought two chain saws on account from Scott's Hardware, $578.
        4 Paid City Service for gas and oil for the truck, $76.
        6 Received revenue for the week, $564.
        7 Paid wages of part-time employee, $121.
        7 Paid for telephone answering service for the month, $61.
       10 Paid City Service for gas and oil for the truck, $59.
       13 Received $628 revenue for the week.
       15 Paid City Chronicle $72 for advertising that was previously re-
            corded.
       18 Spargo withdrew $420 for personal use.
       20 Received revenue for the week, $642.
       21 Paid wages to part-time employee, $132.
       26 Paid utilities for the month, $58.
       26 Paid $24 for city business license.
       30 Paid Midland Truck and Tractor $900 to apply on account.
       30 Paid City Service $47 for gas and oil for the truck plus $18 for a
            wheel alignment for the truck.
       31 Received revenue for the week, $786.
       31 Paid wages of part-time employee, $143.
       31 Spargo withdrew $325 for personal use.

Instructions

1. By reviewing the transactions, formulate a chart of accounts.
2. Label appropriate columns in the combined journal.
3. Record the transactions in the combined journal.
4. Prove the equality of debits and credits on scratch paper.

8 Bank Accounts and Cash Funds

Learning Objectives

After you have completed this chapter, you will be able to do the following:

1. Reconcile a bank statement.

2. Journalize the requisite entries directly from the bank reconciliation.

3. Journalize entries to establish and reimburse Petty Cash Fund.

4. Complete petty cash vouchers and petty cash payments records.

5. Journalize the entries to establish a Change Fund.

6. Journalize transactions involving Cash Short and Over.

A very important aspect of any system of financial accounting, either for an individual or for a business enterprise, is the efficient management of cash. For a business of any size, all cash received during a working day should be deposited at the end of the day, and all disbursements—with the exception of payments from Petty Cash—should be made by check. When we talk about cash, we mean currency, coins, checks, money orders, and bank drafts or bank cashier's checks. Personal checks are accepted on a conditional-payment status, that is, based on the condition that they're valid. In other words, we consider checks to be good until they are proved to be no good.

In this chapter, we're also going to talk about **cash funds**—petty cash funds and change funds—which, in this sense, are separately held stores of cash.

USING A CHECKING ACCOUNT

Although you may be familiar with the process of opening a checking account, making deposits, and writing checks, let's review these and other procedures associated with opening and maintaining a business checking account. We'll discuss signature cards, deposit slips, night deposits, and ways of endorsing checks.

Signature card

When Eugene L. Madison founded East Phoenix Rental Equipment, he opened a checking account in the name of the business. When he made his first deposit, he filled out a **signature card** for the bank's files. Madison gave his accountant the right to sign checks too, so the accountant also signed the card. This card gives the bank a copy of the official signatures of any persons authorized to sign checks. The bank can use it to verify any signatures on checks of East Phoenix Rental Equipment presented for payment. This, of course, helps the bank detect forgeries. Figure 8-1 shows a typical signature card.

Deposit slips

The bank provides **deposit slips** on which customers record the amount of coins and currency they are depositing and list each individual check being deposited. A typical deposit slip is shown in Figure 8-2. For identification purposes, each check should be listed according to its American Bankers Association (ABA) transit number. The **ABA number** is the small

Figure 8-1

Title		Account Number
East Phoenix Rental Equipment		

In consideration of the acceptance by Imlmmllmllmmlm Immmlmllm Imllmlmmlln of my/our account of the type indicated below, I/we agree to be bound by such rules and regulations and/or such schedules of interest, fees and charges applicable to such account as may now or hereafter be adopted by and in effect at said Bank, and also by the provisions printed hereon. It is understood that the acceptance by said Bank of my/our account is subject to the receipt by said Bank of satisfactory credit information.

(1) Sign Here *Eugene L. Madison*

(2) Sign Here *Gloria B. Masters*

Address 3011 N.W. Ventura Street

City Phoenix   State Arizona   Zip 85280

☑ CHECKING   ☐ MULTIPLE MATURITY   ☐ CASH MANAGER

☐ SAVINGS   ☐ GUARANTEED INTEREST   ☐ SAFE DEPOSIT   ☐ OTHER_____
(Multiple Maturity)

IF THIS IS A JOINT ACCOUNT, BOTH OWNERS MUST SIGN ABOVE

Each of the signers guarantees the genuineness of the signature of the other. Each signer also agrees with the other and the Bank that deposits now or hereafter made to this account may be withdrawn in whole or part by either or survivor, and that each may endorse for deposit to this account any instrument payable to the order of either or both. Provisions respecting this agreement shall be modified only upon receipt by the Bank of written notice, signed by both.

fraction located in the upper right corner of a check. The numerator (top of the fraction) indicates the city or state in which the bank is located and the specific bank on which the check is drawn. The denominator (bottom of the fraction) indicates the Federal Reserve District in which the check is cleared and the routing number used by the Federal Reserve Bank. For example,

$$\frac{68\text{-}420}{1210}$$

The 68 identifies the city or state, and the 420 indicates the specific bank within that area. That is all you need to list on the deposit slip. However, for your information, the 12 in the denominator represents the Twelfth

Figure 8-2

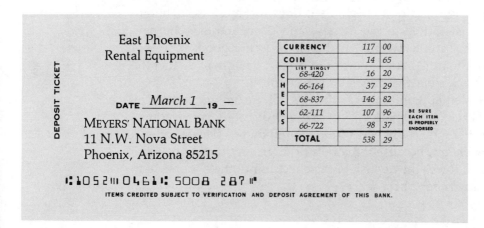

East Phoenix Rental Equipment		CURRENCY	117	00
		COIN	14	65
	C	LIST SINGLY 68-420	16	20
	H	66-164	37	29
DATE *March 1* 19 —	E C	68-837	146	82
MEYERS' NATIONAL BANK	K S	62-111	107	96
11 N.W. Nova Street		66-722	98	37
Phoenix, Arizona 85215		TOTAL	538	29

DEPOSIT TICKET

BE SURE EACH ITEM IS PROPERLY ENDORSED

⑈:⑈1052⑈⑈⑈0461⑈: 5008 287 ⑈⑈

ITEMS CREDITED SUBJECT TO VERIFICATION AND DEPOSIT AGREEMENT OF THIS BANK.

Federal Reserve District, and the 10 represents the routing number used by the Federal Reserve Bank.

The depositor fills out the deposit slip in duplicate, giving one copy to the bank teller and keeping the other copy. (This procedure may vary from bank to bank.)

When the bank receives the deposited checks, it prints the amount of each check on the lower right side of the check in a very distinctive script called **MICR,** which stands for *magnetic ink character recognition*. The routing number used by the Federal Reserve Bank was previously printed on the lower left side of the blank check. The reason banks use this MICR script is that the electronic equipment used to process the checks is able to read the script identifying the bank on which the check is drawn as well as the amount of the check. Clearing checks electronically speeds up the process considerably.

Night Deposits

Most banks provide night depositories so that firms can make deposits after regular banking hours. Depositories are steel-lined chutes into which a firm's representative can drop a bag of cash and checks, knowing that their day's receipts will be safe until the bank opens in the morning.

Endorsements

The bank refuses to accept for deposit a check made out to a firm until someone from the firm has endorsed the check. The **endorsement** may be made by signature or by using a stamp. The endorsement should appear on the back of the left end of a check, as it does in Figure 8-3. The endorsement (1) transfers title to the money, and (2) guarantees the payment of the check. In other words, if the check is not good, NSF (not sufficient funds), then the bank, in order to protect itself, will deduct the amount of the check from the depositor's account.

East Phoenix Rental Equipment endorses all incoming checks by stamping on the back of the checks: "Pay to the Order of Meyers National Bank, For Deposit Only, East Phoenix Rental Equipment." This is called a **restrictive endorsement,** because it restricts or limits any further negotiation of the check; it forces the deposit of the check, since the endorsement is not valid for any other purpose.

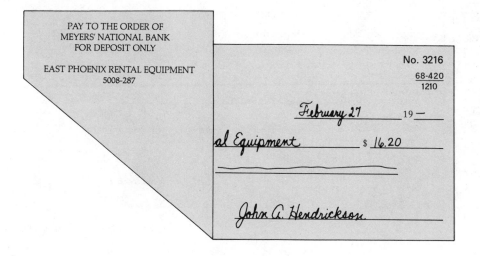

Figure 8-3

PAY TO THE ORDER OF
MEYERS' NATIONAL BANK
FOR DEPOSIT ONLY

EAST PHOENIX RENTAL EQUIPMENT
5008-287

No. 3216

68-420
————
1210

February 27   19 —

al Equipment $ *16.20*

John A. Hendrickson

WRITING CHECKS

As you know, you have to use a check to withdraw money from a checking account. A check represents an order by the depositor, directing the bank to pay money to a designated person or firm: the **payee.**

The checks may be attached to check stubs. Each stub has spaces to record the check number and amount, the date and payee, the purpose of the check, and the beginning and ending balances. *Note well:* The information recorded on the check stub is the basis for the journal entry, so check stubs are vitally important. A person in a hurry, or working under pressure, can sometimes neglect to fill in the check stubs. Therefore, it is best to record all the information on the check stub *before making out the check.*

It goes without saying that all checks should be written carefully, so that no dishonest person can successfully alter them. Write the payee's name on the first long line. Write the amount of the check in figures close to the dollar sign, then write the amount in words at the extreme left of the line provided for this information. Write cents as a fraction of 100. For example, write $727.50 as "seven hundred twenty-seven and 50/100," or $69.00 as "sixty-nine and 00/100." From a legal standpoint, if there is a discrepancy between the amount in figures and the written amount, the written amount prevails. However, as a general practice, the bank gets in touch with the depositor and asks what the correct amount should be.

Many firms use a **check writer,** which is a machine used to imprint the amount in figures and in words on the check itself. Using this machine neatly prevents anyone from altering the amount of the check.

Finally, the depositor's signature on the face of the check should match that of the signature card on file at the depositor's bank.

In Figure 8-4 we see a check, with the accompanying stub, drawn on the account of East Phoenix Rental Equipment.

Figure 8-4

BANK STATEMENTS

Once a month the bank sends all of its customers a **bank statement.** This statement provides the following information about their accounts.

- The balance at the beginning of the month
- Additions in the form of deposits and credit memos
- Deductions in the form of checks and debit memos
- The final balance at the end of the month

A bank statement for East Phoenix Rental Equipment is shown in Figure 8-5. The following code symbols are listed on the statement:

- **CM Credit memo**   Increases or credits to the account, such as notes or accounts left with the bank for collection.
- **DM Debit memo**   Decreases or debits to the account, items returned such as NSF checks and special charges levied by the bank against the account.
- **EC Error correction**   Corrections of errors made by the bank, such as mistakes in transferring figures.
- **OD Overdraft**   An overwithdrawal, resulting in a negative balance in the account.
- **SC Service charge**   The amount charged by the bank for servicing the account, based on the number of items processed and the average balance of the account.

The bank statement is a valuable aid to efficiency because it gives a double record of the Cash account. If a business entity deposits all cash receipts in the bank and makes all payments by check, then the bank is keeping an independent record of the firm's cash. Offhand, you might think that the two balances—the firm's and the bank's—should be equal,

MEYERS NATIONAL BANK
11 N.W. Nova Street
Phoenix, Arizona 85215

STATEMENT OF ACCOUNT	*East Phoenix Rental Equipment* *3011 N.W. Ventura Street* *Phoenix, Arizona 85280*	**ACCOUNT NO.** 5008-287 **STATEMENT DATE** *October 31, 19–*

CHECKS AND OTHER DEBITS			DEPOSITS	DATE	BALANCE
	BALANCE BROUGHT FORWARD FROM LAST STATEMENT			*Oct. 1, 19–*	*7,495.13*
50.00 *200.00*	*400.00*		*921.00*	*Oct. 1*	*7,766.13*
46.00 *174.23*	*671.74*		*1,476.22*	*Oct. 2*	*8,350.38*
846.20 *664.56*			*463.62*	*Oct. 3*	*7,303.24*
719.00 *61.68*	*591.84*		*789.43*	*Oct. 4*	*6,720.15*
36.92 *817.22*	*DM125.00*		*1,063.14*	*Oct. 7*	*6,804.15*
523.00 *786.40*	*374.00*		*1,211.96*	*Oct. 8*	*6,332.71*
943.64			*CM606.00*	*Oct. 30*	*7,812.62*
			873.19	*Oct. 30*	*8,685.81*
843.17 *21.92*	*SC5.50*		*946.78*	*Oct. 31*	*8,762.00*

CHECKING SUMMARY

BEGINNING BALANCE	TOTAL AMOUNT OF CHECKS & DEBITS		TOTAL AMOUNT OF DEPOSITS & CREDITS		SERVICE CHARGE AMOUNT	ENDING BALANCE
	NO.	AMOUNT	NO.	AMOUNT		
7,495.13	*66*	*25,153.41*	*23*	*26,425.78*	*5.50*	*8,762.00*

PLEASE EXAMINE THIS STATEMENT CAREFULLY. REPORT ANY POSSIBLE ERRORS IN 10 DAYS.

CODE SYMBOLS

CM	Credit Memo	OD	Overdraft
DM	Debit Memo	SC	Service Charge
EC	Error Correction		

Figure 8-5

but this is most unlikely. Some transactions may have been recorded in the firm's account before being recorded in the bank's. In addition, there are unavoidable delays (by either the firm or the bank) in recording transactions. Ordinarily, there is a time lag of one day or more between the date a check is written and the date it is presented to the bank for payment. Also, banks usually do not record deposits until the following business day. During this time, deposits made or checks written are recorded in the firm's checkbook, but they are not yet recorded on the bank statement.

The bank usually mails statements to its depositors shortly after the end of the month. In the same envelope with the statement are the **canceled checks** (checks that have been cashed or cleared by the bank) and debit or credit memos. As we mentioned before, debit memos represent deductions and credit memos represent additions to a bank account. Each business entity keeps its accounts from its *own* point of view. As far as the bank is concerned, each customer's deposits are liabilities, in that the bank owes the customer the amount of the deposits. Using T accounts, it looks like this.

Liabilities		Deposits Payable	
−	+	−	+
Debits	Credits	Debits	Credits
		Checks written	Deposits
	Debit	⎰ Service charges	Notes ⎱ Credit
	memos	⎱ NSF checks	collected ⎰ memos

On the customer's books, of course, this comes under the account titled Cash, or Cash in Bank, or simply the name of the bank. Regardless of what title is used for the account, the balance of the account is referred to as the *book balance of Cash.*

Need for Reconciling Bank Balance and Book Balance

The **book balance** is the balance of the Cash account in the general ledger. Since the bank statement balance and the book balance are not equal, a firm makes a **bank reconciliation** to uncover the reasons for the difference between the two balances and to correct any errors that may have been made by either the bank or the firm. This makes it possible to wind up with the same balance in each account, which is called the *adjusted balance,* or *true balance,* of the Cash account.

There are a variety of reasons for differences between the bank statement balance and the customer's cash balance. Here are some of the more usual ones:

- **Outstanding checks** Checks that have been written but that have not yet been received for payment by the time the bank sends out its statement. The depositor, when writing out his or her checks, deducted the amounts from the Cash account in the company's books, which explains the difference.

Objective 1

Reconcile a bank statement.

- **Deposits in transit** A deposit made after the bank statement was issued. Many accountants call this a *late deposit*. The depositor has naturally already added the amount to the Cash account in his or her books.
- **Service charge** A bank charge for services rendered: for issuing checks, for collecting money, for receiving payment of notes turned over to it by the customer for collection, and for other such services. The bank notifies the depositor with a debit memorandum, and immediately deducts the fee from the balance of the bank account.
- **Collections** When the bank acts as a collection agent for its customers by accepting payments on promissory notes, installment accounts, and charge accounts, it adds the proceeds to the customer's bank account and sends a credit memorandum to notify the customer of the transaction.
- **NSF (Not Sufficient Funds) checks** When a bank customer deposits a check, she or he counts it as cash. Occasionally, however, a check is not paid (bounces), and then the bank notifies the customer. The customer must then make a deduction from the Cash account.
- **Errors** In spite of internal control and systems designed to double-check against errors, sometimes either the customer or the bank makes a mistake. Often these errors do not become evident until the bank reconciliation is performed.

Steps in Reconciling the Bank Statement

Follow these steps in reconciling a bank statement:

1. **Canceled checks** Compare the amount of each canceled check with the bank statement, and note any discrepancies. Also, on the stub that matches each canceled check, list the date of the bank statement. In some cases, a bank may not pay a check until one or two months after it was written. If a question arises as to whether or not you have paid a particular bill, you can look at the check stub. Next, you can refer directly to the bank statement to pick up the canceled check as proof of payment.
2. **Deposits** Look over the deposits in transit, or unrecorded deposits listed on the bank reconciliation of the previous month. Compare these with the deposits listed on this month's bank statement. These deposits should all be accounted for; note any discrepancy. Now compare the remaining deposits listed on the current bank statement with deposits written in the firm's accounting records. Consider any deposits not shown on the bank statement as deposits in transit.
3. **Outstanding checks** Next, arrange the canceled checks in the order of the check numbers. Look over the list of outstanding checks left over from the bank reconciliation of the previous month, and note the

checks that have now been returned. Compare each canceled check with the entry in the journal. If the journal is not available, then compare the canceled checks with the check stubs. In either case, use a check mark ($\checkmark$) to indicate that the check has been paid and that the amount is correct. To further verify that money has been sent to the right payee, review the endorsements on the backs of the checks. Any payments that have *not* been checked off, including the outstanding checks from the previous bank reconciliation, are the present outstanding checks. In other words, they were not presented for payment by the time of the cutoff date of the bank statement.

4. **Bank memorandums**   Trace the credit memos and the debit memos to the journal. If the memos have not been recorded, make separate journal entries for them.

As you can see, a bank can be an accountant's best friend. A large firm should require that the reconciliation be prepared by an employee who is not involved in recording business transactions or in handling cash receipts and disbursements.

Examples of Bank Reconciliations

Let's go through the reconciliation process for two firms. First we'll take the case of A. R. Conolly and Company, then we'll look at East Phoenix Rental Equipment.

A. R. Conolly and Company   The bank statement of A. R. Conolly and Company indicates a balance of $2,119 as of March 31. The balance of the Cash account in their ledger as of that date is $1,552. Conolly's accountant has taken the steps we've listed.

1. Verified that canceled checks were recorded correctly on the bank statement.
2. Noted the deposit made on March 31 that was not recorded on the bank statement, $762.
3. Noted outstanding checks: no. 921, $626; no. 985, $69; no. 986, $438.
4. Noted credit memo: note collected by the bank from S. Alden, $200, not recorded in the journal. Noted debit memo: collection charge and service charge not recorded in the journal, $4.

The bank reconciliation may be made on a separate sheet of paper or on the back of the bank statement, since some banks print the main headings on the form. Here are Conolly's bank reconciliation and journal entries. The items in the reconciliation that require journal entries are shown in color in Figure 8-6.

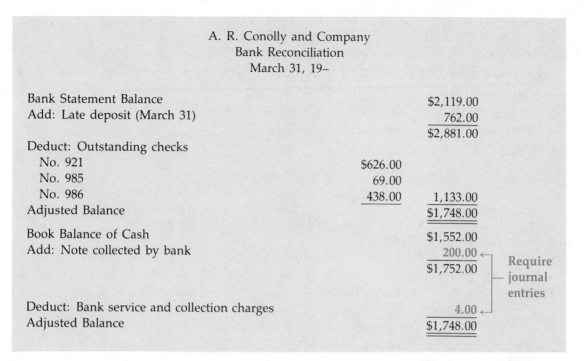

A. R. Conolly and Company
Bank Reconciliation
March 31, 19–

Bank Statement Balance		$2,119.00
Add: Late deposit (March 31)		762.00
		$2,881.00
Deduct: Outstanding checks		
No. 921	$626.00	
No. 985	69.00	
No. 986	438.00	1,133.00
Adjusted Balance		$1,748.00
Book Balance of Cash		$1,552.00
Add: Note collected by bank		200.00
		$1,752.00
Deduct: Bank service and collection charges		4.00
Adjusted Balance		$1,748.00

Require journal entries

Figure 8-6

Objective 2

Journalize the requisite entries directly from the bank reconciliation.

Note that journal entries should be based on the bank reconciliation, since the true balance of Cash is $1,748, whereas the current balance on the firm's books is $1,552. You can't change the balance of an account unless you first make a journal entry and then post the entry to the accounts involved. *Consequently, you have to make journal entries only from the book-balance-of-cash section of the bank reconciliation.* Debit additions to Cash and credit deductions from Cash. A. R. Conolly and Company records the entries in their general journal.

	DATE		DESCRIPTION	POST. REF.	DEBIT	CREDIT
	19– Mar.	31	Cash		2 0 0 00	
			Notes Receivable			2 0 0 00
			Non-interest-bearing note signed			
			by S. Alden was collected by			
			the bank.			
		31	Miscellaneous Expense		4 00	
			Cash			4 00
			Service charge and collection			
			charge levied by the bank.			

GENERAL JOURNAL   PAGE _____

Here service charges and collection charges are recorded in the same account because the amounts are relatively small. However, some accountants use separate expense accounts.

After posting the above entries, the T account for Cash looks like this:

Cash			
Balance	1,552	Mar. 31	4
Mar. 31	200		
	1,752		
Bal. 1,748			

Note that the balance in the T account is now equal to the adjusted balance on the bank reconciliation.

Form of Bank Reconciliation

Now that you have seen an example of a bank reconciliation, let's look at the standard form of a bank reconciliation for a hypothetical company.

Bank Statement Balance (last figure on the statement)		$4,000
Add		
Deposits in transit (late deposits already added to the Cash account)	$300	
Bank errors	20	320
		$4,320
Deduct		
Outstanding checks (they have already been deducted from the Cash account)	$960	
Bank errors	40	1,000
Adjusted balance (the true balance of Cash)		$3,320
Book Balance of Cash (the latest balance of the Cash account if it has been posted up to date; otherwise take the beginning balance of Cash, plus cash receipts and minus cash payments)		$2,850
Add		
Credit memos (additions by the bank not recorded in the Cash account, such as collections of notes)	$500	
Book errors (that understate balance)	40	540
		$3,390

Deduct

Debit memos (deductions by the bank not recorded in the Cash account, such as service charges or collection charges)	$ 20	
Book errors (that overstate balance)	50	70
Adjusted balance (the true balance of Cash)		$3,320

East Phoenix Rental Equipment   The bank statement of East Phoenix Rental Equipment shows a final balance of $8,762 as of October 31 (see Figure 8-7). The present balance of the Cash account in the ledger, after East Phoenix's accountant has posted from the journal, is $7,806.50. The accountant took the following steps:

1. Verified that canceled checks were recorded correctly on the bank statement.
2. Discovered that a deposit of $1,003 made on October 31 was not recorded on the bank statement.

Figure 8-7

East Phoenix Rental Equipment
Bank Reconciliation
October 31, 19–

Bank Statement Balance		$8,762.00
Add: Late deposit (October 31)		1,003.00
		$9,765.00
Deduct: Outstanding checks		
No. 1916	$461.00	
No. 2022	119.00	
No. 2023	827.00	
No. 2024	67.00	1,474.00
Adjusted Balance		$8,291.00
Book Balance of Cash		$7,806.50
Add: Note collected (principal $600.00, interest $6.00, Ryan Plumbing and Heating)	$606.00 ←	
Error in recording Check No. 2001 payable to Mahon, Inc.	9.00 ←	615.00
		$8,421.50
Deduct: Bank service and collection charges	$ 5.50 ←	
NSF check from C. M. Lang Company	125.00 ←	130.50
Adjusted Balance		$8,291.00

Require journal entries

3. Noted outstanding checks: no. 1916, $461; no. 2022, $119; no. 2023, $827; no. 2024, $67.
4. Noted that a credit memo for a note collected by the bank from Ryan Plumbing and Heating, $600 principal plus $6 interest, was not recorded in the journal.
5. Found that check no. 2001 for $523, payable to Mahon, Inc., on account was recorded in the journal as $532. (The correct amount is $523.)
6. Noted that a debit memo for a collection charge and service charge of $5.50 was not recorded in the journal.
7. Noted that debit memo for an NSF check for $125 from C. M. Lang Company was not recorded.

Look at Figure 8-7 to see how each step relates to the bank reconciliation.

The accountant has to make the journal entries shown in Figure 8-8 in order to change the Cash account from the present balance of $7,806.50 to the true balance of $8,291. Again, those items that require journal entries are highlighted in Figures 8-7 and 8-8.

A bank reconciliation form is ordinarily printed on the back of the bank statement. In a typical form, it is assumed that the adjusted balance of the book-balance-of-cash section has already been determined. Conse-

Figure 8-8

GENERAL JOURNAL   PAGE _____

DATE		DESCRIPTION	POST. REF.	DEBIT	CREDIT
19– Oct.	31	Cash		6 0 6 00	
		Notes Receivable			6 0 0 00
		Interest Income			6 00
		Bank collected note signed by			
		Ryan Plumbing and Heating.			
	31	Cash		9 00	
		Accounts Payable			9 00
		Error in recording check no.			
		2001 payable to Mahon, Inc.			
	31	Miscellaneous Expense		5 50	
		Cash			5 50
		Bank service charge and			
		collection charge.			
	31	Accounts Receivable		1 2 5 00	
		Cash			1 2 5 00
		NSF check received from			
		C. M. Lang.			

THIS FORM IS PROVIDED TO HELP YOU BALANCE
YOUR BANK STATEMENT

CHECKS OUTSTANDING—NOT
CHARGED TO ACCOUNT

No.		$		
1916			461	00
2022			119	00
2023			827	00
2024			67	00
TOTAL		$	1,474	00

BEFORE YOU START—

PLEASE BE SURE YOU HAVE ENTERED IN YOUR CHECKBOOK ALL AUTOMATIC TRANSACTIONS SHOWN ON THE FRONT OF YOUR STATEMENT.

YOU SHOULD HAVE ADDED IF ANY OCCURRED:

1. Loan advances.
2. Credit memos.
3. Other automatic deposits.

YOU SHOULD HAVE SUB-TRACTED IF ANY OCCURRED:

1. Automatic loan payments.
2. Automatic savings transfers.
3. Service charges.
4. Debit memos.
5. Other automatic deductions and payments.

BANK BALANCE SHOWN
   ON THIS STATEMENT $ *8,762.00*

ADD
   DEPOSITS NOT SHOWN
     ON THIS STATEMENT
         (IF ANY) $ *1,003.00*

         TOTAL $ *9,765.00*

SUBTRACT—

▶ CHECKS OUTSTANDING $ *1,474.00*

         BALANCE $ *8,291.00*

SHOULD AGREE WITH YOUR CHECKBOOK BALANCE AFTER DEDUCTING SERVICE CHARGE (IF ANY) SHOWN ON THIS STATEMENT.

Please examine immediately and report if incorrect. If no reply is received within 15 days the account will be considered correct.

quently, the bank form only provides for calculating the adjusted bank statement balance of the bank-statement section of the bank reconciliation. The bank form for East Phoenix Rental Equipment is shown in Figure 8-9.

Figure 8-9

Bank reconciliation form

THE PETTY CASH FUND

Day after day, business firms are confronted with transactions involving small immediate payments, such as the cost of a telegram, delivery charges, postage due for mail, or a new typewriter ribbon. If the firm had to go through the usual procedure of making all payments by check, the time consumed would be frustrating and the whole process unduly expensive. For many firms, the cost of writing each check is more than $.50; this includes the cost of an employee's time in writing and reconciling the check. Suppose the mail carrier is at the door with a letter on which there is $.20 postage due. To write a check would be ridiculous. It only makes sense to pay in cash, out of the **Petty Cash Fund.** *Petty* means small; so the firm sets a maximum amount that can be paid out of petty cash. Payments that exceed this maximum must be processed by regular check through the journal.

Establishing the Petty Cash Fund

After the firm has decided on the maximum amount of a payment from petty cash, the next step is to estimate how much cash will be needed during a given period of time, such as a month. Small payments are made during the month from the petty cash fund.

It is also important to consider the element of security when keeping cash in the office. If risk is great, the amount kept in the fund should be small, and the fund should be reimbursed at intervals of perhaps one or two weeks.

East Phoenix Rental Equipment decided to establish a petty cash fund of $50 and put it under the control of the secretary. Accordingly, their accountant writes a check, cashes it at the bank, and records this transaction in the journal as follows.

Objective 3

Journalize entries to establish and reimburse Petty Cash Fund.

			GENERAL JOURNAL				PAGE ____	
DATE			DESCRIPTION	POST. REF.	DEBIT		CREDIT	
19– Sep.	1		*Petty Cash Fund*		5 0 00			
			Cash				5 0 00	
			Established a petty cash fund.					

T accounts for the entry look like this:

Petty Cash Fund			Cash	
+	−		+	−
50				50

Because the Petty Cash Fund is an asset account, it is listed in the balance sheet immediately below Cash. Remember: **The Petty Cash Fund account is debited only once, and this happens when the fund is established initially.**

There is only one exception: When the original amount is not large enough to handle the necessary transactions, the accountant has to make the Petty Cash Fund bigger—maybe change the $50 to $75. But, barring such a change in the size of the fund, Petty Cash is debited only once.

After the accountant cashes that original $50 check, he or she converts it into convenient **denominations,** such as quarters and dimes, and one and five dollar bills. Then the accountant puts the money in a locked drawer in the secretary's desk, telling the secretary not to pay anything larger than $5 out of petty cash.

Payments from the Petty Cash Fund

The secretary now takes the responsibility for the petty cash fund; he or she is designated as the only person who can make payments from it. In case of his or her illness, some other employee should be named as stand-in. A **petty cash voucher** must be used to account for every payment from the fund. The voucher constitutes a receipt signed by the person who authorized the payment and by the person receiving payment. Thus, even for small payments of $5 or less, there would have to be collusion between the payee and the secretary for any theft to occur. Figure 8-10 shows what a petty cash voucher looks like.

Objective 4

Complete petty cash vouchers and petty cash payments records.

Reimbursement of the Petty Cash Fund

When the fund is nearly exhausted, for example at month end, the accountant reimburses the fund for expenditures made to bring the fund back up to the original amount. Consequently, it may be considered to be

Figure 8-10

PETTY CASH VOUCHER

No. _1_   Date _September 2, 19–_

Paid to _Excell Delivery Service_ $ _2.00_

For _Delivery_

Account _Delivery Expense_

Approved by   Payment received by

R. Jason   _C J Comstock_

a revolving fund. If the amount initially put in the Petty Cash Fund is $50 and at the end of the month only $4 is left, the accountant puts $46 in the fund as a reimbursement, thereby bringing it back up to $50 to start the new month.

For example, take voucher no. 1 (shown in Figure 8-10), in which $2 is charged to Delivery Expense. Let's say that, as the month goes by, $12 more is charged to Delivery Expense on other petty cash vouchers. Assume that the total amount spent from the fund during the month for all purposes is $43. At the end of the month, the accountant makes a summarizing entry, debiting the accounts recorded on the petty cash vouchers and crediting Cash. For this month, she or he debits Delivery Expense for $14, debits other accounts for $29, and credits Cash for $43. By doing this, she or he officially journalizes the transactions so that they can be posted to the proper ledger accounts. The accountant then writes a check for $43 payable to Cash, cashes it, and has the secretary put the money in the drawer, bringing the fund back up to the original $50.

Some firms prefer to have a written record on one sheet of paper, so they keep a **petty cash payments record,** with columns in the Distribution of Payments section labeled with the types of expenditures they make most often.

East Phoenix Rental Equipment made the following payments from its petty cash fund during September.

Sep.   2 Paid $2 to Excell Delivery Service, voucher no. 1.
        3 Bought pencils and pens, $3.20, voucher no. 2.
        5 Paid local newspaper for advertising, $5, voucher no. 3.
        7 Paid for mailing packages, $2.90, voucher no. 4.
       10 Eugene L. Madison, the owner, withdrew $5 for personal use,
          voucher no. 5.
       14 Postage due on incoming mail, $.16, voucher no. 6.
       21 Bought typewriter ribbons, $4.10, voucher no. 7.
       22 Paid $3 to Excell Delivery Service, voucher no. 8.
       26 Paid for mailing packages, $3.80, voucher no. 9.
       27 Paid $3.50 to Fast Way Delivery, voucher no. 10.
       29 Bought memo pads, $4.40, voucher no. 11.
       29 Paid for collect telegram, $2.60, voucher no. 12.
       30 Paid $3.20 to Excell Delivery Service, voucher no. 13.
       30 Paid for having windows cleaned, $5, voucher no. 14.

East Phoenix Rental Equipment uses a petty cash payments record to keep track of the payments according to purpose. This is only a supplementary record, *not* a journal. It is merely used as a basis for compiling the journal entry to reimburse the fund. At the end of the month the accountant makes the summarizing entry in order to officially journalize the transactions that have taken place. He or she takes the information directly from the petty cash payments record (shown in Figure 8-11 on the next two pages). The T accounts and the journal entry are shown below on this page.

Note that in the summarizing entry the accountant debits the accounts on whose behalf the payments were made and credits the Cash account. He or she leaves the Petty Cash Fund strictly alone. Then the accountant cashes a check for $47.86 and puts the cash in the secretary's desk drawer, thereby restoring the amount in the Petty Cash Fund to the original $50.

GENERAL JOURNAL

PAGE _____

	DATE		DESCRIPTION	POST. REF.	DEBIT	CREDIT	
1	19– Sep.	30	Office Supplies		11 70		1
2			Delivery Expense		18 40		2
3			Miscellaneous Expense		7 76		3
4			Advertising Expense		5 00		4
5			Eugene L. Madison, Drawing		5 00		5
6			Cash			47 86	6
7			Reimbursed the petty cash fund.				7
8							8

Office Supplies

+	−
11.70	

Cash

+	−
	47.86

Delivery Expense

+	−
18.40	

Eugene L. Madison, Drawing

+	−
5.00	

Miscellaneous Expense

+	−
7.76	

Advertising Expense

+	−
5.00	

	DATE	VOU. NO.	EXPLANATION		PAYMEN
1	Sep.	1	Established fund, check no. 88, $50		
2		2 1	Excell Delivery Service		
3		3 2	Pencils and pens		
4		5 3	Local newspaper		
5		7 4	Postage for mailings		
6		10 5	Eugene L. Madison		
7		14 6	Postage on incoming mail		
8		21 7	Typewriter ribbons		
9		22 8	Excell Delivery Service		
10		26 9	Postage for mailings		
11		27 10	Fast Way Delivery		
12		29 11	Memo pads		
13		29 12	Collect telegram		
14		30 13	Excell Delivery Service		
15		30 14	Cleaning windows		
16		30	Totals		4
17			Balance in Fund	$ 2.14	
18			Reimbursed check no. 136	47.86	
19			Total	$50.00	
20					

THE CHANGE FUND

Anyone who has ever tried to pay for a small item by handing the clerk a $20 bill knows that a firm that carries out numerous cash transactions needs a **Change Fund.**

Establishing the Change Fund

Before setting up a change fund, one has to decide on two things: (1) how much money needs to be in the fund, and (2) what denominations of bills and coins are needed. Like the Petty Cash Fund, **the Change Fund is debited only once: when it is established.** It is left at the initial figure unless the person in charge decides to make it larger. The Change Fund account, like the Petty Cash account, is an asset. It is recorded in the balance sheet immediately below Cash. If the Petty Cash account is larger than the Change Fund account, it precedes the Change Fund.

Figure 8-11

PAGE __1__

	OFFICE SUPPLIES	DELIVERY EXPENSE	MISCELLANEOUS EXPENSE	SUNDRY ACCOUNT	SUNDRY AMOUNT	
DISTRIBUTION OF PAYMENTS						
1						1
2		2 00				2
3	3 20					3
4				Advertising Expense	5 00	4
5		2 90				5
6				E. L. Madison, Drawing	5 00	6
7			16			7
8	4 10					8
9		3 00				9
10		3 80				10
11		3 50				11
12	4 40					12
13			2 60			13
14		3 20				14
15			5 00			15
16	1 1 70	1 8 40	7 76		1 0 00	16
17						17
18						18
19						19
20						20

The owner of East Phoenix Rental Equipment, Mr. Madison, decides to establish a change fund; he decides this at the same time he sets up his petty cash fund. The entries for both transactions look like this.

Objective 5

Journalize the entries to establish a Change Fund.

GENERAL JOURNAL   PAGE _____

	DATE		DESCRIPTION	POST. REF.	DEBIT	CREDIT	
1	19— Sep.	1	Petty Cash Fund		5 0 00		1
2			Cash			5 0 00	2
3			Established a petty cash fund.				3
4							4
5		1	Change Fund		1 0 0 00		5
6			Cash			1 0 0 00	6
7			Established a change fund.				7
8							8

The T accounts for establishing the fund are as follows.

Change Fund		Cash	
+	−	+	−
100			100

So Madison cashes a check for $100 and gets the money in several denominations. He is now prepared to make change in any normal business transactions.

Depositing Cash

At the end of each business day, Madison deposits the cash taken in during the day, but he holds back the amount of the Change Fund, being sure that it's in convenient denominations.

When he makes up the Change Fund depends on what time his shop closes for the day and what time the bank closes. Let's say that on September 1, East Phoenix Rental Equipment has $325 on hand at the end of the day.

$325 Total cash count
− 100 Change fund
$225 New cash

The T accounts look like this.

Cash		Rental Income	
+	−	−	+
225			225

Madison records this in the journal as follows.

GENERAL JOURNAL						PAGE	

	DATE		DESCRIPTION	POST. REF.	DEBIT	CREDIT	
1	19– Sep.	1	Cash		2 2 5 00		1
2			Rental Income			2 2 5 00	2
3			To record revenue earned during				3
4			the day.				4
5							5

Now recall that the amount of the cash deposit is the total cash count less the amount of the Change Fund, so that's how the deposit happens to be $225. On another day the cash count is $327. So Madison deposits $227; the deposit is shown below.

	DATE		DESCRIPTION	POST. REF.	DEBIT	CREDIT	
			GENERAL JOURNAL			PAGE _____	
1	19– Sep.	9	Cash		2 2 7 00		1
2			Rental Income			2 2 7 00	2
3			To record revenue earned during				3
4			the day.				4
5							5

Some business firms label the Cash account *Cash in Bank* and label the Change Fund *Cash on Hand*.

CASH SHORT AND OVER

There is an inherent danger in making change: Human beings make mistakes, especially when there are many customers to be waited on or when the business is temporarily short-handed. Ideally, mistakes should be eliminated. However, because mistakes do happen, accounting records must be set up to cope with the situation. One reason that a business uses a cash register is to detect mistakes in the handling of cash. If, after removing the change fund, the day's receipts are less than the machine reading, then a cash shortage exists. Conversely, when the day's receipts are greater than the machine reading, a cash overage exists. Both shortages and overages are recorded in the same account, which is called Cash Short and Over. (The Cash Short and Over account may also be used to handle shortages and overages in the Petty Cash Fund.) Shortages are considered to be an expense of operating a business and, therefore, are recorded on the debit side of the account. Overages are treated as another form of revenue and so are recorded on the credit side of the account.

Objective 6

Journalize transactions involving Cash Short and Over.

For example, let's say that on September 14 East Phoenix Rental Equipment is faced with the following situation.

Cash Register Tape	Cash Count	Amount of the Change Fund
$281	$378	$100

After deducting the $100 in the Change Fund, Madison will deposit $278. Note that this amount is less than the amount indicated by the cash register; therefore, a cash shortage exists. The following T accounts show how Madison entered this transaction into the books.

Cash		Rental Income		Cash Short and Over	
+	−	−	+		
278			281	3	

The next day, September 15, the pendulum happens to swing in the other direction.

Cash Register Tape	Cash Count	Amount of the Change Fund
$356	$457	$100

The amount to be deposited is $357 ($457 − $100). This figure is $1 greater than the $356 in rental income indicated by the cash register tape. Thus, there is a $1 cash overage on this occasion. The analysis of this transaction is shown below in T accounts.

Cash		Rental Income		Cash Short and Over	
+	−	−	+		
357			356		1

Now let's summarize our discussion of the Cash Short and Over account by drawing these conclusions from the illustration.

1. At the close of the business day, the firm deposits the total day's receipts, holding back the Change Fund.
2. The firm records its rental income as being the amount shown on the cash register tape.
3. If the amount of cash actually received disagrees with the record of receipts, Cash Short and Over takes up the difference. In the first situation just described, there was a shortage of $3, so there was a debit to Cash Short and Over. In the second situation, there was an overage of $1, so there was a credit to Cash Short and Over. It is apparent that as a result of these transactions the account looks like this.

Cash Short and Over	
Shortage 3	Overage 1

East Phoenix Rental Equipment's revenue for September 14 and 15 is recorded in the general journal (Figure 8-12) as follows:

Figure 8-12

GENERAL JOURNAL

PAGE _____

	DATE		DESCRIPTION	POST. REF.	DEBIT	CREDIT	
1	19– Sep.	14	Cash		2 7 8 00		1
2			Cash Short and Over		3 00		2
3			Rental Income			2 8 1 00	3
4			To record revenue earned during				4
5			the day involving a cash				5
6			shortage of $3.00.				6
7							7
8		15	Cash		3 5 7 00		8
9			Rental Income			3 5 6 00	9
10			Cash Short and Over			1 00	10
11			To record revenue earned during				11
12			the day involving a cash				12
13			overage of $1.00.				13
14							14

As far as errors are concerned, one would think that shortages would be offset by overages. However, customers receiving change are more likely to report shortages than overages. Consequently, to the firm shortages predominate. A firm may set a tolerance level for the cashiers. If the shortages consistently exceed the level of tolerance, either fraud is considered or somebody is making entirely too many careless mistakes.

Throughout any fiscal period, the accountant must continually record shortages and overages in the Cash Short and Over account. Let's say that East Phoenix's final balance is $21 on the debit side. East Phoenix winds up with a net shortage of $21.

At the end of the fiscal period, if the account has a debit balance or net shortage, the accountant classifies it as an expense and puts it in the income statement under Miscellaneous Expense. The T account would look like this.

Cash Short and Over

Short		Over	
	3		1
	4		1
	3		2
	7		2
	5		1
	2		2
	3		1
	4		10
	31		
Bal. 21			

Conversely, if the account has a credit balance or net overage, the accountant classifies it as a revenue account and puts it in the income statement under Miscellaneous Income. This is an exception to the policy of recording accounts under their exact account title in financial statements. Rather than attaching plus and minus signs to the Cash Short and Over account immediately, we wait until we find out its final balance.

GLOSSARY

ABA number The number assigned by the American Bankers Association to a given bank. The first part of the numerator denotes the city or state in which the bank is located; the second part denotes the bank on which the check is drawn. The denominator indicates the Federal Reserve District and the routing number used by the Federal Reserve Bank.

Bank reconciliation A process by which an accountant determines whether there is a difference between the balance shown on the bank statement and the balance of the Cash account in the firm's general ledger. The object is to determine the adjusted (or true) balance of the Cash account.

Bank statement Periodic statement that a bank sends to the holder of a checking account listing deposits received and checks paid by the bank, as well as debit and credit memorandums.

Book balance The balance of the Cash account in the general ledger before it is reconciled with the bank statement.

Canceled checks Checks issued by the depositor that have been paid by the bank and listed on the bank statement. They are called canceled checks because they are canceled by a stamp or perforation, indicating that they have been paid.

Cash fund Sums of money set aside for specific purposes.

Change fund A cash fund used by a firm to make change for customers who pay cash for goods or services.

Check writer A machine used to imprint the amount in figures and words on the check itself.

Denominations Varieties of currency and coins, such as $5 bills, $1 bills, quarters, dimes, and nickels.

Deposit in transit A deposit not recorded on the bank statement because the deposit was made between the time of the bank's closing date for compiling items for its statement and the time the statement is received by the depositor; also known as a *late deposit*.

Deposit slips Printed forms provided by a bank so that a customer can list all items being deposited; also known as a *deposit ticket*.

Endorsement The process by which the payee transfers ownership of the check to a bank or another party. A check must be endorsed when deposited in a bank because the bank must have legal title to it in order to collect payment from the drawer of the check (the person or firm who wrote the check). In case the check cannot be collected, the endorser guarantees all subsequent holders (*Exception:* an endorsement "without recourse").

MICR Magnetic ink character recognition; the script the bank uses to print the number of the depositor's account and the bank's number at the bottom of checks and deposit slips. The bank also prints the amount of the check in MICR when the check is deposited. A number written in this script can be read by electronic equipment used by banks in clearing checks.

NSF check A check drawn against an account in which there are *Not Sufficient Funds:* this check is returned by the depositor's bank to the drawer's bank because of nonpayment; also known as a *dishonored check.*

Outstanding checks Checks that have been issued by the depositor and deducted on his or her records but have not reached the bank for payment and deduction by the time the bank issues its statement.

Payee The person to whom a check is payable.

Petty Cash Fund A cash fund used to make small immediate cash payments.

Petty cash payments record A record indicating the amount of each petty cash voucher and the accounts to which they should be charged.

Petty cash voucher A form stating who got what from the Petty Cash Fund, signed by (1) the person in charge of the fund, and (2) the person who received the cash.

Restrictive endorsement An endorsement, such as "Pay to the order of (name of bank), for deposit only," that limits further negotiation of a check. It forces the check's deposit, since the endorsement is not valid for any other purpose.

Service charge The fee the bank charges for handling checks, collections, and other items. It is in the form of a debit memorandum.

Signature card The form a depositor signs to give the bank a sample of his or her signature. The bank uses it to verify the depositor's signature on checks, on cash items that he or she may endorse for deposit, and on other business papers that he or she may present to the bank.

QUESTIONS, EXERCISES, AND PROBLEMS

Discussion Questions

1. What is the purpose of a signature card?
2. What is the purpose of a bank reconciliation?
3. Indicate whether the following items in a bank reconciliation should be (a) added to the cash account balance, (b) deducted from the cash account balance, (c) added to the bank statement balance, (d) deducted from the bank statement balance.

- Deposit in transit
- NSF check
- Outstanding check
- Bank error charging the firm's account with another company's check

4. Describe in order the steps in reconciling a bank statement.
5. Explain the purpose of a petty cash fund. Describe the entries to establish and reimburse the fund.

6. What is the purpose of a petty cash payments record?
7. What does a debit balance in Cash Short and Over represent? Where does it appear in the financial statements? What does a credit balance in Cash Short and Over represent? Where does it appear in the financial statements?

Exercises

Exercise 8-1 Tiny's Restaurant deposits all receipts in the bank on the day received and makes all payments by check. On September 30, the Cash account showed a balance of $443 after all posting was completed. The bank statement received on September 30 had an ending balance of $301. Prepare a bank reconciliation, using the following information, and record the necessary entries in general journal form.

a. The bank included with the September canceled checks a $2 debit memorandum for service charges.
b. Outstanding checks, $194.
c. The September 30 cash receipts, $316, were placed in the bank's night depository after banking hours on that date and were not listed on the bank statement.
d. Check no. 928, returned with the canceled checks, was correctly drawn for $31 in payment of the electric bill and was paid by the bank on September 16, but it had been erroneously recorded in the checkbook and debited to the Utilities Expense account as though it were $13.

Exercise 8-2 The Hinman Company made the following bank reconciliation on April 30 of this year. Record the necessary entries in general journal form.

Bank Reconciliation

Bank Statement Balance		$1,856.00
Add deposit of April 30		145.00
		$2,001.00
Deduct outstanding checks		
No. 191	$200.00	
No. 192	150.00	350.00
Adjusted Balance		$1,651.00
Book Balance of Cash		$1,380.00
Add proceeds of note collected		300.00
		$1,680.00
Deduct: NSF check of Thomas Baxter	$ 27.00	
Collection charge for note	2.00	29.00
Adjusted Balance		$1,651.00

Exercise 8-3   Identify each of the following reconciling items as: (1) an addition to the bank statement balance, (2) a deduction from the bank statement balance, (3) an addition to the book balance of cash, (4) a deduction from the book balance of cash. (None of the transactions reported by bank debit and credit memorandums have been recorded by the depositor.)

a. Check for $100 charged by bank as $1,000.
b. Deposit in transit, $673.15.
c. Outstanding checks, $617.23.
d. Note collected by bank, $525.
e. Check of a customer returned by bank to depositor because of insufficient funds, $31.
f. Bank service charge, $9.20.
g. Check drawn by depositor for $23 but recorded in the checkbook and Cash account as $32.

Exercise 8-4   Make entries in general journal form to record the following.

a. Established a Petty Cash Fund, $80.
b. Reimbursed the Petty Cash Fund for expenditures of $69: store supplies, $21; office supplies, $18; miscellaneous expense, $30.

Exercise 8-5   Make entries in general journal form to record the following.

a. Established a Change Fund, $250.
b. Record the cash sales for the day; the cash in the cash register is $862.

Exercise 8-6   The cash register tape for today indicates $961.16 as sales for the day. The cash count, including a $200 Change Fund, is $1,160.22. Make entries to record how much cash you will deposit in the bank today.

Exercise 8-7   Describe the nature of the entries that have been posted to the following accounts after the Change Fund was established.

Change Fund		Sales		Cash		Cash Short and Over	
Bal. 200			946	944		2	1
			998	999		3	
			1,069	1,066			

Exercise 8-8   The Vaughn Company's Cash account shows a balance of $6,978 as of October 31 of this year. The balance on the bank statement on that date is $10,127.04. Checks for $123, $1,062, and $221.20 are outstanding. The bank statement shows a charge for a check made out by another depositor for $250. The statement also shows a credit of $2,000 for a customer's note that had been left with the bank for collection. Service charges for the month were $7.16. What is the true balance of cash as of October 31?

Problem Set A

Problem 8-1A Marge's Clothes and Things deposits all receipts in the bank and makes all payments by check. On September 30 its Cash in Bank account has a balance of $3,073.60. The bank statement on September 30 shows a balance of $3,321.29. You are given the following information with which to reconcile the bank statement.

a. The reconciliation for August, the previous month, showed three checks outstanding on August 31: no. 786 for $71.50, no. 789 for $117.60, and no. 790 for $49.43. Checks no. 786 and 789 were returned with the September bank statement; however, check no. 790 was not returned.
b. A deposit of $398.36 was placed in the night depository on September 30 and did not appear on the bank statement.
c. Checks no. 801 for $31, no. 803 for $18.40, no. 804 for $103, and no. 805 for $15.62 were written during September but were not returned by the bank.
d. A bank debit memo for service charges, $2.40.
e. A bank credit memo for collection of a note signed by Franklin C. Hough, $404, including $400 principal and $4 interest.
f. You compare the canceled checks with the entries in the check register and find that check no. 797 for $69 was written correctly, payable to M. E. Francis, the owner, for her personal use. However, the check was recorded in the checkbook as $96.

Instructions

1. Prepare a bank reconciliation.
2. Journalize the necessary entries in general journal form, assuming that the debit and credit memos have not been recorded.

Problem 8-2A On April 1 of this year, the Nordic Ski Shop established a Petty Cash Fund, and the following petty cash transactions took place during the month.

Apr. 1 Cashed check no. 1116 for $60 to establish a Petty Cash Fund and put the $60 in a locked drawer in the office.
4 Issued voucher no. 1 for telegram, $3 (Miscellaneous Expense).
7 Issued voucher no. 2 for typewriter ribbons, $4.90.
9 Paid $4.50 for an advertisement in college basketball program, voucher no. 3.
16 Bought postage stamps, $4, voucher no. 4 (Office Supplies).
20 Paid $4.90 to have snow removed from sidewalk in front of store, voucher no. 5 (Miscellaneous Expense).
25 Issued voucher no. 6 for delivery charge on outgoing merchandise, $2.40.
28 L. R. Francis, the owner, withdrew $5 for personal use, voucher no. 7.
29 Paid $1.60 for telegram, voucher no. 8.

Apr.   30 Paid Reliable Delivery Service $4.20 for delivery charges on outgo-
ing merchandise, voucher no. 9.
        30 Issued and cashed check no. 1304 for $34.50 to reimburse Petty
Cash Fund.

Instructions

1. Journalize the entry establishing the Petty Cash Fund in the general
journal.
2. Record the disbursements of petty cash in the petty cash payments record.
3. Journalize the summarizing entry to reimburse the Petty Cash Fund.

Problem 8-3A   During May of this year, the Eastside Cycle Shop has the
following transactions involving its Change Fund, its Cash Short and Over
account, and its cash sales.

May   1 Established a Change Fund, $200, check no. 714.
        6 Recorded cash sales for the week: cash register tape, $1,291; cash
count, $1,490.25.
        13 Recorded cash sales for the week: cash register tape, $1,424.30;
cash count, $1,622.10.
        20 Recorded cash sales for the week: cash register tape, $1,378.25;
cash count, $1,579.15.
        31 Recorded cash sales for the week: cash register tape, $1,813.28;
cash count, $2,009.74.

Instructions

1. Record the entry establishing the Change Fund in the general journal.
2. Record the cash sales in the general journal. (In making deposits, the firm
holds back the amount of the Change Fund.)
3. Post the appropriate entries to the Cash Short and Over ledger account.
Where will the balance of this account appear in the income statement?

Problem 8-4A   On July 31, Riverside Inn receives its bank statement (next
page). The company deposits its receipts in the bank and makes all payments
by check. The debit memo is for a $37 NSF check written by Thomas R. Beeler.
The other debit memo is for a service charge.

The balance of the Cash account as of July 31 is $1,446.82. Outstanding
checks as of July 31 are: no. 1631, $110; no. 1632, $71.19; no. 1633, $163.20.
The accountant notes a deposit of $165.69 that did not appear on the bank
statement.

Instructions

1. Prepare a bank reconciliation as of July 31.
2. Journalize the necessary entries, assuming that the debit memos have not
been recorded.
3. Complete the bank form to determine the adjusted balance of cash.

STANDARD NATIONAL BANK

Riverside Inn
8619 East Castle Blvd.
Chicago, Illinois 60611

ACCOUNT NO.: *761-142-786*
STATEMENT DATE: *July 31, 19–*

Checks and Other Debits		Deposits	Date		Balance
	Balance Brought Forward		*July*	*1*	*1,163 16*
72 50	*167 00*	*491 50*		*3*	*1,415 16*
137 20				*5*	*1,277 96*
236 25	*159 89*	*415 72*		*6*	*1,297 54*
120 00				*8*	*1,177 54*
429 60		*439 16*		*9*	*1,187 10*
		378 20		*11*	*1,565 30*
37 40	*38 49*			*12*	*1,489 41*
		291 76		*15*	*1,781 17*
182 71	*368 70*			*17*	*1,229 76*
96 87		*142 90*		*18*	*1,275 79*
DM 37 00				*22*	*1,238 79*
19 20				*25*	*1,219 59*
DM 3 10		*368 93*		*28*	*1,585 42*

PLEASE EXAMINE THIS STATEMENT CAREFULLY. REPORT ANY POSSIBLE ERRORS IN 10 DAYS.

CODE SYMBOLS

CM	Credit Memo	OD	Overdraft
DM	Debit Memo	SC	Service Charge
EC	Error Correction		

Problem Set B

Problem 8-1B Hagen's Western Store deposits all receipts in the bank each evening and makes all payments by check. On November 30 its Cash in Bank account has a balance of $1,967.65. The bank statement of November 30 shows a balance of $1,920.25. The following information pertains to reconciling the bank statement.

a. The reconciliation for October, the previous month, showed three checks outstanding on October 31: no. 1416 for $85, no. 1419 for $76.50, and no. 1420 for $126. Checks no. 1416 and 1420 were returned with the November bank statement; however, check no. 1419 was not returned.

b. Checks no. 1499 for $39, no. 1516 for $21.60, no. 1517 for $101.50, and no. 1518 for $17 were written during November and have not been returned by the bank.

c. A deposit of $410 was placed in the night depository on November 30 and did not appear on the bank statement.

d. The canceled checks were compared with the entries in the check register, and it was observed that check no. 1487, for $78, was written correctly, payable to C. T. Melton, the owner, for personal use, but was recorded in the checkbook as $87.

e. A bank debit memo for service charges, $3.

f. A bank credit memo for collection of a note signed by T. R. Salmon, $101, including $100 principal and $1 interest.

Instructions

1. Prepare a bank reconciliation.
2. Journalize the necessary entries in general journal form, assuming that the debit and credit memos have not been recorded.

Problem 8-2B On March 1 of this year, Bolen Janitorial Supply Company established a Petty Cash Fund. The following petty cash transactions took place during the month.

Mar. 1 Cashed check no. 956 for $50 to establish a Petty Cash Fund and put the $50 in a locked drawer in the office.
      3 Bought postage stamps, $4, voucher no. 1 (Office Supplies).
      4 Issued voucher no. 2 for telegram, $2 (Miscellaneous Expense).
      6 Issued voucher no. 3 for delivery charges on outgoing merchandise, $5.
      9 B. W. Bolen withdrew $4.50 for personal use, voucher no. 4.
     13 Bought postage stamps, $5, voucher no. 5.
     19 Bought pens for office, $4.90, voucher no. 6.
     23 Paid $3 for trash removal, voucher no. 7 (Miscellaneous Expense).
     28 Paid $5 for window cleaning service, voucher no. 8.
     29 Paid $1.50 for telegram, voucher no. 9.
     31 Issued and cashed check no. 1098 for $34.90 to reimburse Petty Cash Fund.

Instructions

1. Journalize the entry establishing the Petty Cash Fund in the general journal.
2. Record the disbursements of petty cash in the petty cash payments record.
3. Journalize the summarizing entry to reimburse the Petty Cash Fund.

Problem 8-3B Henry's Drive-In made the following transactions during July involving its Change Fund, its Cash Short and Over account, and its cash sales.

Jul. 1 Established a Change Fund, $300, check no. 986.
      7 Recorded cash sales for the week: cash register tape, $1,546; cash count, $1,842.35.
     14 Recorded cash sales for the week: cash register tape, $1,214.10; cash count, $1,511.
     21 Recorded cash sales for the week: cash register tape, $1,482; cash count, $1,783.25.

31 Recorded cash sales for the remainder of the month: cash register
tape, $1,892; cash count, $2,188.50.

Instructions

1. Record the entry establishing the Change Fund in the general journal.
2. Record the cash sales in the general journal. (In making bank deposits, the
   firm holds back the amount of the Change Fund.)
3. Post the appropriate entries to the Cash Short and Over ledger account.
   Where will the balance of this account appear in the income statement?

Problem 8-4B On August 31, Frank's Auto Repair receives its bank statement (next page). The company deposits its receipts in the bank and makes all payments by check. The debit memo for $49 is for an NSF check written by D. Carter. The debit memo for $2 is for a service charge.

The balance of the Cash account as of August 31 is $1,247. Outstanding checks as of August 31 are: no. 928, $119; no. 929, $243. The accountant notes a deposit of $224 that did not appear on the bank statement.

Instructions

1. Prepare a bank reconciliation as of August 31.
2. Journalize the necessary entries, assuming that the debit memos have not
   been recorded.
3. Complete the bank form to determine the adjusted balance of cash.

PARAMOUNT NATIONAL BANK

Frank's Auto Repair
3152 East Senegal Ave.
Toledo, Ohio 44366

ACCOUNT NO.: *168-652-219*

STATEMENT DATE: *August 31, 19–*

CHECKS AND OTHER DEBITS				DEPOSITS		DATE		BALANCE	
		BALANCE BROUGHT FORWARD				Aug.	1	972	00
				326	00		2	1298	00
172	00	76	00				4	1050	00
146	00			412	00		5	1316	00
206	00	139	00				7	971	00
200	00						8	771	00
621	00			437	00		9	587	00
				368	00		14	955	00
37	00	14	00				17	904	00
				419	00		18	1323	00
533	00						23	790	00
				398	00		24	1188	00
94	00			291	00		28	1385	00
DM 49	00	DM 2	00				31	1334	00

PLEASE EXAMINE THIS STATEMENT CAREFULLY. REPORT ANY POSSIBLE ERRORS IN 10 DAYS.

CODE SYMBOLS

CM	Credit Memo	OD	Overdraft
DM	Debit Memo	SC	Service Charge
EC	Error Correction		

9 Payroll Accounting: Employee Earnings and Deductions

Learning Objectives

After you have completed this chapter, you will be able to do the following:

1. Calculate total earnings based on an hourly, piece-rate, or commission basis.

2. Determine deductions from tables of employees' income tax withholding.

3. Complete a payroll register.

4. Journalize the payroll entry from a payroll register.

5. Maintain employees' individual earnings records.

Up to now, we've been recording employees' wages as a debit to Salaries or Wages Expense and a credit to Cash, but we've really been talking only about **gross pay.** We haven't said a word about the various deductions that we all know are taken out of our gross pay before we get to the **net pay** or take-home pay. In this chapter we'll be talking about types and amounts of deductions and how to enter them in payroll records, as well as journal entries for recording the payroll and paying the employees.

OBJECTIVES OF PAYROLL RECORDS AND ACCOUNTING

There are two primary reasons for maintaining accurate payroll records. First, we must collect the necessary data to compute the compensation for each employee for each payroll period.

Second, we must provide information needed to complete the various government reports—federal and state—that are required of all employers. All business enterprises, both large and small, are required by law to withhold certain amounts from employees' pay for taxes, to make payments to government agencies by specified deadlines, and to submit reports on official forms. Because governments impose penalties if the requirements are not met, employers are vitally concerned with payroll accounting. Anyone going into accounting, or involved with the management of any business, should be thoroughly acquainted with payroll accounting.

EMPLOYER/EMPLOYEE RELATIONSHIPS

Payroll accounting is concerned only with employees and their compensations, withholdings, records, reports, and taxes. *Note:* There is a distinction between an employee and an independent contractor. An **employee** is one who is under the direction and control of the employer, such as a secretary, bookkeeper, sales clerk, vice president, controller, and so on. An **independent contractor,** on the other hand, is someone who is engaged for a definite job or service who may choose her or his own means of doing the work (*examples:* an appliance repair person, a plumber, a CPA firm). Payments made to independent contractors are in the form of fees or charges. Independent contractors submit bills or invoices for the work they do. The invoice is paid in a lump sum and is not subject to any withholding or payroll taxes.

LAWS AFFECTING COMPENSATION OF EMPLOYEES

Both federal and state laws require the employer to act as a collecting agent and deduct specified amounts from employees' gross earnings. The employer sends the withholdings to the appropriate government agencies, along with reports substantiating the figures. In addition, certain payroll taxes, based on the total wages paid to employees, are levied on the employer. Let's look at some of the more important laws that pertain to compensation of employees.

Federal Income Tax Withholding

The **Current Tax Payment Act** requires employers not only to withhold the tax and then pay it to the Internal Revenue Service, but also to keep records of the names and addresses of persons employed, their earnings and withholdings, and the amounts and dates of payment. The employer has to submit reports to the Internal Revenue Service on a quarterly basis (Form 941) and to the employee on an annual basis (W-2 form). With few exceptions, this requirement applies to employers of one or more persons. We'll discuss these reports and the related deposits in Chapter 10.

Federal Insurance Contributions Act (FICA)

This act, passed in 1935, provides for retirement pensions after a worker reaches age 62, disability benefits for any worker who becomes disabled (and for her or his dependents), and a health insurance program or Medicare after age 65. Both the employee and the employer have to pay **FICA taxes,** which are commonly referred to as Social Security taxes. The employer withholds FICA taxes from employees' wages and pays them to the Internal Revenue Service. The employer has to match the amount of FICA tax withheld from the employees' wages, and the employer's share is recorded under Payroll Tax Expense. We'll cover this in Chapter 10, as our concern here is with employees' deductions.

FICA tax rates apply to the gross earnings of an employee during the calendar year. After an employee has paid FICA tax on the maximum taxable earnings, the employer stops deducting FICA tax until the next calendar year begins. Congress has frequently changed the schedule of rates and taxable incomes. A rate of 7.1 percent applied to earnings up to $36,000, or a maximum of $2,556, will be assumed and used in this text for the examples and the problems. (Future changes in FICA tax rates are already on the books: 1985, 7.05 percent; 1986, 7.15 percent; 1988, 7.51

percent; 1990, 7.65 percent. The earnings base will increase automatically with growth in average earnings.)

The employer is required to keep records of the following information.

1. **Personal data on employee**   Name, address, Social Security number, date of birth
2. **Data on wage payments**   Dates and amounts of payments, and payroll periods
3. **Amount of taxable wages paid**   Total amount earned so far during the year
4. **Amount of tax withheld from each employee's earnings**

Every three months the employer has to submit reports to the Internal Revenue Service, recording the information on Form 941, the same form that is used to report the income tax withheld. The employer's payment to the Internal Revenue Service consists of (1) the employee's share of the FICA tax, (2) the employer's matching portion of the FICA tax, and (3) the employee's income tax withheld. We'll talk about this in detail in Chapter 10.

Fair Labor Standards Act

The **Fair Labor Standards Act (Wages and Hours Law)** specifies that employers engaged in interstate commerce must pay their employees overtime at the rate of 1½ times the regular rate (time-and-a-half) for hours worked in excess of 40 per week. Frequently, union contracts stipulate additional overtime pay for work performed on Sundays and holidays. The act provides that certain management and supervisory employees are exempt from its regulations—these exempt employees are usually referred to as salaried personnel.

Federal Unemployment Tax Act (FUTA)

The purpose of the Federal Unemployment Tax Act is to provide financial support for the maintenance of government-run employment offices throughout the country. **FUTA taxes** are paid by employers only.

The federal unemployment tax is based on the total earnings of each employee during the calendar year. Congress has frequently changed the rates and the taxable income base.

For the examples and problems in this text, we will assume that employers pay an effective federal unemployment tax rate of .8 percent (.008) of the first $7,000 of earnings of each employee during the calendar year (January 1 through December 31).

Reports to the federal government (Form 940) must be submitted annually. We'll discuss these reports in Chapter 10.

State Unemployment Taxes

Each state is responsible for paying its own unemployment compensation benefits. The revenue provided by **state unemployment taxes** is used exclusively for this purpose. However, there is considerable variation among the states concerning the tax rates and the amount of taxable income. The minimum tax rate levied by any state is 2.7 percent based on the taxable income stipulated in the Federal Unemployment Tax Act. States require employers to file reports on a quarterly, or three-month, basis, listing employees' names, amount of wages paid to each employee, and a computation of the unemployment tax. We'll discuss these reports in Chapter 10.

Our example of payroll accounting deals with the firm of Harding and Associates. This business is located in the state of Washington, which has an assumed unemployment tax rate of 3 percent on the first $12,000 of wages paid to each employee during the calendar year (January 1 through December 31). This tax is paid by employers only.

Workers' Compensation Laws

Workers' compensation laws protect employees and their dependents against losses due to death or injury incurred on the job. Most states require employers either to contribute to a state compensation insurance fund or to buy similar insurance from a private insurance company. The employer ordinarily pays the cost of the insurance premiums. The premium rates vary according to the degree of danger inherent in each job category and the employer's number of accidents. The employer has to keep records of job descriptions and classifications, as well as claims of insured persons.

State and City Income Taxes

Besides requiring employers to deduct money from employees' earnings for federal income taxes, two-thirds of the states require employers to deduct money to pay state income taxes. A number of cities also require withholding for *city* income taxes. When these laws are in effect, the employer handles the reporting and payments in much the same way as for federal income taxes. Separate liability accounts may be set up for employees' state and city income taxes withheld.

HOW EMPLOYEES GET PAID

Employees may be paid a salary or wages, depending on the type of work and the period of time covered. Money paid to a person for managerial or administrative services is usually called a salary, and the time period covered is generally a month or a year. Money paid for either skilled or unskilled labor is usually called wages, and the time period covered is hours or weeks. Wages may also be paid on a piecework basis. In practice, the words *salaries* and *wages* are somewhat interchangeable. A company may supplement an employee's salary or wage by commissions, bonuses, cost-of-living adjustments, and profit-sharing plans. As a rule, employees are paid by check or in cash. However, their compensation may take the form of merchandise, lodging, meals, or other property as well. When the compensation is in these forms, one has to determine the fair value of property or service given in payment for an employee's labor.

Calculating Total Earnings

When compensation is based on the amount of time worked, the accountant of course has to have a record of the number of hours worked by each employee. When there are only a few employees, this can be accomplished by means of a book record. When there are many employees, time clocks are the traditional method. Nowadays, for computer-operated time-keeping systems, employers use punched cards.

Objective 1

Calculate total earnings based on an hourly, piece-rate, or commission basis.

Wages

Let's take the case of Graham C. Laboe, who works for Harding and Associates. His regular rate of pay is $12 per hour. The company pays time-and-a-half for hours worked in excess of 40. In addition, it pays him double time for any work he does on Sundays and holidays. Laboe has a ½-hour lunch break during an 8½-hour day. He is not paid for the lunch break. His time card for the week is shown in Figure 9-1.

Laboe's gross wages can be computed by one of two methods. The first method works like this:

40 hours at straight time	40 × $12 per hour = $480
2 hours overtime on Thursday	2 × $18 per hour = 36
1 hour overtime on Friday	1 × $18 per hour = 18
5 hours overtime on Saturday	5 × $18 per hour = 90
4 hours overtime on Sunday	4 × $24 per hour = 96
Total gross wages	$720

Figure 9-1

TIME CARD

Name   _Laboe, Graham C._

Week ending _Nov. 7, 19–_

Day	In	Out	In	Out	Hours Worked	
					Regular	Overtime
M	7^{57}	12^{00}	12^{30}	4^{32}	8	
T	7^{56}	12^{06}	12^{36}	4^{37}	8	
W	7^{57}	12^{02}	12^{31}	4^{31}	8	
T	8^{00}	12^{11}	12^{40}	6^{32}	8	2
F	8^{00}	12^{03}	12^{33}	5^{33}	8	1
S	7^{59}	1^{02}				5
S	7^{55}	12^{04}				4

The second method of calculating gross wages is often used when machine accounting is involved.

52 hours at straight time: 52 × $12 per hour = $624
Overtime premium:

8 hours × $ 6 per hour premium = $48	
4 hours × $12 per hour premium = $\underline{48}$	
Total overtime premium	$\underline{96}$
Total gross wages	$\underline{\underline{\$720}}$

Salaries

Employees who are paid a regular salary may also be entitled to premium pay for overtime. It is necessary to figure out their regular hourly rate of pay before you can determine their overtime rate. Let's consider the case of Donna Garcia, who gets a salary of $1,872 per month. She is entitled to overtime pay for all hours worked in excess of 40 during a week at the rate of 1½ times her regular hourly rate. This past week she worked 44 hours, so we calculate her overtime pay as follows.

$1,872 per month × 12 months = $22,464 per year
$22,464 per year ÷ 52 weeks = $432 per week
$432 per week ÷ 40 hours = $10.80 per regular hour

Earnings for 44 hours:
40 hours at straight time   40 × $10.80 = $432.00
 4 hours overtime   4 × $16.20 =   64.80
Total gross earnings $496.80

Piece Rate

Workers under the piece-rate system are paid at the rate of so much per unit of production. For example, Peter Ryan, an apple picker, gets paid $8 for picking a bin of apples. If he picks 6 bins during the day, his total earnings are 6 × $8 = $48.

Commissions and Bonuses

Some salespersons are paid on a purely commission basis. However, a more common arrangement is a salary plus a commission or bonus. Assume that Rosie Perkins receives an annual salary of $9,600. Her employer agrees to pay her a 6 percent commission on all sales during the year in excess of $120,000. Her sales for the year total $210,000. Her bonus amounts to $90,000 × .06 = $5,400. Therefore her total earnings are $9,600 + $5,400 = $15,000.

DEDUCTIONS FROM TOTAL EARNINGS

Anyone who has ever earned a paycheck has encountered some of the many types of deductions that account for the shrinkage. The most usual deductions are due to the following.

1. Federal income tax withholding
2. State income tax withholding
3. FICA tax (Social Security), employee's share
4. Purchase of U.S. savings bonds
5. Union dues
6. Medical and life insurance premiums
7. Contributions to a charitable organization
8. Repayment of personal loans from the company credit union
9. Savings through the company credit union

Employees' Federal Income Tax Withholding

The amount of federal income tax withheld from an employee's wages depends on the amount of her or his total earnings and the number of exemptions claimed. An **exemption** is the amount of an individual's earnings that is exempt from income taxes (nontaxable). An employee is entitled to one personal exemption, plus an additional exemption if he or she is over 65 or blind, and an exemption for each dependent. Each employee has to fill out an **Employee's Withholding Allowance Certificate (Form W-4),** shown in Figure 9-2.

The employer retains this form, as authorization to withhold money for the employee's federal income tax.

For convenience, most employers use the wage-bracket withholding tables in *Circular E, Employer's Tax Guide,* an Internal Revenue Service publication, to determine the amount of federal tax to be withheld for each employee. These tables cover monthly, semimonthly, biweekly, weekly, and daily payroll periods; they are also subdivided on the basis of married and unmarried persons.

In order to determine the tax to be withheld from an employee's gross wages, first locate the wage bracket in the first two columns of the table. Next, find the column for the number of exemptions claimed and read down this column until you get to the wage-bracket line. A portion of the weekly federal income tax withholding table for married persons is reproduced in Figure 9-3.

Assume that Graham C. Laboe, who claims three exemptions, has $720 gross wages for the week. At first sight, it appears that $720 could fall in

Objective 2

Determine deductions from tables of employees' income tax withholding.

Figure 9-2

Form **W-4**	Department of the Treasury—Internal Revenue Service **Employee's Withholding Allowance Certificate**	OMB No. 1545-0010

| **1** Type or print your full name Graham C. Laboe | **2** Your social security number 543–24–1680 |

| Home address (number and street or rural route) 1582 North Pierce Street City or town, State, and ZIP code Spokane, WA 99204 | **3** Marital Status | ☐ Single ☒ Married ☐ Married, but withhold at higher Single rate **Note:** If married, but legally separated, or spouse is a nonresident alien, check the Single box. |

4 Total number of allowances you are claiming (from line F of the worksheet on page 2) 3

5 Additional amount, if any, you want deducted from each pay . . . . $

6 I claim exemption from withholding because (see instructions and check boxes below that apply):

  a ☐ Last year I did not owe any Federal income tax and had a right to a full refund of **ALL** income tax withheld, **AND**

  b ☐ This year I do not expect to owe any Federal income tax and expect to have a right to a full refund of

    ALL income tax withheld. If both a and b apply, enter the year effective and ''EXEMPT'' here . . . ▶   Year

  c   If you entered ''EXEMPT'' on line 6b, are you a full-time student? . . . . ☐Yes ☐No

Under penalties of perjury, I certify that I am entitled to the number of withholding allowances claimed on this certificate, or if claiming exemption from withholding, that I am entitled to claim the exempt status

Employee's signature ▶ *Graham C. Laboe.*   Date ▶ February 1   , 19 --

7 Employer's name and address (**Employer: Complete 7, 8, and 9 only if sending to IRS**) | **8** Office code | **9** Employer identification number

MARRIED Persons—WEEKLY Payroll Period

And the wages are—		And the number of withholding allowances claimed is—										
At least	But less than	0	1	2	3	4	5	6	7	8	9	10 or more
		The amount of income tax to be withheld shall be—										
$310	$320	$42.70	$39.10	$35.40	$31.80	$28.10	$24.80	$21.70	$18.70	$15.60	$12.50	$9.40
320	330	44.60	41.00	37.30	33.70	30.00	26.40	23.30	20.30	17.20	14.10	11.00
330	340	46.50	42.90	39.20	35.60	31.90	28.30	24.90	21.90	18.80	15.70	12.60
340	350	48.40	44.80	41.10	37.50	33.80	30.20	26.50	23.50	20.40	17.30	14.20
350	360	50.30	46.70	43.00	39.40	35.70	32.10	28.40	25.10	22.00	18.90	15.80
360	370	52.70	48.60	44.90	41.30	37.60	34.00	30.30	26.70	23.60	20.50	17.40
370	380	55.10	50.50	46.80	43.20	39.50	35.90	32.20	28.60	25.20	22.10	19.00
380	390	57.50	52.80	48.70	45.10	41.40	37.80	34.10	30.50	26.80	23.70	20.60
390	400	59.90	55.20	50.60	47.00	43.30	39.70	36.00	32.40	28.70	25.30	22.20
400	410	62.30	57.60	53.00	48.90	45.20	41.60	37.90	34.30	30.60	26.90	23.80
410	420	64.70	60.00	55.40	50.80	47.10	43.50	39.80	36.20	32.50	28.80	25.40
420	430	67.10	62.40	57.80	53.20	49.00	45.40	41.70	38.10	34.40	30.70	27.10
430	440	69.50	64.80	60.20	55.60	51.00	47.30	43.60	40.00	36.30	32.60	29.00
440	450	71.90	67.20	62.60	58.00	53.40	49.20	45.50	41.90	38.20	34.50	30.90
450	460	74.30	69.60	65.00	60.40	55.80	51.20	47.40	43.80	40.10	36.40	32.80
710	720	155.30	148.20	141.10	134.00	127.80	121.70	115.50	109.40	103.20	97.80	92.60
720	730	159.00	151.90	144.80	(137.70)	131.00	124.90	118.70	112.60	106.40	100.50	95.30
730	740	162.70	155.60	148.50	141.40	134.30	128.10	121.90	115.80	109.60	103.50	98.00
740	750	166.40	159.30	152.20	145.10	138.00	131.30	125.10	119.00	112.80	106.70	100.70
750	760	170.10	163.00	155.90	148.80	141.70	134.50	128.30	122.20	116.00	109.90	103.70
760	770	173.80	166.70	159.60	152.50	145.40	138.20	131.50	125.40	119.20	113.10	106.90
770	780	177.50	170.40	163.30	156.20	149.10	141.90	134.80	128.60	122.40	116.30	110.10
780	790	181.20	174.10	167.00	159.90	152.80	145.60	138.50	131.80	125.60	119.50	113.30
790	800	184.90	177.80	170.70	163.60	156.50	149.30	142.20	135.10	128.80	122.70	116.50
800	810	188.60	181.50	174.40	167.30	160.20	153.00	145.90	138.80	132.00	125.90	119.70
810	820	192.30	185.20	178.10	171.00	163.90	156.70	149.60	142.50	135.40	129.10	122.90
820	830	196.00	188.90	181.80	174.70	167.60	160.40	153.30	146.20	139.10	132.30	126.10
830	840	199.70	192.60	185.50	178.40	171.30	164.10	157.00	149.90	142.80	135.70	129.30
840	850	203.40	196.30	189.20	182.10	175.00	167.80	160.70	153.60	146.50	139.40	132.50
850	860	207.10	200.00	192.90	185.80	178.70	171.50	164.40	157.30	150.20	143.10	136.00
		37 percent of the excess over $860 plus—										
$860 and over		209.00	201.90	194.70	187.60	180.50	173.40	166.30	159.20	152.00	144.90	137.80

Figure 9-3

either the $710–$720 bracket or the $720–$730 bracket. However, note the headings of the bracket columns: "At least" and "But less than." A strict interpretation of the $710–$720 bracket really means $710–$719.99. Therefore $720 must be included in the $720–$730 bracket. As can be seen from the table, $137.70 should be withheld.

Many states that levy state income taxes also furnish employers with withholding tables. Other states use a fixed percentage of the federal income tax withholding as the amount to be withheld for state taxes.

Employees' FICA Tax Withholding (Social Security)

To determine the FICA tax for each employee, simply multiply the FICA taxable wages by the FICA tax rate.

Let's get back to Graham C. Laboe, who had gross wages of $720 for the week ending November 7. Suppose that the total accumulated gross wages Laboe earned this year prior to this payroll period were $25,316. His total gross wages including this payroll period were $26,036 ($25,316 + $720), which is well below the $36,000 assumed maximum taxable income. Therefore, multiply the FICA taxable wages ($720) by the FICA tax rate (7.1 percent).

$720 × .071 = $51.12

Of course, if Laboe's gross earnings prior to this payroll period had been greater than $36,000, then there would be *no* FICA tax deduction. (Tables for FICA tax withholding are published in the Internal Revenue Service's *Circular E, Employer's Tax Guide*.)

PAYROLL REGISTER

The payroll register is a form that summarizes the information about employees' wages and salaries for a given payroll period. In Figure 9-4 we see a payroll register that shows the data for each employee on a separate line. This would be suitable for a firm, such as Harding and Associates, that has a small number of employees.

Objective 3

Complete a payroll register.

State Unemployment Taxable Earnings Column

The columns marked Taxable Earnings refer to the amount of pay that is subject to taxation. The employer uses the information in these columns to calculate the amount of unemployment taxes as well as the employer's portion of FICA. (We'll discuss these calculations in Chapter 10.)

For the present, however, we are concerned only with recording the amount of taxable income (the amount on which the actual tax is figured). First, let's take the State Unemployment Taxable Earnings column. Remember, however, that taxable earnings may differ from one state to another. Harding and Associates operates in the state of Washington, which has an assumed unemployment tax based on the first $12,000 paid to each employee during the calendar year (January 1 through December 31). After an employee's earnings top $12,000 in one year, the employer no longer pays state unemployment tax on that employee. For example, Graham C. Laboe's total earnings before the payroll period ended November 7 were $25,316 (as shown in his earnings record in Figure 9-7). Since he has already earned more than $12,000, no amount is recorded in the State

	NAME	TOTAL HOURS	EARNINGS			TAXABLE EARNINGS			
			REGULAR	OVERTIME	TOTAL	STATE UNEMPL.	FEDERAL UNEMPL.	FICA	FEDERAL INCOME TA
1	Anderson, Dennis L.	45	4 0 0 00	7 5 00	4 7 5 00	2 4 0 00		4 7 5 00	7 4
2	Bowlen, Ralph P.	46	3 2 0 00	7 2 00	3 9 2 00	3 9 2 00	3 9 2 00	3 9 2 00	5 0
3	Daniels, John N.	49	4 0 0 00	1 3 5 00	5 3 5 00			5 3 5 00	8 0
4	Drew, Nancy R.	40	3 6 0 00		3 6 0 00	3 6 0 00	3 6 0 00	3 6 0 00	4 4
5	Farrell, Steven L.	40	3 8 4 00		3 8 4 00	3 8 4 00	3 8 4 00	3 8 4 00	4 8
6	Harwood, Lance C.	40	9 5 0 00		9 5 0 00				2 2 8
7	Laboe, Graham C.	52	4 8 0 00	2 4 0 00	7 2 0 00			7 2 0 00	1 3 7
8	Lyman, Mary C.	40	6 0 0 00		6 0 0 00			6 0 0 00	1 0 4
9	Miller, Robert M.	44	4 4 0 00	6 6 00	5 0 6 00			5 0 6 00	8 2
10	Olsen, Marvin C.	45	4 0 0 00	7 5 00	4 7 5 00	2 4 0 00		4 7 5 00	7 4
11	Stanfield, John D.	40	8 5 0 00		8 5 0 00				1 8 5
12	Tucker, Norma P.	52	4 8 0 00	2 1 6 00	6 9 6 00			6 9 6 00	1 2 7
13			6 0 6 4 00	8 7 9 00	6 9 4 3 00	1 6 1 6 00	1 1 3 6 00	5 1 4 3 00	1 2 4 0
14									

Unemployment Taxable Earnings column. A blank space indicates that the employee has already earned more than $12,000 (prior to this payroll period) so far this year. On the other hand, Ralph P. Bowlen's total earnings so far this year, including the $392 during this pay period, amount to $8,460. Because his earnings are still less than $12,000, the entire $392 is recorded in the State Unemployment Taxable Earnings column. Dennis L. Anderson's cumulative earnings prior to this week were $11,760. As a result, only $240 of this week's earnings are taxable for state unemployment, to bring him up to the $12,000 maximum. After this week, none of Anderson's earnings will be taxable for state unemployment.

Federal Unemployment Taxable Earnings Column

Regarding the Federal Unemployment Taxable Earnings column, we assume a tax rate of .8 percent on the first $7,000 paid to each employee during the calendar year. After a given employee's earnings top $7,000 in one year, the employer doesn't have to pay any more federal unemployment tax on that employee. For example, Laboe has already earned more than $7,000 during the year, so no amount is recorded in the Federal Unemployment Taxable Earnings column. On the other hand, Steven L. Farrell's cumulative earnings so far this year, including the $384 during this pay period, amount to $6,242. Consequently, the entire $384 is placed in the Federal Unemployment Taxable Earnings column as well as in the State Unemployment Taxable Earnings column.

| | | | | OTHER | | | PAYMENTS | | EXPENSE ACCOUNT DEBITED | | |
FICA	U.S. BONDS	UNION DUES	MEDICAL INSURANCE	CODE	AMOUNT	TOTAL	NET AMOUNT	CK. NO.	SALES SALARY EXPENSE	OFFICE SALARY EXPENSE	
33 73	20 00	10 00	16 00	CC	4 00	158 23	316 77	273	475 00		1
27 83		10 00	16 00			104 43	287 57	274	392 00		2
37 99	32 00	10 00	20 00	CC	6 00	186 29	348 71	275		535 00	3
25 56		10 00	16 00			96 46	263 54	276		360 00	4
27 26		10 00	16 00			101 96	282 04	277	384 00		5
	40 00		20 00	CC	6 00	294 00	656 00	278	950 00		6
51 12	10 00		20 00	CC	6 00	234 82	485 18	279	720 00		7
42 60	10 00		20 00	CC	5 00	182 50	417 50	280	600 00		8
35 93		10 00	16 00			144 53	361 47	281	506 00		9
33 73		10 00	20 00	AR	40 00	178 23	296 77	282	475 00		10
			20 00	CC	6 00	211 80	638 20	283	850 00		11
49 42		10 00	16 00	CC	4 00	207 02	488 98	284		696 00	12
665 17	112 00	90 00	216 00		77 00	2100 27	4842 73		5352 00	1591 00	13
											14

Figure 9-4

FICA Taxable Earnings Column

We have assumed a FICA tax rate of 7.1 percent on the first $36,000. In the case of Graham C. Laboe, his total earnings so far this year, including the $720 during this pay period, amount to $26,036 (see Laboe's individual earnings record, Figure 9-7). Consequently, the entire $720 is listed as FICA taxable. On the line of Lance C. Harwood, there is a blank, indicating that he has already earned more than $36,000 before this pay period.

As we said, the three taxable earnings columns are used to calculate the employer's payroll tax expense, which is discussed in Chapter 10. However, the FICA Taxable Earnings column is also used to determine the amount of the *employees'* FICA tax deductions. For example, to find Laboe's FICA deduction multiply $720 (FICA taxable) by 7.1 percent (FICA tax rate): $720 × .071 = $51.12.

Deductions Columns

The federal income tax withholding and the FICA (Social Security) deductions are employee deductions required by law; the others are usually voluntary. One could set up special columns for any frequently used deductions. Here, Community Chest and Accounts Receivable are included as other deductions.

The Net Amount column represents the employee's take-home pay. The last two columns show the distribution of the salary accounts to be debited. Harding and Associates uses Sales Salary Expense and Office Salary Expense. The sum of these two columns equals the total earnings.

Figure 9-5

	DATE		DESCRIPTION	POST. REF.	DEBIT				CREDIT				
1	19– Nov.	7	Sales Salary Expense		5 3 5 2	00							1
2			Office Salary Expense		1 5 9 1	00							2
3			Employees' Income Tax Payable					1 2 4 0	10		3
4			FICA Tax Payable ($5,143 × .071)					3 6 5	17		4
5			Employees' Bond Deductions								5
6			Payable					1 1 2	00		6
7			Employees' Union Dues Payable					9 0	00		7
8			Employees' Medical Insurance								8
9			Payable					2 1 6	00		9
10			Employees' Community Chest								10
11			Payable					3 7	00		11
12			Accounts Receivable					4 0	00		12
13			Salaries Payable					4 8 4 2	73		13
14			Payroll register, page 68, for week								14
15			ended November 7.								15
16											16
17											17
18											18

GENERAL JOURNAL   PAGE __31__

The Payroll Entry

Because the payroll register summarizes the payroll data for the period, it seems logical that it should be used as the basis for recording the payroll in the ledger accounts. Since the payroll register does not have the status of a journal, a journal entry is necessary. Figure 9-5 shows the entry in general journal form. (The calculation is given purely as further explanation; it is not ordinarily a part of the journal entry.)

Note that a firm records the total cost to the company for services of employees as debits to the salary expense accounts. To pay the employees, the firm now makes the following journal entry.

Objective 4

Journalize the payroll entry from a payroll register.

	7	Salaries Payable	4 8 4 2	73		
		Cash			4 8 4 2	73
		Paid salaries for week ended				
		November 7. Issued check no.				
		667 payable to special payroll				
		bank account.				

In the two journal entries, the debit and credit to the Salaries Payable account cancel out each other. It would be possible to combine the two entries by making one credit to Cash. If a combined journal were in use, both of the above entries would be recorded in it, instead of in the general journal.

A firm having a large number of employees would probably open a special payroll account with its bank. One check drawn on the regular bank account is made payable to the special payroll account for the amount of the total net pay for a payroll period. All payroll checks for the period are then written on the special payroll account. With the use of the special payroll account, if employees delay cashing their paychecks, then the checks do not have to be listed on the bank reconciliation of the firm's regular bank account. Balances of Employees' Bond Deductions Payable, Employees' Union Dues Payable, and other employee deductions are paid out of the firm's regular bank account.

Small businesses that have just a few workers will not find it worthwhile to use a special payroll bank account. Instead, these firms will use their regular bank account to write the employees' payroll checks, crediting Cash directly rather than crediting Salaries Payable.

PAYCHECK

All the data needed to make out a payroll check are available in the payroll register. Graham C. Laboe's paycheck is shown in Figure 9-6.

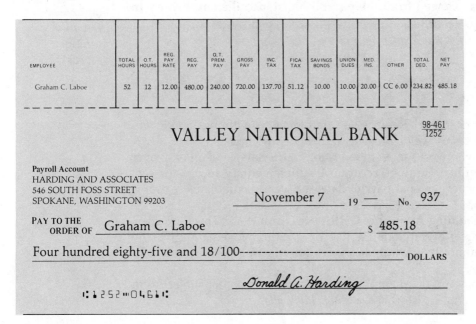

Figure 9-6

EMPLOYEE	TOTAL HOURS	O.T. HOURS	REG. PAY RATE	REG. PAY	O.T. PREM. PAY	GROSS PAY	INC. TAX	FICA TAX	SAVINGS BONDS	UNION DUES	MED. INS.	OTHER	TOTAL DED.	NET PAY
Graham C. Laboe	52	12	12.00	480.00	240.00	720.00	137.70	51.12	10.00	10.00	20.00	CC 6.00	234.82	485.18

VALLEY NATIONAL BANK 98-461 1252

Payroll Account
HARDING AND ASSOCIATES
546 SOUTH FOSS STREET
SPOKANE, WASHINGTON 99203

November 7 19 — No. 937

PAY TO THE ORDER OF Graham C. Laboe $ 485.18

Four hundred eighty-five and 18/100------------------------------------ DOLLARS

Donald A. Harding

⑆1252⑈0461⑉

NAME _Laboe, Graham Charles_

ADDRESS _1582 North Pierce Street_

Spokane, Washington 99204

MALE _X_   FEMALE _____

MARRIED _X_   SINGLE _____

PHONE NO. _663-2556_   DATE OF BIRTH _9/19/39_

LINE NO.	PERIOD ENDED	DATE PAID	HOURS WORKED		EARNINGS			ACCUMULATED EARNINGS	INCOME TAX
			REG.	O.T.	REGULAR	OVERTIME	TOTAL		
40	10/3	10/4	40		480 00	144 00	624 00	23 162 00	105
41	10/10	10/11	40	2	480 00	36 00	516 00	23 678 00	74
42	10/17	10/18	40	2	480 00	36 00	516 00	24 194 00	74
43	10/24	10/24	40	5	480 00	90 00	570 00	24 764 00	91
44	10/30	11/1	40	4	480 00	72 00	552 00	25 316 00	85
45	11/7	11/8	40	12	480 00	240 00	720 00	26 036 00	137

Employees' Individual Earnings Records

To comply with government regulations, a firm has to keep current data on each employee's accumulated earnings, deductions, and net pay. The information is transferred from the payroll register to the **employee's individual earnings record** each payday. Figure 9-7 shows a portion of the earnings record for Graham C. Laboe.

Objective 5

Maintain employees' individual earnings records.

GLOSSARY

Current Tax Payment Act Requires an employer to withhold employees' federal income tax as well as to pay and report the tax.

Employee One who works for compensation in the service of an employer.

Employee's individual earnings record A supplementary record for each employee showing personal payroll data and yearly cumulative earnings and deductions.

Employee's Withholding Allowance Certificate (Form W-4) This form specifies the number of exemptions claimed by each employee and gives the employer the authority to withhold money for an employee's income taxes and FICA taxes.

Exemption An amount of an employee's annual earnings not subject to income tax. The term is also called a _withholding allowance_.

EARNINGS RECORD

EMPLOYEE NO. _5_

SOC. SEC. NO. _543-24-1680_

PAY RATE _$12.00_

EQUIVALENT HOURLY RATE _$12.00_

DATE TERMINATED _____

CLASSIFICATION FOR WORKMEN'S COMPENSATION INSURANCE _Warehouse_

DATE EMPLOYED _2/1/—_

NO. OF EXEMPTIONS _3_

PER HOUR _X_

PER WEEK _____

PER DAY _____

PER MONTH _____

	DEDUCTIONS								PAID	
FICA	BONDS	UNION DUES	HOSPITAL INSURANCE	OTHER CODE	OTHER AMOUNT	TOTAL		NET AMOUNT	CK. NO.
4 4 30	1 0 00	1 0 00	2 0 00	cc	6 00	1 9 5 50	4 2 8 50	887
3 6 64	1 0 00	1 0 00	2 0 00	cc	6 00	1 5 7 54	3 5 8 46	889
3 6 64	1 0 00	1 0 00	2 0 00	cc	6 00	1 5 7 54	3 5 8 46	901
4 0 47	1 0 00	1 0 00	2 0 00	cc	6 00	1 7 7 57	3 9 2 43	913
3 9 19	1 0 00	1 0 00	2 0 00	cc	6 00	1 7 0 89	3 8 1 11	925
5 1 12	1 0 00	1 0 00	2 0 00	cc	6 00	2 3 4 82	4 8 5 18	937

Figure 9-7

Fair Labor Standards Act (Wages and Hours Law) An act requiring employers whose products are involved in interstate commerce to pay their employees time-and-a-half for all hours worked in excess of 40 per week.

FICA taxes Social Security taxes paid by both employers and employees under the provisions of the Federal Insurance Contributions Act. The proceeds are used to pay old-age and disability pensions.

FUTA taxes Taxes paid only by employers under the provisions of the Federal Unemployment Tax Act. The proceeds are used to pay part of the costs of the federal-state unemployment programs.

Gross pay The total amount of an employee's pay before any deductions.

Independent contractor Someone who is engaged for a definite service who may choose her or his own means of doing the work; not an employee of the firm for which the service is provided. (*Examples:* appliance repair person, plumber, freelance artist, CPA firm.)

Net pay Gross pay minus deductions.

State unemployment taxes Taxes paid by employers only. The proceeds are used to pay unemployment benefits.

Workers' compensation laws State laws guaranteeing benefits for employees who are injured or killed on the job.

QUESTIONS, EXERCISES, AND PROBLEMS

Discussion Questions

1. Distinguish between an employee and an independent contractor.
2. Suggest seven possible deductions from total earnings of an employee.

3. Explain the requirements of the Fair Labor Standards Act.
4. What are the main provisions of the Federal Insurance Contributions Act?
5. What is a wage-bracket withholding table?
6. Describe how a special payroll bank account is useful in paying the wages of employees.
7. What information is included in an employee's individual earnings record, and what is its function?

Exercises

Exercise 9-1 Using the table in Figure 9-3 (page 254), determine the amount of federal income tax an employer should withhold weekly for married employees with the following wages and exemptions.

	Total Weekly Wages	Number of Exemptions	Amount of Withholding
a	$315.52	1	_____
b	$712.16	5	_____
c	$710.00	6	_____

Exercise 9-2 Henry R. Gallo works for the Central Roofing Corporation, which must abide by the Fair Labor Standards Act. It must pay its employees time-and-a-half for all hours worked per week in excess of 40. Gallo's pay rate is $9.20 per hour. His wages are subject to federal income tax and FICA deductions at the rate of 7.1 percent. He claims four income tax exemptions. Gallo has a ½-hour lunch during an 8½-hour day. His time card is shown below.

TIME CARD

Name _Henry R. Gallo_

Week ending _March 11, 19–_

Day	In	Out	In	Out	Hours Worked Regular	Hours Worked Overtime
M	7^{56}	12^{09}	12^{39}	4^{32}	8	
T	7^{52}	12^{05}	12^{35}	5^{04}	8	½
W	7^{59}	12^{20}	12^{40}	5^{03}	8	½
T	8^{00}	12^{08}	12^{38}	4^{34}	8	
F	7^{56}	12^{09}	12^{39}	6^{33}	8	2
S	8^{00}	11^{01}				3
S						

Complete the following.

a. _____ hours at straight time × $9.20 per hour $_____
b. _____ hours overtime × $13.80 per hour $_____
c. Total gross wages $_____
d. Federal income tax withholding
   (from tax tables in Figure 9-3, page 254) $_____
e. FICA withholding at 7.1 percent $_____
f. Total withholding $_____
g. Net pay $_____

Exercise 9-3 On January 31, Sato and Company's column totals of its payroll register showed that its sales employees had earned $4,560 and its office employees had earned $960. FICA taxes were withheld at an assumed rate of 7.1 percent. Other deductions consisted of federal income tax, $501.60; U.S. savings bonds, $240; and hospital insurance, $320. Determine the amount of FICA taxes to be withheld and record the general journal entry for the payroll, crediting Salaries Payable for the net pay.

Exercise 9-4 Sandra Lund works for Fine Fabrics, a company engaged in interstate commerce, which is subject to the provisions of the Fair Labor Standards Act. Fine Fabrics has just adopted a four-day, 40-hour workweek.

Lund's pay rate is $7.40 per hour. During the four-day week, her working hours were as follows: Monday, 12 hours; Tuesday, 10 hours; Wednesday, 11½ hours; Thursday, 10½ hours. Compute the amount of her gross earnings for the week.

Exercise 9-5 The following information was taken from the records of Rasmussen Tea Company, which is subject to the Fair Labor Standards Act, for the first week of January.

NAME	HOURLY RATE	HOURS WORKED REG.	HOURS WORKED O.T.	TOTAL EARNINGS	DEDUCTIONS FEDERAL INCOME TAX	FICA	SAVINGS BONDS	HOSPITAL INSURANCE	TOTAL	NET PAY
Murray, A.	7.50	40	6				4 00	16 00		
Smith, B.	7.90	40	8				10 00	18 00		

Using the table in Figure 9-3 (page 254), determine the income tax withheld. The FICA tax rate is 7.1 percent. Murray and Smith claim two exemptions each. In general journal form, record the payroll entry, debiting Wages Expense for the amount of the total earnings and crediting Cash for the net pay.

Exercise 9-6 June Ames is employed by the Solar Company. During the week ended July 7, she worked 9 hours on Monday and 7 hours each day during the remaining four days of the five-day week. The existing union contract defines overtime as time worked over 8 hours each day. She earns $10 per hour and time-and-a-half for overtime. Ames's deductions include the following.

Federal income tax withheld $50.50
Union dues withheld   12.00
Medical insurance withheld   20.00

Her total earnings through July 1 were $9,800. Assume that the FICA tax is 7.1 percent of the first $36,000 earned during the calendar year. Compute Ames's total earnings and the net amount of her check for the week.

Exercise 9-7 The Booker Camera Company has two employees. The information shown below was taken from their individual earnings record cards for the month of October. Determine the missing amounts, assuming that the FICA tax is 7.1 percent.

	Davis	Finch
Regular earnings	$?	$670.00
Overtime earnings	30.00	?
Total earnings	?	684.00
FICA taxes withheld	?	48.56
Federal income taxes withheld	140.00	132.00
State income taxes withheld	10.00	?
Medical insurance withheld	15.00	15.00
Total deductions	216.83	204.56
Net amount paid	513.17	479.44

Exercise 9-8 Assume the employees in Exercise 9-7 are paid from the firm's regular bank account. Journalize the payroll entry in general journal form.

Problem Set A

Problem 9-1A Jan R. Franco, an employee of Carpets, Inc., worked 47 hours during the week of February 15 to 21. Her rate of pay is $8.40 per hour, and she gets time-and-a-half for work in excess of 40 hours per week. She is married and claims one exemption on her W-4 form. Her wages are subject to the following deductions.

a. Federal income tax (use the table in Figure 9-3, page 254)
b. FICA tax at 7.1 percent
c. Union dues, $6.20
d. Medical insurance, $17.20

Instructions

Compute her regular pay, overtime pay, gross pay, and net pay.

Problem 9-2A The Falcon Motor Inn has the following payroll information for the week ended April 26.

Name	Daily Time M	T	W	T	F	S	S	Pay Rate	Federal Income Tax	Union Dues	Earnings at End of Previous Week
Baker, Loren	8	0	0	8	10	8	8	5 40	28 60	4 00	3,960 00
Collier, Douglas	0	0	8	8	8	8	8	3 50	14 00	4 00	2,172 60
Edwards, Roberta	8	8	8	8	4	0	8	4 00	19 20	4 00	2,548 22
Stanski, Louise	0	4	8	8	8	8	8	4 00	22 50	4 00	3,980 10
Tolliver, Elwood	8	8	4	8	8	0	8	4 50	22 60	4 00	861 30

The firm is subject to the Fair Labor Standards Act regarding minimum wages. However, being a motel, it is exempt from paying time-and-a-half for 44 hours or less. In this case, all hours are compensated at the regular rate. For each employee, taxable earnings for FICA are based on the first $36,000, and taxable earnings for unemployment insurance (state and federal) are based on the first $7,000.

Instructions

1. Complete the payroll register, using 7.1 percent for calculating FICA tax withholding.
2. Prepare a general journal entry to record the payroll. The firm's general ledger contains a Wages Expense account and a Wages Payable account.
3. Assuming that the firm uses a special payroll bank account, make the entry in the general journal to record check no. 53.

Problem 9-3A   The Illinois Products Company is subject to the Fair Labor Standards Act and, accordingly, pays its employees time-and-a-half for all hours worked in excess of 40 per week. The following information is available from time cards and employee's individual earnings records for the pay period ended February 28.

Name	Clock Card No.	Daily Time M	T	W	T	F	S	S	Regular Rate	Income Tax Exemp.	Union Dues	Medical Insurance	Earnings at End of Previous Week
Bush, Paula C.	69	8	8	8	10	9	0	0	7 20	1	6 00	13 60	2,298 00
Carlson, John D.	70	8	8	8	8	8	5	0	7 20	3	6 00	15 00	2,388 00
Dodge, R. C.	71	8	10	8	9	8	0	0	7 70	5	6 00	15 40	2,446 00
Klein, Louis A.	72	8	8	9	8	8	2	0	7 70	4	6 00	15 20	2,424 00
Lewis, David	73	8	8	8	8	8	0	0	9 00	4	6 00	15 20	2,736 00

For each employee, taxable earnings for FICA are based on the first $36,000, and taxable earnings for unemployment insurance (state and federal) are based on the first $7,000.

Instructions

1. Complete the payroll register, using the wage-bracket income tax withholding tables in Figure 9-3 (page 254). The FICA tax is 7.1 percent. Assume that all employees are married.
2. Prepare a general journal entry to record the payroll. The firm's general ledger contains a Wages Expense account and a Wages Payable account.
3. Assume that the firm uses a special payroll bank account and issues check no. 113.

Problem 9-4A   The Brewster Trailer Company is subject to the Fair Labor Standards Act and, accordingly, pays its employees time-and-a-half for all hours worked in excess of 40 per week. The following information is available from the time books and employee's individual earnings records for the pay period ended December 10.

Name	Pay Rate	Hours Worked	Federal Income Tax	Union Dues	Medical Insurance	Earnings at End of Previous Week
Cooper, C. R.	$7.20 per hour	41	37 40	8 00	13 00	14,600 00
Crane, J. P.	$400 per week	40	53 00		13 00	19,600 00
Kimball, A. L.	$350 per week	40	43 00		14 00	17,150 00
Woods, C. N.	$6.50 per hour	42	31 70	8 00	11 00	6,920 00

For each employee, taxable earnings for FICA are based on the first $36,000, and taxable earnings for unemployment insurance are based on the first $7,000 (state and federal).

Instructions

1. Complete the payroll register, using a FICA tax of 7.1 percent.
2. Prepare a general journal entry to record the payroll and the payment of the employees. Assume that the company issues individual checks out of its regular bank account beginning with check no. 864.

Problem Set B

Problem 9-1B   James Noble, an employee of Andrews Motors, worked 46 hours during the week of March 16 to 22. His rate of pay is $9.20 per hour, and he receives time-and-a-half for all work in excess of 40 hours per week. Noble is married and claims two exemptions on his W-4 form. His wages are subject to the following deductions.

a. Federal income tax (use the table in Figure 9-3, page 254)
b. FICA tax at 7.1 percent
c. Union dues, $7.40
d. Medical insurance, $25.50

Instructions

Compute his regular pay, overtime pay, gross pay, and net pay.

Problem 9-2B The Lakeside Motel has the following payroll information for the week ended April 18.

Name	Daily Time M	T	W	T	F	S	S	Pay Rate	Federal Income Tax	Union Dues	Earnings at End of Previous Week
Albers, John	0	8	8	8	8	8	0	5 60	26 60	4 00	3,510 00
Conrad, Jean	8	8	8	8	8	0	0	7 10	41 60	4 00	2,392 00
Johnson, Donna	0	0	8	8	8	8	8	4 00	20 70		1,280 00
Mennen, Roy	0	4	8	8	8	8	8	4 00	19 20		1,686 00
Palmer, Ronald	8	8	8	8	8	4	0	6 20	39 20	4 00	3,430 00

The firm is subject to the Fair Labor Standards Act regarding minimum wages. However, being a motel, it is exempt from paying time-and-a-half for 44 hours of work or less. In this case, all hours are compensated at the regular rate. For each employee, taxable earnings for FICA are based on the first $36,000, and taxable earnings for unemployment insurance (state and federal) are based on the first $7,000. The amounts of employees' income tax withheld are given.

Instructions

1. Complete the payroll register, using 7.1 percent of earnings for calculating FICA tax withholding.
2. Prepare a general journal entry to record the payroll. The firm's general ledger contains a Wages Expense account and a Wages Payable account.
3. Assuming that the firm uses a special payroll bank account, make the entry in the general journal to record check no. 53.

Problem 9-3B The Rhode Island Products Company is subject to the Fair Labor Standards Act and, accordingly, pays time-and-a-half for all hours worked in excess of 40 per week. The following information is available from the time cards and employees' individual earnings records for the pay period ended March 16.

Name	Clock Card No.	Daily Time M	T	W	T	F	S	S	Regular Rate	Income Tax Exemption	Union Dues	Medical Insurance	Earnings at End of Previous Week
Clark, C. R.	76	8	8	8	10	8	0	0	7 80	2	5 00	9 60	2,580 00
Dillon, L. C.	77	8	8	8	8	8	0	0	8 55	2	5 00	9 60	1,815 00
Evans, M. E.	78	8	8	8	8	8	4	4	7 50	4	5 00	10 50	3,255 00
Keller, D. N.	79	8	8	9	9	8	6	0	7 80	3	5 00	10 00	3,345 00
Norton, T. C.	80	8	8	8	8	8	0	0	9 00	4	5 00	10 50	3,480 00

For each employee, taxable earnings for FICA are based on the first $36,000, and taxable earnings for unemployment insurance (state and federal) are based on the first $7,000.

Instructions

1. Complete the payroll register, using the wage-bracket income tax withholding table in Figure 9-3 (page 254). The FICA tax is 7.1 percent. Assume that all employees are married.
2. Prepare a general journal entry to record the payroll. The firm's general ledger contains a Wages Expense account and a Wages Payable account.
3. Assume that the firm uses a special payroll bank account and issues check no. 113.

Problem 9-4B   The Quincy Insurance Company is subject to the Fair Labor Standards Act and, accordingly, pays its employees time-and-a-half for all hours worked in excess of 40 per week. The following information is available from Quincy's time book and the employee's individual earnings records for the payroll period ended December 8.

Name	Pay Rate	Hours Worked	Federal Income Tax		Union Dues		Medical Insurance		Earnings at End of Previous Week	
Glenn, D. N.	$7.10 per hour	46	41	10	6	00	14	00	16,950	00
Sharp, D. L.	$460.00 per week	40	72	00			16	00	22,540	00
Vaughn, J. A.	$325.00 per week	40	41	00			12	00	15,925	00
Wise, T. C.	$5.90 per hour	48	42	70	6	00	12	00	6,946	00

For each employee, taxable earnings for FICA are based on the first $36,000, and taxable earnings for unemployment are based on the first $7,000 (state and federal).

Instructions

1. Complete the payroll register, using a FICA tax of 7.1 percent.
2. Prepare a general journal entry to record the payroll and the payment of the employees. Assume that the company issues individual checks out of its regular bank account beginning with check no. 716.

10 Payroll Accounting: Employer's Taxes, Payments, and Reports

Learning Objectives

After you have completed this chapter, you will be able to do the following:

1. Journalize the entry to record payroll tax expense.

2. Journalize the entry for the deposit of employees' income taxes withheld and FICA taxes (both employees' withheld and employer's matching share).

3. Journalize the entries for the payment of employer's state and federal unemployment taxes.

4. Complete Employer's Quarterly Federal Tax Return, Form 941.

5. Prepare W-2 forms and W-3 forms.

6. Prepare state and federal unemployment insurance reports and the related journal entries.

7. Calculate the premium for workers' compensation insurance, and prepare the entry for payment in advance.

8. Determine the amount of adjustment for workers' compensation insurance at end of year, and record adjustment.

In Chapter 9, we talked about the computing and recording of such pay-roll data as gross pay, employees' income tax withheld, employees' FICA tax withheld, and various deductions requested by employees. Now we're going to get around to the payment of these withholdings and the taxes levied on the employer based on total payroll.

EMPLOYER'S IDENTIFICATION NUMBER

As you know quite well, everyone who works has a Social Security number, a number that is a vital part of his or her federal income tax returns. For an employer, a counterpart to the Social Security number is the **employer identification number.** Each employer of one or more persons is required to have such a number, and it must be listed on all reports and payments of employees' federal income tax withholding and FICA taxes.

EMPLOYER'S PAYROLL TAXES

An employer's payroll taxes are levied on the employer on the basis of the gross wages paid to the employees. Payroll taxes—like property taxes—are an expense of doing business. Harding and Associates records these taxes in the Payroll Tax Expense account and debits the account for the company's FICA taxes as well as for state and federal unemployment taxes. In T account form Payroll Tax Expense for Harding and Associates would look like the following example.

Payroll Tax Expense	
+	−
FICA (employer's matching portion)	Closed at the end of the year along with
Federal Unemploy-ment Tax	all other expense accounts
State Unemploy-ment Tax	

As you can see, FICA tax (employer's share), **federal unemployment tax,** and **state unemployment tax** are included under the "umbrella" of Payroll Tax Expense. The unemployment taxes are levied on the employer only.

Employer's Matching Portion of FICA Tax

The FICA tax is imposed on both employer and employee. The firm's accountant deducts the employee's share from gross wages and records it in the payroll entry under FICA Tax Payable (the same liability account as shown in Chapter 9). Next, he or she determines the employer's share by multiplying the employer's FICA tax rate (assumed to be 7.1 percent) times the total FICA-taxable earnings (gross annual earnings for the calendar year for each employee up to an assumed $36,000). In this text, we shall assume that the same tax rate applies to both the employer and the employee. The accountant gets the FICA-taxable earnings figure from the payroll register. In Figure 10-1 we take another look at the Taxable Earnings columns from the payroll register for the week ended November 7, 19–, shown in Figure 9-4.

By T accounts, the entry to record the employer's portion of the FICA tax looks like this.

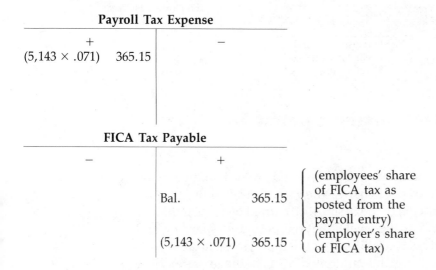

Note particularly that the FICA Tax Payable account is often used for the tax liability of both the employer and the employee. This is logical because both FICA taxes are paid at the same time and the same place. There might be a slight difference between the employer's and the employee's share of FICA taxes, due to the rounding-off process (or to slightly different rates, as in 1984). In our example, the accountant calculates the employee's share by taking 7.1 percent (assumed rate) of the taxable earnings of each worker, then adding these figures to find the total amount due for all employees. At the same time, she or he determines the employer's share by taking 7.1 percent of the total taxable earnings of all the employees. The two figures may vary, but only by a few cents.

Figure 10-1

Amount of employees' earnings that are less than $7,000 per employee for the year

Amount of employees' earnings that are less than $12,000 per employee for the year (Many states use $7,000 for each employee.)

Amount of employees' earnings that are less than $36,000 per employee for the year

	TAXABLE EARNINGS		
STATE UNEMPLOYMENT	FEDERAL UNEMPLOYMENT	FICA	
2 4 0 00		4 7 5 00	
3 9 2 00	3 9 2 00	3 9 2 00	
		5 3 5 00	
3 6 0 00	3 6 0 00	3 6 0 00	
3 8 4 00	3 8 4 00	3 8 4 00	
		7 2 0 00	
		6 0 0 00	
		5 0 6 00	
2 4 0 00		4 7 5 00	
		6 9 6 00	
1 6 1 6 00	1 1 3 6 00	5 1 4 3 00	

Employer's state unemployment tax
$1,616 × .03 = $48.48

Employer's federal unemployment tax
$1,136 × .008 = $9.09

Employer's FICA tax
5,143 × .071 = $365.15

Employer's Federal Unemployment Tax (FUTA)

The employer's federal unemployment tax is levied on the employer only. Congress may from time to time change the rate. But for now, let's assume a rate of .8 percent (.008) of the first $7,000 earned by each employee during the calendar year. For the weekly payroll period for Harding and Associates, the tax liability is $9.09 ($1,136 of unemployment taxable earnings taken from the payroll register multiplied by .008, the tax rate). By T accounts, the entry is as follows.

Payroll Tax Expense		Federal Unemployment Tax Payable	
+	−	−	+
(1,136 × .008) 9.09			(1,136 × .008) 9.09

Employer's State Unemployment Tax

This tax, like the federal unemployment tax, is paid by the employer only. The rate of the state unemployment tax varies considerably among the states. During recent years, with the trend toward higher unemployment benefits, many states have adopted a base of at least $7,000 and rates of 2.7 percent or higher. However, let us assume here that Harding and Associates is subject to a rate of 3 percent of the first $12,000 of each employee's earnings. As shown in the portion of the payroll register illustrated in Figure 10-1, $1,616 of earnings are subject to the state unemployment tax. Accordingly, by T accounts, the state unemployment tax based on taxable earnings is as follows.

Payroll Tax Expense		State Unemployment Tax Payable	
+	−	−	+
(1,616 × .03) 48.48			(1,616 × .03) 48.48

To make things clearer in the foregoing discussion, figures for the three employer's payroll taxes have been presented separately. Now let's combine this information into one entry, which follows the regular payroll entry. Harding and Associates pays its employees weekly, so it also makes its Payroll Tax Expense entry weekly.

Objective 1

Journalize the entry to record payroll tax expense.

GENERAL JOURNAL   PAGE _31_

	DATE		DESCRIPTION	POST. REF.	DEBIT	CREDIT	
17	19– Nov.	7	Payroll Tax Expense		4 2 2 72		17
18			FICA Tax Payable			3 6 5 15	18
19			Federal Unemployment Tax Payable			9 09	19
20			State Unemployment Tax Payable			4 8 48	20
21			To record employer's share of				21
22			FICA tax and employer's federal				22
23			and state unemployment taxes.				23
24							24
25							25
26							26
27							27

JOURNAL ENTRIES FOR RECORDING PAYROLL

At this point let us restate in general journal form the entries that have been recorded, using the payroll register illustrated in Chapter 9 (Figure 9-4) as the source of information. First, we record the payroll entry.

1	19– Nov.	7	Sales Salary Expense		5	3	5	2	00								1
2			Office Salary Expense		1	5	9	1	00								2
3			Employees' Income Tax Payable							1	2	4	0	10			3
4			FICA Tax Payable								3	6	5	17			4
5			Employees' Bond Deductions														5
6			Payable								1	1	2	00			6
7			Employees' Union Dues Payable									9	0	00			7
8			Employees' Medical Insurance														8
9			Payable								2	1	6	00			9
10			Employees' Community Chest														10
11			Payable									3	7	00			11
12			Accounts Receivable									4	0	00			12
13			Salaries Payable							4	8	4	2	73			13
14			Payroll register page 68, for week														14
15			ended November 7.														15
16																	16

Next, the entry to record the employer's payroll taxes is journalized.

17		7	Payroll Tax Expense		4	2	2	72							17
18			FICA Tax Payable							3	6	5	15		18
19			Federal Unemployment Tax Payable									9	09		19
20			State Unemployment Tax Payable								4	8	48		20
21			To record employer's share of												21
22			FICA tax and employer's federal												22
23			and state unemployment taxes.												23
24															24

Finally, Harding and Associates, on the basis of the previous entry, issues one check payable to a payroll bank account. To pay its employees, it will draw separate payroll checks on this payroll bank account.

25		7	Salaries Payable		4	8	4	2	73						25
26			Cash							4	8	4	2	73	26
27			To record payment of employees												27
28			(by issuing one check payable												28
29			to payroll bank account).												29
30															30

As stated previously, in the first payroll entry, small employers will credit Cash directly instead of Salaries Payable.

PAYMENTS OF FICA TAXES AND EMPLOYEES' INCOME TAX WITHHOLDING

After an employer has paid the employees, he or she has to make payments in the form of federal tax deposits for (1) employees' federal income taxes withheld, (2) employees' FICA taxes withheld, and (3) the employer's share of FICA taxes. These deposits, which put the employers on a pay-as-you-go basis, are made during the three-month quarter.

For *large-sized employers,* if the combined total of undeposited employees' income taxes and FICA taxes levied on both employees and employer is greater than $3,000 for an **eighth-of-a-month period** (approximately three or four days), the employer has to make deposits within three banking days after the end of the period and must include at least 95 percent of the tax liability. Note that these amounts are cumulative. These eighth-of-a-month periods end on the 3rd, 7th, 11th, 15th, 19th, 22nd, 25th, and last day of any month. For example, assume that an employer has $4,950 of undeposited taxes for an eighth-of-a-month period ending on Friday, September 7. Since the banks are traditionally closed on Saturday and Sunday, the employer would have to make the deposit by Wednesday, September 12.

For *medium-sized employers,* if the total undeposited income taxes and FICA taxes for any *month* is between $500 and $3,000, the employer has to make the deposit within fifteen days after the end of the month.

But now suppose you're just a *small-sized employer,* and the total amount of your undeposited income taxes and FICA taxes at the end of the calendar **quarter** (three months) is less than $500; you don't have to make a deposit until you submit your quarterly return, Form 941. Now, remember that we're talking about a quarter (three months). You keep records on the basis of a calendar year, with the first quarter ending March 31, the second quarter ending June 30, the third quarter ending September 30, and the fourth quarter ending December 31. (If taxes are less than $500 at the end of a single month, they can be carried over to the following month within the quarter.)

Harding and Associates, for the week ended November 7, had the following taxes due:

Employees' income tax withheld	$1,240.10
Employees' FICA taxes withheld	365.17
Employer's FICA tax	365.15
Total	$1,970.42

Because Harding's tax liability is less than $3,000, it is not necessary to make a federal tax deposit at this time.

Assume that for the week ended November 14 Harding and Associates had the following taxes due:

Employees' income tax withheld	$1,364.11
Employees' FICA taxes withheld	401.68
Employer's FICA tax	401.68
Total	$2,167.47

The total cumulative liability for the two-week period is now $4,137.89 ($1,970.42 + $2,167.47). Because the total cumulative liability is greater than $3,000, it is necessary for the firm to make a federal tax deposit at the end of the second week, or within three banking days thereafter.

Harding receives a federal tax deposit card (preprinted with the company's name and tax number) from the Internal Revenue Service. The accountant records the amount of the deposit and the name of the bank where the deposit is to be submitted (any authorized commercial bank or Federal Reserve bank). The deposits are forwarded to the U.S. Treasury. The entry in general journal form to record the deposit of two weeks' taxes looks like this.

Objective 2

Journalize the entry for the deposit of employees' income taxes withheld and FICA taxes.

1	19– Nov.	15	Employees' Income Tax Payable	2 6 0 4 21		1
2			FICA Tax Payable	1 5 3 3 68		2
3			Cash		4 1 3 7 89	3
4			Issued check to record payment			4
5			of federal tax deposit.			5
6						6
7						7
8						8
9						9

The T accounts are as follows.

Employees' Income Tax Payable			
Nov. 15	2,604.21	Nov. 7	1,240.10
		Nov. 14	1,364.11

FICA Tax Payable			
Nov. 15	1,533.68	Nov. 7	365.17
		Nov. 7	365.15
		Nov. 14	401.68
		Nov. 14	401.68

Cash		
	Nov. 15	4,137.89

PAYMENTS OF STATE UNEMPLOYMENT INSURANCE

States differ with regard to both the rate and the taxable base for unemployment insurance. The state tax is usually due by the end of the month following the end of the calendar quarter. Here's the general journal entry made by Harding and Associates for the first quarter (January, February, and March).

1	19– Apr.	27	State Unemployment Tax Payable	2 0 3 0 69		1
2			Cash		2 0 3 0 69	2
3			To record payment of state			3
4			unemployment tax.			4
5						5
6						6
7						7
8						8
9						9
10						10

The T accounts are as follows.

State Unemployment Tax Payable		Cash	
–	+	+	–
Apr. 27 2,030.69	Apr. 27 Bal. 2,030.69		Apr. 27 2,030.69

The balance in State Unemployment Tax Payable is the result of weekly entries recording payroll tax expense.

PAYMENTS OF FEDERAL UNEMPLOYMENT INSURANCE

The FUTA tax is calculated quarterly, during the month following the end of each calendar quarter. **If the accumulated tax liability is greater than $100, the tax is deposited in a commercial bank or Federal Reserve bank, accompanied by a preprinted federal tax deposit card,** like the form used to deposit employees' federal income tax withholding and FICA taxes. The due date for this deposit is the last day of the month following the end of the quarter, the same as the due dates for the Employer's Quarterly Federal Tax Return and for state unemployment taxes.

19– Apr.	27	Federal Unemployment Tax Payable		4 7 6 30*				
		Cash				4 7 6 30		
		To record payment of federal						
		unemployment tax.						

*The calculation of $476.30 is shown on page 283.

The T accounts are as follows.

Federal Unemployment Tax Payable		Cash	
–	+	+	–
Apr. 27 476.30	Apr. 27 Bal. 476.30		Apr. 27 476.30

The balance in Federal Unemployment Tax Payable is taken from the weekly entries recording payroll tax expense.

Employer's Quarterly Federal Tax Return (Form 941)

This return, which applies to federal income taxes withheld and FICA taxes, must be filed by the end of the month following the end of the quarter. Consequently, the due dates for a calendar-year taxpayer are: first quarter, April 30; second quarter, July 31; third quarter, October 31; fourth quarter, January 31. Once an employer has secured an identification number and has filed his or her first return, the Internal Revenue Service sends forms directly to the employer. These forms will have the employer's name, address, and identification number filled in.

Objective 4

Complete Employer's Quarterly Federal Tax Return, Form 941.

Harding's sources of information for its Employer's Quarterly Federal Tax Return are the payroll registers and the general ledger accounts. Its Form 941 for the fourth quarter is shown in Figure 10-2. Note that in the illustration the taxable FICA wages are multiplied by 14.2 percent (the 7.1 percent portion contributed by the employees plus the 7.1 percent matching portion contributed by the employer). Also note the tax deposit section indicating the amount and date of each deposit. In this case, the deposits are up to date and no payment is due. However, if an amount is shown on line 15 for undeposited taxes due, the entry for payment is a debit to Employees' Income Tax Payable, a debit to FICA Tax Payable (employees' and employer's share), and a credit to Cash.

Employer's Quarterly Federal Tax Return
► For Paperwork Reduction Act Notice, see page 2.

OMB No. 1545-0029

T	
FF	
FD	
FP	
I	
T	

Your name, address, employer identification number, and calendar quarter of return. (If not correct, please change.)

Name (as distinguished from trade name)
Donald A. Harding

Trade name, if any
Harding and Associates

Address and ZIP code
546 South Foss Street
Spokane, WA 99203

Date quarter ended
December 31, 19--

Employer identification number
64-7218463

If address is different from prior return, check here ►

Record of Federal Tax Liability
(Complete if line 13 is $500 or more)

See the instructions under rule 4 on page 4 for details before checking these boxes.

Check only if you made eighth-monthly deposits using the 95% rule. ► ☐

Check only if you are a first-time 3-banking-day depositor. ► ☐

If you are not liable for returns in the future, write "FINAL" . . . . ►

Date final wages paid . . . . ►

Complete for First Quarter Only

1 **a** Number of employees (except household) employed in the pay period that includes March 12th . . ► **12**

b If you are a subsidiary corporation AND your parent corporation files a consolidated Form 1120, enter parent corporation's employer identification number (EIN) ►

Date wages paid		Tax liability
Day		
1st-3rd	A	
4th-7th	B	2,153.68
8th-11th	C	
12th-15th	D	2,028.56
16th-19th	E	
20th-22nd	F	2,244.60
23rd-25th	G	
26th-last	H	2,212.82
I Total ►		8,639.66
1st-3rd	I	
4th-7th	J	1,970.42
8th-11th	K	
12th-15th	L	2,167.47
16th-19th	M	
20th-22nd	N	2,005.36
23rd-25th	O	
26th-last	P	2,151.19
II Total ►		8,294.44
1st-3rd	Q	
4th-7th	R	2,225.52
8th-11th	S	
12th-15th	T	2,228.36
16th-19th	U	
20th-22nd	V	2,177.80
23rd-25th	W	
26th-last	X	1,870.70
III Total ►		8,502.38
IV Total for quarter (add lines I, II, and III)		25,436.48

(First month of quarter / Second month of quarter / Third month of quarter)

2	Total wages and tips subject to withholding, plus other compensation . . . ►	85,426	40
3	**a** Income tax withheld from wages, tips, pensions, annuities, sick pay, gambling, etc. . . . ►	13,305	93
	b Backup withholding . . . . ►	0	
	c Total income tax withheld (add lines 3a and 3b) ►	13,305	93
4	Adjustment of withheld income tax for preceding quarters of calendar year:		
	a From wages, tips, pensions, annuities, sick pay, gambling, etc. . . . ►	0	
	b From backup withholding . . . ►	0	
	c Total adjustments (add lines 4a and 4b) . ►	0	
5	Adjusted total of income tax withheld (line 3c as adjusted by line 4c)	13,305	93
6	Taxable social security wages paid: $ 85,426 40 X 14.2% (.142) . .	12,130	55
7	**a** Taxable tips reported: $ 0 X 7.1% (.071) . .	0	
	b Tips deemed to be wages (see instructions): $ 0 X 7.1% (.071) . .	0	
8	Total social security taxes (add lines 6, 7a, and 7b) . .	12,130	55
9	Adjustment of social security taxes (see instructions) ►	0	
10	Adjusted total of social security taxes	12,130	55
11	Total taxes (add lines 5 and 10) . . . . ►	25,436	48
12	Advance earned income credit (EIC) payments, if any ►	0	
13	Net taxes (subtract line 12 from line 11). This must equal line IV (plus line IV of Schedule A (Form 941) if you have treated backup withholding as a separate liability.) .	25,436	48
14	Total deposits for quarter, including any overpayment applied from a prior quarter, from your records . . . . ►	25,436	48
15	Undeposited taxes due (subtract line 14 from line 13). Enter here and pay to Internal Revenue Service . . . ►	0	

16 If line 14 is more than line 13, enter overpayment here ► $ and check if to be: ☐ Applied to next return, or ☐ Refunded.

Under penalties of perjury, I declare that I have examined this return, including accompanying schedules and statements, and to the best of my knowledge and belief it is true, correct, and complete.

Signature ► *Donald A. Harding*   Title ► Owner   Date ► 1/29/19--

Please file this form with your Internal Revenue Service Center (see instructions on "Where to File").   Form **941** (Rev.   )

Figure 10-2

Withholding Statements for Employees (W-2 forms)

Objective 5

Prepare W-2 forms and W-3 forms.

The employer has to furnish W-2 forms to employees on or before the January 31 following the close of the preceding year or within 30 days after an employee leaves service. The source of the information on the W-2 form is the employee's individual earnings record. Graham C. Laboe's earnings record, presented in Chapter 9, will be our source for this example (see Figure 9-7). The accountant fills out Form W-2 (Figure 10-3) in quadruplicate and gives copies B and C to the employee.

Notice the squares in block 5. Statutory employees are life insurance and traveling salespersons; legal representatives include attorneys and parents; 942 employees include household workers; subtotal is used if the employer is submitting more than forty-one W-2 forms. Block 7 shows the total paid to employees as advance earned income credit payments. For qualifying low-income taxpayers, earned income credit is a deduction from income tax owed.

Figure 10-3

1 Control number 22222	For Paperwork Reduction Act Notice, see back of Copy D. OMB No. 1545-0008	For Official Use Only	
2 Employer's name, address, and ZIP code	3 Employer's identification number 64–7218463	4 Employer's State number 462–718	

Harding and Associates
546 South Foss Street
Spokane, WA 99203

5 Stat. employee ☐ Deceased ☐ Legal rep. ☐ 942 emp. ☐ Subtotal ☐ Void ☐

6 Allocated tips

7 Advance EIC payment

| 8 Employee's social security number 543–24–1680 | 9 Federal income tax withheld $5,768.29 | 10 Wages, tips, other compensation $30,161.00 | 11 Social security tax withheld $2,141.43 |

12 Employee's name (first, middle, last)
Graham Charles Laboe

13 Social security wages $30,161.00

14 Social security tips

1582 North Pierce Street
Spokane, WA 99204

16 °

17 State income tax   18 State wages, tips, etc.   19 Name of State

20 Local income tax   21 Local wages, tips, etc.   22 Name of locality

15 Employee's address and ZIP code

Form **W-2 Wage and Tax Statement** 19   Copy A For Social Security Administration * See Instructions for Forms W-2 and W-2P   Department of the Treasury Internal Revenue Service

Employer's Annual Federal Income Tax Reports

Harding sends copy A of each employee's W-2 form to the District Director of Internal Revenue on or before February 28. The accountant attaches these to Form W-3, the Transmittal of Income and Tax Statements, shown in Figure 10-4.

To sum up thus far: The employer must submit the following at the end of the calendar year: (1) Employer's Quarterly Federal Tax Return for the fourth quarter, (2) copy A of all employees' W-2 forms, and (3) Form W-3. The employer keeps copy D of the W-2 forms.

1 Control number		33333	OMB No. 1545-0008			

	Kind of Payer and Tax Statements Transmitted ▶	2 941/941E □ Military □ 943 □ CT-1 □ 942 □ Medicare Fed. emp. □		3 W-2 ☒ W-2P □	4	5 Number of statements attached 12
6 Allocated tips		7 Advance EIC payments 0		8		
9 Federal income tax withheld 61,093.22		10 Wages, tips, and other compensation 343,220.32		11 Social security (FICA) tax withheld 23,048.04		
12 Employer's State number 462–718		13 Social security (FICA) wages 324,620.32		14 Social security (FICA) tips 0		
15 Employer's identification number 64— 7218463				16 Establishment number 0		
17 Employer's name Harding and Associates				18 Gross annuity, pension, etc. (Form W-2P) 0		
546 South Foss Street Spokane, WA 99203				20 Taxable amount (Form W-2P) 0		
19 Employer's address and ZIP code (If available, place label over boxes 15, 17, and 19.)				21 Income tax withheld by third-party payer 0		

Under penalties of perjury, I declare that I have examined this return and accompanying documents, and to the best of my knowledge and belief, they are true, correct, and complete. In the case of documents without recipients' identifying numbers, I have complied with the requirements of the law in attempting to secure such numbers from the recipients.

Signature ▶ *Donald A. Harding*   Title ▶ Owner   Date ▶1/31/--

Form **W-3** Transmittal of Income and Tax Statements

Department of the Treasury
Internal Revenue Service

Figure 10-4

Reports and Payments of State Unemployment Insurance

Figure 10-5 shows the state unemployment insurance return for Harding and Associates for the first quarter with an assumed state rate of 3 percent on the first $12,000 paid to each employee during the calendar year. The source for the wage report section is the employees' individual earnings records.

Various states differ with regard to both the rate and the taxable base for unemployment insurance. The state tax is usually due by the end of the month following the end of the calendar quarter; the due dates consequently coincide with the due dates for Form 941.

Here is the general journal entry made by Harding and Associates for the first quarter (January, February, and March).

Objective 6

Prepare state and federal unemployment insurance reports and the related journal entries.

	19– Apr.	27	State Unemployment Tax Payable		2 0 3 0 69			1
2			Cash			2 0 3 0 69		2
3			To record payment of state					3
4			unemployment tax.					4

	2. FEDERAL I.D. NO.	TAX OFFICE	EMP. CLASS	3. CALENDAR QUARTER ENDING DATE			TAX RATE %	4. EMPLOYMENT SEC. NO.	
				MO.	DAY	YR.		ACCOUNT	BR
	64-7218463	15	7	3	31	–	3.0	462-718	810

STATE OF WASHINGTON
EMPLOYMENT SECURITY DEPARTMENT
OLYMPIA, WASHINGTON 98504

EMPLOYER'S QUARTERLY REPORT OF EMPLOYEE'S WAGES

ATTACH ADDITIONAL WAGE LISTING HERE

▶ READ INSTRUCTIONS ON BACK OF PAGE 3 BEFORE COMPLETING THIS FORM.

▶ IF ANY BUSINESS CHANGES HAVE OCCURRED, COMPLETE PAGE 3.

1. EMPLOYER'S NAME AND ADDRESS

Donald A. Harding
Harding and Associates
546 South Foss Street
Spokane, WA 99203

LINE	5. EMPLOYEE'S SOCIAL SECURITY NUMBER			6. EMPLOYEE'S NAME LAST FIRST INITIAL	7. HOURS WORKED THIS QTR.	8. TOTAL WASHINGTON WAGES PAID THIS QUARTER	
L1	533	16	7285	Anderson, Dennis L.	582	2,840	00
L2	541	27	6982	Bowlen, Ralph P.	598	2,620	00
L3	539	87	1643	Daniels, John N.	572	5,980	00
L4	533	98	5379	Drew, Nancy R.	520	2,756	00
L5	526	71	8478	Farrell, Steven L.	520	2,150	00
L6	541	19	6143	Harwood, Lance C.	520	11,400	00
L7	543	24	1680	Laboe, Graham C.	520	7,176	00
L8	533	62	1745	Lyman, Mary C.	520	7,200	00
L9	541	38	9394	Miller, Robert M.	598	5,769	50
L10	540	29	7162	Olsen, Marvin C.	582	2,422	00
L11	538	12	2796	Stanfield, John D.	520	10,200	00
L12	529	92	8131	Tucker, Norma P.	572	7,176	00

	NO. OF PAGES	9. NO. OF EMPLOYEES	10.	WAGES	
TOTALS FOR THIS PAGE		12		67,689	50
	11.	12.	13.		
GRAND TOTALS ALL PAGES	1	12		67,689	50

PAGE 1 - ORIGINAL
EMPLOYMENT SECURITY DEPARTMENT COPY

— **DO NOT DETACH**

DO NOT DETACH

EMS 5208

▶ ATTACH CHECK HERE

25. EMPLOYER'S NAME AND ADDRESS

Donald A. Harding
Harding and Associates
546 South Foss Street
Spokane, WA 99203

STATE OF WASHINGTON
EMPLOYMENT SECURITY DEPARTMENT
OLYMPIA, WASHINGTON 98504

EMPLOYER'S QUARTERLY TAX REPORT

▶ DO NOT MAKE ENTRIES IN THE SHADED AREAS.

PAGE 1 - ORIGINAL
EMPLOYMENT SECURITY DEPARTMENT COPY

COMPUTATION OF PAYMENT

		FOR DEPARTMENT USE		
14. TOTAL WAGES (SAME AS ITEM 13)			67,689	50
15. EXCESS WAGES			0	
16. TAXABLE WAGES (ITEM 14 LESS ITEM 15)			67,689	50
17. TAX DUE YOUR TAX RATE 3% TIMES ITEM 16			2,030	69
18. PENALTY - LATE PAYMENT (MINIMUM PENALTY - $2.00)			0	
19. INTEREST			0	
20. ADJUSTMENT (ATTACH STATEMENT OF ACCOUNT - FORM EMS 5229)			0	
21. PENALTY - LATE REPORT ($10.00)			0	
22. REMITTANCE (MAKE CHECKS PAYABLE TO: EMPLOYMENT SECURITY DEPARTMENT)			2,030	69

	1ST MONTH	2ND MONTH	3RD MONTH
23. NUMBER OF COVERED EMPLOYEES	12	12	12

24. I CERTIFY THAT THE INFORMATION CONTAINED IN THIS REPORT IS TRUE AND CORRECT AND THAT NO PART OF THE TAX REPORTED WAS OR IS TO BE DEDUCTED FROM WORKERS WAGES.

SIGNATURE *Donald A. Harding*   TITLE Owner

DATE April 27, 19--   TELEPHONE NO. (509) 272-4414

FOR DEPARTMENTAL USE				26. ANNUAL TAXABLE WAGE BASE EACH EMPLOYEE	27. FEDERAL I.D. NO.	TAX OFFICE	EMP. CLASS	28. CALENDAR QUARTER ENDING DATE			29. TAX RATE %	30. EMPLOYMENT SEC. NO.	
DATE RECEIVED	TAX	PENALTY	INTEREST					MO.	DAY	YR.		ACCOUNT	BR
				$12,000	64-7218463	15	7	3	31	–	3.0	462-718	810
RECEIVED BY		AUDITED BY											

Figure 10-5

REPORTS AND PAYMENTS OF FEDERAL UNEMPLOYMENT INSURANCE

Each employer who is subject to the Federal Unemployment Tax Act, as outlined in Chapter 9, must submit an Employer's Annual Federal Unemployment Tax Return, Form 940, not later than the January 31 following the close of the calendar year. This deadline may be extended until February 10 if the employer has made deposits paying the FUTA tax liability in full. The FUTA tax is calculated quarterly, during the month following the end of each calendar quarter. **If the accumulated tax liability is greater than $100, the tax is deposited in a commercial bank or Federal Reserve bank, accompanied by a preprinted federal tax deposit card.** The due date for this deposit is the last day of the month following the end of the quarter, the same as the dates for the Employer's Quarterly Federal Tax Return and state unemployment taxes.

The accountant computes the tax liability for the first quarter as follows: Suppose that unemployment-taxable earnings are $59,537.50 and that the FUTA tax rate is .8 percent. Then $59,537.50 × .008 = $476.30. As stated on page 278, the entry for the deposit of the tax, in general journal form, is as follows.

19– Apr.	27	Federal Unemployment Tax Payable	4 7 6 30	
		Cash		4 7 6 30
		To record payment of federal		
		unemployment tax.		

Unemployment taxable earnings for the second quarter are $15,240, which means a tax liability of $121.92. As the year goes on, many employees' total earnings will pass the $7,000 mark and the firm's tax liability will be reduced accordingly.

Harding does not have to make a deposit following the third quarter because the total accumulated liability is less than $100. Harding can pay the unpaid tax liability of $73.78 ($51.62 for the third quarter, and $22.16 for the fourth quarter) when the Employer's Annual Federal Unemployment Tax Return (Form 940) is filed.

Figure 10-6 presents the annual return (Form 940) for Harding and Associates. The employer should complete the quarterly state unemployment tax return for the last quarter of the year before he or she tries to prepare the Employer's Annual Federal Unemployment Tax Return. Data from the state returns are the source of information for the federal Form 940.

Form 940

Department of the Treasury
Internal Revenue Service

Employer's Annual Federal Unemployment (FUTA) Tax Return

▶ For Paperwork Reduction Act Notice, see page 2.

OMB No. 1545-0028

19 –

T	
FF	
FD	
FP	
I	
T	

If Incorrect, make any necessary change. ▶

Name (as distinguished from trade name)
Donald A. Harding

Trade name, if any
Harding and Associates

Address and ZIP code
546 South Foss Street
Spokane, WA 99203

Calendar Year
19 –

Employer identification number
64-7218463

A Did you pay all required contributions to your State unemployment fund by the due date of Form 940? . . . . ☒ Yes ☐ No

If you check the "Yes" box, enter amount of contributions paid to your State unemployment fund . . . . . . ▶ $ 9,856 56

B Are you required to pay contributions to only one State? . . . . ☒ Yes ☐ No

If you checked the "Yes" box, (1) Enter the name of the State where you are required to pay contributions . . . . . ▶ Washington

(2) Enter your State reporting number(s) as shown on State unemployment tax return . . . . . . ▶ 462-718

PART I.—Computation of Taxable Wages and Credit Reduction (To Be Completed by All Taxpayers)

1	Total payments (including exempt payments) during the calendar year for services of employees	**1**	343,220	32
2	Exempt payments. (Explain each exemption shown, attaching additional sheets if necessary) ▶	Amount paid		
		2		
3	Payments for services in excess of $7,000. Enter only the excess over the first $7,000 paid to individual employees exclusive of exempt amounts entered on line 2. Do not use State wage limitation	**3** 259,220 32		
4	Total exempt payments (add lines 2 and 3)	**4**	259,220	32
5	**Total taxable wages** (subtract line 4 from line 1). (If any portion is exempt from State contributions, see instructions)▶	**5**	84,000	00
6	Credit reduction for unpaid advances to the States listed. Enter the wages included on line 5 above for each State and multiply by the rate shown.			

(a) AR _____ x .006 _____	(g) MI _____ x .006 _____	(m) VT _____ x .006 _____
(b) CT _____ x .007 _____	(h) MN _____ x .006 _____	(n) WV _____ x .006 _____
(c) DE _____ x .006 _____	(i) NJ _____ x .006 _____	**Outside the U.S.**
(d) DC _____ x .011 _____	(j) OH _____ x .006 _____	(o) PR _____ x .006 _____
(e) IL _____ x .007 _____	(k) PA _____ x .007 _____	(p) VI _____ x .006 _____
(f) KY _____ x .003 _____	(l) RI _____ x .006 _____	

7	Total credit reduction (add lines 6(a) through 6(p) and enter on line 2, Part II or line 4, Part III) . . . . . ▶	**7**	0

PART II.—Tax Due or Refund (Complete if You Checked the "Yes" Boxes in Both Items A and B Above)

1	FUTA tax. Multiply the wages on line 5, Part I, by .008 and enter here	**1**	672	00
2	Enter amount from line 7, Part I	**2**	0	
3	**Total FUTA tax** (add lines 1 and 2)	**3**	672	00
4	Less: Total FUTA tax deposited for the year from your records	**4**	598	22
5	**Balance due** (subtract line 4 from line 3—if over $100, see Part IV instructions). Pay to IRS . . . ▶	**5**	73	78
6	**Overpayment** (subtract line 3 from line 4). Check if to be: ☐ Applied to next return, or ☐ Refunded . . . ▶	**6**		

PART III.—Tax Due or Refund (Complete if You Checked the "No" Box in Either Item A or Item B Above. Also complete Part V)

1	Gross FUTA tax. Multiply the wages on line 5, Part I, by .035	**1**	
2	Maximum credit. Multiply the wages on line 5, Part I, by .027.	**2**	
3	Enter the smaller of the amount on line 11, Part V, or line 2, Part III	**3**	
4	Enter amount from line 7, Part I	**4**	
5	**Credit allowable** (subtract line 4 from line 3)	**5**	
6	Total FUTA tax (subtract line 5 from line 1)	**6**	
7	Less: Total FUTA tax deposited for the year from your records	**7**	
8	**Balance due** (subtract line 7 from line 6—if over $100, see Part IV instructions). Pay to IRS . . . ▶	**8**	
9	**Overpayment** (subtract line 6 from line 7).Check if to be: ☐ Applied to next return, or ☐ Refunded . . . ▶	**9**	

PART IV.—Record of Quarterly Federal Tax Liability for Unemployment Tax (Do not include State liability)

Quarter	First	Second	Third	Fourth	Total for Year
Liability for quarter .	$476.30	$121.92	$51.62	$22.16	$672.00

If you will not have to file returns in the future, write "Final" here (see general instruction "Who Must File") . . . . . ▶

Under penalties of perjury, I declare that I have examined this return, including accompanying schedules and statements, and to the best of my knowledge and belief, it is true, correct, and complete, and that no part of any payment made to a State unemployment fund claimed as a credit was or is to be deducted from the payments to employees.

Date ▶ 1/26/--   Signature ▶ *Donald A. Harding*   Title (Owner, etc.) ▶ Owner

Form **940**

Figure 10-6

WORKERS' COMPENSATION INSURANCE

Objective 7

Calculate the premium for workers' compensation insurance, and prepare the entry for payment in advance.

As we said in Chapter 9 when we were describing the laws affecting employment, most states require employers to provide **workers' compensation insurance** or industrial accident insurance, either through plans administered by the state or through private insurance companies authorized by the state. The employer usually has to pay all the premiums. The premium rate varies with the amount of risk the job entails and the company's number of accidents. Handling molten steel ingots is a lot more dangerous than typing reports. So it is very important that employees be identified properly according to the insurance premium classifications. For example, the rate for office work may be .15 percent of the payroll for office work; the rate for industrial labor in heavy manufacturing may be 3.5 percent of the payroll for that category. These same figures may be expressed as $.15 per $100 of payroll and $3.50 per $100 of payroll.

Generally, the employer pays a premium in advance, based on the estimated payrolls for the year. After the year ends, the employer knows the exact amounts of the payrolls and can calculate the exact premium. At this time, depending on the difference between the estimated and the exact premium, the employer either pays an additional premium or gets a credit for overpayment.

At Harding and Associates, there are two types of work classifications: office work and sales work. At the beginning of the year, the firm's accountant computed the estimated annual premium, based on the predicted payrolls for the year, as follows.

Classification	Predicted Payroll	Rate (Percent)	Estimated Premium
Office work	$ 76,000	.15	$ 76,000 × .0015 = $ 114
Sales work	280,000	.5	280,000 × .005 = 1,400
			Total estimated premium $1,514

As shown by T accounts, the accountant made the following entry.

Prepaid Insurance, Workers' Compensation				Cash	
+	−			+	−
Jan. 10 1,514					Jan. 10 1,514

Then, at the end of the calendar year, the accountant calculated the exact premium.

Classification	Exact Payroll	Rate (Percent)	Exact Premium
Office work	$ 78,000	.15	$ 78,000 × .0015 = $ 117.00
Sales work	286,512	.5	286,512 × .005 = 1,432.56
			Total exact premium $1,549.56

Therefore, the amount of the unpaid premium is

$1,549.56	Total exact premium
1,514.00	Less total estimated premium paid
$ 35.56	Additional premium owed

Now the accountant makes an adjusting entry, similar to the adjusting entry for expired insurance; this entry appears on the work sheet. The accountant then makes an additional adjusting entry for the extra premium owed. By T accounts, the entries are as follows.

Objective 8

Determine the amount of adjustment for workers' compensation insurance at end of year, and record adjustment.

Workers' Compensation Insurance Expense

+	−
Dec. 31 Adj. 1,514.00	
Dec. 31 Adj. 35.56	

Prepaid Insurance, Workers' Compensation

+	−
Jan. 10 Bal. 1,514	Dec. 31 Adj. 1,514

Workers' Compensation Insurance Payable

−	+
	Dec. 31 Adj. 35.56

Harding and Associates will pay this amount of unpaid premium in January, together with the estimated premium for the next year.

ADJUSTING FOR ACCRUED SALARIES AND WAGES

Assume that $800 of salaries accrue for the time between the last payday and the end of the year. The adjusting entry is the same as that introduced in Chapter 5.

DATE	DESCRIPTION	POST. REF.	DEBIT	CREDIT	
1	*Adjusting Entry*				1
2	Salary Expense		8 0 0 00		2
3	Salaries Payable			8 0 0 00	3

Salaries Payable is considered a liability account, as are employees' withholding taxes and deductions payable. Actually, federal income taxes and FICA taxes levied on employees do not legally become effective until the employees are paid. Therefore, for the purpose of recording the adjusting entry, one includes the entire liability of the gross salaries and wages under Salaries Payable or Wages Payable. In other words, in the adjusting entry, such accounts as Employees' Income Tax Payable, FICA Tax Payable (employees' share), and Employees' Union Dues Payable, are not used.

Adjusting Entry for Accrual of Payroll Taxes

As we have seen, the following taxes come under the Payroll Tax Expense account: the employer's share of the FICA tax, the state unemployment tax, and the federal unemployment tax. The employer becomes liable for these taxes only when the employees are actually paid, rather than at the time the liability to the employees is incurred. From the standpoint of legal liability, there should be no adjusting entry for Payroll Tax Expense. From the standpoint of the income statement, however, failure to make this entry means that this accrued expense for payroll taxes is not included; thus the expenses are understated and the net income is overstated, although by a rather inconsequential amount. Although the legal element is not consistent with good accounting practice, we have to abide by the law.

TAX CALENDAR

Now let's put it all together: Assume that the employer's combined monthly totals of employees' FICA taxes, employer's FICA tax, and employees' income tax withheld are usually greater than $500 and less than $3,000. So the accountant, in order to keep up with the task of paying and reporting the various taxes, compiles a chronological list of the due dates. We are including only the payroll taxes here; however, sales taxes and property taxes should also be listed. When you think about the penalties for nonpayment of taxes by the due dates, this chronological list seems to be well worth the trouble.

Jan. 10 Pay estimated annual premium for workers' compensation insurance. (This is an approximate date, as it varies among the
states.)

31 Complete Employer's Quarterly Federal Tax Return, Form 941,
for the fourth quarter and pay employees' income tax withholding, employees' FICA tax withholding, and employer's
FICA tax for wages paid during the month of December.

31 Issue copies B and C of Wage and Tax statement, Form W-2, to
employees.

31 Pay state unemployment tax liability for the previous quarter
and submit state return, employer's tax report.

31 Pay federal unemployment tax liability for previous year and
submit Form 940, Employer's Annual Federal Unemployment
Tax Return.

Feb. 15 Make federal tax deposit for employees' income tax withholding, employees' FICA tax withholding, and employer's FICA
tax for wages paid during the month of January.

28 Complete Transmittal of Income and Tax Statements, Form
W-3, and attach copy A of W-2 forms for employees.

Mar. 15 Make federal tax deposit for employees' income tax withholding, employees' FICA tax withholding, and employer's FICA
tax for wages paid during the month of February.

Apr. 30 Pay state unemployment tax liability for the previous quarter
and submit state return, employer's tax report.

30 Complete Employer's Quarterly Federal Tax Return, Form 941,
for the first quarter, and pay employees' income tax withholding, employees' FICA tax withholding, and employer's FICA
tax for wages paid during the month of March.

30 Make federal tax deposit for federal unemployment tax liability
if it exceeds $100.

PAYROLL SUMMARY

An employer's taxes (with assumed rates) based on the payroll are as
follows. Remember that rates are always subject to change.

1. FICA tax, 7.1 percent of taxable income (the first $36,000 for each em-
ployee)
2. Federal unemployment tax, .8 percent of taxable income (the first
$7,000 for each employee)
3. State unemployment tax, which varies from state to state, approximately 3 percent of taxable income (approximately the first $12,000 for
each employee)

After recording each payroll entry from the payroll register, the accountant makes the following type of entry to record the employer's payroll taxes.

17			Payroll Tax Expense	4 2 2 72			17
18			FICA Tax Payable		3 6 5 15	18
19			Federal Unemployment Tax			19
20			Payable		9 09	20
21			State Unemployment Tax Payable		4 8 48	21
22			To record employer's share of			22
23			FICA tax and employer's federal			23
24			and state unemployment taxes.			24
25						25

Payment of the tax liabilities and sample journal entries are as follows.

1. Payment of the combined amounts of employees' income tax withheld, employees' FICA tax withheld, and employer's FICA tax falls into three brackets:

   a. **Large**   If at the end of any eighth of a month (approximately three or four days) the cumulative amount of undeposited taxes so far for the calendar quarter (three months) is $3,000 or more, deposit the taxes within three banking days after the end of the period. The Internal Revenue Service divides any month into eight periods ending on the 3rd, 7th, 11th, 15th, 19th, 22nd, 25th, and last day of the month.

   b. **Medium**   If at the end of any month (except the last month of a quarter) the cumulative amount of undeposited taxes for the quarter is at least $500 but less than $3,000, deposit the taxes within fifteen days after the end of the month. For the last month of the quarter, make the payment by the end of the next month.

   c. **Small**   If at the end of a calendar month or calendar quarter (three months) the total amount of undeposited taxes is less than $500, make the payment when submitting the Employer's Quarterly Federal Tax Return.

1	19– Nov.	15	Employees' Income Tax Payable	2 6 0 4 21			1
2			FICA Tax Payable	1 5 3 3 68			2
3			Cash		4 1 3 7 89	3
4			Issued check to record payment			4
5			of federal tax deposit.			5
6						6
7						7
8						8

2. State unemployment tax is paid on a quarterly basis. Payment is due by the end of the next month following the end of the calendar quarter.

	19– Apr.	27	State Unemployment Tax Payable		2 0 3 0 69			
1					2 0 3 0 69			1
2			Cash			2 0 3 0 69		2
3			To record payment of state					3
4			unemployment tax.					4
5								5
6								6
7								7
8								8

3. If the amount of the accumulated federal unemployment tax liability exceeds $100, pay the tax by the end of the next month following the end of the quarter. If the federal unemployment tax payable is less than $100 at the end of the year, pay it by January 31 of the next year.

	19– Apr.	27	Federal Unemployment Tax Payable		4 7 6 30			
1					4 7 6 30			1
2			Cash			4 7 6 30		2
3			To record payment of federal					3
4			unemployment tax.					4
5								5
6								6

4. Workers' compensation insurance is based on a state plan or private insurance. At the beginning of the year, pay the premium in advance based on the estimated annual payroll. At the end of the year, when you know the actual payroll, adjust for the exact amount of the premium.

GLOSSARY

Eighth-of-a-month period A period used to determine the due date of tax deposits, designated by the Internal Revenue Service as follows: from the 1st to the 3rd of the month, from the 4th to the 7th of the month, from the 8th to the 11th of the month, from the 12th to the 15th of the month, from the 16th to the 19th of the month, from the 20th to the 22nd of the month, from the 23rd to the 25th of the month, and from the 26th to the last day of the month. (All dates are inclusive.)

Employer identification number The number assigned each employer by the Internal Revenue Service for use in the submission of reports and payments for FICA taxes and federal income tax withheld.

Federal unemployment tax A tax levied on the employer only, amounting to .8 percent of the first $7,000 of total earnings paid to each employee during the calendar year. This tax is used to supplement state unemployment benefits.

Payroll Tax Expense A general expense account used for recording the employer's matching portion of the FICA tax, the federal unemployment tax, and the state unemployment tax.

Quarter A three-month interval of the year, also referred to as a *calendar quarter*, as follows: first quarter, January, February, and March; second quarter, April, May, and June; third quarter, July, August, and September; fourth quarter, October, November, and December.

State unemployment tax A tax levied on the employer only. Rates differ among the various states; however, they are generally 2.7 percent or higher of the first $7,000 of total earnings paid to each employee during the calendar year. The proceeds are used to pay subsistence benefits to unemployed workers.

Workers' compensation insurance This insurance, usually paid for by the employer, provides benefits for employees injured or killed on the job. The rates vary according to the degree of risk inherent in the job. The plans may be sponsored by states or by private firms. The employer pays the premium in advance at the beginning of the year, based on the estimated payroll, and rates are adjusted after the exact payroll is known.

QUESTIONS, EXERCISES AND PROBLEMS

Discussion Questions

1. What payroll taxes are included under Payroll Tax Expense?
2. What information concerning the employee is included on a W-2 form?
3. How many copies of a W-2 form are prepared? To whom are the copies given?
4. What are Forms 940 and 941? How often are they prepared, and what are the due dates?
5. Explain the deposit requirement for federal unemployment insurance.
6. Generally, what is the time schedule for payment of premiums of workers' compensation insurance?
7. Explain the advantage of establishing a tax calendar.

Exercises

Exercise 10-1 The earnings for the calendar year for the employees of Computer Services are as follows.

Employee	Cumulative Earnings
Bach, Ralph P.	$ 12,400.00
Lindahl, Doreen C.	37,500.00
Luhr, Alan D.	36,200.00
Weist, Terry D.	18,400.00
	$104,500.00

The employees had to pay FICA tax during the year at the rate of 7.1 percent on the first $36,000 of their earnings; the employer had to pay a matching FICA tax. Unemployment insurance rates were 2.7 percent for the state and .8 percent for the federal government on the first $7,000 of an employee's earnings.

a. Determine the taxable earnings for FICA, state unemployment, and federal unemployment.
b. Determine the amount of taxes paid by the employees.
c. Determine the total amount of payroll taxes paid by the employer.
d. What percentage of the employer's total payroll of $104,500 was represented by payroll taxes?

Exercise 10-2 The salary expense of the Erskine Company this year was $150,000, of which $30,000 was not subject to FICA tax and $60,000 was not subject to state and federal unemployment taxes. Calculate Erskine's payroll tax expense for the year, using the following rates: FICA, 7.1 percent; state unemployment, 3 percent; federal unemployment, .8 percent.

Exercise 10-3 On January 13, at the end of the second weekly pay period during the year, the totals of Cooper Transfer's payroll register showed that its driver employees had earned $2,200 and its office employees had earned $600. The employees were to have FICA taxes withheld at the rate of 7.1 percent of the first $36,000, plus $275 of federal income taxes, and $90 of union dues.

a. Calculate the amount of FICA taxes to be withheld, and write the general journal entry to record the payroll.
b. Write the general journal entry to record the employer's payroll taxes, assuming that the state unemployment tax rate is 2.7 percent of the first $7,000 paid each employee, and that the federal unemployment tax is .8 percent of the same base.

Exercise 10-4 The payroll for the Quinn Company is as follows.

Gross earnings of employees	$100,000
Earnings subject to FICA tax	88,000
Earnings subject to federal unemployment tax	26,000
Earnings subject to state unemployment tax	26,000

Assuming that the payroll is subject to a FICA tax of 7.1 percent (.071), a state unemployment tax of 2.7 percent (.027), and a federal unemployment tax of .8 percent (.008), give the entry in general journal form to record the payroll tax expense.

Exercise 10-5 The following information on earnings and deductions for the pay period ended December 14 is from J. C. Willms and Company's payroll records.

Name	Gross Pay	Earnings to End of Previous Week
Fowler, Earl C.	$190.00	$ 2,500.00
Minski, Carl A.	720.00	36,000.00
Woods, Norma M.	200.00	10,000.00
Zimmer, Axel L.	210.00	10,500.00

Prepare a general journal entry to record the employer's payroll taxes. The FICA tax is 7.1 percent of the first $36,000 of earnings for each employee. The state unemployment tax rate is 3 percent of the first $7,000 of earnings of each employee, and the federal unemployment tax is .8 (.008) percent of the same base.

Exercise 10-6   On March 31 Dover Company's selected payroll accounts are as follows.

FICA Tax Payable		State Unemployment Tax Payable	
	Mar. 31 980.04		Mar. 31 414.11
	Mar. 31 980.02		

Federal Unemployment Tax Payable		Employees' Federal Income Tax Payable	
	Mar. 31 112.14		Mar. 31 1,819.82

Prepare general journal entries to record payment of the taxes.

Apr.   14 Record payment of federal tax deposit of FICA and income tax.
    30 Record payment of state unemployment tax.
    30 Record deposit of federal unemployment tax.

Exercise 10-7   Suppose that you are an accountant for a small business, and you get a premium notice for workers' compensation insurance, stipulating the rates for the coming year. You have estimated that the year's premium will be as follows.

Classification	Estimated Wages and Salaries	Rate	Estimated Premium
Office work	$ 9,000	.10%	$ 9.00
Sales work	36,000	.78%	280.80
Warehouse work	9,000	1.80%	162.00
		Total estimated premium	$451.80

On January 27 the owner issued a check for $451.80. Record the entry in general journal form.

Exercise 10-8 Still with reference to Exercise 10-7, at the end of the year the exact figures for the payroll are as follows.

Classification	Estimated Wages and Salaries	Rate	Estimated Premium	
Office work	$ 9,000	.10%		$ 9.00
Sales work	37,800	.78%		294.84
Warehouse work	9,600	1.80%		172.80
			Total actual premium	$476.64
			Less estimated premium paid	451.80
			Balance of premium due	$ 24.84

Record the adjusting entries for the insurance expired as well as for the additional premium due.

Problem Set A

Problem 10-1A Robert Johnson and Company had the following payroll for the week ended June 24.

Salaries		Deductions	
Sales salaries	$1,640.00	Income tax withheld	$230.00
Office salaries	280.00	FICA tax withheld	136.32
	$1,920.00	U.S. Savings Bonds	150.00
		Medical insurance	160.00

Assumed tax rates are as follows.

a. FICA tax, 7.1 percent (.071) on the first $36,000 for each employee
b. State unemployment tax, 2.7 percent (.027) on the first $7,000 for each employee
c. Federal unemployment tax, .8 percent (.008) on the first $7,000 for each employee

Instructions

Record the following entries in general journal form.

1. The payroll entry as of June 24
2. The entry to record the employer's payroll taxes as of June 24, assuming that the total payroll is subject to the FICA tax and that $1,410 is subject to unemployment taxes
3. The payment of the employees as of June 27, assuming that Johnson and Company issues one check payable to a payroll bank account

Problem 10-2A   The column totals of the payroll register of Rivera and Son, for the week ended January 14 of this year, show that the sales employees have earned $1,700 and the office employees $300. Rivera has deducted from the salaries of employees $336 for income taxes, $85 for medical insurance, $68 for union dues, and FICA tax at the rate of 7.1 percent (.071) on the first $36,000 of their earnings.

Instructions

Record the following entries in general journal form:

1. The payroll entry as of January 14
2. The entry to record the employer's payroll taxes as of January 14, assuming 2.7 percent (.027) of $7,000 for state unemployment insurance and .8 percent (.008) of $7,000 for federal unemployment insurance
3. The payment of the employees as of January 16, assuming that Rivera issues one check payable to a payroll bank account

Problem 10-3A   For the third quarter of the year, Sprague Company, 2116 Highland Street, Boston, MA 02102, received Form 941 from the Director of Internal Revenue. The identification number of Sprague Company is 66-7125961. Its payroll for the quarter ended September 30 is as follows.

NAME	TOTAL EARNINGS	TAXABLE EARNINGS UNEMPLOYMENT INSURANCE	TAXABLE EARNINGS FICA	FICA WITHHELD	INCOME TAX WITHHELD
Lange, M. C.	3 6 4 8 00		3 6 4 8 00	2 5 9 01	4 8 9 60
Larken, A. L.	3 4 5 6 00		3 4 5 6 00	2 4 5 38	4 7 6 80
McBride, F. C.	2 9 9 2 00	4 1 6 00	2 9 9 2 00	2 1 2 43	3 5 0 40
Randich, P. G.	3 1 3 6 00	1 2 8 00	3 1 3 6 00	2 2 2 65	3 6 9 60
Webb, A. L.	1 9 2 0 00	1 9 2 0 00	1 9 2 0 00	1 3 6 32	2 3 3 60
	15 1 5 2 00	2 4 6 4 00	15 1 5 2 00	10 7 5 79	19 2 0 00

The company has had five employees throughout the year. Assume that the FICA tax payable by the employees is 7.1 percent of the first $36,000 of their earnings and that the FICA tax payable by the employer is also 7.1 percent of the first $36,000 paid to the employees. Sprague Company has submitted the following federal tax deposits and written the accompanying checks.

On August 14, for the July Payroll	On September 12, for the August Payroll	On October 14, for the September Payroll
Employees' income	Employees' income	Employees' income
tax withheld $ 608.00	tax withheld $ 672.00	tax withheld $ 640.00
Employees' FICA	Employees' FICA	Employees' FICA
tax withheld 340.66	tax withheld 376.03	tax withheld 359.10
Employer's FICA tax 340.66	Employer's FICA tax 376.03	Employer's FICA tax 359.10
$1,289.32	$1,424.06	$1,358.20

Instructions

Complete Form 941 dated October 28. Record the tax liability and deposits (the same amounts) in the spaces marked "Total."

Problem 10-4A The Martin Company has the following balances in its general ledger as of March 1 of this year.

a. FICA tax payable (liability for February), $948.56
b. Employees' income tax payable (liability for February), $1,004.91
c. Federal unemployment tax payable (liability for January and February), $106.88
d. State unemployment tax payable (liability for January and February), $360.72
e. Medical insurance payable (liability for January and February), $1,244

The company completed the following transactions involving the payroll during March and April.

Mar. 12 Issued check for $1,953.47, payable to the Security Bank and Trust, for the monthly deposit of February FICA taxes and employees' federal income tax withheld.

12 Issued check for $106.88, payable to the Security Bank and Trust, for the deposit of February federal unemployment tax.

31 Recorded the payroll entry in the general journal from the payroll register for March. The payroll register has the following column totals.

Sales salaries	$5,600.00	
Office salaries	1,080.00	
Total earnings		$6,680.00
Employees' income tax deductions	$1,004.91	
Employees' FICA tax deductions	474.28	
Medical insurance deductions	622.00	
Total deductions		2,101.19
Net pay		$4,578.81

31 Recorded payroll taxes in the general journal. Employees' FICA tax is 7.1 percent, employer's is 7.1 percent, state unemployment insurance is 2.7 percent, and federal unemployment insurance is .8 percent.

31 Issued check for $4,578.81 payable to a payroll bank account.

Apr. 14 Issued check for $1,866, payable to Noble Insurance Company, in payment of employees' medical insurance for January, February, and March.

14 Issued check for $541.08, payable to the State Tax Commission, for state unemployment taxes for January, February, and March. The check was accompanied by the quarterly tax return.

14 Issued check for $1,953.47, payable to the Security Bank and Trust, for the monthly deposit of March FICA taxes and employees' federal income tax withheld.

Instructions

Record the transactions listed above in the general journal.

Problem Set B

Problem 10-1B The Draper Clinical Laboratory had the following payroll for the week ended June 15.

Salaries		Deductions	
Technicians' salaries	$1,860.00	Income tax withheld	$287.00
Office salaries	390.00	FICA tax withheld	159.75
	$2,250.00	U.S. Savings Bonds	160.00
		Medical insurance	180.00

Assumed tax rates are as follows.

a. FICA tax, 7.1 percent (.071) on the first $36,000 for each employee
b. State unemployment tax, 2.7 percent (.027) on the first $9,000 for each employee
c. Federal unemployment tax, .8 percent (.008) on the first $7,000 for each employee

Instructions

Record the following entries in general journal form.

1. The payroll entry as of June 15
2. The entry to record the employer's payroll taxes as of June 15, assuming that the total payroll is subject to the FICA tax and that $1,400 is subject to unemployment taxes
3. The payment of the employees as of June 18, assuming that Draper Clinical Laboratory issued one check payable to a payroll bank account

Problem 10-2B The column totals of the payroll register of the Sheridan Chair Company for the week ended January 28 of this year show that the sales employees have earned $1,920 and the office employees $360. Sheridan has deducted from the salaries of employees $296 for income taxes, $90 for medical insurance, $72 for union dues, and FICA tax at the rate of 7.1 percent (.071) on the first $36,000 of their earnings.

Instructions

Record the following entries in general journal form:

1. The payroll entry as of January 28
2. The entry to record the payroll taxes as of January 28, assuming 2.7 percent (.027) for state unemployment insurance and .8 percent (.008) for federal unemployment insurance on the first $7,000
3. The payment of the employees as of January 31, assuming that Sheridan issues one check payable to a payroll bank account

Problem 10-3B Nowell Machine Shop, of 3216 Stanich Boulevard, Los Angeles, California 90028, received Form 941 from the Director of Internal Revenue. The identification number for Nowell Machine Shop is 75-3959166. Its payroll for the quarter ended September 30 is as follows.

NAME	TOTAL EARNINGS	TAXABLE EARNINGS UNEMPLOYMENT INSURANCE	TAXABLE EARNINGS FICA	FICA WITHHELD	INCOME TAX WITHHELD
Ballard, F. N.	5 0 5 9 20		5 0 5 9 20	3 5 9 20	6 8 4 80
Carrier, M. A.	3 8 1 4 40		3 8 1 4 40	2 7 0 83	5 0 5 60
Couch, H. E.	3 0 6 5 60		3 0 6 5 60	2 1 7 66	4 0 4 80
Edwards, J. A.	3 4 7 2 00		3 4 7 2 00	2 4 6 51	4 7 0 40
Goode, D. L.	2 3 6 1 60	1 6 7 6 80	2 3 6 1 60	1 6 7 67	3 1 8 40
	17 7 7 2 80	1 6 7 6 80	17 7 7 2 80	1 2 6 1 87	2 3 8 4 00

The company has had five employees during the year. Assume that the employees have paid a FICA tax of 7.1 percent on the first $36,000 of their earnings and that the employer has paid the same percentage on their earnings. F. R. Nowell, the owner, has submitted the following federal tax deposits and written the accompanying checks.

On August 12, for the July Payroll	On September 13, for the August Payroll	On October 12, for the September Payroll
Employees' income tax withheld $ 754.02	Employees' income tax withheld $ 789.98	Employees' income tax withheld $ 840.00
Employees' FICA tax withheld 384.38	Employees' FICA tax withheld 411.48	Employees' FICA tax withheld 466.01
Employer's FICA tax 384.38	Employer's FICA tax 411.48	Employer's FICA tax 466.01
$1,522.78	$1,612.94	$1,772.02

Instructions

Complete Form 941 dated October 28. Record the tax liability and deposits (the same amounts) in the spaces marked "Total."

Problem 10-4B The Lafke Company has the following balances in its general ledger as of March 1 of this year.

a. FICA tax payable (liability for February), $1,931.20
b. Employees' federal income tax payable (liability for February), $2,040
c. Federal unemployment tax payable (liability for the months of January and February), $217.60
d. State unemployment tax payable (liability for the months of January and February), $734.40
e. Medical insurance payable (liability for January and February), $1,608

The company completed the following transactions involving the payroll during March and April.

Mar. 3 Issued check for $3,971.20 to Common Bank and Trust, for monthly deposit of February FICA taxes and employees' federal income tax withheld.

31 Recorded the payroll entry in the general journal from the payroll register for March. The payroll register had the following column totals.

Sales salaries	$10,400.00	
Office salaries	3,200.00	
Total earnings		$13,600.00
Employees' federal income tax deductions	$ 2,016.00	
Employees' FICA tax deductions	965.60	
Medical insurance deductions	804.00	
Total deductions		3,785.60
Net pay		$ 9,814.40

31 Recorded payroll taxes in the general journal. Employees' FICA tax is 7.1 percent, employer's is 7.1 percent, state unemployment insurance is 2.7 percent, and federal unemployment insurance is .8 percent.

31 Issued check for $9,814.40, payable to a payroll bank account.

31 Issued check for $108.80, payable to Common Bank and Trust for deposit of federal unemployment tax for January and February.

Apr. 3 Issued check for $3,947.20, payable to Common Bank and Trust, for monthly deposit of March FICA taxes and employees' federal income tax withheld.

6 Issued check for $2,412, payable to Fidelity Insurance Company, in payment of employees' medical insurance for January, February, and March.

14 Issued check for $1,101.60, payable to the State Tax Commission, for state unemployment taxes for January, February, and March. The check was accompanied by the quarterly tax return.

Instructions

Record the transactions listed above in the general journal.

REVIEW OF T ACCOUNT PLACEMENT AND REPRESENTATIVE TRANSACTIONS CHAPTERS 7 THROUGH 10

Review of T-account Placement

The following sums up the placement of T accounts covered in Chapters 7 through 10 in relation to the fundamental accounting equation.

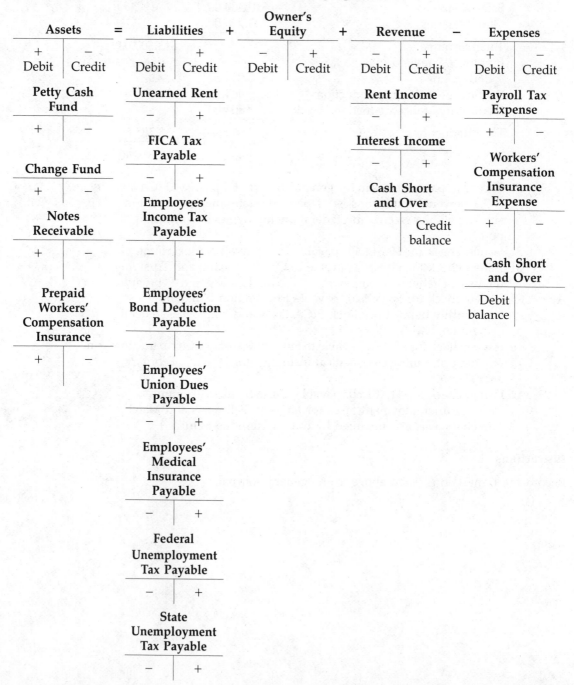

Review of Representative Transactions

The following summarizes the recording of transactions covered in Chapters 7 through 10, along with a classification of the accounts involved.

Transaction	Accounts Involved	Class.	Increase or Decrease	Therefore Debit or Credit	Financial Statement
Established a Petty Cash Fund	Petty Cash Fund Cash	A A	I D	Debit Credit	Bal. Sheet Bal. Sheet

Reimbursed Petty Cash Fund	Expenses or
	   Assets or
	   Drawing
	Cash
		E,
		A,
		OE
		A
			I
			
			D
				Debit
				
				Credit
					Balance Sheet,
					State. of O.E.,
					or Inc. Stat.
					Bal. Sheet

Established a Change Fund	Change Fund Cash	A A	I D	Debit Credit	Bal. Sheet Bal. Sheet
Recorded cash sales (amount on cash register tape was larger than cash count)	Cash Cash Short and Over Sales	A E R	I — I	Debit Debit Credit	Bal. Sheet Inc. State. Inc. State.

Recorded cash sales (amount on cash register tape was less than cash count)	Cash
	   Sales
	   Cash Short and Over
		A
		R
		R
			I
			I
			—
				Debit
				Credit
				Credit
					Bal. Sheet
					Inc. State.
					Inc. State.

Recorded service charges on bank account	Miscellaneous General
	   Expense
	   Cash
		E
		A
			I
			D
				Debit
				Credit
					Inc. State.
					Bal. Sheet

Recorded NSF check received from customer	Accounts Receivable Cash	A A	I D	Debit Credit	Bal. Sheet Bal. Sheet

Transaction	Accounts Involved	Class.	Increase or Decrease	Therefore Debit or Credit	Financial Statement
Recorded interest-bearing note receivable collected by our bank	Cash	A	I	Debit	Bal. Sheet
	Notes Receivable	A	D	Credit	Bal. Sheet
	Interest Income	R	I	Credit	Inc. State.
Recorded the payroll entry from the payroll register	Sales Salary Expense	E	I	Debit	Inc. State.
	Office Salary Expense	E	I	Debit	Inc. State.
	FICA Tax Payable	L	I	Credit	Bal. Sheet
	Employees' Income Tax Payable	L	I	Credit	Bal. Sheet
	Employees' Bond Deduction Payable	L	I	Credit	Bal. Sheet
	Employees' Union Dues Payable	L	I	Credit	Bal. Sheet
	Salaries Payable	L	I	Credit	Bal. Sheet
Issued check payable to payroll bank account	Salaries Payable	L	D	Debit	Bal. Sheet
	Cash	A	D	Credit	Bal. Sheet
Recorded employer's payroll taxes	Payroll Tax Expense	E	I	Debit	Inc. State.
	FICA Tax Payable	L	I	Credit	Bal. Sheet
	State Unemployment Tax Payable	L	I	Credit	Bal. Sheet
	Federal Unemployment Tax Payable	L	I	Credit	Bal. Sheet
Recorded deposit of FICA taxes and employees' income tax withheld	Employees' Income Tax Payable	L	D	Debit	Bal. Sheet
	FICA Tax Payable	L	D	Debit	Bal. Sheet
	Cash	A	D	Credit	Bal. Sheet
Recorded deposit of federal unemployment tax	Federal Unemployment Tax Payable	L	D	Debit	Bal. Sheet
	Cash	A	D	Credit	Bal. Sheet

Transaction	Accounts Involved	Class.	Increase or Decrease	Therefore Debit or Credit	Financial Statement
Paid state unemploy-ment tax	State Unemployment Tax Payable	L	D	Debit	Bal. Sheet
	Cash	A	D	Credit	Bal. Sheet
Paid for workers' compensation insurance in advance	Prepaid Workers' Compensation Insurance	A	I	Debit	Bal. Sheet
	Cash	A	D	Credit	Bal. Sheet
Adjusting entry for workers' compensation insurance, assuming an additional amount is owed	Workers' Compensation Insurance Expense	E	I	Debit	Inc. State.
	Prepaid Workers' Compensation Insurance	A	D	Credit	Bal. Sheet
	Workers' Compensation Insurance Payable	L	I	Credit	Bal. Sheet

11 Accounting for Merchandise: Sales

Learning Objectives

After you have completed this chapter, you will be able to do the following:

1. Record transactions in sales journals.

2. Post from sales journals to an accounts receivable ledger and a general ledger.

3. Prepare a schedule of accounts receivable.

4. Post directly from sales invoices to an accounts receivable ledger and a general ledger.

By now you've had enough experience to complete the full accounting cycle for service-type and professional enterprises. To enlarge your accounting knowledge, let us now introduce accounting systems for merchandising enterprises. The same general principles of double-entry accounting prevail. This chapter describes specific accounts of merchandising firms; such a merchandising firm could be anything from a dress shop to a supermarket. The sales journal and the accounts receivable ledger are also presented. Just as we used NuWay Cleaners as a continuous example of a service-type business, we shall use C. L. Frederickson Plumbing Supply as an example of a merchandising business.

SPECIAL JOURNALS

In our previous descriptions of the accounting process, we have intentionally shown the entire procedure. In other words, we have taken the long way home, but there are certain shortcuts available. Moreover, as far as understanding accounting is concerned, if you fully understand the long way, it's relatively easy to learn the shortcuts. The reverse is not true; you cannot readily understand the entire system if you are exposed to shortcuts only.

Any accounting system must be as efficient as possible. As a matter of fact, accounting is a means, or tool, by which to measure efficiency in a business. Consequently, one should take shortcuts wherever one can do so without sacrificing internal control (discussed in detail in Chapter 12).

As we shall see, **special journals** provide one shortcut. Using a two-column general journal for recording transactions that take place day after day is extremely time-consuming, because each individual debit and credit entry must be posted separately. Special journals make it easier to handle specialized transactions and delegate work. The following table lists the special journals that we shall introduce separately in the next few chapters.

When any of these four journals are used, the general journal must also be used to record any *non*specialized transactions—in other words, any transactions that the special journals cannot handle. In this case the letter designation for the general journal is J.

Chapter	Special Journal	Letter Designation	Specialized Transaction
11	Sales journal	S	Sales of merchandise on account only
12	Purchases journal	P	Purchase of merchandise on account only
13	Cash receipts journal	CR	All cash received from any source
13	Cash payments journal	CP	All cash paid out for any purpose

SPECIFIC ACCOUNTS FOR MERCHANDISING FIRMS

A service or professional enterprise, such as the ones we have encountered, depends for its revenue on the rendering of services; a service or professional enterprise uses such accounts as Income from Services or Professional Fees. A merchandising business, on the other hand, depends for its revenue on the sale of goods or merchandise, recording the amount of the sale under the account titled Sales.

Merchandise inventory consists of a stock of goods that a firm buys and intends to resell, in the same physical condition, at a profit. Merchandise should be differentiated from other assets, such as equipment and supplies, which are acquired for use in the business and are not for resale.

Because the merchandising firm has to record transactions involving the purchase, handling, and sale of its merchandise, it uses accounts and procedures that we have not yet discussed. Let's look at the fundamental accounting equation with the new T accounts that are introduced in this chapter, as well as the T accounts introduced in Chapters 12 and 13 (which are shown in color).

Assets		=	Liabilities		+	Owner's Equity		+	Revenue		−	Expenses	
+	−		−	+		−	+		−	+		+	−
Debit	Credit		Debit	Credit		Debit	Credit		Debit	Credit		Debit	Credit

Merchandise Inventory		Sales Tax Payable							Sales		Purchases	
+	−	−	+						−	+	+	−

									Sales Returns and Allowances		Purchases Returns and Allowances	
									+	−	−	+

									Sales Discount		Purchases Discount	
									+	−	−	+

The **Sales** account, as we have said, is a revenue account; it records the sale of merchandise.

The **Purchases** account records the cost of merchandise acquired for resale. Remember that the Purchases account is used strictly for the buying of merchandise. The plus and minus signs are the same as the signs for Merchandise Inventory. Purchases is placed under the heading of Expenses only because the accountant closes it, along with the expense accounts, at the end of the fiscal period.

The **Sales Returns and Allowances** account records the physical return of merchandise by customers or a reduction in a bill because merchandise was damaged. It is treated as a deduction from Sales.

The **Purchases Returns and Allowances** account records the firm's return of merchandise it has purchased or a reduction in the bill due to damaged merchandise. It is treated as a deduction from Purchases.

The **Sales Discount** and **Purchases Discount** accounts record cash discounts granted for prompt payments, in accordance with the credit terms. We'll discuss these accounts along with cash journals in Chapter 13.

The T accounts for returns and allowances and for discounts are shown in color to emphasize that we are treating them as deductions from the related accounts placed above them. We list these accounts as deductions because they appear as deductions in the financial statements. Their relationship is similar to that between the Drawing account and the Capital account; remember that we deduct Drawing from Capital in the statement of owner's equity.

The firm's accountant makes entries involving Merchandise Inventory only when the firm takes an actual physical count of the goods in stock; otherwise the accountant leaves this account strictly alone.

The type of transaction most frequently encountered in a merchandising business is the sale of merchandise. Some businesses sell on a cash-and-carry basis only; others sell only on credit. Many firms offer both arrangements. The same general types of entries pertain to retail and wholesale enterprises. Here are some examples.

Sale of merchandise for cash, $100.

Cash		Sales	
+	−	−	+
100			100

Debit Cash and credit Sales; record this in the cash receipts journal.

Sale of merchandise on account, $200.

Accounts Receivable		Sales	
+	−	−	+
200			200

Debit Accounts Receivable and credit Sales; record this in the sales journal.

HANDLING SALES ON ACCOUNT

Sales are only recorded in response to a customer order. The routines for processing orders and recording sales vary with the type and size of the business.

In a retail business, a salesperson usually prepares a sales ticket—either in duplicate or triplicate—for a sale on account. One copy is given to the customer, and another to the accounting department, where it will serve as the basis for an entry in the sales journal. A third copy may be used as a record of sales—when one is computing sales commissions or is involved in inventory control, for example.

In a wholesale business, the company usually receives a written order from a customer or from a salesperson who obtained the order from the customer. The order must then be approved by the credit department, after which it is sent to the billing department, where the sales invoice is prepared. Like a sales ticket, the sales invoice may be made out in duplicate or triplicate.

For our model business, we shall use C. L. Frederickson Plumbing Supply, a wholesaler. One of its invoices is shown in Figure 11-1.

We shall introduce the sales journal by looking at three transactions on the books of C. L. Frederickson Plumbing Supply.

Figure 11-1

C. L. FREDERICKSON PLUMBING SUPPLY
1968 N.E. Allen Street
Portland, OR 97201

INVOICE

Sold To: T. L. Long Co.
620 S.W. Kennedy Street
Portland, OR 97110

Date: *August 1, 19–*
Invoice No.: *320*
Order No.: *5384*
Shipped By: *Their truck*
Terms: *2/10, n/30*

Quantity	Description	Unit Price	Total
1,000	*¾" galv. pipe, 10'*	*.32*	*320.00*
50	*1½" cast-iron 90° reg. elbow*	*.96*	*48.00*
40	*1½" cast-iron 90° street elbow*	*1.40*	*56.00*
			424.00

Aug. 1 Sold merchandise on account to T. L. Long Company, invoice no. 320, $424.

 3 Sold merchandise on account to Maley, Inc., invoice no. 321, $116.

 6 Sold merchandise on account to Abel Plumbing and Heating, invoice no. 322, $94.

We can use T accounts to visualize these transactions.

Accounts Receivable		Sales	
+	−	−	+
424			424
116			116
94			94

If the transactions were recorded in a general journal, they would appear as they do in Figure 11-2.

Next the journal entries would be posted to the accounts in the general ledger, as shown here. (In each of the following ledger accounts, assume that there were no beginning balances.)

GENERAL LEDGER

ACCOUNT _Accounts Receivable_   ACCOUNT NO. _113_

	DATE	ITEM	POST. REF.	DEBIT	CREDIT	BALANCE DEBIT	BALANCE CREDIT	
1	19– Aug. 1		23	4 2 4 00		4 2 4 00		1
2	3		23	1 1 6 00		5 4 0 00		2
3	6		23	9 4 00		6 3 4 00		3
4								4

ACCOUNT _Sales_   ACCOUNT NO. _411_

	DATE	ITEM	POST. REF.	DEBIT	CREDIT	BALANCE DEBIT	BALANCE CREDIT	
1	19– Aug. 1		23		4 2 4 00		4 2 4 00	1
2	3		23		1 1 6 00		5 4 0 00	2
3	6		23		9 4 00		6 3 4 00	3
4								4

Figure 11-2

GENERAL JOURNAL

PAGE __23__

	DATE		DESCRIPTION	POST. REF.	DEBIT	CREDIT	
1	19– Aug.	1	Accounts Receivable	113	4 2 4 00		1
2			Sales	411		4 2 4 00	2
3			Invoice no. 320, T. L. Long				3
4			Company.				4
5							5
6		3	Accounts Receivable	113	1 1 6 00		6
7			Sales	411		1 1 6 00	7
8			Invoice no. 321, Maley, Inc.				8
9							9
10		6	Accounts Receivable	113	9 4 00		10
11			Sales	411		9 4 00	11
12			Invoice no. 322, Abel Plumbing				12
13			and Heating.				13
14							14

Obviously, there is a great deal of repetition in both journalizing and posting. The credit sales require three separate journal entries, three debit postings to Accounts Receivable, and three credit postings to Sales. We have presented all of this to show the advantages of the sales journal. Using a *sales journal* eliminates all this repetition.

THE SALES JOURNAL

The **sales journal** records sales of merchandise *on account only*. This specialized type of transaction calls for debits to Accounts Receivable and credits to Sales. Let's see how to record the three transactions for C. L. Frederickson Plumbing Supply in the sales journal *instead of* in the general journal.

Objective 1

Record transactions in sales journals.

SALES JOURNAL

PAGE __38__

	DATE	INV. NO.	CUSTOMER'S NAME	POST. REF.	ACCOUNTS RECEIVABLE DR., SALES CR.	
1	19– Aug.	1 320	T. L. Long Company		4 2 4 00	1
2		3 321	Maley, Inc.		1 1 6 00	2
3		6 322	Abel Plumbing and Heating		9 4 00	3
4						4

Because *one* money column is headed *Accounts Receivable Debit and Sales Credit*, each transaction requires only a single line. Repetition is avoided, and all entries for sales of merchandise on account are found in one place.

Listing the invoice number makes it easier to check the details of a particular sale at a later date.

Posting from the Sales Journal

Using the sales journal also saves time and space in posting to the ledger accounts. The transactions involving the sales of merchandise on account for the entire month of August are shown in Figure 11-3.

Objective 2

Post from sales journals to an accounts receivable ledger and a general ledger.

	DATE		INV. NO.	CUSTOMER'S NAME	POST. REF.	ACCOUNTS RECEIVABLE DR., SALES CR.	
1	19– Aug.	1	320	T. L. Long Company		4 2 4 00	1
2		3	321	Maley, Inc.		1 1 6 00	2
3		6	322	Abel Plumbing and Heating		9 4 00	3
4		9	323	Manning Service Company		9 6 1 00	4
5		11	324	Craig and Fraser Hardware		8 6 00	5
6		16	325	Home Hardware Company		2 1 5 00	6
7		20	326	Henning's Plumbing		2 9 3 00	7
8		23	327	Baker Building Supplies		5 6 0 00	8
9		24	328	Craig and Fraser Hardware		2 8 6 00	9
10		28	329	Home Hardware Company		7 5 00	10
11		30	330	Baker Building Supplies		3 8 7 00	11
12		31	331	T. L. Long Company		5 6 00	12
13		31	332	Robert D. Bishop, Inc.		8 7 1 00	13
14		31				4 4 2 4 00	14
15						(113)(411)	15
16							16
17							17

SALES JOURNAL   PAGE 38

Figure 11-3

Because all the entries are a debit to Accounts Receivable and a credit to Sales, one can now make a single posting to these accounts for the amount of the total as of the last day of the month. In the Posting Reference columns of the ledger accounts, the letter S designates the sales journal.

GENERAL LEDGER

ACCOUNT Accounts Receivable   ACCOUNT NO. 113

	DATE		ITEM	POST. REF.	DEBIT	CREDIT	BALANCE DEBIT	BALANCE CREDIT	
1	19– Aug.	31		S38	4 4 2 4 00		4 4 2 4 00		1
2									2

	DATE	ITEM	POST. REF.	DEBIT	CREDIT	BALANCE DEBIT	BALANCE CREDIT	
1	19– Aug. 31		S38		4 4 2 4 00		4 4 2 4 00	1
2								2

After posting to the Accounts Receivable account, go back to the sales journal and record the account number in parentheses directly below the total. The account number for the account being debited (Accounts Receivable) goes on the left. The account number for the account being credited (Sales) goes on the right. Again, as a precaution, don't record these account numbers until you have completed the postings.

If you should find an error, do not erase it. If the error is caught in a journal entry before it is posted to the ledger, simply draw a single line through the error (with a ruler), write in the correct information, and add your initials. If an amount is entered incorrectly in the ledger (although the journal entry is correct), follow the same procedure. However, if an entry has been posted to the wrong accounts in the ledger, then you must prepare a new journal entry correcting the first one.

Sales Journal Provision for Sales Tax

Most states and some cities levy a **sales tax** on retail sales of goods and services. The retailer collects the sales tax from customers and later pays it to the tax authorities.

When goods or services are sold on credit, the sales tax is charged to the customer and recorded at the time of the sale. The sales journal must be designed to handle this type of transaction. For example, if a retail store sells an item for $100 and the sales tax is 4 percent, the transaction would be recorded in T accounts like this.

Accounts Receivable		Sales		Sales Tax Payable	
+	–	–	+	–	+
104			100		4

The accountant debits Sales Tax Payable and credits Cash when the sales tax is paid to the government.

Because we want to illustrate a sales journal for a retail merchandising firm operating in a state having a sales tax, we shall talk about the transactions of Milner and Salter Fabrics. Its sales journal is presented on the next page.

SALES JOURNAL

	DATE	INV. NO.	CUSTOMER'S NAME	POST. REF.	ACCOUNTS RECEIVABLE DEBIT	SALES TAX PAYABLE CREDIT	SALES CREDIT	
1	19– Apr. 1	9382	B. T. Lawson		1 6 64	64	1 6 00	1
2	1	9383	Culver Apartments		2 2 88	88	2 2 00	2
3	1	9384	Richard Gladdon		5 2 00	2 00	5 0 00	3
4	2	9385	T. R. Sears		1 2 48	48	1 2 00	4
10	30	10121	Paul Murphy		1 2 4 80	4 80	1 2 0 00	10
11	30				2 5 1 6 80	9 6 80	2 4 2 0 00	11
12					(1 1 3)	(2 1 4)	(4 1 1)	12
13								13

Each column is posted to the ledger accounts as a total at the end of the month. After posting the figures, the accountant records the account numbers in parentheses immediately below the totals.

GENERAL LEDGER

ACCOUNT **Accounts Receivable**   ACCOUNT NO. 113

	DATE	ITEM	POST. REF.	DEBIT	CREDIT	BALANCE DEBIT	BALANCE CREDIT	
1	19– Apr. 30		S96	2 5 1 6 80		2 5 1 6 80		1
2								2

ACCOUNT **Sales Tax Payable**   ACCOUNT NO. 214

	DATE	ITEM	POST. REF.	DEBIT	CREDIT	BALANCE DEBIT	BALANCE CREDIT	
1	19– Apr. 30		S96		9 6 80		9 6 80	1
2								2

ACCOUNT **Sales**   ACCOUNT NO. 411

	DATE	ITEM	POST. REF.	DEBIT	CREDIT	BALANCE DEBIT	BALANCE CREDIT	
1	19– Apr. 30		S96		2 4 2 0 00		2 4 2 0 00	1
2								2
3								3

THE ACCOUNTS RECEIVABLE LEDGER

Accounts Receivable, as we have seen, represents the total amount owed to a business by its charge customers.

There is a major deficiency with the account, however. The business can't tell at a glance *how much each* individual charge customer owes, which handicaps the credit department. To correct this shortcoming, businesses keep a separate account for each charge customer.

When a business has very few charge customers, it is possible to have a separate Accounts Receivable account in the general ledger for each charge customer. However, if there are many charge customers (which is the usual case), such an arrangement is too cumbersome. When each charge customer's account is included, the trial balance is very long, and of course, the possibility for errors increases accordingly.

It is more practical to have a separate book containing a list of all the charge customers and each one's respective balance. This is called the **accounts receivable ledger.** In the accounts receivable ledger, the individual charge customer accounts are listed in alphabetical order. Most accountants prefer a loose-leaf binder so that they can insert accounts for new customers and remove other accounts; they don't use account numbers.

The Accounts Receivable account should still be maintained in the general ledger; when all the postings are up to date, the balance of this account should equal the total of all the individual balances of the charge customers. The Accounts Receivable account in the general ledger is called a **controlling account.** The accounts receivable *ledger*, containing the accounts or listing of all the charge customers, is really a special ledger, called a **subsidiary ledger**. Figure 11-4 diagrams the interrelationship of these books.

The accountant posts the individual amounts to the accounts receivable ledger every day, so that this ledger will have up-to-date information. At the end of the month, the accountant posts the total of the sales journal (in Figure 11-4 it happens to be $2,900) to the general ledger accounts as a debit to the Accounts Receivable (controlling) account and a credit to the Sales account. As indicated in Figure 11-4, the balance of the Accounts Receivable (controlling) account at the end of the month must equal the total of the balances of the charge customer accounts in the accounts receivable ledger. The schedule of accounts receivable is merely a listing of charge customers' individual balances.

After you post the amount from the sales journal to the charge customer's account in the accounts receivable ledger, put a check mark ($\sqrt{}$) in the Posting Reference column of the sales journal.

Let us now look at the sales journal of C. L. Frederickson Plumbing Supply for August with the daily postings that its accountant has made to the accounts receivable ledger, as well as the schedule of accounts

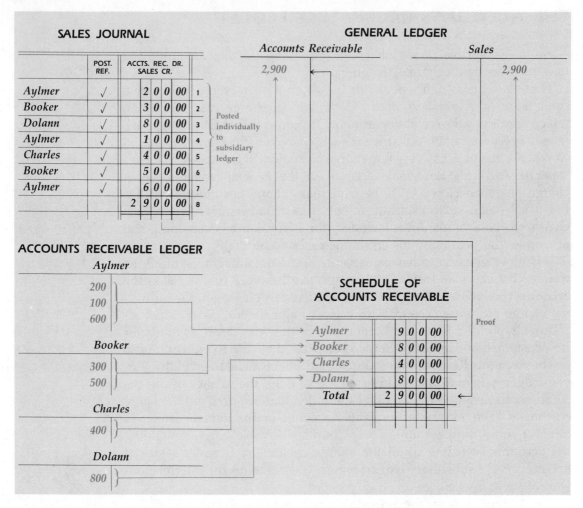

Figure 11-4

	DATE	INV. NO.	CUSTOMER'S NAME	POST. REF.	ACCOUNTS RECEIVABLE DR., SALES CR.	
	SALES JOURNAL			PAGE _38_		
1	19– Aug. 1	320	*T. L. Long Company*	√	4 2 4 00	1
2	3	321	*Maley, Inc.*	√	1 1 6 00	2
3	6	322	*Abel Plumbing and Heating*	√	9 4 00	3
4	9	323	*Manning Service Company*	√	9 6 1 00	4
5	11	324	*Craig and Fraser Hardware*	√	8 6 00	5
6	16	325	*Home Hardware Company*	√	2 1 5 00	6
7	20	326	*Henning's Plumbing*	√	2 9 3 00	7
8	23	327	*Baker Building Supplies*	√	5 6 0 00	8
9	24	328	*Craig and Fraser Hardware*	√	2 8 6 00	9
10	28	329	*Home Hardware Company*	√	7 5 00	10
11	30	330	*Baker Building Supplies*	√	3 8 7 00	11
12	31	331	*T. L. Long Company*	√	5 6 00	12
13	31	332	*Robert D. Bishop, Inc.*	√	8 7 1 00	13
14	31				4 4 2 4 00	14
15					(113)(411)	15

Figure 11-5

receivable. These entries are shown in Figure 11-5 and the ledger accounts that follow.

ACCOUNTS RECEIVABLE LEDGER

NAME _Abel Plumbing and Heating_

ADDRESS _1015 Broadway, S.W._

Seattle, WA 98102

DATE		ITEM	POST. REF.	DEBIT	CREDIT	BALANCE
19— Aug.	6		S38	9 4 00		9 4 00

NAME _Baker Building Supplies_

ADDRESS _17 No. Second St._

Renton, WA 98055

DATE		ITEM	POST. REF.	DEBIT	CREDIT	BALANCE
19— Aug.	23		S38	5 6 0 00		5 6 0 00
	30		S38	3 8 7 00		9 4 7 00

NAME _Robert D. Bishop, Inc._

ADDRESS _2168 Main St._

Kent, WA 98031

DATE		ITEM	POST. REF.	DEBIT	CREDIT	BALANCE
19— Aug.	31		S38	8 7 1 00		8 7 1 00

NAME Craig and Fraser Hardware
ADDRESS 2005 N. Powder St.
Everett, WA 98201

DATE		ITEM	POST. REF.	DEBIT	CREDIT	BALANCE
19— Aug.	11		S38	8 6 00		8 6 00
	24		S38	2 8 6 00		3 7 2 00

NAME Henning's Plumbing
ADDRESS 21680 S.E. Twelfth Ave.
Portland, OR 97208

DATE		ITEM	POST. REF.	DEBIT	CREDIT	BALANCE
19— Aug.	20		S38	2 9 3 00		2 9 3 00

NAME Home Hardware Company
ADDRESS 7810 N.W. Cherburg St.
Portland, OR 97206

DATE		ITEM	POST. REF.	DEBIT	CREDIT	BALANCE
19— Aug.	16	•	S38	2 1 5 00		2 1 5 00
	28		S38	7 5 00		2 9 0 00

NAME T. L. Long Company
ADDRESS 620 S.W. Kennedy St.
Portland, OR 97110

DATE		ITEM	POST. REF.	DEBIT	CREDIT	BALANCE
19— Aug.	1		S38	4 2 4 00		4 2 4 00
	31		S38	5 6 00		4 8 0 00

NAME __Maley, Inc.__
ADDRESS __1720 Ninth St., N.W.__
__Seattle, WA 98107__

DATE	ITEM	POST. REF.	DEBIT	CREDIT	BALANCE
19– Aug. 3		S38	1 1 6 00		1 1 6 00

NAME __Manning Service Company__
ADDRESS __2720 N.W. 43rd Ave.__
__Portland, OR 97210__

DATE	ITEM	POST. REF.	DEBIT	CREDIT	BALANCE
19– Aug. 9		S38	9 6 1 00		9 6 1 00

Assuming that these were the only transactions involving charge customers, the accountant prepares a schedule of accounts receivable, listing the balance of each charge customer.

Objective 3

Prepare a schedule of accounts receivable.

C. L. Frederickson Plumbing Supply
Schedule of Accounts Receivable
August 31, 19–

Abel Plumbing and Heating	$	9 4 00
Baker Building Supplies		9 4 7 00
Robert D. Bishop, Inc.		8 7 1 00
Craig and Fraser Hardware		3 7 2 00
Henning's Plumbing		2 9 3 00
Home Hardware Company		2 9 0 00
T. L. Long Company		4 8 0 00
Maley, Inc.		1 1 6 00
Manning Service Company		9 6 1 00
Total Accounts Receivable	$	4 4 2 4 00

Again we assume that there were no previous balances in the customers' accounts. Under this circumstance, the Accounts Receivable (controlling) account in the general ledger will have the same balance, $4,424, as the schedule of accounts receivable.

GENERAL LEDGER

ACCOUNT *Accounts Receivable*   ACCOUNT NO. 113

	DATE	ITEM	POST. REF.	DEBIT	CREDIT	BALANCE DEBIT	BALANCE CREDIT	
1	19– Aug. 31		S38	4 4 2 4 00		4 4 2 4 00		1
2								2

SALES RETURNS AND ALLOWANCES

The Sales Returns and Allowances account handles two types of transactions having to do with merchandise that has previously been sold. A *return* is a physical return of the goods. An *allowance* is a reduction from the original price because the goods were defective or damaged. It may not be economically worthwhile to have customers return the goods; each situation is a special case. In order to avoid writing a separate letter each time to inform customers of their account adjustments, businesses use a special form called a **credit memorandum,** such as the one in Figure 11-6.

The Sales Returns and Allowances account is considered to be a deduction from Sales. Using an account separate from Sales provides a better record of the total returns and allowances. Accountants deduct Sales Returns and Allowances from Sales in the income statement, as we shall see later. Let's consider this situation by using T accounts.

Transaction (a)   On August 24, C. L. Frederickson sold merchandise on account to Craig and Fraser Hardware, $286, and recorded this in the sales journal.

Figure 11-6

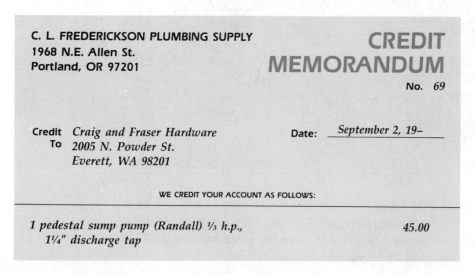

C. L. FREDERICKSON PLUMBING SUPPLY
1968 N.E. Allen St.
Portland, OR 97201

CREDIT
MEMORANDUM

No. 69

Credit   *Craig and Fraser Hardware*   Date: *September 2, 19–*
To   *2005 N. Powder St.*
        Everett, WA 98201

WE CREDIT YOUR ACCOUNT AS FOLLOWS:

1 pedestal sump pump (Randall) ⅓ h.p.,   45.00
   1¼" discharge tap

Transaction (b) On September 2, Craig and Fraser Hardware returned $45 worth of the merchandise. C. L. Frederickson issued credit memorandum no. 69 (see Figure 11-6).

Assets	=	Liabilities	+	Owner's Equity	+	Revenue	−	Expenses
+ −		− +		− +		− +		+ −
Debit Credit		Debit Credit		Debit Credit		Debit Credit		Debit Credit

Accounts Receivable		Sales	
+	−	−	+
(a) 286	(b) 45		(a) 286

	Sales Returns and Allowances	
	+	−
	(b) 45	

C. L. Frederickson's accountant debits Sales Returns and Allowances because C. L. Frederickson has greater returns and allowances than it did before. The accountant credits Accounts Receivable because the charge customer (Craig and Fraser) owes less than before.

One uses the word *credit* in "credit memorandum" because one credits Accounts Receivable. Suppose that during September, C. L. Frederickson Plumbing Supply issues two credit memorandums and makes the following entries in the general journal.

GENERAL JOURNAL PAGE 27

	DATE		DESCRIPTION	POST. REF.	DEBIT	CREDIT	
1	19– Sep.	2	Sales Returns and Allowances		4 5 00		1
2			Accounts Receivable, Craig and				2
3			Fraser Hardware			4 5 00	3
4			Credit memorandum no. 69.				4
5							5
6		2	Sales Returns and Allowances		1 1 6 00		6
7			Accounts Receivable, Home				7
8			Hardware Company			1 1 6 00	8
9			Credit memorandum no. 70.				9
10							10

The general journal entry serves as the posting source for crediting the Accounts Receivable controlling account in the general ledger. It also serves as the posting source for updating the accounts receivable ledger and therefore includes the name of the charge customer. If the balance of the Accounts Receivable (controlling) account is to equal the total of the individual balances in the accounts receivable ledger, one must post to *both* the Accounts Receivable account in the general ledger *and* the account of Craig and Fraser Hardware in the accounts receivable ledger. To take care of this double posting, one puts a slant line in the Posting Reference column. When the amount has been posted as a credit to the general ledger account, the accountant puts the account number of Accounts Receivable in the left part of the Posting Reference column. After the account of Craig and Fraser Hardware has been posted as a credit, the accountant puts a check mark in the right portion of the Posting Reference column, then posts Sales Returns and Allowances in the usual manner. Here are the entries with posting completed.

GENERAL JOURNAL   PAGE ___27___

	DATE		DESCRIPTION	POST. REF.	DEBIT	CREDIT	
1	19– Sep.	2	Sales Returns and Allowances	412	4 5 00		1
2			Accounts Receivable, Craig and				2
3			Fraser Hardware	113/√		4 5 00	3
4			Credit memorandum no. 69.				4
5							5
6		2	Sales Returns and Allowances	412	1 1 6 00		6
7			Accounts Receivable, Home				7
8			Hardware Company	113/√		1 1 6 00	8
9			Credit memorandum no. 70.				9
10							10

GENERAL LEDGER

ACCOUNT ___Accounts Receivable___   ACCOUNT NO. ___113___

	DATE		ITEM	POST. REF.	DEBIT	CREDIT	BALANCE DEBIT	BALANCE CREDIT	
1	19– Aug.	31		S38	4 4 2 4 00		4 4 2 4 00		1
2	Sep.	2		J27		4 5 00	4 3 7 9 00		2
3		2		J27		1 1 6 00	4 2 6 3 00		3
4									4

ACCOUNT	Sales Returns and Allowances					ACCOUNT NO. 412	

	DATE	ITEM	POST. REF.	DEBIT	CREDIT	BALANCE DEBIT	BALANCE CREDIT	
1	19– Sep. 2		J27	45 00		45 00		1
2	2		J27	1 16 00		1 61 00		2
3								3
4								4

ACCOUNTS RECEIVABLE LEDGER

NAME _Craig and Fraser Hardware_

ADDRESS _2005 N. Powder St._
Everett, WA 98201

DATE	ITEM	POST. REF.	DEBIT	CREDIT	BALANCE
19– Aug. 11		S38	86 00		86 00
24		S38	2 86 00		3 72 00
Sep. 2		J27		45 00	3 27 00

NAME _Home Hardware Company_

ADDRESS _7810 N.W. Cherburg St._
Portland, OR 97206

DATE	ITEM	POST. REF.	DEBIT	CREDIT	BALANCE
19– Aug. 16		S38	2 15 00		2 15 00
28		S38	75 00		2 90 00
Sep. 2		J27		1 16 00	1 74 00

If a customer who returns merchandise to a retail store was originally charged a sales tax, the sales tax must be returned to the customer. To illustrate, first, refer to the sales journal of Milner and Salter Fabrics on page 314 involving sales taxes. On April 3, assume that B. T. Lawson returns the merchandise bought on April 1 for $16 plus $.64 sales tax. The general journal entry for the return is on the next page.

GENERAL JOURNAL

PAGE __12__

	DATE		DESCRIPTION	POST. REF.	DEBIT	CREDIT	
1	19– Apr.	3	Sales Returns and Allowances		1 6 00		1
2			Sales Tax Payable		64		2
3			Accounts Receivable, B. T. Lawson			1 6 64	3
4			Credit memorandum no. 371.				4
5							5

POSTING DIRECTLY FROM SALES INVOICES

An accountant can take a further shortcut by posting directly from sales invoices or sales slips. The accountant posts to the charge customer accounts in the accounts receivable ledger daily, directly from carbon copies of the sales invoices or sales slips. He or she writes the *invoice number* rather than the journal page number in the Posting Reference column. Then, at the end of the month, the accountant brings the Accounts Receivable (controlling) account in the general ledger up to date by totaling all the sales invoices for the month, then making a general journal entry debiting Accounts Receivable and crediting Sales.

Let's use a different firm to show how this procedure works. The Marsden Sports Equipment Company posts directly from its sales invoices; the total of its sales invoices for December is $17,296. Its accountant journalizes and posts the entry as follows.

Objective 4

Post directly from sales invoices to an accounts receivable ledger and a general ledger.

GENERAL JOURNAL

PAGE __36__

	DATE		DESCRIPTION	POST. REF.	DEBIT	CREDIT	
1	19– Dec.	31	Accounts Receivable	113	17 2 9 6 00		1
2			Sales	411		17 2 9 6 00	2
3			Summarizing entry for the total				3
4			of the sales invoices for the				4
5			month.				5
6							6

GENERAL LEDGER

ACCOUNT __Accounts Receivable__   ACCOUNT NO. __113__

	DATE	ITEM	POST. REF.	DEBIT	CREDIT	BALANCE DEBIT	BALANCE CREDIT	
1	19– Dec. 31		J36	17 2 9 6 00		17 2 9 6 00		1
2								2

ACCOUNT __Sales__   ACCOUNT NO. __411__

	DATE	ITEM	POST. REF.	DEBIT	CREDIT	BALANCE DEBIT	BALANCE CREDIT	
1	19– Dec. 31		J36		17 2 9 6 00		17 2 9 6 00	1
2								2

This is called a *summarizing entry* because it summarizes the credit sales for one month. Because the company's accountant posts the entry to the accounts in the general ledger, there is no need for a sales journal; the one summarizing entry in the general journal records the total sales for the month.

One invoice and the corresponding entry in the accounts receivable ledger might look like Figure 11-7.

Figure 11-7

MARSDEN SPORTS EQUIPMENT COMPANY
1610 Alhambra Blvd.
San Diego, CA 92002

INVOICE

Sold To   *Garcia and Cranston, Sporting Goods*
1600 Santa Clara Ave.
San Francisco, CA 94133

Date: *Dec. 4, 19–*
Invoice No.: *6075*
Order No.: *359*
Shipped By: *Express Collect*
Terms: *2/10, n/30*

Quantity	Description	Unit Price	Total
10	*Molded unicellular foam ski/life vest (Davis) lg.*	16.80	168.00

ACCOUNTS RECEIVABLE LEDGER

NAME   *Garcia and Cranston, Sporting Goods*

ADDRESS   *1600 Santa Clara Ave.*

San Francisco, CA 94133

DATE		ITEM	POST. REF.	DEBIT	CREDIT	BALANCE
19– Dec.	4		6075	1 6 8 00		1 6 8 00

The $168 would, of course, be posted to the general ledger as a part of the total comprising the monthly summarizing entry.

GLOSSARY

Accounts receivable ledger   A subsidiary ledger that lists the individual accounts of charge customers in alphabetical order.

Controlling account   An account in the general ledger that summarizes the balances of a subsidiary ledger.

Credit memorandum   A written statement indicating a seller's willingness to reduce the amount of a buyer's debt. The seller records the amount of the credit memorandum under the Sales Returns and Allowances account.

Merchandise inventory   A stock of goods that a firm buys with the intent of reselling the goods in the same physical condition.

Purchases   An account for recording the cost of merchandise acquired for resale.

Purchases Discount   An account that records cash discounts granted by suppliers in return for prompt payment; it is treated as a deduction from Purchases.

Purchases Returns and Allowances   An account that records allowances and cash refunds granted by a supplier for returned or defective merchandise; it is treated as a deduction from Purchases.

Sales   A revenue account for recording the sale of merchandise.

Sales Discount   An account that records a deduction from the original price, granted by the seller to the buyer for the prompt payment of an invoice.

Sales journal   A special journal for recording the sale of merchandise on account only.

Sales Returns and Allowances   The account a seller uses to record the amount of a reduction granted to a customer either for the physical return of merchandise previously sold to the customer or as compensation for merchandise that is defective or damaged. This account is usually evidenced by a credit memorandum issued by the seller.

Sales tax A tax levied by a state or local government on the sale of goods. The tax is paid by the consumer but collected by the merchant.

Special journals Books of original entry in which one records specialized types of transactions.

Subsidiary ledger A group of accounts representing individual subdivisions of a controlling account.

QUESTIONS, EXERCISES, AND PROBLEMS

Discussion Questions

1. What information typically appears on a sales invoice?
2. What kind of ledger is an accounts receivable ledger? Are account numbers used? Why or why not?
3. Why does a business with a large number of charge customers need an accounts receivable ledger?
4. What is a schedule of accounts receivable?
5. What is the difference between a sales return and a sales allowance?
6. Why is it worthwhile to set up an account for sales returns and allowances instead of debiting Sales for any transaction involving a return or allowance?
7. Describe the method of posting directly from sales invoices.

Exercises

Exercise 11-1 Label the blanks as debit or credit.

					ACCOUNTS RECEIVABLE	SALES TAX PAYABLE	SALES
DATE	SALES SLIP	CUSTOMER's NAME	POST. REF.	(___)	(___)	(___)

SALES JOURNAL PAGE ____

Exercise 11-2 Describe how the following sales journal of Bancroft Company would be posted to the ledgers.

SALES JOURNAL PAGE 26

	DATE	INV. NO.	CUSTOMER'S NAME	POST. REF.	ACCOUNTS RECEIVABLE DR., SALES CR.	
1	19— Nov. 2	723	Sanderson Company		2 2 1 62	1
2	6	724	J. C. Farnsworth		1 6 4 2 00	2
3	12	725	A. R. Dombroski		1 2 6 8 71	3
4	20	726	Bannion and Worthy		3 6 8 4 00	4
5	30	727	Craig and Luckman		1 8 7 4 68	5
6	30				8 6 9 1 01	6
7						7

Exercise 11-3 Record the following transactions in general journal form.

a. Sold merchandise on account to L. B. Simpson, invoice no. 318, $120.
b. Issued credit memo no. 18 to L. B. Simpson for merchandise returned, $20.
c. Received full payment from L. B. Simpson.

Exercise 11-4 Describe the transactions recorded in the following T accounts.

Cash		Accounts Receivable			
(b)	210	**(a)**	210	**(b)**	210

Sales		Sales Tax Payable	
(a)	200	**(a)**	10

Exercise 11-5 Post the following entry to the general ledger and subsidiary ledger accounts.

GENERAL JOURNAL   PAGE 43

	DATE		DESCRIPTION	POST. REF.	DEBIT	CREDIT	
1	19– May	1	Sales Returns and Allowances		1 2 1 16		1
2			Accounts Receivable, J. B. Stokes			1 2 1 16	2
3			Issued credit memo no. 129.				3
4							4

GENERAL LEDGER

ACCOUNT Accounts Receivable   ACCOUNT NO. 113

	DATE		ITEM	POST. REF.	DEBIT	CREDIT	BALANCE DEBIT	BALANCE CREDIT	
1	19– May	1	Balance	✓			6 3 2 1 70		1
2									2

ACCOUNT Sales Returns and Allowances   ACCOUNT NO. 412

	DATE		ITEM	POST. REF.	DEBIT	CREDIT	BALANCE DEBIT	BALANCE CREDIT	
1	19– May	1	Balance	✓	3 2 9 80		3 2 9 80		1
2									2

ACCOUNTS RECEIVABLE LEDGER

ACCOUNT J. B. Stokes

	DATE	INVOICE NO.	ITEM	POST. REF.	DEBIT	CREDIT	BALANCE	
1	19– Apr. 30	761		S26	4 9 2 60		4 9 2 60	1
2								2

Exercise 11-6   A business firm uses carbon copies of its sales invoices to record sales of merchandise on account and carbon copies of its credit memorandums to record its sales returns and allowances. During September, the firm issued 214 invoices for $82,729.82 and 12 credit memorandums for $1,768.20. Present the summarizing entries, dated September 30, in general journal form to record the sales and sales returns and allowances for the month.

Exercise 11-7   An accountant made the following errors in journalizing sales of merchandise on account in a single-column sales journal and posting to the general ledger and accounts receivable ledger. The errors were discovered at the end of the month before the closing entries were journalized and posted. Describe how to correct the errors.

a. The sales journal was footed correctly as $34,760, but it was posted as a debit and credit of $34,670.
b. A sale of $56 to T. R. Prentice was posted to his account as $5.60.
c. A sale of $72 to A. C. Freese was entered in the sales journal correctly, but it was posted to Freese's account as $27.

Exercise 11-8   Record the following transactions in general journal form.

a. Sold merchandise for cash to Paul Bremmer, $100 plus 5 percent sales tax.
b. Bremmer returned $20 of the merchandise; issued credit memo no. 323, and paid Bremmer $21 in cash, $20 for the amount of the returned merchandise plus $1 for the amount of the sales tax.

Problem Set A

Problem 11-1A   Martin Brothers sells scaffolding equipment on a wholesale basis. The following transactions took place during March of this year.

Mar. 1 Sold merchandise on account to Duncan Construction Company, invoice no. 623, $482.
     7 Sold merchandise on account to T. R. Gibson Company, invoice no. 624, $386.
     8 Issued credit memorandum no. 41 to Richards Company for merchandise returned, $46.
    13 Sold merchandise on account to Spencer and Lucas, invoice no. 625, $106.

Mar. 15 Sold merchandise on account to Snyder and Pierce, invoice no. 626, $933.

20 Sold merchandise on account to Sprague Painting, invoice no. 627, $481.

24 Issued credit memorandum no. 42 to Snyder and Pierce for merchandise returned, $97.

26 Sold merchandise on account to Richards Company, invoice no. 628, $398.

29 Sold merchandise on account to Spencer and Lucas, invoice no. 629, $861.

30 Issued credit memorandum no. 43 to Spencer and Lucas for damage to merchandise, $43.

Instructions

1. Record these sales of merchandise on account in the sales journal. Record the sales returns and allowances in the general journal.
2. Immediately after recording each transaction, post to the accounts receivable ledger.
3. Post the amounts from the general journal daily. Post the sales journal amount as a total at the end of the month.
4. Prepare a schedule of accounts receivable.

Problem 11-2A Margold Electronics, which opened for business during May of this year, had the following sales of merchandise on account and sales returns and allowances during the month.

May 3 Sold merchandise on account to Dempsey Automotive Electric, invoice no. 1, $272.65.

9 Sold merchandise on account to William T. Brocklin, invoice no. 2, $318.

11 Sold merchandise on account to L. T. Barber, Inc., invoice no. 3, $864.20.

16 Sold merchandise on account to N. C. Farmer, invoice no. 4, $788.16.

17 Issued credit memorandum no. 1, $26, to William T. Brocklin for merchandise returned.

22 Sold merchandise on account to Dempsey Automotive Electric, invoice no. 5, $976.70.

24 Issued credit memorandum no. 2, $118.10, to L. T. Barber, Inc., for merchandise returned.

27 Sold merchandise on account to N. C. Farmer, invoice no. 6, $227.18.

29 Sold merchandise on account to William T. Brocklin, invoice no. 7, $698.

30 Sold merchandise on account to Dempsey Automotive Electric, invoice no. 8, $163.72.

31 Issued credit memorandum no. 3, $44, to L. T. Barber, Inc., for merchandise damaged in transit.

Instructions

1. Record these sales of merchandise on account in the sales journal. Record the sales returns and allowances in the general journal.
2. Immediately after recording each transaction, post to the accounts receivable ledger.
3. Post the amounts from the general journal daily. Post the sales journal amount as a total at the end of the month.
4. Prepare a schedule of accounts receivable. Compare the balance of the Accounts Receivable controlling account with the total of the schedule of accounts receivable.

Problem 11-3A Hall's Camera sells merchandise on a retail basis. Most sales are for cash; however, a few steady customers have charge accounts. The salesclerks fill out sales slips for each sale. The state government levies a 5 percent retail sales tax, which is collected by the retailer. Hall's Camera's charge sales for November are as follows:

Nov. 3 Sold a Tendex Four-speed Projector with f/1.5 zoom lens to A. T. Albers, sales slip no. 238, $180, plus sales tax of $9, total $189.

5 Sold a Nasha K-3 Autowinder to Sheila Nelson, sales slip no. 263, $70, plus sales tax of $3.50, total $73.50.

10 Sold a Simpson Automatic-opening Screen to Roger Scott, sales slip no. 271, $48, plus sales tax of $2.40.

15 Sold a Tendex 35mm Auto Camera with Auto Focus (N16) to C. T. Abernathy, $260, plus sales tax, sales slip no. 282.

16 Giffin Photos bought a Miko SL Portrait Camera with Semco tripod and two Semco light stands on account, sales slip no. 296, $800, plus sales tax.

19 Giffin Photos returned the Semco tripod and two Semco light stands. Hall's Camera allowed full credit on the sale, $140, plus $7 sales tax, sales slip no. 296.

20 The Daily Chronicle bought ten Kadette 35mm Autofocus Viewfinder Cameras (K6), $1,100, plus sales tax, sales slip no. 303.

22 Allowed the Daily Chronicle credit, $110 plus tax, because of a defective camera, sales slip no. 303.

Instructions

1. Record these sales of merchandise on account in either the sales journal or the general journal.
2. Immediately after recording each transaction, post to the accounts receivable ledger.
3. Post the amounts from the general journal daily. Post the sales journal amount as a total at the end of the month.
4. Prepare a schedule of accounts receivable.

Problem 11-4A Worthington Company uses carbon copies of its charge sales invoices as a sales journal and posts to the accounts receivable ledger directly from the sales invoices. The invoices are totaled at the end of the month; an entry is made in the general journal summarizing the charge sales for the month. The charge sales invoices for March are as follows.

Mar.   2 T. R. Timmins Company, invoice no. 3912, $348.
       7 Northern Novelty Company, invoice no. 3925, $104.
       9 Harold J. Townsend, invoice no. 3936, $542.
      11 Vance and Harris, invoice no. 3944, $744.
      16 Coolidge and Roe, Inc., invoice no. 3962, $148.
      21 Prentice and Thomas, Inc., invoice no. 3978, $432.
      25 Perez Specialty Company, invoice no. 3989, $539.
      27 Singleton Amusement, invoice no. 3999, $268.
      31 Northern Novelty Company, invoice no. 4011, $189.

Instructions

1. Post to the accounts receivable ledger directly from the sales invoices, listing the invoice number in the Posting Reference column.
2. Record the summarizing entry in the general journal for the total amount of the sales invoices.
3. Post the general journal entry to the appropriate accounts in the general ledger.
4. Prepare a schedule of accounts receivable.

Problem Set B

Problem 11-1B   Martin Brothers sells scaffolding equipment on a wholesale basis. The following transactions took place during April of this year.

Apr.   1 Sold merchandise on account to Duncan Construction Company, invoice no. 621, $457.
       6 Sold merchandise on account to T. R. Gibson Company, invoice no. 622, $353.
       7 Issued credit memorandum no. 30 to Richards Company for merchandise returned, $34.
      12 Sold merchandise on account to Spencer and Lucas, invoice no. 623, $98.
      14 Sold merchandise on account to Snyder and Pierce, invoice no. 624, $921.
      19 Sold merchandise on account to Sprague Painting, invoice no. 625, $469.
      23 Issued credit memorandum no. 31 to Snyder and Pierce for merchandise returned, $96.
      25 Sold merchandise on account to Richards Company, invoice no. 626, $392.
      29 Sold merchandise on account to Spencer and Lucas, invoice no. 627, $872.
      30 Issued credit memorandum no. 32 to Spencer and Lucas for damage to merchandise, $29.

Instructions

1. Record these sales of merchandise on account in the sales journal. Record the sales returns and allowances in the general journal.
2. Immediately after recording each transaction, post to the accounts receivable ledger.
3. Post the amounts from the general journal daily. Post the sales journal amount as a total at the end of the month.
4. Prepare a schedule of accounts receivable.

Problem 11-2B   Margold Electronics, which opened for business during October of this year, had the following sales of merchandise on account and sales returns and allowances during the month.

Oct.   6 Sold merchandise on account to Dempsey Automotive Electric, invoice no. 1, $260.

9 Sold merchandise on account to William T. Brocklin, invoice no. 2, $315.

11 Sold merchandise on account to L. T. Barber, Inc., invoice no. 3, $870.

16 Sold merchandise on account to N. C. Farmer, invoice no. 4, $776.

17 Issued credit memorandum no. 1, $48, to William T. Brocklin for merchandise returned.

21 Sold merchandise on account to Dempsey Automotive Electric, invoice no. 5, $964.

23 Issued credit memorandum no. 2 to L. T. Barber, Inc., for merchandise returned, $120.

27 Sold merchandise on account to N. C. Farmer, invoice no. 6, $229.

29 Sold merchandise on account to William T. Brocklin, invoice no. 7, $694.

30 Sold merchandise on account to Dempsey Automotive Electric, invoice no. 8, $161.

31 Issued credit memorandum no. 3 to L. T. Barber, Inc., for damage done to merchandise during shipping, $40.

Instructions

1. Record the above sales of merchandise on account in the sales journal. Record the sales returns and allowances in the general journal.
2. Immediately after recording each transaction, post to the accounts receivable ledger.
3. Post the amounts from the general journal daily. Post the sales journal amount as a total at the end of the month.
4. Prepare a schedule of accounts receivable. Compare the balance of the Accounts Receivable controlling account with the total of the schedule of accounts receivable.

Problem 11-3B   Pasara's Camera sells merchandise on a retail basis. Most sales are for cash; however, a few steady customers have charge accounts.

The salesclerks fill out sales slips for each sale. The state government levies a 5 percent retail sales tax, which is collected by the retailer. Pasara's Camera's charge sales for November are as follows.

Nov.   4 Sold a Pasha Electro 35mm PTN Rangefinder camera with f/1.6 lens to Sheila Nelson, sales slip no. 217, $160, plus sales tax of $8, total $168.

6 Sold a Tendex SV Flash to A. T. Albers, sales slip no. 262, $80, plus sales tax of $4, total $84.

12 Sold Giffin Photos a Laashi TN Portrait Camera with Semte tripod and two Semte light stands, sales slip no. 272, $600, plus sales tax of $30.

14 Sold a Rognor 3 C Tele-Converter to Roger Scott, sales slip no. 284, $60, plus sales tax.

18 Sold the Daily Chronicle two Bannion DE-2 35mm cameras with f/1.7 lens and two Bannion C Strobes, $900, plus sales tax, sales slip no. 294.

21 Giffin Photos returned a Semte tripod and two Semte light stands from sales slip no. 272. Pasara's Camera allowed full credit on the sale of $180 and the related sales tax of $9.

27 C. T. Abernathy bought a Bannion 28mm f/2.8 Wide Angle Lens for $240, plus sales tax, sales slip no. 306.

30 Allowed the Daily Chronicle credit for the return of two Bannion C Strobes, $80, plus tax, purchased on sales slip no. 294.

Instructions

1. Record the transactions in either the sales journal or the general journal.
2. Immediately after recording each transaction, post to the accounts receivable ledger.
3. Post the amounts from the general journal daily. Post the sales journal amount as a total at the end of the month.
4. Prepare a schedule of accounts receivable.

Problem 11-4B   Best-Goods Company uses carbon copies of its charge sales invoices as a sales journal and posts to the accounts receivable ledger directly from the sales invoices. At the end of the month, the accountant totals the invoices and makes an entry in the general journal summarizing the charge sales for the month. The charge sales invoices are as follows.

Mar.   3 T. R. Timmins Company, invoice no. 2016, $360.

9 Northern Novelty Company, invoice no. 2019, $789.

12 Harold J. Townsend, invoice no. 2021, $219.

16 Vance and Harris, invoice no. 2024, $1,068.

17 Coolidge and Roe, Inc., invoice no. 2025, $724.

19 Prentice and Thomas, Inc., invoice no. 2027, $191.

25 Perez Specialty Company, invoice no. 2028, $783.

29 Singleton Amusement Company, invoice no. 2039, $860.

30 Northern Novelty Company, invoice no. 2040, $1,216.

Instructions

1. Post to the accounts receivable ledger directly from the sales invoices, listing the invoice number in the Posting Reference column.
2. Record the summarizing entry in the general journal for the total amount of the sales invoices.
3. Post the general journal entry to the appropriate accounts in the general ledger.
4. Prepare a schedule of accounts receivable.

12 Accounting for Merchandise: Purchases

Learning Objectives

After you have completed this chapter, you will be able to do the following:

1. Record transactions in a one-column purchases journal.

2. Post from a one-column purchases journal to an accounts payable ledger and a general ledger.

3. Prepare a schedule of accounts payable.

4. Journalize transactions involving transportation charges on incoming goods.

5. Post directly from purchase invoices to an accounts payable ledger and a general ledger.

We've been talking about the procedures, accounts, and special journals used to record the *selling* of merchandise. Now let's talk about those same elements as they apply to the *buying* of merchandise. We'll be dealing with the Purchases account and with Purchases Returns and Allowances. In this chapter you'll see that Accounts Payable is a controlling account, just as you saw in Chapter 11 that Accounts Receivable is a controlling account.

PURCHASING PROCEDURES

When you think of the great variety in types and sizes of merchandising firms, it comes as no surprise to learn that there is also considerable variety in the procedures used to buy goods for resale. Some purchases may be for cash; however, in most cases, purchases are on a credit basis. In a small retail store, the owner may do the buying. In large retail and wholesale concerns, department heads or division managers do the buying, after which the Purchasing Department goes into action: placing purchase orders, following up the orders, receiving the goods, and seeing that deliveries are made to the right departments. The Purchasing Department also acts as a source of information on current prices, price trends, quality of goods, prospective suppliers, and reliability of suppliers.

The Purchasing Department normally requires that any buying orders be in writing, in the form of a **purchase requisition.** After the purchase requisition is approved, the Purchasing Department sends a **purchase order** to the supplier. A purchase order is the company's written offer to buy certain goods. The accountant does not make any entry at this point, because the supplier has not yet indicated acceptance of the order. A purchase order is made out in triplicate: One copy goes to the supplier, one stays in the Purchasing Department (as proof of what was ordered), and one goes to the department that sent out the requisition (telling them that the goods they wanted have indeed been ordered).

To continue with the accounts of C. L. Frederickson Plumbing Supply: The Pipe Department submits a purchase requisition to the Purchasing Department as shown in Figure 12-1.

The Purchasing Department completes the bottom part of the purchase requisition and then sends out a purchase order, as shown in Figure 12-2.

The seller now sends an **invoice** to the buyer. This invoice should arrive in advance of the goods (or at least *with* the goods). From the seller's point of view, this is a sales invoice. If the sale is on credit, as we saw in Chapter 11, the seller's accountant makes an entry debiting Accounts Receivable and crediting Sales. To the buyer, this is a purchase invoice, so

Figure 12-1

C. L. FREDERICKSON
1968 N.E. Allen St.
Portland, OR 97201

PURCHASE REQUISITION

No. C-726

Department _Pipe_

Advise on delivery _Mr. Holloway_

Date of request _July 2, 19–_

Date required _Aug. 5, 19–_

Quantity	Description
1,000'	Flexible copper tubing ⅝", Type L, (50' roll)

Approved by _Ronald Schmidt_   Requested by _J. H. Holloway_

FOR PURCHASING DEPT. USE ONLY

Purchase Order No. _7918_

Date _July 5, 19–_

Issued to: _Darvik, Inc._
1616 Madera Ave.
Los Angeles, CA 90026

Figure 12-2

C. L. FREDERICKSON PLUMBING SUPPLY
1968 N.E. Allen St.
Portland, OR 97201

PURCHASE ORDER

To: _Darvik, Inc._
1616 Madera Ave.
Los Angeles, CA 90026

Date: _July 5, 19–_
Order No.: _7918_
Shipped By: _Freight Truck_
Terms: _2/10, n/30_

Quantity	Description	Unit Price	Total
1,000'	Flexible copper tubing ⅝", Type L (50' roll)	.42	420.00

Ronald Schmidt

the buyer's accountant makes an entry debiting Purchases and crediting Accounts Payable. C. L. Frederickson Plumbing Supply receives an invoice (Figure 12-3) from Darvik, Inc.

Let us now extract from the fundamental accounting equation (recall Chapter 11) the T accounts involved in buying merchandise. Again, color is used to emphasize the accounts that are deductions from Purchases.

Assets	=	Liabilities	+	Owner's Equity	+	Revenue	−	Expenses
+ | −		− | +		− | +		− | +		+ | −
Debit | Credit		Debit | Credit		Debit | Credit		Debit | Credit		Debit | Credit

Purchases

+	−

Purchases Returns and Allowances

−	+

Purchases Discount

−	+

Figure 12-3

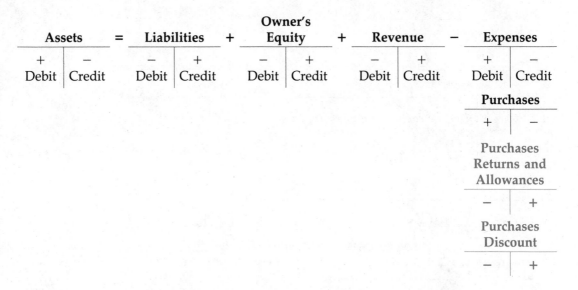

DARVIK, INC.
1616 Madera Ave.
Los Angeles, CA 90026

INVOICE

Sold To: C. L. Frederickson Plumbing Supply
1968 N.E. Allen St.
Portland, OR 97201

Date: July 31, 19–
No.: 2706
Order No.: 7918
Shipped By: Western Freight Line
Terms: 2/10, n/30

Quantity	Description	Unit Price	Total
1,000'	Flexible copper tubing ⅝", Type L (50' roll)	.42	420.00

Bear in mind that the Purchases account is used exclusively for the buying of merchandise intended for resale. *If the firm buys anything else, the accountant records the amount under the appropriate asset or expense account.* At the end of the fiscal period, the balance in the Purchases account represents the total cost of merchandise bought during the period. As we said in Chapter 11, Purchases is classified as an expense only for the sake of convenience. The classification is permissible because Purchases is closed at the end of the fiscal period along with the expense accounts.

Purchases Returns and Allowances is a deduction from Purchases. A separate account is set up to keep track of the amount of the returns and of the reductions in bills due to damaged merchandise. In the income statement, we treat Purchases Returns and Allowances and Purchases Discount as deductions from Purchases; so, for consistency they are presented below Purchases in the fundamental accounting equation just shown.

To get back to C. L. Frederickson Plumbing Supply: as in Chapter 11, we'll record three transactions in the general journal. Then—just to reemphasize the advantage of special journals as opposed to the general journal—we'll record the same three transactions in a special journal.

During the first week in August, the following transactions took place.

Aug. 2 Bought merchandise on account from Darvik, Inc., their invoice no. 2706, dated July 31; terms 2/10, n/30; $420.
   3 Bought merchandise on account from Reiter and Simon Company, their invoice no. 982, dated August 2, terms net 30 days, $760.
   5 Bought merchandise on account from Alman Manufacturing Company, their invoice no. 10611, dated August 3; terms 2/10, n/30; $692.

Let's take a minute to explain the credit terms in the transactions. The notation "net 30 days" means that the bill is due within 30 days after the date of the invoice. The notation "2/10, n/30" refers to the **purchases discount** or cash discount. It means that the seller offers a 2 percent discount if the bill is paid within 10 days after the date of the invoice, and that the whole bill must be paid within 30 days after the invoice date. We will be working with these credit terms in Chapter 13.

For the present, we are concerned with recording the purchases. Let's visualize these transactions in terms of T accounts.

Purchases		Accounts Payable	
+	−	−	+
420			420
760			760
692			692

Figure 12-4

GENERAL JOURNAL

PAGE __22__

	DATE		DESCRIPTION	POST. REF.	DEBIT	CREDIT	
1	19– Aug.	2	Purchases	511	4 2 0 00		1
2			Accounts Payable	211		4 2 0 00	2
3			Darvik, Inc., their invoice no.				3
4			2706, terms 2/10, n/30, dated				4
5			July 31.				5
6							6
7		3	Purchases	511	7 6 0 00		7
8			Accounts Payable	211		7 6 0 00	8
9			Reiter and Simon Company, their				9
10			invoice no. 982, terms net 30				10
11			days, dated August 2.				11
12							12
13		5	Purchases	511	6 9 2 00		13
14			Accounts Payable	211		6 9 2 00	14
15			Alman Manufacturing Company,				15
16			their invoice no. 10611, terms				16
17			2/10, n/30, dated August 3.				17
18							18
19							19
20							20
21							21

If these transactions are recorded in the general journal, they look like Figure 12-4, above.

Next the general journal entries would be posted to the general ledger.

GENERAL LEDGER

ACCOUNT __Accounts Payable__   ACCOUNT NO. __211__

	DATE		ITEM	POST. REF.	DEBIT	CREDIT	BALANCE DEBIT	BALANCE CREDIT	
1	19– Aug.	1	Balance	√				3 5 6 00	1
2		2		22		4 2 0 00		7 7 6 00	2
3		3		22		7 6 0 00		1 5 3 6 00	3
4		5		22		6 9 2 00		2 2 2 8 00	4
5									5
6									6
7									7
8									8

GENERAL LEDGER

ACCOUNT _Purchases_   ACCOUNT NO. __511__

	DATE		ITEM	POST. REF.	DEBIT	CREDIT	BALANCE DEBIT	BALANCE CREDIT	
1	19— Aug.	1	_Balance_	✓			20 6 1 2 00		1
2		2		22	4 2 0 00		21 0 3 2 00		2
3		3		22	7 6 0 00		21 7 9 2 00		3
4		5		22	6 9 2 00		22 4 8 4 00		4
5									5

PURCHASES JOURNAL

Objective 1

Record transactions in a one-column purchases journal.

The above repetition can be avoided if the accountant uses a **purchases journal** instead of the general journal. The purchases journal is used to record the purchase of merchandise _on account only_. In each case, with this special type of transaction, the accountant debits Purchases and credits Accounts Payable.

PURCHASES JOURNAL   PAGE __29__

	DATE		SUPPLIER'S NAME	INVOICE NO.	INVOICE DATE	TERMS	POST. REF.	PURCHASES DR., ACCOUNTS PAYABLE CR.	
1	19— Aug.	2	_Darvik, Inc._	2706	7/31	2/10, n/30		4 2 0 00	1
2		3	_Reiter and Simon_						2
3			_Company_	982	8/2	n/30		7 6 0 00	3
4		5	_Alman Manufacturing_						4
5			_Company_	10611	8/3	2/10, n/30		6 9 2 00	5
6									6

Note that the one money column is headed Purchases Debit, Accounts Payable Credit.

Posting from the Purchases Journal to the General Ledger

Objective 2

Post from a one-column purchases journal to an accounts payable ledger and a general ledger.

Figure 12-5 shows the journal entries for all transactions involving the purchase of merchandise on account for August.

The next step in the accounting cycle is posting. Since all the entries are debits to Purchases and credits to Accounts Payable, one can post the totals to these accounts at the end of the month.

Figure 12-5

PURCHASES JOURNAL
PAGE 29

	DATE		SUPPLIER'S NAME	INVOICE NO.	INVOICE DATE	TERMS	POST. REF.	PURCHASES DR., ACCOUNTS PAYABLE CR.	
1	19– Aug.	2	Darvik, Inc.	2706	7/31	2/10, n/30		4 2 0 00	1
2		3	Reiter and Simon						2
3			Company	982	8/2	n/30		7 6 0 00	3
4		5	Alman Manufacturing						4
5			Company	10611	8/3	2/10, n/30		6 9 2 00	5
6		9	Sullivan Manufacturing						6
7			Company	B643	8/6	1/10, n/30		1 6 5 00	7
8		18	Tru-Fit Valve, Inc.	46812	8/17	n/60		2 2 8 00	8
9		25	Donaldson and Farr	1024	8/23	2/10, n/30		3 7 6 00	9
10		26	Darvik, Inc.	2801	8/25	n/30		4 0 6 00	10
11		31						3 0 4 7 00	11
12								(511)(211)	12
13									13

In the Posting Reference column of the ledger accounts, P designates the purchases journal. After posting to the ledger accounts, the accountant goes back to the purchases journal and records the account numbers in parentheses directly below the total, placing the account number for the account being debited on the left. **Transactions involving the buying**

GENERAL LEDGER

ACCOUNT Accounts Payable   ACCOUNT NO. 211

	DATE		ITEM	POST. REF.	DEBIT	CREDIT	BALANCE DEBIT	BALANCE CREDIT	
1	19– Aug.	1	Balance	√				3 5 6 00	1
2		31		P29		3 0 4 7 00		3 4 0 3 00	2
3									3

GENERAL LEDGER

ACCOUNT Purchases   ACCOUNT NO. 511

	DATE		ITEM	POST. REF.	DEBIT	CREDIT	BALANCE DEBIT	BALANCE CREDIT	
1	19– Aug.	1	Balance	√			20 6 1 2 00		1
2		31		P29	3 0 4 7 00		23 6 5 9 00		2
3									3

of supplies or other assets should *not* be recorded in the purchases journal, because the purchases journal may be used only for the purchases of merchandise for resale.

THE ACCOUNTS PAYABLE LEDGER

In Chapter 11 we called the Accounts Receivable account in the general ledger a *controlling* account, and we saw that the accounts receivable ledger consists of an individual account for each charge customer. We also saw that the accountant posts to the accounts receivable ledger every day.

Accounts Payable is a parallel case; it, too, is a controlling account in the general ledger. The accounts payable ledger is a subsidiary ledger, and it consists of individual accounts for all the creditors. Again, in the accounts payable ledger, posting is done daily. After posting to the individual creditors' accounts, the accountant puts a check mark ($\surd$) in the Posting Reference column of the purchases journal. After he or she has finished all the posting to the controlling account at the end of the period, the total of the schedule of accounts payable should equal the balance of the Accounts Payable (controlling) account. Incidentally, one always uses the three-column form for the accounts payable ledger. Because the T account for Accounts Payable is

Accounts
Payable

−	+

it follows that the three-column form looks like this.

Accounts Payable Ledger

Debit	Credit	Balance
−	+	+

Now let's see the purchases journal (Figure 12-6) and the postings to the ledger (Figure 12-7).

Note that in the accounts payable ledger—as in the accounts receivable ledger—the accounts of the individual creditors are listed in alphabetical order. Accountants usually use a loose-leaf binder with no page numbers or account numbers.

Figure 12-6

PURCHASES JOURNAL

PAGE _29_

	DATE		SUPPLIER'S NAME	INVOICE NO.	INVOICE DATE	TERMS	POST. REF.	PURCHASES DR., ACCOUNTS PAYABLE CR.	
1	19—Aug.	2	Darvik, Inc.	2706	7/31	2/10, n/30	√	4 2 0 00	1
2		3	Reiter and Simon						2
3			Company	982	8/2	n/30	√	7 6 0 00	3
4		5	Alman Manufacturing						4
5			Company	10611	8/3	2/10, n/30	√	6 9 2 00	5
6		9	Sullivan Manufacturing						6
7			Company	B643	8/6	1/10, n/30	√	1 6 5 00	7
8		18	Tru-Fit Valve, Inc.	46812	8/17	n/60	√	2 2 8 00	8
9		25	Donaldson and Farr	1024	8/23	2/10, n/30	√	3 7 6 00	9
10		26	Darvik, Inc.	2801	8/25	n/30	√	4 0 6 00	10
11		31						3 0 4 7 00	11
12								(511)(211)	12
13									13

Figure 12-7

ACCOUNTS PAYABLE LEDGER

NAME __Alman Manufacturing Company__

ADDRESS __2510 Madeira Ave.__
__San Francisco, CA 94130__

DATE		ITEM	POST. REF.	DEBIT	CREDIT	BALANCE
19—Aug.	5		P29		6 9 2 00	6 9 2 00

NAME __Darvik, Inc.__

ADDRESS __1616 Madera Ave.__
__Los Angeles, CA 90026__

DATE		ITEM	POST. REF.	DEBIT	CREDIT	BALANCE
19—Aug.	2		P29		4 2 0 00	4 2 0 00
	26		P29		4 0 6 00	8 2 6 00

NAME __Donaldson and Farr__

ADDRESS __1600 S.W. Yelm St.__
__Portland, OR 97216__

DATE		ITEM	POST. REF.	DEBIT	CREDIT	BALANCE
19—Aug.	25		P29		3 7 6 00	3 7 6 00

Figure 12-7
(continued)

NAME___Reiter and Simon Company

ADDRESS___21325 186th Ave. No.

Seattle, WA 98101

DATE		ITEM	POST. REF.	DEBIT	CREDIT	BALANCE
19— Jul.	27		P28		1 8 0 00	1 8 0 00
Aug.	3		P29		7 6 0 00	9 4 0 00

NAME___Sullivan Manufacturing Company

ADDRESS___1068 Casino Ave.

Los Angeles, CA 90023

DATE		ITEM	POST. REF.	DEBIT	CREDIT	BALANCE
19— Aug.	9		P29		1 6 5 00	1 6 5 00

NAME___Tru-Fit Valve, Inc.

ADDRESS___1620 Minard St.

San Francisco, CA 94130

DATE		ITEM	POST. REF.	DEBIT	CREDIT	BALANCE
19— Jul.	29		P28		1 7 6 00	1 7 6 00
Aug.	18		P29		2 2 8 00	4 0 4 00

PURCHASES RETURNS AND ALLOWANCES

This account, as the title implies, handles either a return of merchandise previously purchased or an allowance made for merchandise that arrived in damaged condition. In both cases there is a reduction in the amount owed to the supplier. The buyer sends a letter or printed form to the supplier, who acknowledges the reduction by sending a **credit memorandum.** The buyer should wait for notice of the agreed deduction before making an entry.

The Purchases Returns and Allowances account is considered to be a deduction from Purchases. Using a separate account provides a better record of the total returns and allowances. Purchases Returns and Allowances is deducted from the Purchases account in the income statement. (We'll talk about this point later.) For now, let's look at an example consisting of two entries on the books of C. L. Frederickson Plumbing Supply.

Transaction (a)   On August 5, bought merchandise on account from Alman Manufacturing Co., their invoice no. 10611 of August 3; terms 2/10, n/30; $692. Recorded this as a debit to Purchases and a credit to Accounts Payable. On August 6, returned $70 worth of the merchandise. Made no entry.

Transaction (b)   On August 8, received credit memorandum no. 629 from Alman Manufacturing Company for $70. Recorded this as a debit to Accounts Payable and a credit to Purchases Returns and Allowances.

Assets		=	Liabilities		+	Owner's Equity		+	Revenue		−	Expenses	
+	−		−	+		−	+		−	+		+	−
Debit	Credit		Debit	Credit		Debit	Credit		Debit	Credit		Debit	Credit

Accounts Payable

−	+
(b) 70	(a) 692

Purchases

+	−
(a) 692	

Purchases Returns and Allowances

−	+
	(b) 70

Purchases Returns and Allowances is credited because C. L. Frederickson has more returns and allowances than before. Accounts Payable is debited because C. L. Frederickson owes less than before.

. Suppose that C. L. Frederickson Plumbing Supply returned merchandise on two occasions during August and received credit memorandums from the suppliers; the entries are recorded in the general journal.

	DATE		DESCRIPTION	POST. REF.	DEBIT	CREDIT	
1	19– Aug.	8	Accounts Payable, Alman				1
2			Manufacturing Company		7 0 00		2
3			Purchases Returns and Allowances			7 0 00	3
4			Credit memo 629, invoice				4
5			no. 10611.				5
6							6
7		12	Accounts Payable, Sullivan				7
8			Manufacturing Company		3 6 00		8
9			Purchases Returns and Allowances			3 6 00	9
10			Credit memo 482, invoice				10
11			no. B643.				11
12							12
13							13

In these entries, Accounts Payable is followed by the name of the individual creditor's account. The accountant must post to both the Accounts Payable controlling account and the individual creditor's account in the accounts payable ledger. The journal entries are shown below as they appear when the posting is completed. The account numbers in the Posting Reference column indicate postings to the accounts in the general ledger, and the check marks indicate postings to the accounts in the accounts payable ledger.

	DATE		DESCRIPTION	POST. REF.	DEBIT	CREDIT	
1	19– Aug.	8	Accounts Payable, Alman				1
2			Manufacturing Company	211/✓	7 0 00		2
3			Purchases Returns and Allowances	512		7 0 00	3
4			Credit memo 629, invoice				4
5			no. 10611.				5
6							6
7		12	Accounts Payable, Sullivan				7
8			Manufacturing Company	211/✓	3 6 00		8
9			Purchases Returns and Allowances	512		3 6 00	9
10			Credit memo 482, invoice				10
11			no. B643.				11
12							12
13							13

GENERAL LEDGER

ACCOUNT _Purchases Returns and Allowances_   ACCOUNT NO. _512_

	DATE	ITEM	POST. REF.	DEBIT	CREDIT	BALANCE DEBIT	BALANCE CREDIT	
1	19– Aug. 1	Balance					6 9 2 00	1
2	8		J27		7 0 00		7 6 2 00	2
3	12		J27		3 6 00		7 9 8 00	3
4								4

GENERAL LEDGER

ACCOUNT _Accounts Payable_   ACCOUNT NO. _211_

	DATE	ITEM	POST. REF.	DEBIT	CREDIT	BALANCE DEBIT	BALANCE CREDIT	
1	19– Aug. 1	Balance	√				3 5 6 00	1
2	8		J27	7 0 00			2 8 6 00	2
3	12		J27	3 6 00			2 5 0 00	3
4								4

ACCOUNTS PAYABLE LEDGER

NAME _Alman Manufacturing Company_

ADDRESS _2150 Madeira Ave._

San Francisco, CA 94130

DATE	ITEM	POST. REF.	DEBIT	CREDIT	BALANCE
19– Aug. 5		P29		6 9 2 00	6 9 2 00
8		J27	7 0 00		6 2 2 00

NAME _Sullivan Manufacturing Company_

ADDRESS _1068 Casino Ave._

Los Angeles, CA 90023

DATE	ITEM	POST. REF.	DEBIT	CREDIT	BALANCE
19– Aug. 9		P29		1 6 5 00	1 6 5 00
12		J27	3 6 00		1 2 9 00

Schedule of Accounts Payable

Assuming that no other transactions involved Accounts Payable, the schedule of accounts payable would appear as follows. Note that the balances of the creditors' accounts, with the exception of the accounts for Alman Manufacturing Company and Sullivan Manufacturing Company, are taken from the accounts payable ledger shown in Figure 12-7.

C. L. Frederickson Plumbing Supply
Schedule of Accounts Payable
August 31, 19–

Alman Manufacturing Company	$ 622 00
Darvik, Inc.	826 00
Donaldson and Farr	376 00
Reiter and Simon Company	940 00
Sullivan Manufacturing Company	129 00
Tru-Fit Valve, Inc.	404 00
Total Accounts Payable	$3297 00

The Accounts Payable controlling account in the general ledger is now posted up to date.

GENERAL LEDGER

ACCOUNT _Accounts Payable_   ACCOUNT NO. _211_

	DATE	ITEM	POST. REF.	DEBIT	CREDIT	BALANCE DEBIT	BALANCE CREDIT	
1	19– Aug. 1	Balance	✓				356 00	1
2	8		J27	70 00			286 00	2
3	12		J27	36 00			250 00	3
4	31		P29		3047 00		3297 00	4
5								5
6								6
7								7

TRANSPORTATION CHARGES ON INCOMING MERCHANDISE AND OTHER ASSETS

When a firm buys merchandise, the total of the purchase invoice may include the transportation charges. If it does, this means that the supplier is selling on the basis of **FOB destination.** In other words, the supplier loads the goods *free on board* (FOB) the carrier and ships them to the customer without charge. Since the supplier is paying the freight charges, these charges naturally have to be included in the selling price of the goods.

For example, C. L. Frederickson Plumbing Supply (remember, it's in Portland) buys pipe fittings from a supplier in Chicago. A note on the supplier's invoice indicates that the terms are FOB Portland (destination). The total of the invoice is $1,200, and C. L. Frederickson knows that this figure includes the freight charges but does not account for them separately. We show this situation by T accounts as follows.

Purchases		Accounts Payable	
+	–	–	+
1,200			1,200

What happens when the transportation charges are separate? In that case, there's a note on the invoice that the terms are **FOB shipping point.** This term means that the supplier will load the goods free on board the carrier at the shipping point, but any freight charges from there on have to be paid by the buyer.

Suppose, for example, that C. L. Frederickson Plumbing Supply buys lavatories from a manufacturer in Detroit with terms FOB Detroit (shipping point). Now the total of the invoice is $1,750, but in this case C. L. Frederickson Plumbing Supply has to pay the freight charges from Detroit to Portland separately. The lavatories are shipped by rail, and C. L. Frederickson pays the railroad $125. In our minds we can picture the T accounts this way.

Objective 4

Journalize transactions involving transportation charges on incoming goods.

Purchases		Accounts Payable		Cash	
+	–	–	+	+	–
1,750			1,750		125
125					

Any merchandising concern must base its markups on the *delivered* cost of the merchandise. So, for this reason, **the buyer debits any freight charges on incoming merchandise to Purchases.** Thus the Purchases account represents both the *cost* of the merchandise and the *freight charges* the buyer has to pay for transporting the goods. In the case of FOB destination, the freight charges have already been included in the total price of the merchandise and debited to the Purchases account when recording the invoice. In the case of FOB shipping point, the buyer pays the freight charges separately and debits the Purchases account at the time of payment. So, with both FOB destination and FOB shipping point, the freight charges on incoming merchandise all wind up in the Purchases account.

Any firm that sells on the basis of FOB destination must be able to cover all its costs, which of course include freight costs. Therefore the firm must include freight costs when it sets the price for its goods. There is an interesting legal point here. Ordinarily, unless the title is definitely retained by the seller, whoever pays the freight charges on the goods has title to the goods during shipment.

Some business firms, instead of debiting Purchases for freight charges on incoming merchandise, set up an expense account entitled Freight In or Transportation In. In the income statement, the accountant adds the balance of this account to the balance of the Purchases account to determine the *delivered* cost of the purchases. However, here we shall follow the policy of debiting Purchases for freight charges on incoming merchandise.

Any shipping charges involved in the buying of any other assets, such as supplies or equipment, are debited to their respective asset accounts. For example, C. L. Frederickson Plumbing Supply bought display cases on account, at a cost of $2,700 plus freight charges of $90. As a convenience, the seller of the display cases paid the transportation costs for C. L. Frederickson Plumbing Supply and then added the $90 to the invoice price of the cases. Let's visualize this by means of T accounts.

Store Equipment			Accounts Payable		
+		−		−	+
2,790					2,790

On the other hand, if C. L. Frederickson had paid the freight charges separately, the entry for the payment would be a debit to Store Equipment for $90 and a credit to Cash for $90.

POSTING DIRECTLY FROM PURCHASE INVOICES

Posting from purchase invoices is a shortcut like posting from sales invoices (described in Chapter 11). The accountant posts to the individual creditors' accounts daily, directly from the purchase invoices. The suppliers' invoice numbers are recorded in the Posting Reference column in place of the journal page number. The Accounts Payable controlling account in the general ledger is brought up to date at the end of the month by making a summarizing entry in the general journal. The accountant debits Purchases and any asset accounts that may be involved and credits Accounts Payable.

Objective 5

Post directly from purchase invoices to an accounts payable ledger and a general ledger.

Since posting directly from purchase invoices is a variation of the accounting system, we shall use a different example: Sam's Towing and Trailer Service. This firm sorts its purchase invoices for the month and finds that the totals are as follows: purchase of merchandise, $8,610; store supplies, $168; office supplies, $126; store equipment, $520. The accountant then makes a summarizing entry in the general journal, as follows.

GENERAL JOURNAL
PAGE 37

	DATE	DESCRIPTION	POST. REF.	DEBIT	CREDIT	
1	19– Oct. 31	Purchases	511	8 6 1 0 00		1
2		Store Supplies	114	1 6 8 00		2
3		Office Supplies	115	1 2 6 00		3
4		Store Equipment	121	5 2 0 00		4
5		Accounts Payable	211		9 4 2 4 00	5
6		Summarizing entry for total				6
7		purchase of goods on account.				7
8						8

The accountant posts the above entry to the general ledger accounts.

GENERAL LEDGER

ACCOUNT Store Supplies   ACCOUNT NO. 114

	DATE	ITEM	POST. REF.	DEBIT	CREDIT	BALANCE DEBIT	BALANCE CREDIT	
1	19– Oct. 31		J37	1 6 8 00		1 6 8 00		1
2								2

ACCOUNT Office Supplies   ACCOUNT NO. 115

	DATE	ITEM	POST. REF.	DEBIT	CREDIT	BALANCE DEBIT	BALANCE CREDIT	
1	19– Oct. 31		J37	1 2 6 00		1 2 6 00		1
2								2

ACCOUNT Store Equipment   **ACCOUNT NO.** 121

	DATE	ITEM	POST. REF.	DEBIT	CREDIT	BALANCE DEBIT	BALANCE CREDIT	
1	19– Oct. 31		J37	5 2 0 00		5 2 0 00		1
2								2

ACCOUNT Accounts Payable   **ACCOUNT NO.** 211

	DATE	ITEM	POST. REF.	DEBIT	CREDIT	BALANCE DEBIT	BALANCE CREDIT	
1	19– Oct. 31		J37		9 4 2 4 00		9 4 2 4 00	1
2								2

ACCOUNT Purchases   **ACCOUNT NO.** 511

	DATE	ITEM	POST. REF.	DEBIT	CREDIT	BALANCE DEBIT	BALANCE CREDIT	
1	19– Oct. 31		J37	8 6 1 0 00		8 6 1 0 00		1
2								2

This procedure does away with the need for a purchases journal, and it also includes the buying of any assets on account in the same summarizing entry. An example of an invoice is shown in Figure 12-8.

Sam's Towing and Trailer Service posts the amount of the invoice to the account of the supplier in the accounts payable ledger.

ACCOUNTS PAYABLE LEDGER

NAME Reinbold Electronics
ADDRESS 9600 Alhambra St.
San Francisco, CA 94132

DATE	ITEM	POST. REF.	DEBIT	CREDIT	BALANCE
19– Oct. 7		13168		1 7 6 00	1 7 6 00

Sam's Towing and Trailer Service will also include the $176 figure in the summarizing entry recorded in the general journal, debiting Purchases and crediting Accounts Payable. Note that the supplier's invoice number is recorded in the Post. Ref. column in the Reinbold Electronics account.

Figure 12-8

REINBOLD ELECTRONICS
9600 Alhambra St.
San Francisco, CA 94132

INVOICE

Sold To	Sam's Towing and Trailer Service 2716 Brighton Road Burlingame, CA 94011	Date:	Oct. 4, 19–
		No.:	13168
		Order No.:	1635
		Shipped By:	Pacific Express Co.
		Terms:	1/10, n/30

Quantity	Description	Unit Price	Total
20	Mobile home antenna—TV	8.80	176.00

SUBSIDIARY LEDGERS

The place of subsidiary ledgers in the accounting cycle is shown in Figure 12-9. The figure also shows how the schedules of accounts receivable and accounts payable fit into the accounting cycle.

INTERNAL CONTROL

We have already spoken briefly about the efficient management of cash in Chapter 8. We stated that all payments should be made either by check or from the petty cash fund, and all cash received should be deposited in the bank at the end of the day. The handling of cash in this manner is an example of **internal control.** When there is internal control, plans and procedures for the control of operations are made a part of the accounting system. Doing this is necessary when the owner or management must delegate authority. The owner has to take measures to (1) protect assets against fraud and waste, (2) provide for accurate accounting data, (3) promote an efficient operation, and (4) encourage adherence to management policies. We'll be talking about the concept of internal control quite often in the rest of the text.

Figure 12-9
The Accounting Cycle

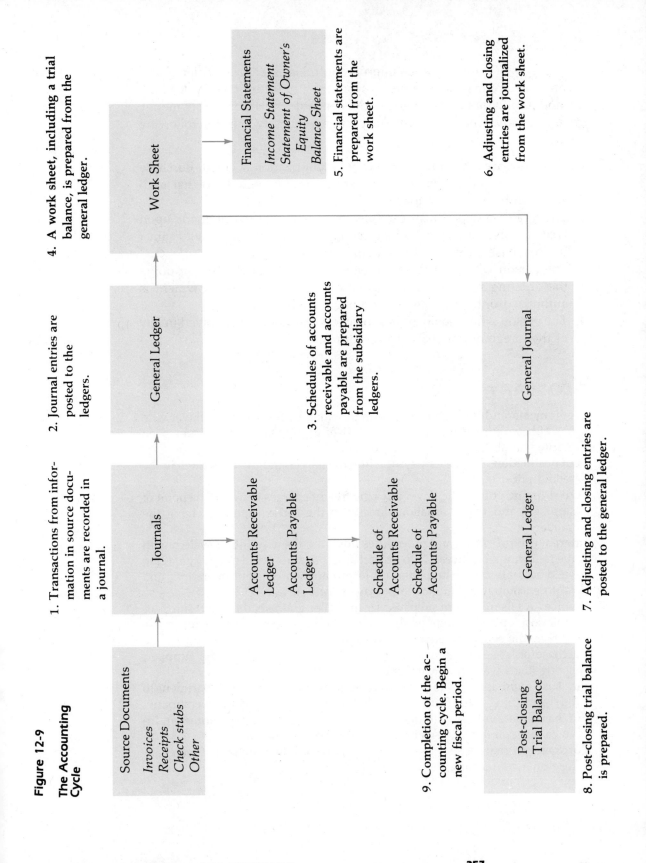

1. Transactions from information in source documents are recorded in a journal.

Source Documents
Invoices
Receipts
Check stubs
Other

2. Journal entries are posted to the ledgers.

Journals

General Ledger

3. Schedules of accounts receivable and accounts payable are prepared from the subsidiary ledgers.

Accounts Receivable Ledger
Accounts Payable Ledger

Schedule of Accounts Receivable
Schedule of Accounts Payable

4. A work sheet, including a trial balance, is prepared from the general ledger.

Work Sheet

Financial Statements
Income Statement
Statement of Owner's Equity
Balance Sheet

5. Financial statements are prepared from the work sheet.

6. Adjusting and closing entries are journalized from the work sheet.

General Journal

7. Adjusting and closing entries are posted to the general ledger.

General Ledger

8. Post-closing trial balance is prepared.

Post-closing Trial Balance

9. Completion of the accounting cycle. Begin a new fiscal period.

Internal Control of Purchases

Purchases is one area in which internal control is essential. Efficiency and security require most companies to work out careful procedures for buying and paying for goods. This is understandable, as large sums of money are usually involved. The control aspect generally involves the following measures.

1. Purchases are made only after proper authorization is given. Purchase requisitions and purchase orders are all prenumbered, so that each form can be accounted for.
2. The receiving department carefully checks and counts all goods upon receipt. Later the report of the receiving department is verified against the purchase order and the purchase invoice.
3. The person who authorizes the payment is neither the person doing the ordering nor the person actually writing the check. Payment is authorized only after the verifications have been made.
4. The person who actually writes the check has not been involved in any of the foregoing purchasing procedures.

GLOSSARY

Credit memorandum A business form provided by the seller to a buyer who has either returned a purchase (or part of a purchase) for credit or been granted an allowance for damaged goods.

FOB destination The seller pays the freight charges and includes them in the selling price.

FOB shipping point The buyer pays the freight charges between the point of shipment and the destination directly to the carrier upon receiving the goods.

Internal control Plans and procedures built into the accounting system with the following objectives: (1) to protect assets against fraud and waste, (2) to yield accurate accounting data, (3) to promote an efficient operation, and (4) to encourage adherence to management policies.

Invoice A business form prepared by the seller that lists the items shipped, their cost, and the mode of shipment. The buyer considers it a purchase invoice; the seller considers it a sales invoice.

Purchase order A written order from the buyer of goods to the supplier, listing items wanted as well as terms of the transaction.

Purchase requisition A form used to request the Purchasing Department to buy something. This form is intended for internal use within a company.

Purchases discount A cash discount allowed for prompt payment of an invoice; for example, 2 percent if the bill is paid within 10 days.

Purchases journal A special journal used to record the purchase of merchandise on account only.

Purchases Returns and Allowances The account used by the buyer to record a reduction granted by the supplier either for the return of merchandise or as compensation for damage to the merchandise. The entry in the buyer's account is based on a credit memorandum received from the supplier.

QUESTIONS, EXERCISES, AND PROBLEMS

Discussion Questions

1. How many copies of a purchase order are usually made, and who receives each copy?
2. What business document authorizes the recording of a purchase transaction?
3. What does a check mark in the Posting Reference column of a purchases journal indicate?
4. How will an error in posting to an individual creditor's account generally be detected?
5. Why is it necessary for a business firm to account for transportation charges on incoming merchandise?
6. When an owner delegates authority, what measures must be taken to maintain control over the operations?
7. Describe the four procedures that most companies follow to maintain internal control of purchases?

Exercises

Exercise 12-1 Label the blanks in the column headings as debit or credit.

PURCHASES JOURNAL						PAGE _____
DATE	SUPPLIER'S NAME	INVOICE NO.	INVOICE DATE	TERMS	POST. REF.	PURCHASES (_____) ACCOUNTS PAYABLE (_____)

Exercise 12-2 Record the following transactions in general journal form.

a. Bought merchandise on account from Drexel Company, invoice no. 7197, FOB shipping point, $416.
b. Paid Acme Fast Freight for shipping charges on the above purchase, $36.

Exercise 12-3 On the above purchase, the markup is 20 percent of cost. Determine the selling price of the new merchandise.

Exercise 12-4 Record the following transactions in general journal form.

a. Bought merchandise on account from Bingham and Harvey, invoice no. D716, $640.
b. Received credit memo no. 216 from Bingham and Harvey for merchandise returned on invoice no. D716, $30.
c. Issued a check to Bingham and Harvey in full payment of invoice no. D716.

Exercise 12-5 A business firm that posts directly from its purchase invoices sorts the invoices for the month and finds that the totals are as follows: purchases of merchandise, $7,624; store supplies, $118; office supplies, $97; office equipment, $136. Record the summarizing entry in general journal form.

Exercise 12-6 Describe the transactions in the following T accounts.

Cash	Purchases	Purchases Returns and Allowances	Accounts Payable
(c) 670	(a) 720	(b) 50	(b) 50 | (a) 720
			(c) 670

Exercise 12-7 Record the following transactions in general journal form.

a. Bought a desk for use in the office from Modern Office Supply, invoice no. D419, $240.
b. Paid Mountain States Freight Company for shipping the desk, $9.

Exercise 12-8 Post the following entry to the general ledger and subsidiary ledger accounts.

GENERAL JOURNAL   PAGE __44__

	DATE	DESCRIPTION	POST. REF.	DEBIT	CREDIT	
1	19– Jun. 15	Accounts Payable, L. B. Dixon				1
2		Company		3 7 40		2
3		Purchases Returns and Allowances			3 7 40	3
4		Received credit memo no. 1087.				4
5						5
6						6
7						7
8						8
9						9
10						10
11						11

GENERAL LEDGER

ACCOUNT *Accounts Payable*   ACCOUNT NO. _212_

	DATE	ITEM	POST. REF.	DEBIT	CREDIT	BALANCE DEBIT	BALANCE CREDIT	
1	19– Jun. 1	Balance	√				1 6 5 4 20	1
2								2

ACCOUNT *Purchases Returns and Allowances*   ACCOUNT NO. _512_

	DATE	ITEM	POST. REF.	DEBIT	CREDIT	BALANCE DEBIT	BALANCE CREDIT	
1	19– Jun. 1	Balance	√				8 4 20	1
2								2

ACCOUNTS PAYABLE LEDGER

NAME *L. B. Dixon Company*

ADDRESS _____

	DATE	ITEM	POST. REF.	DEBIT	CREDIT	BALANCE
	19– May 27		G729		1 2 8 00	1 2 8 00

Problem Set A

Problem 12-1A Morgan and Stern, Jewelers, uses a single-column purchases journal. On January 1 of this year, the balances in the ledger accounts are Accounts Payable, $400.86; Purchases, zero. In addition to a general ledger, Morgan and Stern uses an accounts payable ledger. Transactions for January related to the buying of merchandise are as follows.

Jan. 5 Bought sixty Soules Mortenson Automatic Day/Date watches in Karecki yellow cases from Spencer Watch Company, invoice no. 2117D, dated January 4, terms net 60 days, $5,920.

7 Bought ten Precision Chronograph ILD watches from Bell and Taylor, invoice no. C3946, dated January 7; terms 2/10, n/30; $482.

8 Bought four Farrell Deep Diver watches from Ferrano Imports, invoice no. 15148, dated January 8, terms net 30 days, $268.

11 Bought ten Unico Boy's Sport watches, model 14K, from Cooper and Larkin, invoice no. 359FE, dated January 9; terms 1/10, n/30; $282.

Jan. 19 Bought ten Mercer Antiqued Gold-tone Vest Chains from Ferrano Imports, invoice no. 15224, dated January 18, terms net 30 days, $73.60.

24 Purchased ten Tenser PCL Pocket watches from Spencer Watch Company, invoice no. 2218D, dated January 23, terms net 60 days, $1,326.

29 Bought two Fidelity Diamond Sharon watches from Campbell Manufacturing Company, invoice no. 764LC, dated January 27; terms 2/10, n/30; $293.16.

31 Bought one Champton Diamond Minuet watch from Simmons, Inc., invoice no. 36049, dated January 28; terms 2/10, n/30; $326.82.

Instructions

1. Open the following accounts in the accounts payable ledger and record the January 1 balances, if any, as given: Bell and Taylor, $128; Campbell Manufacturing Company, $74.16; Cooper and Larkin; Ferrano Imports; Simmons, Inc., $198.70; Spencer Watch Company.
2. Record the balance of $400.86 as of January 1 in the Accounts Payable controlling account.
3. Record the transactions in the purchases journal beginning with page 72.
4. Post to the accounts payable ledger.
5. Post to the Accounts Payable controlling account and the Purchases account.
6. Prepare a schedule of accounts payable, and compare the balance of the Accounts Payable controlling account with the total of the schedule of accounts payable.

Problem 12-2A The Heathwood Gift Shop had the following purchases of merchandise and supplies and related returns and allowances during March.

Mar. 3 Bought merchandise on account from Merrill Pottery Company, invoice no. 8792, dated March 1; terms 2/10, n/30; $682.

4 Bought merchandise on account from Danville Supply Company, invoice no. 21863D, dated March 2; terms net 30 days; $583.20.

7 Bought merchandise on account from Dawes and Son, invoice no. 28860, dated March 7; terms net 30 days; $291.72.

11 Bought office supplies on account from Nielson Office Supply, invoice no. 3849, dated March 11; terms net 30 days; $169.48.

13 Received credit memo no. 316 from Merrill Pottery Company for merchandise returned, $22.

15 Bought merchandise on account from Unique Card Company, invoice no. 77281, dated March 15; terms 1/10, n/30; $789.60.

20 Bought office equipment on account from Carlton Equipment Company, invoice no. 6582, dated March 18; terms net 30 days; $717.

25 Bought merchandise on account from Unique Card Company, invoice no. 77472, dated March 25; terms 1/10, n/30; $989.60.

28 Received credit memo no. 49 from Danville Supply Company for merchandise returned, $73.

Mar. 29 Bought merchandise on account from Merrill Pottery Company, invoice no. 8871, dated March 28; terms 2/10, n/30; $1,273.10.

30 Bought store supplies on account from Lassiter and Foss, invoice no. 87616, dated March 30; terms net 30 days; $41.

30 Bought merchandise on account from Dawes and Son, invoice no. 29143, dated March 29; terms net 30 days; $142.30.

30 Bought merchandise on account from Danville Supply Company, invoice no. 21914D, dated March 28; terms net 30 days; $348.16.

Instructions

1. Open the following accounts in the general ledger and enter the March 1 balances as given.

113	Store Supplies	$ 315.18
114	Office Supplies	136.32
121	Office Equipment	4,775.00
211	Accounts Payable	2,744.01
511	Purchases	6,881.19
512	Purchases Returns and Allowances	262.46

2. Open the following accounts in the accounts payable ledger and enter the balances, if any, in the Balance columns as of March 1: Carlton Equipment Company; Danville Supply Company; Dawes and Son, $924.18; Lassiter and Foss; Merrill Pottery Company, $1,480; Nielson Office Supply; Unique Card Company, $339.83.

3. Record the transactions either in the general journal, page 31, or the purchases journal, page 9, as appropriate.

4. Post the entries to the creditors' accounts in the accounts payable ledger immediately after you record each journal entry.

5. Post the entries to the general ledger after you record each general journal entry.

6. Post the total of the purchases journal at the end of the month.

7. Prepare a schedule of accounts payable, and compare the balance of the Accounts Payable controlling account with the total of the schedule of accounts payable.

Problem 12-3A Frankhurst Products Company records sales of merchandise daily by posting directly from its sales invoices to the accounts receivable ledger. At the end of the month it makes a summarizing entry in the general journal. It records purchases of goods on account the same way, daily, posting directly from the invoices to the accounts payable ledger and making a summarizing entry in the general journal at the end of the month. Sales of merchandise and purchases of goods on account during October of this year were as follows.

Sales of merchandise

Oct. 4 Allentown Specialty Shop, no. 3216, $348.17.

7 I. D. Miller, no. 3217, $548.19.

11 R. D. Blanchard and Company, no. 3218, $918.65.

15 Myron and Nelson, no. 3219, $1,080.72.

Oct. 22 Lane P. Jackson, no. 3220, $877.25.
24 Eldon P. Wenzel, no. 3221, $967.60.
25 Rex P. Ruller, no. 3222, $1,110.
28 Dante and Rubin, no. 3223, $540.35.
30 Myron and Nelson, no. 3224, $318.
31 I. D. Miller, no. 3225, $225.70.

Purchases of goods on account

Oct. 3 Denham and Lancaster, merchandise, no. C1189, $566.
7 Dugan Wood Products, merchandise, no. 23229, $1,400.
9 Precision Manufacturing Company, merchandise, no. 83118, $3,870.
10 Singleton Supply Company, office supplies, no. AD776, $112.
19 C. C. Russo and Company, merchandise, no. C1146, $129.76.
26 Nelson and Nelson, store supplies, no. S9825, $54.60.
28 Dugan Wood Products, merchandise, no. 23313, $2,874.
31 Denton Equipment Company, store equipment, no. 31192, $210.

Instructions

1. Record the summarizing entry for the sales of merchandise on account in the general journal.
2. Record the summarizing entry for the purchase of goods on account in the general journal.

Problem 12-4A The following transactions relate to the Pembrook Company during March of this year. Terms of sale are 2/10, n/30.

Mar. 1 Sold merchandise on account to Arthur Yeager, invoice no. 16116, $800.
3 Bought merchandise on account from Newton Manufacturing Company, invoice no. A1121, March 1; terms 1/10, n/30; $450.
9 Sold merchandise on account to Anderson and Low, invoice no. 16117, $1,250.
11 Bought merchandise on account from N. D. Stonewall Company, invoice no. 7892, dated March 10; terms 2/10, n/30; $4,300.
14 Received credit memo no. 84 for merchandise returned to N. D. Stonewall Company, for $110, related to invoice no. 7892.
17 Sold merchandise on account to Martin Dahl, invoice no. 16118, $840.
17 Issued credit memo no. 26 to Anderson and Low, for merchandise returned, $80, related to invoice no. 16117.
26 Bought merchandise on account from George T. Williams and Son, invoice no. 9986, dated March 25; 2/10, EOM (within 10 days after the end of the month); $1,600.
28 Bought office supplies on account from Freeport Stationery Company, invoice no. R2686, dated March 28, 30 days net, $65.
29 Sold merchandise on account to Sutton and Thomas, invoice no. 16119, $2,960.
30 Issued credit memo no. 27 to Sutton and Thomas for merchandise returned, $190, related to invoice no. 16119.

Instructions

1. Open the following accounts in the accounts receivable ledger, and enter the March 1 balances, if any, in the Balance columns as given: Anderson and Low, $417; Dahl, Martin; Sutton and Thomas, $983; Yeager, Arthur.
2. Open the following accounts in the accounts payable ledger, and enter the March 1 balances, if any, in the Balance columns as given: Freeport Stationery Company; Newton Manufacturing Company; N. D. Stonewall Company, $378; George T. Williams and Son.
3. Record the transactions in the sales, purchases, and general journals as appropriate.
4. Post to the accounts receivable ledger daily.
5. Post to the accounts payable ledger daily.
6. Post to the general ledger provided.
7. Prepare a schedule of accounts receivable.
8. Prepare a schedule of accounts payable.
9. Compare the totals of the schedules with the balances of the controlling accounts.

Problem Set B

Problem 12-1B   Stevens Appliance uses a single-column purchases journal. On January 1 of this year, the balances of the ledger accounts are Accounts Payable, $539.06; Purchases, zero. In addition to a general ledger, Stevens Appliance also uses an accounts payable ledger. Transactions for January related to the buying of merchandise are as follows.

Jan.   3 Bought eighty Mulholland Two-Burner Buffet Ranges from Skelton, Inc., invoice no. 2718C, dated January 2, terms net 60 days, $2,376.

5 Bought ten White Swan Immersible Griddles from Shattuck Company, invoice no. 27418, dated January 2; terms 2/10, n/30; $325.

8 Bought ten Supra Deluxe Waffle Bakers from Thomas and Finch, invoice no. 321AC, dated January 5; terms 1/10, n/30; $264.

11 Bought twenty-four Simpo Popcorn Pumpers, Model 2800, from Ulmer Company, invoice no. C8741, dated January 10; terms 2/10, n/30; $480.

15 Bought four Trendo Automatic Egg Cookers, Model 24-10, from Foster Products Company, invoice no. 2621, dated January 14, terms net 30 days, $98.

23 Bought forty Sebas Hot Baskets, Model BC1, from Skelton, Inc., invoice no. 2823C, dated January 21; terms net 60 days; $980.

29 Bought ten Trendo Pizza Baker/Grills, Model 5122, from Foster Products Company, invoice no. 2719, dated January 28, terms net 30 days, $263.

30 Bought ten Isenware 6½ qt. Electric Woks, Model 210, from Penfield Manufacturing Company, invoice no. 732AL, dated January 27; terms 2/10, n/30; $286.

Instructions

1. Open the following accounts in the accounts payable ledger and record the balances, if any, as of January 1: Foster Products Company; Penfield Manufacturing Company, $143.17; Shattuck Company, $167.19; Skelton, Inc.; Thomas and Finch, $228.70; Ulmer Company.
2. Record the balance of $539.06 in the Accounts Payable controlling account as of January 1.
3. Record the transactions in the purchases journal beginning with page 81.
4. Post to the accounts payable ledger.
5. Post to the Accounts Payable controlling account and the Purchases account.
6. Prepare a schedule of accounts payable, and compare the balance of the Accounts Payable controlling account with the total of the schedule of accounts payable.

Problem 12-2B   The Remco Gift Shop bought the following merchandise and supplies and had the following returns and allowances during May of this year.

May   2 Bought merchandise on account from Trevino Pottery Company, invoice no. 9761, dated May 1; terms 2/10, n/30; $680.
      4 Bought merchandise on account from Tenet Card Company, invoice no. 16728, dated May 1; terms 1/10, n/30; $268.
      6 Bought merchandise on account from Dow Supply Company, invoice no. 21792D, dated May 5, terms net 30 days, $586.
     10 Bought office supplies on account from Drexel and Son, invoice no. 2995C, dated May 10, terms net 30 days, $162.
     12 Received credit memorandum no. 746 from Tenet Card Company for merchandise returned, $26.
     16 Bought merchandise on account from Axel Printing Company, invoice no. 99821, dated May 15; terms 1/10, n/30; $580.
     21 Bought office equipment on account from Dalton Equipment Company, invoice no. 6616, dated May 18; terms net 30 days; $624.
     26 Bought merchandise on account from Tenet Card Company, invoice no. 17118, dated May 23; terms 1/10, n/30; $982.
     27 Received credit memorandum no. 28C from Dow Supply Company for merchandise returned, $76.
     28 Bought merchandise on account from Trevino Pottery Company, invoice no. 10096, dated May 27; terms 2/10, n/30; $1,642.
     29 Bought store supplies on account from Towne and Truvall, invoice no. 98621, dated May 29, terms net 30 days, $32.

Instructions

1. Open the following accounts in the general ledger and enter the May 1 balances as given:

113	Store Supplies	$ 210
114	Office Supplies	121
121	Office Equipment	4,680
211	Accounts Payable	2,788

| 511 | Purchases | 6,984 |
| 512 | Purchases Returns and Allowances | 270 |

2. Open the following accounts in the accounts payable ledger and enter the balances in the Balance columns as of May 1: Axel Printing Company; Dalton Equipment Company; Dow Supply Company, $1,800; Drexel and Son; Tenet Card Company, $28; Towne and Truvall; Trevino Pottery Company, $960.
3. Record the transactions in either the general journal, starting on page 27, or the purchases journal, listing them on page 6, as appropriate.
4. Post the entries to the creditors' accounts in the accounts payable ledger immediately after you make each journal entry.
5. Post the entries in the general journal immediately after you make each journal entry.
6. Post the total of the purchases journal at the end of the month.
7. Prepare a schedule of accounts payable, and compare the balance of the Accounts Payable controlling account with the total of the schedule of accounts payable.

Problem 12-3B   The Trotter Products Company records sales of merchandise daily by posting directly from its sales invoices to the accounts receivable ledger. At the end of the month, a summarizing entry is made in the general journal. The purchase of goods on account is recorded in a similar manner. Each day's posting is done directly from the invoices to the accounts payable ledger, and a summarizing entry is made in the general journal at the end of the month. Sales of merchandise and purchases of goods on account during September of this year were as follows.

Sales of merchandise

Sep.   3 Arnold Store Corp., no. 2611, $2,300.
       6 T. D. Mitchell, no. 2612, $3,400.
      10 C. A. Howard and Company, no. 2613, $1,612.
      14 Bartor and Bartell, no. 2614, $2,680.
      21 Franklin P. Ellis, no. 2615, $1,470.
      23 George H. Anderson, no. 2616, $424.
      24 Daniel B. Tyne, no. 2617, $2,900.
      27 Marshall and Miner, no. 2618, $640.
      28 T. D. Mitchell, no. 2619, $1,876.
      30 Bartor and Bartell, no. 2620, $1,920.
      30 Marshall and Miner, no. 2621, $3,268.

Purchases of goods on account

Sep.   2 Lanham Corp., merchandise, no. 6382, $2,170.
      6 Unique Wood Products, merchandise, no. 2198A, $1,800.
      8 Modern Manufacturing Company, merchandise, no. 82116, $4,620.
      16 Slessor and Smith, store supplies, no. D9682, $210.
      25 B. R. Rogers and Company, store supplies, no. 9621, $180.
      28 Lanham Corp., merchandise, no. B726, $3,960.
      30 Unique Wood Products, merchandise, no. 2716A, $4,215.
      30 Johnson Equipment Company, store equipment, no. 72116, $325.

Instructions

1. Record the summarizing entry for sales of merchandise on account in the general journal.
2. Record the summarizing entry for the purchase of goods on account in the general journal.

Problem 12-4B   The transactions described below relate to the Snyder Supply Company during March of this year. Terms of sale are 2/10, n/30.

Mar.   1 Sold merchandise on account to Spangler Hardware, invoice no. 36442, $762.

   4 Bought merchandise on account from Northern Manufacturing Company, invoice no. C1149, dated March 4; 1/10, n/30; $320.

   8 Sold merchandise on account to Meadowland Department Store, invoice no. 36443, $942.

   10 Bought merchandise on account from Superior Products Company, invoice no. 9119, dated March 10; 2/10, n/30; $3,776.75.

   13 Received credit memo no. 96 for merchandise returned from Roxford and Son for $341, related to invoice no. D1198.

   16 Sold merchandise on account to Nancy Girard, invoice no. 36444, $442.70.

   17 Issued credit memo no. 31 to Meadowland Department Store for merchandise related to invoice no. 36443, $96.

   25 Bought merchandise on account from Danforth Manufacturing Company, invoice no. B4491, dated March 23; 2/10, n/30; $1,562.

   27 Bought office supplies on account from Hosford and Randall Company, invoice no. D3179, dated March 26, 30 days net, $56.20.

   27 Sold merchandise on account to Hadley Specialty Company, invoice no. 36445, $3,006.

   30 Issued credit memo no. 32 to Hadley Specialty Company for merchandise related to invoice no. 36445, $258.

Instructions

1. Open the following accounts in the accounts receivable ledger, and enter the March 1 balances, if any, in the Balance columns as given: Girard, Nancy; Hadley Specialty Company, $1,400; Meadowland Department Store; Spangler Hardware.
2. Open the following accounts in the accounts payable ledger, and enter the March 1 balances, if any, in the Balance columns as given: Danforth Manufacturing Company; Hosford and Randall; Northern Manufacturing Company; Roxford and Son, $378; Superior Products Company.
3. Record the transactions in the sales, purchases, and general journals.
4. Post to the accounts receivable ledger daily.
5. Post to the accounts payable ledger daily.
6. Post to the general ledger provided.
7. Prepare a schedule of accounts receivable.
8. Prepare a schedule of accounts payable.
9. Compare the totals of the schedules with the balances of the controlling accounts.

13 Cash Receipts and Cash Payments

Learning Objectives

After you have completed this chapter, you will be able to do the following:

1. Record transactions for a retail merchandising business in a cash receipts journal.

2. Post from a cash receipts journal to a general ledger and an accounts receivable ledger.

3. Determine cash discounts according to credit terms, and record cash receipts from charge customers who are entitled to deduct the cash discount.

4. Record transactions for a wholesale merchandising business in a cash receipts journal.

5. Record transactions in a cash payments journal for a service enterprise.

6. Record transactions in a cash payments journal for a merchandising enterprise.

7. Record transactions in a check register.

8. Record transactions involving trade discounts.

We have seen that using a sales journal and a purchases journal enables an accountant to carry out the journalizing and posting processes much more efficiently. These special journals make it possible to post column totals rather than individual figures. This procedure also makes possible a more efficient division of labor, because the journalizing functions can be delegated to different persons. The *cash receipts journal* and *cash payments journal* further extend these advantages.

CASH RECEIPTS JOURNAL

The **cash receipts journal** records all transactions in which cash comes in, or increases. When the cash receipts journal is used, all transactions in which cash is debited *must* be recorded in it. It may be used for a service as well as a merchandising business. To get acquainted with the cash receipts journal, let's list some typical transactions of a retail merchandising business that result in an increase in cash. To get a better picture of the transactions, let's record them immediately in T accounts.

Objective 1

Record transactions for a retail merchandising business in a cash receipts journal.

May 3: Sold merchandise for cash, $100, plus $4 sales tax.

Cash	Sales	Sales Tax Payable
+ $\quad$ −	− $\quad$ +	− $\quad$ +
104	$\qquad$ 100	$\qquad$ 4

May 4: Sold merchandise, $100 plus $4 sales tax, and the customer used a **bank charge card.** Millions of people use these cards every day and pay the bank directly at the end of the month. The firm, on the other hand, deposits the bank credit card receipts every day. The bank *deducts a discount* and credits the firm's account with cash. This discount is often 2 percent of the total of sales plus sales tax. The firm therefore records the amount of the discount under Credit Card Expense. (From the amount that would ordinarily be debited to Cash, deduct the bank charge, consisting of 2 percent of the total of sales plus sales tax, and debit this amount to Credit Card Expense instead of to Cash: $104 \times .02 = \$2.08$ credit card expense; $\$100 + \$4 - \$2.08 = \$101.92$.)

Cash	Credit Card Expense	Sales Tax Payable	Sales
+ $\quad$ −	+ $\quad$ −	− $\quad$ +	− $\quad$ +
101.92	2.08	$\qquad$ 4	$\qquad$ 100

May 5: Collected cash on account from J. C. Rowe, a charge customer, $208.

Cash		Accounts Receivable	
+	–	+	–
208			208

May 7: The owner, A. P. Hall, invested cash in the business, $3,000.

Cash		A. P. Hall, Capital	
+	–	–	+
3,000			3,000

May 8: Sold equipment for cash at cost, $150.

Cash		Equipment	
+	–	+	–
150			150

Now let's appraise these five transactions: The first three would occur frequently; the last two could conceivably take place, but they would be rather infrequent. If one is designing a cash receipts journal, it is logical to include a Cash Debit column because all the transactions involve an increase in cash. If a business regularly collects cash from charge customers, there should be an Accounts Receivable Credit column. If a firm often sells merchandise for cash and collects a sales tax, there should be a Sales Credit column and a Sales Tax Payable Credit column. If the business honors bank charge cards, there should be a Credit Card Expense Debit column to take care of the amount deducted by the bank.

However, the credit to A. P. Hall, Capital, and the credit to Equipment occur very seldom, so it wouldn't be practical to set up special columns for them. They can be handled adequately by a Sundry Credit column, which can be used for credits to all accounts that have no special column.

Now let's record the same transactions in a cash receipts journal (see Figure 13-1 on page 372). First we'll repeat the transactions:

May   3 Sold merchandise for cash, $100, plus $4 sales tax.
        4 Sold merchandise, $100 plus $4 sales tax, and the customer used a bank charge card. Discount charged by the bank is 2 percent of the amount of the total of sales plus sales tax.
        5 Collected cash from J. C. Rowe, a charge customer, on account, $208.

CASH RECEIPTS JOURNAL

DATE	ACCOUNT CREDITED	POST. REF.	SUNDRY ACCOUNTS CREDIT	ACCOUNTS RECEIVABLE CREDIT	SALES CREDIT	SALES TAX PAYABLE CREDIT	CREDIT CARD EXPENSE DEBIT	CASH DEBIT	
19— May 3	Sales				100 00	4 00		104 00	1
4	Sales				100 00	4 00	2 08	101 92	2
5	J. C. Rowe			208 00				208 00	3
7	A. P. Hall, Capital		3000 00					3000 00	4
8	Equipment		150 00					150 00	5
									6

Figure 13-1

CASH RECEIPTS JOURNAL

DATE	ACCOUNT CREDITED	POST. REF.	SUNDRY ACCOUNTS CREDIT	ACCOUNTS RECEIVABLE CREDIT	SALES CREDIT	SALES TAX PAYABLE CREDIT	CREDIT CARD EXPENSE DEBIT	CASH DEBIT	
19— May 3	Sales	—			100 00	4 00		104 00	1
4	Sales	√			100 00	4 00	2 08	101 92	2
5	J. C. Rowe	√		208 00				208 00	3
7	A. R. Hall, Capital	311	3000 00					3000 00	4
8	Equipment	121	150 00					150 00	5
11	Notes Payable	211	300 00					300 00	6
16	Sales	—			200 00	8 00		208 00	7
21	Sales	—			50 00	2 00	1 04	50 96	8
26	Kenneth Ralston	√		6 2 40				6 2 40	9
28	Sales	—			40 00	1 60		41 60	10
31	Sales	—			150 00	6 00	3 12	152 88	11
31	Sylvia Harlow	√		2 6 00				2 6 00	12
31			3450 00	296 40	640 00	25 60	6 24	4405 76	13
			(√)	(113)	(411)	(213)	(513)	(111)	14
									15

Figure 13-2

May   7 The owner, A. P. Hall, invested cash in the business, $3,000.
      8 Sold equipment for cash at cost, $150.

Posting from the Cash Receipts Journal

At the end of the month we can post the special columns in the cash receipts journal as totals to the general ledger accounts. These include Accounts Receivable Credit, Sales Credit, Sales Tax Payable Credit, Credit Card Expense Debit, and Cash Debit. We post the items in the Sundry Accounts Credit column individually; we post the figures in the Accounts Receivable Credit column separately to accounts in the accounts receivable ledger. The posting letter designation for the cash receipts journal is CR.

Here are some other transactions made during the month that involve increases in cash. (Remember that these transactions are for a retail business.)

Objective 2

Post from a cash receipts journal to a general ledger and an accounts receivable ledger.

May   11 Borrowed $300 from the bank, receiving cash and giving the bank a promissory note.
      16 Sold merchandise for cash, $200, plus $8 sales tax.
      21 Sold merchandise for cash, $50, plus $2 sales tax; customer used a bank charge card. Credit card expense charge is 2 percent of sales plus tax.
      26 Collected cash from Kenneth Ralston, a charge customer, on account, $62.40.
      28 Sold merchandise for cash, $40, plus $1.60 sales tax.
      31 Sold merchandise for cash, $150, plus $6 sales tax; customer used a bank charge card. Credit card expense charge is 2 percent of sales plus tax.
      31 Collected cash from Sylvia Harlow, a charge customer, on account, $26.

Let us assume that all the month's transactions involving debits to Cash have now been recorded in the cash receipts journal. The cash receipts journal (Figure 13-2) and the T accounts on page 374 illustrate the postings to the general ledger and the accounts receivable ledger.

Individual amounts in the Accounts Receivable credit column of the cash receipts journal are posted daily. Individual amounts in the Sundry credit column are posted daily. Totals are posted at the end of the month.

Accounts Receivable Ledger		General Ledger	

Accounts Receivable Ledger

Sylvia Harlow

+	−
	May 31 26

J. C. Rowe

+	−
	May 5 208

Kenneth Ralston

+	−
	May 26 62.40

General Ledger

A. P. Hall, Capital

−	+
	May 7 3,000

Equipment

+	−
	May 8 150

Notes Payable

−	+
	May 11 300

Cash

+	−
May 31 4,405.76	

Credit Card Expense

+	−
May 31 6.24	

Sales Tax Payable

−	+
	May 31 25.60

Sales

−	+
	May 31 640

Accounts Receivable

+	−
	May 31 296.40

In the Posting Reference column, the check marks (√) indicate that the amounts in the Accounts Receivable Credit column have been posted to the individual charge customers' accounts as credits. The account numbers show that the amounts in the Sundry Accounts Credit column have been posted separately to the accounts described in the Account Credited column. A check mark (√) also goes under the total of the Sundry column, where it means "do not post—the figures have already been posted separately." A check mark in our example thus has two meanings: (1) *the individual account has been posted in the subsidiary ledger*, as in the Accounts Receivable Credit column; and (2) *the total is not to be posted*, as in the Sundry column.

A dash in the Posting Reference column indicates that an individual amount is being posted as a part of a column total. For example, the $100 credit to Sales on May 3 will be posted as a part of the $640 total.

Let's say it's the end of the month. We total the columns, then check the accuracy of the footings by proving that the sum of the debit totals equals the sum of the credit totals. This process is referred to as **crossfooting** the journal. It must be done before one posts the totals to the general ledger accounts.

	Debit Totals
Cash	$4,405.76
Credit Card Expense	6.24
	$4,412.00

	Credit Totals
Sundry Accounts	$3,450.00
Accounts Receivable	296.40
Sales	640.00
Sales Tax Payable	25.60
	$4,412.00

After posting the total amounts of the special columns, write the general ledger account number in parentheses below the total in the appropriate column.

CREDIT TERMS

The seller always stipulates credit terms: How much credit can be allowed to a customer? And how much time should the customer be given to pay the full amount? The **credit period** is the time the seller allows the buyer before full payment has to be made. Retailers generally allow 30 days.

Wholesalers and manufacturers often specify a **cash discount** in their credit terms. A cash discount is the amount a customer can deduct if she or he pays the bill within a short time. The discount is based on the total amount of the invoice after deducting any returns and allowances. Naturally this discount acts as an incentive for charge customers to pay their bills promptly.

Let's say that a wholesaler offers customers credit terms of 2/10, n/30. These terms mean that the customer gets a 2 percent discount if the bill is paid within 10 days after the invoice date. If the bill is not paid within the 10 days, then the entire amount is due within 30 days after the invoice date. Other cash discounts that may be used are the following.

Objective 3

Determine cash discounts according to credit terms, and record cash receipts from charge customers who are entitled to deduct the cash discount.

- **1/15, n/60** The seller offers a 1 percent discount if the bill is paid within 15 days after the invoice date, or the whole bill must be paid within 60 days after the invoice date.
- **2/10, EOM, n/60** The seller offers a 2 percent discount if the bill is paid within 10 days after the end of the month, and the whole bill must be paid within 60 days after the invoice date.

A wholesaler or manufacturer offering a cash discount adopts a single cash discount as a credit policy and makes this available to all its customers. The seller considers cash discounts as **sales discounts;** the buyer, on the other hand, considers cash discounts as purchases discounts. In this section we are concerned with the sales discount. The Sales Discount account, like Sales Returns and Allowances, is a deduction from Sales.

To illustrate, we return to C. L. Frederickson Plumbing Supply. We'll record the following transactions in T accounts so we can see them at a glance.

Transaction (a) August 1: Sold merchandise on account to T. L. Long Company, invoice no. 320; terms 2/10, n/30; $424.

Transaction (b) August 10: Received check from T. L. Long Company for $415.52 in payment of invoice no. 320, less cash discount ($424.00 − $8.48 = $415.52).

Assets		=	Liabilities		+	Owner's Equity		+	Revenue		−	Expenses	
+	−		−	+		−	+		−	+		+	−
Debit	Credit		Debit	Credit		Debit	Credit		Debit	Credit		Debit	Credit

Accounts Receivable			Sales	
+	−		−	+
(a) 424.00	(b) 424.00			(a) 424.00

Cash			Sales Discount	
+	−		+	−
(b) 415.52			(b) 8.48	

Objective 4

Record transactions for a wholesale merchandising business in a cash receipts journal.

Since C. L. Frederickson Plumbing Supply offers this cash discount to all its customers, and since charge customers often pay their bills within the discount period, C. L. Frederickson sets up a Sales Discount Debit column in the cash receipts journal. Note that C. L. Frederickson Plumbing Supply is a wholesaler. Therefore, a column for Sales Tax Payable is not used, since few states levy a tax on sales at the wholesale level.

	DATE	ACCOUNT CREDITED	POST. REF.	SUNDRY ACCOUNTS CREDIT	ACCOUNTS RECEIVABLE CREDIT	SALES CREDIT	SALES DISCOUNT DEBIT	CASH DEBIT	
1	19– Aug. 10	T. L. Long Co.			4 2 4 00		8 48	4 1 5 52	1
2									2

Several other transactions of C. L. Frederickson Plumbing Supply involve increases in cash during August. Remember that the standard credit terms for all charge customers are 2/10, n/30.

Aug.   15 Cash sales for first half of the month, $460.

16 Received check from Abel Plumbing and Heating for $92.12 in payment of invoice no. 322, less cash discount ($94.00 − $1.88 = $92.12).

17 Received payment on a promissory note given by John R. Stokes, $300 principal, plus $3 interest. (The amount of the interest is recorded in Interest Income.)

21 Received check from Craig and Fraser Hardware for $84.28 in payment of invoice no. 324, less cash discount ($86.00 − $1.72 = $84.28).

23 Sold store equipment for cash at cost, $126.

26 C. L. Frederickson, the owner, invested an additional $4,000 cash in the business.

26 Received a check from Home Hardware Company for $97.02 in payment of invoice no. 325, less the amount of credit memorandum no. 70, $99, less cash discount ($215 − $116 = $99; $99.00 × .02 = $1.98; $99.00 − $1.98 = $97.02).

30 Received check from Henning's Plumbing for $287.14 in payment of invoice no. 326, less cash discount ($293.00 − $5.86 = $287.14).

31 Cash sales for second half of the month, $620.

31 Received check from Maley, Inc., in payment of invoice no. 321, for $116. (This is longer than the 10-day period, so they missed the cash discount.)

C. L. Frederickson records these transactions in its cash receipts journal (Figure 13-3, next page).

After that has been done, the company's accountant proves the equality of debits and credits:

Debit Totals		**Credit Totals**	
Cash	$6,601.08	Sundry Accounts	$4,429.00
Sales Discount	19.92	Accounts Receivable	1,112.00
	$6,621.00	Sales	1,080.00
			$6,621.00

CASH RECEIPTS JOURNAL

DATE	ACCOUNT CREDITED	POST. REF.	SUNDRY ACCOUNTS CREDIT	ACCOUNTS RECEIVABLE CREDIT	SALES CREDIT	SALES DISCOUNT DEBIT	CASH DEBIT	
19— Aug. 10	T. L. Long Company			4 2 4 00		8 48	4 1 5 52	1
15	Sales				4 6 0 00		4 6 0 00	2
16	Abel Plumbing and Heating			9 4 00		1 88	9 2 12	3
17	Notes Receivable		3 0 0 00					4
	Interest Income		3 00				3 0 3 00	5
21	Craig and Fraser Hardware			8 6 00		1 72	8 4 28	6
23	Store Equipment		1 2 6 00				1 2 6 00	7
26	C. L. Frederickson, Capital		4 0 0 0 00				4 0 0 0 00	8
26	Home Hardware Company			9 9 00		1 98	9 7 02	9
30	Henning's Plumbing			2 9 3 00		5 86	2 8 7 14	10
31	Sales				6 2 0 00		6 2 0 00	11
31	Maley, Inc.			1 1 6 00			1 1 6 00	12
31			4 4 2 9 00	1 1 1 2 00	1 0 8 0 00	19 92	6 6 0 1 08	13
								14
								15
								16
								17
								18
								19
								20
								21
								22
								23
								24

Figure 13-3

CASH PAYMENTS JOURNAL: SERVICE ENTERPRISE

The cash payments journal, as the name implies, records all transactions in which cash goes out, or decreases. When the cash payments journal is used, all transactions in which cash is credited *must* be recorded in it. It may be used for a service as well as a merchandising business.

To get acquainted with the cash payments journal, let's list some typical transactions of a service firm (such as a dry cleaner or a bowling alley) or a professional enterprise that result in a decrease in cash. So that you'll see the transactions at a glance, let's record them directly in T accounts.

May 2: Paid C. C. Hardy Company, a creditor, on account, check no. 63, $220.

Accounts Payable		Cash	
−	+	+	−
220			220

May 4: Bought supplies for cash, check no. 64, $90.

Supplies		Cash	
+	−	+	−
90			90

May 5: Paid wages for two weeks, check no. 65, $1,216 (previously recorded in the payroll entry).

Wages Payable		Cash	
−	+	+	−
1,216			1,216

May 6: Paid rent for the month, check no. 66, $350.

Rent Expense		Cash	
+	−	+	−
350			350

Now let's appraise these four transactions. The first one would occur very often, as payments to creditors are made several times a month. Of the last three transactions, the debit to Wages Payable might occur twice a month, the debit to Rent Expense once a month, and the debit to Supplies only occasionally.

It is logical to include a Cash Credit column in a cash payments journal, because all transactions recorded in it involve a decrease in cash. Since payments to creditors are made often, there should also be an Accounts Payable Debit column. One can set up any other column that is used often enough to warrant it. Otherwise, a Sundry Debit column takes care of all the other transactions.

Now let's record these same transactions in a cash payments journal and include a column entitled Check Number. If you think a moment, you'll see that this is consistent with good management of cash. All expenditures but Petty Cash expenditures should be paid for by check. First let's repeat the transactions.

Objective 5

Record transactions in a cash payments journal for a service enterprise.

May 2 Paid C. C. Hardy Company, a creditor, on account, check no. 63, $220.

4 Bought supplies for cash, check no. 64, $90.

5 Paid wages for two weeks, check no. 65, $1,216 (previously recorded in the payroll entry).

6 Paid rent for the month, check no. 66, $350.

CASH PAYMENTS JOURNAL

PAGE 62

	DATE	CK. NO.	ACCOUNT DEBITED	POST. REF.	SUNDRY ACCOUNTS DEBIT	ACCOUNTS PAYABLE DEBIT	CASH CREDIT	
1	19– May 2	63	C. C. Hardy					1
2			Company			2 2 0 00	2 2 0 00	2
3	4	64	Supplies		9 0 00		9 0 00	3
4	5	65	Wages Payable		1 2 1 6 00		1 2 1 6 00	4
5	6	66	Rent Expense		3 5 0 00		3 5 0 00	5
6								6

Note that you list all checks in consecutive order, even those checks that must be voided. In this way, *every* check is accounted for, which is necessary for internal control.

At the end of the month, post the special columns as totals to the general ledger accounts; do not post the total of the Sundry Accounts Debit column. A check mark (√) is written below the total of the Sundry Accounts Debit column to indicate that the total amount is not posted. Post the figures in this column individually, then place the account number in the Posting Reference column. Post the amounts in the Accounts Payable Debit column separately to individual accounts in the accounts payable ledger. After posting, put a check mark (√) in the Posting Reference column. The posting letter designation for the cash payments journal is CP. Other transactions involving decreases in cash during May are as follows.

May 7 Paid a three-year premium for fire insurance, check no. 67, $360.

9 Paid Treadwell, Inc., a creditor, on account, check no. 68, $418.

11 Issued check no. 69 in payment of delivery expense, $62.

14 Paid Johnson and Son, a creditor, on account, check no. 70, $110.

16 Issued check no. 71 to the Melton State Bank, for a Note Payable, $660, $600 on the principal and $60 interest.

19 Voided check no. 72.

19 Bought equipment from Burns Company for $800, paying $200 down. Issued check no. 73. The rest of this entry is recorded in the general journal as explained below.

20 Paid wages for two weeks, check no. 74, $1,340 (previously recorded in the payroll entry).

22 Issued check no. 75 to Peter R. Morton Advertising Agency for advertising, $94.

26 Paid telephone bill, check no. 76, $26.

31 Issued check for freight bill on equipment purchased on May 19, check no. 77, $28.

31 Paid Teller and Noble, a creditor, on account, check no. 78, $160.

These transactions are recorded in the cash payments journal as illustrated in Figure 13-4.

Figure 13-4

CASH PAYMENTS JOURNAL

PAGE 62

	DATE	CK. NO.	ACCOUNT DEBITED	POST. REF.	SUNDRY ACCOUNTS DEBIT	ACCOUNTS PAYABLE DEBIT	CASH CREDIT	
1	19– May 2	63	C. C. Hardy Co.	✓		2 2 0 00	2 2 0 00	1
2	4	64	Supplies	113	9 0 00		9 0 00	2
3	5	65	Wages Payable	411	1 2 1 6 00		1 2 1 6 00	3
4	6	66	Rent Expense	412	3 5 0 00		3 5 0 00	4
5	7	67	Prepaid Insurance	114	3 6 0 00		3 6 0 00	5
6	9	68	Treadwell, Inc.	✓		4 1 8 00	4 1 8 00	6
7	11	69	Delivery Expense	413	6 2 00		6 2 00	7
8	14	70	Johnson and Son	✓		1 1 0 00	1 1 0 00	8
9	16	71	Notes Payable	211	6 0 0 00			9
10			Interest Expense	414	6 0 00		6 6 0 00	10
11	19	72	Void	✓				11
12	19	73	Equipment	✓	2 0 0 00		2 0 0 00	12
13	20	74	Wages Payable	411	1 3 4 0 00		1 3 4 0 00	13
14	22	75	Advertising Expense	415	9 4 00		9 4 00	14
15	26	76	Telephone Expense	416	2 6 00		2 6 00	15
16	31	77	Equipment	121	2 8 00		2 8 00	16
17	31	78	Teller and Noble	✓		1 6 0 00	1 6 0 00	17
18	31				4 4 2 6 00	9 0 8 00	5 3 3 4 00	18
19					(✓)	(2 1 1)	(1 1 1)	19
20								20

When the purchase of an asset involves a cash down payment with the remainder on account, it is necessary to record the transactions in two journals. For example, this transaction: Bought equipment for $800 from Burns Company, paying $200 down with the remainder to be paid in 30 days. In the general journal, debit Equipment for $800, credit Accounts Payable, Burns Company for $600, and credit Cash for $200. In the Posting Reference column of this entry, place a check mark on the line with Cash so that the $200 credit to Cash will not be posted. Record the second entry in the cash payments journal, debiting Equipment for $200 in the Sundry Accounts Debit column and crediting Cash for $200 in the Cash Credit column. In the Posting Reference column of this entry, place a check mark on the line with Equipment so that the $200 debit to Equipment will not be posted. The net result is that Equipment is debited for the full amount of $800, Cash is credited for $200, and Accounts Payable is credited for $600. The general journal entry looks like this.

	GENERAL JOURNAL				PAGE __94__
	DATE	DESCRIPTION	POST. REF.	DEBIT	CREDIT
1	19– May 19	Equipment	121	8 0 0 00		1
2		Accounts Payable, Burns Company	211√		6 0 0 00	2
3		Cash	√		2 0 0 00	3
4		Payment is due in 30 days.				4
5						5

Let us return to the cash payments journal. At the end of the month, after totaling the columns, check the accuracy of the footings by proving that the sum of the debit totals equals the sum of the credit totals. Since you have posted the individual amounts in the Sundry Debit column to the general ledger, the only posting that remains is the credit to the Cash account for $5,334 and the debit to the Accounts Payable (controlling) account for $908.

	Debit Totals		Credit Totals
Sundry	$4,426.00	Cash	$5,334.00
Accounts Payable	908.00		
	$5,334.00		

The posting is summarized in the following T accounts. Individual amounts in the Accounts Payable Debit column and the general journal are posted daily to the subsidiary ledger. Individual amounts in the Sundry debit column of the special journal and individual amounts in the general journal are posted daily to the general ledger. Totals of the Cash Credit column and the Accounts Payable Debit column are posted at the end of the month.

Accounts Payable Ledger

C. C. Hardy Company

−		+
May 2	220	

Johnson and Son

−		+
May 14	110	

Teller and Noble

−		+
May 31	160	

Treadwell, Inc.

−		+
May 9	418	

Burns Company

−		+	
		May 19	600

General Ledger

Cash

+		−	
		May 31	5,334

Supplies

+		−
May 4	90	

Accounts Payable

−		+	
May 31	908	May 19	600

Wages Payable

−		+
May 5	1,216	
20	1,340	

Rent Expense

+		−
May 6	350	

Prepaid Insurance

+		−
May 7	360	

Delivery Expense

+		−
May 11	62	

Notes Payable

−		+
May 16	600	

Interest Expense

+		−
May 16	60	

Equipment

+		−
May 19	800	
31	28	

Advertising Expense

+		−
May 22	94	

Telephone Expense

+		−
May 26	26	

CASH PAYMENTS JOURNAL: MERCHANDISING ENTERPRISE

There is one slight difference between the **cash payments journal** for a merchandising enterprise and that for a service enterprise. This difference has to do with the cash discounts available to a merchandising business. Recall that a cash discount is the amount that the buyer may deduct from the bill; this acts as an incentive to make the buyer pay the bill promptly. The buyer considers the cash discount to be a Purchases Discount, because it relates to his or her purchase of merchandise. The Purchases Discount account, like Purchases Returns and Allowances, is treated as a deduction from Purchases in the buyer's income statement.

Let us return to C. L. Frederickson Plumbing Supply and assume that the following transactions take place. To demonstrate the debits and credits, let's show some typical transactions in the form of T accounts.

Objective 6

Record transactions in a cash payments journal for a merchandising enterprise.

Transaction (a) August 2: Bought merchandise on account from Darvik, Inc., their invoice no. 2706, dated July 31; terms 2/10, n/30; $420.

Transaction (b) August 8: Issued check no. 76 to Darvik, Inc., in payment of invoice no. 2706 less the cash discount of $8.40, $411.60.

Assets		=	Liabilities		+	Owner's Equity		+	Revenue		−	Expenses	
+	−		−	+		−	+		−	+		+	−
Debit	Credit		Debit	Credit		Debit	Credit		Debit	Credit		Debit	Credit

Cash		Accounts Payable			Purchases	
+	−	−	+		+	−
	(a) 411.60	(b) 420	(a) 420		(a) 420	

Purchases Discount	
−	+
	(b) 8.40

Any well-managed business takes advantage of a purchases discount whenever possible. So if a discount is generally available to the business, it is worthwhile to set up a special Purchases Discount credit column in the cash payments journal.

DATE	CK. NO.	ACCOUNT NAME	POST. REF.	SUNDRY ACCOUNTS DEBIT	ACCOUNTS PAYABLE DEBIT	PURCHASES DISCOUNT CREDIT	CASH CREDIT	
1	19– Aug. 8	76	Darvik, Inc.			4 2 0 00	8 40	· 4 1 1 60	1
2									2

Here are some other transactions of C. L. Frederickson Plumbing Supply involving decreases in cash during August. Note that credit terms vary among the different creditors.

Aug. 10 Paid wages for two-week period, check no. 77, $1,680 (previously recorded in the payroll entry).

11 Issued check no. 78 to Alman Manufacturing Company, in payment of invoice no. 10611, less return; less cash discount, 2/10, n/30; $609.56 ($692 − $70 = $622; $622.00 × .02 = $12.44; $622.00 − $12.44 = $609.56).

12 Bought supplies for cash, issued check no. 79 payable to Davenport Office Supplies, $70.

15 Issued check no. 80 to Sullivan Manufacturing Company in payment of their invoice no. B643, less return; less cash discount, 1/10, n/30; $127.71 ($165 − $36 = $129; $129.00 × .01 = $1.29; $129.00 − $1.29 = $127.71).

16 Bought merchandise for cash, check no. 81, payable to Jones Sheet and Tube, $200.

19 Issued check no. 82 to Reliable Express Company for freight cost on merchandise purchased, $60.

23 Voided check no. 83.

23 Issued check no. 84 to American Fire Insurance Company for insurance premium for one year, $120.

25 Paid wages for two-week period, check no. 85, $1,750 (previously recorded in the payroll entry).

27 Paid F. R. Waller for merchandise he returned on a cash sale, check no. 86, $46.

31 Issued check no. 87 to Reiter and Simon Company in payment of invoice no. 982, net 30 days, $760.

Now let's record these transactions in the cash payments journal (Figure 13-5). After that has been done, C. L. Frederickson's accountant proves the equality of debits and credits:

Debit Totals		Credit Totals	
Sundry	$3,926.00	Cash	$5,834.87
Accounts Payable	1,931.00	Purchases Discount	22.13
	$5,857.00		$5,857.00

CASH PAYMENTS JOURNAL

	DATE	CK. NO.	ACCOUNT NAME	POST. REF.	SUNDRY ACCOUNTS DEBIT	ACCOUNTS PAYABLE DEBIT	PURCHASES DISCOUNT CREDIT	CASH CREDIT	
1	19— Aug. 8	76	Darvik, Inc.			4 2 0 00	8 40	4 1 1 60	1
2	10	77	Wages Payable		1 6 8 0 00			1 6 8 0 00	2
3	11	78	Alman Manufacturing Co.			6 2 2 00	1 2 44	6 0 9 56	3
4	12	79	Supplies		7 0 00			7 0 00	4
5	15	80	Sullivan Manufacturing Co.			1 2 9 00	1 29	1 2 7 71	5
6	16	81	Purchases		2 0 0 00			2 0 0 00	6
7	19	82	Purchases		6 0 00			6 0 00	7
8	23	83	Void						8
9	23	84	Prepaid Insurance		1 2 0 00			1 2 0 00	9
10	25	85	Wages Payable		1 7 5 0 00			1 7 5 0 00	10
11	27	86	Sales Returns and						11
12			Allowances		4 6 00			4 6 00	12
13	31	87	Reiter and Simon						13
14			Company			7 6 0 00		7 6 0 00	14
15	31				3 9 2 6 00	1 9 3 1 00	2 2 13	5 8 3 4 87	15
16									16

Figure 13-5

CHECK REGISTER

Instead of using a cash payments journal as a book of original entry, one can use a check register. The check register is merely a large checkbook with perforations that make it easy to tear out the checks. The page opposite the checks has columns labeled for special accounts, such as Bank Credit (in place of Cash), Accounts Payable Debit, and so on. The checks are prenumbered, and each check issued is recorded on the columnar sheet. This is common practice for a small business in which the owner writes the checks himself or herself. One posts directly from the check register.

Suppose C. L. Frederickson Plumbing Supply had used a check register instead of the cash payments journal. Its August transactions would appear as they do in Figure 13-6.

You can see for yourself that the difference between the cash payments journal and the check register is minor. Recall that one substitutes the Bank Credit column for the Cash Credit column. The check register lists the payee of the check. The Accounts Payable Debit column and the Purchases Discount Credit column are included to handle payments to creditors.

Two additional columns, Deposits and Bank Balance, can be added, to give a current balance of the Valley National Bank or Cash account. The posting process for each book of original entry is the same.

Objective 7

Record transactions in a check register.

DATE	CK. NO.	PAYEE	ACCOUNT DEBITED	POST. REF.	SUNDRY ACCOUNTS DEBIT	ACCOUNTS PAYABLE DEBIT	PURCHASES DISCOUNT CREDIT	VALLEY BANK CREDIT	
19— Aug.									
8	76	Darvik, Inc.	Darvik, Inc.			4 2 0 00	8 40	4 1 1 60	1
10	77	Payroll	Wages Payable		1 6 8 0 00			1 6 8 0 00	2
11	78	Alman Manufacturing	Alman Manufacturing			6 2 2 00	1 2 44	6 0 9 56	3
12	79	Davenport	Supplies		7 0 00			7 0 00	4
15	80	Sullivan Mfg. Co.	Sullivan Mfg. Co.			1 2 9 00	1 29	1 2 7 71	5
16	81	Jones Sheet and Tube	Purchases		2 0 0 00			2 0 0 00	6
19	82	Reliable Express Co.	Purchases		6 0 00			6 0 00	7
23	83	Void							8
23	84	American Fire	Prepaid Insurance		1 2 0 00			1 2 0 00	9
25	85	Payroll	Wages Payable		1 7 5 0 00			1 7 5 0 00	10
27	86	F. R. Waller	Sales Ret. and Allow.		4 6 00			4 6 00	11
31	87	Reiter & Simon Co.	Reiter & Simon Co.			7 6 0 00		7 6 0 00	12
31					3 9 2 6 00	1 9 3 1 00	2 2 13	5 8 3 4 87	13
									14
									15
									16
									17
									18
									19
									20
									21
									22
									23

Figure 13-6

In a small business, the owner or manager usually signs all the checks. However, if the owner delegates the authority to sign checks to some other person, that person should *not* have access to the accounting records. Why? Well, this helps to prevent fraud, because a dishonest employee could conceal a cash disbursement in the accounting records. In other words, for a medium- to large-size business, it's worth a manager's while to keep a separate book, which in this case is the cash payments journal. One person writes the checks; another person records the checks in the cash payments journal. In this way, one person acts as a check on the other. There would have to be collusion between the two people for embezzlement to take place. Again, this precaution is consistent with a good system of internal control.

TRADE DISCOUNTS

Manufacturers and wholesalers of many lines of products publish annual catalogs listing their products at retail prices. These concerns offer their customers substantial reductions (often as much as 40 percent) from the list or catalog prices. The reductions from the list prices are called **trade discounts.** Remember, firms grant cash discounts for prompt payment of invoices. Trade discounts are *not related* to cash payments. Manufacturers and wholesalers use trade discounts to avoid reprinting catalogs when selling prices change. They simply issue a new list of trade discounts to be applied to the catalog prices, effectively changing prices.

Objective 9

Record transactions involving trade discounts.

Firms may quote trade discounts as a single percentage. Example: A distributor of furnaces grants a single discount of 40 percent off the listed catalog price of $8,000. In this case, the selling price is calculated as follows.

List or catalog price	$8,000
Less trade discount of 40% ($8,000 × .4)	3,200
Selling price	$4,800

Neither the seller nor the buyer records trade discounts in the accounts; they enter only the selling price. By T accounts, the furnace distributor records the sale like this:

Accounts Receivable		Sales	
+	−	−	+
4,800			4,800

The buyer records the purchase as follows:

Purchases			Accounts Payable	
+	−	−	+	
4,800			4,800	

Firms may also quote trade discounts as a chain, or series of percentages. For example, a distributor of automobile parts grants discounts of 30 percent, 10 percent, and 10 percent off the listed catalog price of $900. In this case, the selling price is calculated as follows.

List or catalog price	$900.00
Less first trade discount of 30% ($900 × .3)	270.00
Remainder after first discount	$630.00
Less second trade discount of 10% ($630 × .1)	63.00
Remainder after second discount	$567.00
Less third discount of 10% ($567 × .1)	56.70
Selling price	$510.30

By T accounts, the automobile parts distributor records the sale as follows:

Accounts Receivable			Sales	
+	−	−	+	
510.30			510.30	

The buyer records the purchase as follows:

Purchases			Accounts Payable	
+	−	−	+	
510.30			510.30	

In the situation involving a chain of discounts, the additional discounts are granted for large-volume transactions, either in dollar amount or in size of shipment, such as carload lots.

Cash discounts could also apply in situations involving trade discounts. Example: Suppose that the credit terms of the above sale include a cash discount of 2/10, n/30, and the buyer pays the invoice within 10 days. The seller applies the cash discount to the selling price. By T accounts, the seller records the transaction as

Cash		Sales Discount		Accounts Receivable	
+	−	+	−	+	−
500.09		10.21			510.30

Types of Transactions

Sale of merchandise on account	Purchase of merchandise on account	Receipt of cash	Payment of cash	All other

Evidenced by Source Documents

Sales invoice	Purchase invoice	Credit card receipts / Cash / Checks	Check stub	Miscellaneous

Types of Journals

Sales journal	Purchases journal	Cash receipts journal	Cash payments journal	General journal

Posting to Ledger Accounts

Sales journal	Purchases journal	Cash receipts journal	Cash payments journal	General journal
Individual amounts posted daily to the accounts receivable ledger and the total posted monthly to the general ledger.	*Individual amounts posted daily to the accounts payable ledger and the total posted monthly to the general ledger.*	*Individual amounts in the Accounts Receivable credit column posted daily to the accounts receivable ledger. Individual amounts in the Sundry columns posted daily to the general ledger. Totals of special columns posted monthly.*	*Individual amounts in the Accounts Payable debit column posted daily to the accounts payable ledger. Individual amounts in the Sundry columns posted daily to the general ledger. Totals of special columns posted monthly.*	*Entries posted daily to the subsidiary ledgers and the general ledger.*

Figure 13-7

Choice of the Correct Journal

The buyer records the transaction as

Cash		Purchases Discount		Accounts Payable	
+	−	−	+	−	+
	500.09		10.21	510.30	

We have now looked at four special journals and the general journal. It is very important for a business to select and use the journals that will provide the most efficient accounting system possible. Figure 13-7 summarizes the applications of and correct procedures for using the journals we have discussed.

GLOSSARY

Bank charge card A bank credit card, like the credit cards used by millions of private citizens. The card holder pays what she or he owes directly to the issuing bank. The business firm deposits the credit card receipts; the amount of the deposit equals the total of the receipts, less a discount deducted by the bank.

Cash discount The amount a customer can deduct for paying a bill within a specified period of time; to encourage prompt payment. Not all sellers offer cash discounts.

Cash payments journal A special journal used to record all transactions in which cash goes out, or decreases.

Cash receipts journal A special journal used to record all transactions that increase cash.

Credit period The time the seller allows the buyer before full payment on a charge sale must be made.

Crossfooting The process of totaling columns in a journal or work sheet to make sure that the sum of the debit totals equals the sum of the credit totals.

Sales discount The cash discount from the seller's point of view; in the buyer's books this is a *purchases discount*.

Trade discounts Substantial reductions from the list or catalog prices of goods, granted by the seller.

QUESTIONS, EXERCISES, AND PROBLEMS

Discussion Questions

1. Describe the posting procedure for a cash receipts journal that has a Sundry Accounts credit column and several special columns including an Accounts Receivable credit column.

2. When a cash receipts journal and a cash payments journal are used, how does one determine the exact balance of cash on a specific date during the month?
3. What does "1/10, n/30" mean?
4. Is the normal balance of Sales Discount a debit or a credit?
5. In a cash receipts journal, both the Accounts Receivable credit column and the Cash debit column were erroneously under added by $100. How will this error be discovered?
6. Explain the difference between the handling of delivery costs on merchandise sold and the handling of freight costs on merchandise purchased.
7. What is the difference between a cash discount and a trade discount?

Exercises

Exercise 13-1 Describe the transactions recorded in the following T accounts.

Cash	Sales Tax Payable	Accounts Receivable	Sales
(b) 208	(a) 8	(a) 208 | (b) 208	(a) 200

Exercise 13-2 Record the transactions listed below in general journal form.

Aug.   2 Sold merchandise on account to T. Clancy; 2/10, n/30; $800.
       4 Issued credit memo no. 493 to T. Clancy for damaged merchandise, $35.
      12 Received a check from T. Clancy in full payment of bill.

Exercise 13-3 Describe the transaction recorded in the following T accounts.

Cash	Sales Tax Payable	Sales	Credit Card Expense
102.90	5	100	2.10

Exercise 13-4 Record the transactions listed here in general journal form.

Mar.   9 Bought merchandise on account from Columbia Electrical Supply; 2/10, n/30; $1,500.
      21 Received a credit memo for $100 for defective goods returned.
Apr.   8 Paid Columbia Electrical Supply in full of account.

Exercise 13-5 Label the blanks in the column heads as debit or credit.

CASH PAYMENTS JOURNAL   PAGE _____

	DATE	CK. NO.	ACCOUNT NAME	POST. REF.	SUNDRY ACCOUNTS	ACCOUNTS PAYABLE	PURCHASES DISCOUNT	CASH	
1									1
2									2
3									3
4									4

Exercise 13-6 Describe the transactions recorded in the following T accounts.

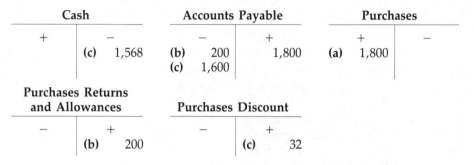

Cash			Accounts Payable			Purchases	
+	−	−		+	+		−
	(c) 1,568	(b) 200		1,800	(a) 1,800		
		(c) 1,600					

Purchases Returns and Allowances			Purchases Discount	
−	+	−		+
	(b) 200			(c) 32

Exercise 13-7 Shown below is a page from a special journal.

1. What kind of journal is this?
2. Explain each of the transactions.
3. Explain the notations in the Posting Reference column.
4. Explain the notations below the column totals.

	DATE	ACCOUNT CREDITED	POST. REF.	SUNDRY ACCOUNTS CREDIT	ACCOUNTS RECEIVABLE CREDIT	SALES CREDIT	SALES DISCOUNT DEBIT	CASH DEBIT	
1	19– May 2	Della Simpson	√		5 0 0 00		1 0 00	4 9 0 00	1
2	7	Sales	–			7 1 0 00		7 1 0 00	2
3	11	Notes Payable	211	2 5 0 0 00				2 5 0 0 00	3
4	21	Harry Walls	√		2 1 0 00			2 1 0 00	4
5	31	L. R. Lee,							5
6		Capital	311	5 0 0 0 00				5 0 0 0 00	6
7				7 5 0 0 00	7 1 0 00	7 1 0 00	1 0 00	8 9 1 0 00	7
8				(√)	(1 1 3)	(4 1 1)	(4 1 3)	(1 1 1)	8
9									9

Exercise 13-8 Record the transactions listed here in general journal form.

Jun. 1 Sold merchandise on account to the Bayliss Company; 2/10, n/30; $460.

  9 Purchased merchandise on account from the Mueller Company; 1/10, n/30, F.O.B. shipping point; $720.

Jun. 10 Paid freight charges on the merchandise purchased from the Mueller Company, $10.

10 Received payment from the Bayliss Company, less the cash discount.

12 Received a credit memo from the Mueller Company for defective merchandise returned, $70.

18 Paid the Mueller Company in full.

Problem Set A

Problem 13-1A Sommerset and Vaughn, a retail sales concern, sells on the bases of (1) cash, (2) charge accounts, and (3) bank credit cards. The following transactions involved cash receipts for the firm during April of this year. The state imposes a 4 percent sales tax on retail sales.

Apr. 7 Total cash sales for the week, $900, plus $36 sales tax.

7 Total sales for the week paid for by bank credit cards, $800, plus $32 sales tax. The bank charges 2 percent on the total of the sales plus tax ($832 × .02 = $16.64).

8 N. T. Nolan, the owner, invested an additional $2,000.

11 Collected cash from Robert Stone, a charge customer, $47.80.

12 Sold store equipment for cash, at cost, $160.

14 Total cash sales for the week, $1,100, plus $44 sales tax.

14 Total sales for the week paid for by bank credit cards, $600, plus $24 sales tax.

18 Borrowed $1,600 from the bank, receiving cash and giving the bank a promissory note.

20 Collected cash from Ruth Aiken, a charge customer, $52.

21 Total sales for the week paid for by bank credit cards, $700, plus $28 sales tax.

21 Total cash sales for the week, $1,600, plus $64 sales tax.

23 Received cash as refund for return of merchandise bought, $90.

25 Collected cash from J. R. Finch, a charge customer, $104.

30 Total sales for the week paid for by bank credit cards, $160.00, plus $6.40 sales tax.

30 Collected cash from Nathan Turnbull, a charge customer, $72.80.

30 Total cash sales for the week, $1,550, plus $62 sales tax.

Instructions

1. Open the following accounts in the accounts receivable ledger and record the April 1 balances as given: Ruth Aiken, $52.00; J. R. Finch, $124.00; Stella Roe, $76.48; Robert Stone, $47.80; Nathan Turnbull, $72.80; C. R. Zellers, $81.20. Place a check mark in the Posting Reference column.
2. Record a balance of $454.28 in the Accounts Receivable controlling account as of April 1.
3. Record the transactions in the cash receipts journal beginning with page 57.
4. Post daily to the accounts receivable ledger.

5. Total and rule the cash receipts journal.
6. Prove the equality of debit and credit totals.
7. Post to the Accounts Receivable account in the general ledger.

Problem 13-2A The H. G. Seton Company sells snacks wholesale, primarily to vending-machine operators. Terms of sales on account are 2/10, n/30, FOB shipping point. The following selected transactions involving cash receipts and sales of merchandise took place in May of this year.

May   1 Received $490 cash from P. Kline in payment of April 23 invoice of $500, less cash discount.
      4 Received $840 cash in payment of $800 note receivable and interest of $40.
      7 Sold merchandise on account to F. Stevens, invoice no. 871, $360.
      8 Received $686 in cash from Donald Pihl in payment of April 30 invoice of $700, less cash discount.
   14 Received cash from F. Stevens in payment of invoice no. 871, less discount.
   15 Cash sales for the first half of May, $2,772.
   18 Received $152 in cash from Randy Sims in payment of April 14 invoice, no discount.
   21 Sold merchandise on account to S. T. Thompson, invoice no. 898, $416.
   24 Received $218 cash refund for return of defective equipment bought in April for cash.
   27 Sold merchandise on account to C. C. Cummins, invoice no. 921, $432.
   31 Cash sales for the second half of May, $2,027.

Instructions

1. Journalize the transactions for May in the cash receipts journal and the sales journal.
2. Total and rule the journals.

Problem 13-3A The Matthews Bookstore uses a check register to keep track of expenditures. The following transactions occurred during February of this year.

Feb.   2 Issued check no. 3118 to National Book Company for their invoice no. 1113B, $520, less cash discount of $10.40, $509.60.
      3 Paid freight bill to Newton Express Company for merchandise purchased, check no. 3119, $47.
      5 Paid rent for month of February, check no. 3120, to Standard Realty, $215.
   10 Paid for advertising in *Campus News*, check no. 3121, $42.
   11 Paid Piedmont Publishing Company, check no. 3122, for their invoice no. C755 in the amount of $1,000 less 1 percent cash discount of $10, $990.
   16 Paid wages for the first half of month, check no. 3123, $426 (payroll entry previously recorded).

Feb. 20 R. Matthews, the owner, withdrew cash for personal use, check no. 3124, $425.

26 Made payment to Fenway National Bank on bank loan, check no. 3125, consisting of $600 on principal and $20 interest, $620.

28 Issued to Southern Publishing Company, check no. 3126, for their invoice no. 3126 (no discount previously recorded), $358.

28 Voided check no. 3127.

28 Paid wages for the second half of month, check no. 3128, $426 (payroll entry previously recorded).

28 Received and paid telephone bill, check no. 3129, payable to Nationwide Telephone Company, $32.

Instructions

1. Record the transactions in the check register.
2. Total and rule the check register.
3. Prove the equality of the debit and credit totals.

Problem 13-4A The following transactions were completed by Thompson Electronics Supply during January, the first month of this fiscal year. Terms of sale are 2/10, n/30.

Jan. 2 Paid rent for month, check no. 6981, $825.

2 J. M. Thompson, the owner, invested an additional $3,360 in the business.

4 Bought merchandise on account from Meyer and Company, their invoice no. A691, dated January 2; 2/10, n/30; $4,065.

4 Received check from Worden Appliance for $1,470 in payment of invoice for $1,500, less discount.

4 Sold merchandise on account to C. R. Larsen, invoice no. 6483, $975.

6 Received check from Metcalf and Schafer for $955.50 in payment of $975 invoice, less discount, $19.50.

7 Issued check no. 6982 to Hunter and Jared, in payment of their invoice no. C1271, for $900, less discount, $882.

7 Bought supplies on account from Conley Office Supply, their invoice no. 1906B, $127.20.

7 Sold merchandise on account to Bridges and Spear, invoice no. 6484, $1,275.

9 Issued credit memo no. 43 to C. R. Larsen, for merchandise returned, $45.

11 Cash sales for January 1 to 10, $6,663.90.

11 Issued check no. 6983 to Meyer and Company in payment of their invoice, $4,065, less discount; $3,983.70.

14 Sold merchandise on account to Worden Appliance, invoice no. 6485, $2,850.

14 Received check from C. R. Larsen, $911.40, in payment of $975 invoice, less return of $45, less discount, $18.60.

18 Bought merchandise on account from Chapman Products, their invoice no. 7281D, dated January 16; 2/10, n/60; $5,610.

Jan. 21 Issued check no. 6984, for advertising, $397.50.

21 Cash sales for January 11 to 20, $5,347.50.

23 Received credit memo no. 163 from Chapman Products for merchandise returned, $144.

23 Paid Acme Fast Freight, check no. 6985, for transportation of merchandise purchased, $117.

29 Sold merchandise on account to Allen Supply, invoice no. 6486, $2,796.

31 Cash sales for January 21 to 31, $5,980.50.

31 Issued check no. 6986, for miscellaneous expenses, $67.50.

31 Recorded payroll entry from the payroll register: total salaries, $8,700; employees' income tax withheld, $1,218; FICA tax withheld, $522.

31 Recorded the payroll taxes: FICA, $522; state unemployment tax, $348; federal unemployment tax, $69.60.

31 Issued check no. 6987, for salaries for the month, $6,960.

31 J. M. Thompson, the owner, withdrew cash for personal use, check no. 6988, $1,455.

Instructions

1. Journalize the transactions.
2. Post daily all entries involving customer accounts to the accounts receivable ledger.
3. Post daily all entries involving creditor accounts to the accounts payable ledger.
4. Post daily those entries involving the Sundry columns and the general journal to the general ledger.
5. Add the columns of the special journals, and prove the equality of debit and credit totals on scratch paper.
6. Post the appropriate totals of the special journals to the general ledger.
7. Prepare a trial balance.
8. Prepare a schedule of accounts receivable and a schedule of accounts payable. Do the totals equal the balances of the related controlling accounts?

Problem Set B

Problem 13-1B Flegel and Rossiter, a retail store, sells on the bases of (1) cash, (2) charge accounts, and (3) bank credit cards. The following transactions involve cash receipts for the firm for March of this year. The state imposes a 4 percent sales tax on retail sales.

Mar. 8 Total cash sales for the week, $850, plus $34 sales tax.

8 Total sales from bank credit cards for the week, $900, plus $36 sales tax. The bank charges 2 percent of the total sales plus tax ($936 × .02 = $18.72).

12 C. T. Kohler, the owner, invested an additional $2,364.

13 Sold office equipment for cash, at cost, $183.

13 Collected cash from Robert Alston, a charge customer, $26.92.

Mar. 15 Total cash sales for the week, $1,296.52, plus $51.86 sales tax.

15 Total sales for the week on the basis of bank credit cards, $720.00, plus $28.80 sales tax.

19 Collected cash from Betsy Wagoner, a charge customer, $39.26.

20 Borrowed $2,780 from the bank, receiving cash and giving the bank a promissory note.

22 Total cash sales for the week, $1,627.00, plus $65.08 sales tax.

22 Total sales from bank credit cards for the week, $740.00, plus $29.60 sales tax.

23 Collected cash from T. E. French, a charge customer, $116.76.

25 Flegel and Rossiter received cash as a refund for the return of merchandise they purchased, $186.

28 Collected cash from Norbert Truman, a charge customer, $71.56.

31 Total sales from bank credit cards for the week, $176.40, plus $7.06 sales tax.

31 Total cash sales for the week, $1,927.84, plus $77.11 sales tax.

Instructions

1. Open the following accounts in the accounts receivable ledger and record the March 1 balances as given: Robert Alston, $46.92; T. E. French, $116.76; Megan Green, $53.23; Douglas Lowe, $89.76; Norbert Truman, $71.56; Betsy Wagoner, $39.26. Place a check mark in the Posting Reference column.
2. Record balance of $417.49 in the Accounts Receivable controlling account as of March 1.
3. Record the transactions in the cash receipts journal beginning with page 14.
4. Post daily to the accounts receivable ledger.
5. Total and rule the cash receipts journal.
6. Prove the equality of debit and credit totals.
7. Post to the Accounts Receivable account in the general ledger.

Problem 13-2B Parkins Company sells snacks wholesale, primarily to vending machine operators. Terms of sales on account are 2/10, n/30, FOB shipping point. The following transactions involving cash receipts and sales of merchandise took place in May of this year.

May 1 Received cash from G. Payne in payment of April 22 invoice of $1,000, less cash discount; $980.

3 Received $660 cash in payment of a $600 note receivable and interest of $60.

6 Received cash from J. R. Potter in payment of April 29 invoice of $600, less cash discount; $588.

7 Sold merchandise on account to N. Olson, invoice no. 286, $400.

15 Cash sales for the first half of May, $2,160.

16 Received cash from N. Olson in payment of invoice no. 286, less discount.

19 Received cash from Ralph Porter in payment of April 16 invoice, no discount, $160.

May 20 Sold merchandise on account to P. R. Thresher, invoice no. 298, $810.

23 Received cash refund for return of defective equipment bought in April for cash, $216.

26 Sold merchandise on account to T. E. Bannister, invoice no. 306, $460.

31 Cash sales for the second half of May, $3,290.

Instructions

1. Journalize the transactions for May in the cash receipts journal and the sales journal.
2. Total and rule the journals.

Problem 13-3B The Runyan Bookshop uses a check register to keep track of expenditures. The following transactions occurred during February of this year.

Feb. 2 Issued check no. 6210 to Amalgamated Publishers for the amount of their invoice no. 68172 for $640.00, less 2 percent cash discount of $12.80, $627.20.

3 Paid freight bill to Midway Express Company, books purchased, check no. 6211, $40.

5 Paid rent for the month, to Beale Land Company, check no. 6212, $190.

10 Paid for advertising in *Campus News,* check no. 6213, $40.

11 Issued check no. 6214 to New England Book Company for their invoice no. A3322 for $860 less 1 percent cash discount of $8.60, $851.40.

16 Paid wages for the first half of February, check no. 6215, $320 (payroll entry previously recorded).

20 N. D. Runyan, the owner, withdrew $200 for personal use, check no. 6216.

25 Made payment on bank loan to Coast National Bank, check no. 6217, consisting of $400 on the principal and $40 interest, $440.

28 Paid Midwest Publishing Company for their invoice no. 7768 (no discount previously recorded), check no. 6218, $940.

28 Voided check no. 6219.

28 Paid wages for the second half of February, check no. 6220, $320 (payroll entry previously recorded).

Instructions

1. Record the transactions in the check register.
2. Total and rule the check register.
3. Prove the equality of the debit and credit totals.

Problem 13-4B The following transactions were completed by Thompson Electronics Supply during January, the first month of this fiscal year. Terms of sale are 2/10, n/30.

Jan. 2 J. M. Thompson, the owner, invested an additional $3,300 in the business.

2 Paid rent for the month, check no. 6981, $900.

4 Bought merchandise on account from Meyer and Company, their invoice no. A691, dated January 2; 2/10, n/30; $4,260.

4 Received check from Worden Appliance, in payment of $1,500 invoice, less discount, $30; $1,470.

4 Sold merchandise on account to C. R. Larsen, invoice no. 6483, $1,125.

6 Received check from Metcalf and Moody for $955.50 in payment of $975.00 invoice, less discount, $19.50.

7 Issued check no. 6982 to Hunter and Jared, in payment of their invoice no. C1272 for $750, less discount of $15, $735.

7 Bought supplies on account from Conley Office Supply, their invoice no. 1906B, $147.

7 Sold merchandise on account to Bridges and Spear, invoice no. 6484, $1,335.

9 Issued credit memo no. 43 to C. R. Larsen, for merchandise returned, $75.

11 Cash sales for January 1 to 10, $6,771.

11 Paid Meyer and Company, check no. 6983, in payment of $4,260.00 invoice, less discount of $85.20, $4,174.80.

14 Sold merchandise on account to Worden Appliance, invoice no. 6485, $2,925.

18 Bought merchandise on account from Chapman Products, their invoice no. 7281D, dated January 16; 2/10, n/60; $7,395.

21 Issued check no. 6984, for advertising, $423.

21 Cash sales for January 11 to 20, $5,985.

23 Paid Acme Fast Freight, check no. 6985, for transportation of merchandise purchased, $129.

23 Received credit memo no. 163 from Chapman Products, for merchandise returned, $637.50.

29 Sold merchandise on account to Allen Supply, invoice no. 6486, $2,910.

31 Cash sales, January 21 to 31, $6,642.

31 Issued check no. 6986, for miscellaneous expenses, $73.50.

31 Recorded payroll entry from the payroll register: total salaries, $9,150; employees' income tax withheld, $1,281; FICA tax withheld, $549.

31 Recorded the payroll taxes: FICA, $549; state unemployment tax, $366; federal unemployment tax, $73.20.

31 Issued check no. 6987, for salaries for the month, $7,320.

31 J. M. Thompson, the owner, withdrew cash for personal use, check no. 6988, $1,425.

Instructions

1. Journalize the transactions.
2. Post daily all entries involving customer accounts to the accounts receivable ledger.

3. Post daily all entries involving creditor accounts to the accounts payable ledger.
4. Post daily those entries involving the Sundry columns and the general journal to the general ledger.
5. Add the columns of the special journals. Prove the equality of debit and credit totals on scratch paper.
6. Post the appropriate totals from the special journals to the general ledger.
7. Prepare a trial balance.
8. Prepare a schedule of accounts receivable and a schedule of accounts payable. Do the totals equal the balances of the related controlling accounts?

14 Work Sheet and Adjusting Entries for a Merchandising Business

Learning Objectives

After you have completed this chapter, you will be able to do the following:

1. Complete a work sheet for a merchandising business involving adjustments for merchandise inventory, unearned revenue, depreciation, expired insurance, supplies used, and accrued wages or salaries.

2. Journalize the adjusting entries for a merchandising business.

For quite some time we've been talking about keeping special journals and accounts for a merchandising enterprise. Now let's take another step forward in the accounting cycle for a merchandising business: let's make *adjustments* and prepare *work sheets*.

The columnar classifications and procedures for completing the work sheet are basically the same as those described in Chapter 5. A merchandising business—like a service business—requires adjustments for supplies used, expired insurance, depreciation, and accrued wages. However, one adjustment applies exclusively to a merchandising enterprise: the adjustment for merchandise inventory. Still another adjustment, which could apply to either a merchandising or a service business, is the adjustment for unearned revenue. Previously, in introducing the work sheet, we included the Adjusted Trial Balance columns as a means of verifying that the accounts were in balance after recording the adjustments. To reduce the size of the work sheet, we will now eliminate the Adjusted Trial Balance columns. The account balances after the adjustments will be carried directly into the Income Statement and Balance Sheet columns of the work sheet.

This chapter will also discuss the work sheet with respect to handling the specialized accounts of a merchandising business.

ADJUSTMENT FOR MERCHANDISE INVENTORY

When we introduced the Merchandise Inventory account in Chapter 11, we put it under the heading of assets and said that in our example the balance of the account is changed only after a **physical inventory** (or actual count) has been taken. This is consistent with a system of periodic inventories in which one records the purchase of merchandise as a debit to Purchases for the amount of the cost, and the sale of merchandise as a credit to Sales for the amount of the selling price.

Consider this example: A firm has a Merchandise Inventory balance of $18,000, which represents the cost of the inventory at the beginning of the fiscal period. At the end of the fiscal period, the firm takes an actual count of the stock on hand and determines the cost of the ending inventory to be $22,000. Naturally, in any business, goods are constantly being bought, sold, and replaced. Evidently the reason that the cost of the ending inventory is larger than the cost of the beginning inventory is that the firm bought more than it sold. When we adjust the Merchandise Inventory account, we want to install the new figure of $22,000 in the account. We do this by a two-step process.

Objective 1

Complete a work sheet for a merchandising business involving adjustments for merchandise inventory, unearned revenue, depreciation, expired insurance, supplies used, and accrued wages or salaries.

Step 1 Eliminate or close the Merchandise Inventory account into Income Summary by the amount of the beginning inventory. (Transfer the balance into Income Summary.)

Let's look at this entry in the form of T accounts.

Merchandise Inventory		Income Summary	
Bal. 18,000	Adj. 18,000	Adj. 18,000	

①

We handle this just as we handle the closing of any other account, by balancing off the account, or making the balance equal to zero. We treat the entry as a credit to Merchandise Inventory and then do the opposite to Income Summary, which means we debit this account.

Step 2 Enter the ending Merchandise Inventory, because one must record on the books the cost of the asset remaining on hand. (Add on the ending inventory.)

Let's repeat the T accounts, showing Step 1 and adding Step 2.

Merchandise Inventory		Income Summary	
Bal. 18,000	Adj. 18,000	Adj. 18,000	Adj. 22,000
Adj. 22,000			

①
②

In step 2, we debit Merchandise Inventory (recording the asset on the plus side of the account), and we do the opposite to Income Summary.

The reason for adjusting the Merchandise Inventory account in these two steps is that both the beginning and the ending figures appear separately in the income statement (see page 430), which is prepared directly from the Income Statement columns of the work sheet. This method of adjusting the inventory is considered to be more meaningful than taking a shortcut and adjusting for the difference between the beginning and the ending inventory values, since the amount of the difference does not appear as a distinct figure in the income statement.

ADJUSTMENT FOR UNEARNED REVENUE

Let us now introduce another adjusting entry: **unearned revenue.** As we said, this entry could pertain to a service as well as to a merchandising business. Occasionally, cash is received in advance for services to be performed in the future. For example, a dining hall sells meal tickets in advance, a concert association sells season tickets in advance, a magazine receives subscriptions in advance, and an insurance company receives premiums in advance. If the amounts to be received by each of these organizations will be earned during the present fiscal period, the amounts should be credited to revenue accounts. On the other hand, if the amounts to be received will *not* be earned during the present fiscal period, the amounts should be credited to unearned revenue accounts. An unearned revenue account is classified as a liability because an organization is liable for the amount received in advance until it is earned.

To illustrate, assume that Mark Publishing Company receives $60,000 in cash for subscriptions covering two years and records them originally as debits to Cash and credits to Unearned Subscriptions. At the end of the year, Mark finds that $44,000 of the subscriptions have been earned. Accordingly, Mark's accountant makes an adjusting entry, debiting Unearned Subscriptions and crediting Subscriptions Income. In other words, the accountant takes the earned portion out of Unearned Subscriptions and adds it to Subscriptions Income. T accounts show the situation as follows.

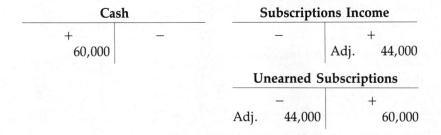

To take another example, suppose that C. L. Frederickson offers a course in plumbing repairs for home owners and apartment managers. On November 1, C. L. Frederickson receives $900 in fees for a three-month course. Because C. L. Frederickson's present fiscal period ends on December 31, the three months' worth of fees received in advance will not be earned during this fiscal period. Therefore, C. L. Frederickson's accountant records the transaction as a debit to Cash of $900 and a credit to Unearned Course Fees of $900. Unearned Course Fees is a liability account because C. L. Frederickson must complete the how-to course or refund a portion of the money it collected. Any account beginning with the word *Unearned* is always a liability.

On December 31, because two months' worth of course fees have now been earned, C. L. Frederickson's accountant makes an adjusting entry to transfer $600 (⅔ of $900) from Unearned Course Fees to Course Fees Income. By T accounts, the situation looks like this:

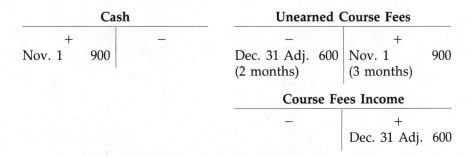

Cash		
+		−
Nov. 1 900		

Unearned Course Fees	
−	+
Dec. 31 Adj. 600	Nov. 1 900
(2 months)	(3 months)

Course Fees Income	
−	+
	Dec. 31 Adj. 600

C. L. Frederickson Plumbing Supply's chart of accounts is presented below. The account-number arrangement will be discussed in Chapter 15.

Assets (100–199)
111 Cash
112 Notes Receivable
113 Accounts Receivable
114 Merchandise Inventory
115 Supplies
116 Prepaid Insurance
121 Equipment
122 Accumulated Depreciation, Equipment
125 Building
126 Accumulated Depreciation, Building
127 Land

Liabilities (200–299)
211 Notes Payable
212 Accounts Payable
213 Wages Payable
217 Unearned Course Fees
221 Mortgage Payable

Owner's Equity (300–399)
311 C. L. Frederickson, Capital
312 C. L. Frederickson, Drawing
313 Income Summary

Revenue (400–499)
411 Sales
412 Sales Returns and Allowances
413 Sales Discount
421 Course Fees Income
422 Interest Income

Expenses (500–599)
511 Purchases
512 Purchases Returns and Allowances
513 Purchases Discount
521 Wages Expense
522 Depreciation Expense, Equipment
523 Supplies Expense
531 Depreciation Expense, Building
532 Taxes Expense
533 Insurance Expense
534 Interest Expense

Before we demonstrate how to record adjustments, let's first look at the trial balance section of C. L. Frederickson Plumbing Supply's work sheet (Figure 14-1). Notice that the adjustments for supplies used, insurance expired, depreciation, and accrued wages are the same type of adjustment we discussed for a service business in earlier chapters.

	ACCOUNT NAME	TRIAL BALANCE		ADJUSTMENTS		
		DEBIT	CREDIT	DEBIT	CREDIT	
1	Cash	21 9 2 2 00				1
2	Notes Receivable	4 0 0 0 00				2
3	Accounts Receivable	29 3 6 0 00				3
4	Merchandise Inventory	63 0 0 0 00				4
5	Supplies	1 4 4 0 00				5
6	Prepaid Insurance	9 6 0 00				6
7	Equipment	33 6 0 0 00				7
8	Accum. Depreciation, Equipment		16 4 0 0 00			8
9	Building	100 0 0 0 00				9
10	Accum. Depreciation, Building		32 0 0 0 00			10
11	Land	12 0 0 0 00				11
12	Notes Payable		3 0 0 0 00			12
13	Accounts Payable		36 4 0 0 00			13
14	Unearned Course Fees		9 0 0 00			14
15	Mortgage Payable		8 0 0 0 00			15
16	C. L. Frederickson, Capital		146 5 7 4 00			16
17	C. L. Frederickson, Drawing	19 2 0 0 00				17
18	Sales		176 1 8 0 00			18
19	Sales Returns and Allowances	8 4 0 00				19
20	Sales Discount	1 8 8 0 00				20
21	Interest Income		1 2 0 00			21
22	Purchases	85 6 0 0 00				22
23	Purchases Returns and Allowances		8 3 2 00			23
24	Purchases Discount		1 2 4 8 00			24
25	Wages Expense	45 8 0 0 00				25
26	Taxes Expense	1 9 6 0 00				26
27	Interest Expense	9 2 00				27
28		421 6 5 4 00	421 6 5 4 00			28

Figure 14-1

DATA FOR THE ADJUSTMENTS

The data for adjustments are as follows.

a–b. Ending merchandise inventory, $58,800
   c. Course fees earned, $600
   d. Ending supplies inventory, $412
   e. Insurance expired, $320
   f. Additional year's depreciation of equipment, $4,800
   g. Additional year's depreciation of building, $4,000
   h. Wages owed but not paid to employees at end of year, $1,220

Listing the adjustment data appears to be a relatively minor task. In a business situation, however, one must take actual physical counts of the inventories and match them up with costs. One must check insurance policies to determine the amount of insurance that has expired. Finally, one must systematically write off, or depreciate, the cost of equipment and buildings. Incidentally, for income tax and accounting purposes, land cannot be depreciated. Even if the building and lot were bought as one package for one price, the buyer must separate the cost of the building from the cost of the land. For real estate taxes, the county assessor appraises the building and the land separately. If there is no other qualified appraisal available, one can use the assessor's ratio or percentage as a basis for separating building cost and land cost.

Now let's look at these adjustments in the form of T accounts.

Merchandise Inventory			Income Summary	
+	**−**		(a) Adj. 63,000	(b) Adj. 58,800
Bal. 63,000	(a) Adj. 63,000			
(b) Adj. 58,800				

Unearned Course Fees			Course Fees Income	
−	**+**		**−**	**+**
(c) Adj. 600	Bal. 900			(c) Adj. 600

Supplies			Supplies Expense	
+	**−**		**+**	**−**
Bal. 1,440	(d) Adj. 1,028		(d) Adj. 1,028	

Prepaid Insurance			Insurance Expense	
+	**−**		**+**	**−**
Bal. 960	(e) Adj. 320		(e) Adj. 320	

Accumulated Depreciation, Equipment			Depreciation Expense, Equipment	
−	**+**		**+**	**−**
	Bal. 16,400		(f) Adj. 4,800	
	(f) Adj. 4,800			

Accumulated Depreciation, Building			Depreciation Expense, Building	
−	**+**		**+**	**−**
	Bal. 32,000		(g) 4,000	
	(g) 4,000			

Wages Payable			Wages Expense	
−	**+**		**+**	**−**
	(h) 1,220		Bal. 45,800	
			(h) 1,220	

We now record these in the Adjustments columns of the work sheet, using the same letters to identify the adjustments (see Figure 14-2).

COMPLETION OF THE WORK SHEET

Now we carry the account balances from the Trial Balance and Adjustments columns directly to the Income Statement and Balance Sheet columns. In the interest of efficiency and to save space, we do away with the Adjusted Trial Balance columns. In the earlier presentation they acted as a teaching device and as an intermediate checkpoint to prove that the accounts were in balance before we carried them forward. Obviously, however, the Adjusted Trial Balance columns are not necessary to complete the work sheet. For the sake of efficiency and economy, therefore, we often eliminate the Adjusted Trial Balance columns.

Figure 14-2

	ACCOUNT NAME	TRIAL BALANCE DEBIT	TRIAL BALANCE CREDIT	ADJUSTMENTS DEBIT	ADJUSTMENTS CREDIT	
1	Cash	21 9 2 2 00				1
2	Notes Receivable	4 0 0 0 00				2
3	Accounts Receivable	29 3 6 0 00				3
4	Merchandise Inventory	63 0 0 0 00		(b)58 8 0 0 00	(a)63 0 0 0 00	4
5	Supplies	1 4 4 0 00			(d) 1 0 2 8 00	5
6	Prepaid Insurance	9 6 0 00			(e) 3 2 0 00	6
7	Equipment	33 6 0 0 00				7
8	Accum. Depreciation, Equipment		16 4 0 0 00		(f) 4 8 0 0 00	8
9	Building	100 0 0 0 00				9
10	Accum. Depreciation, Building		32 0 0 0 00		(g) 4 0 0 0 00	10
11	Land	12 0 0 0 00				11
12	Notes Payable		3 0 0 0 00			12
13	Accounts Payable		36 4 0 0 00			13
14	Unearned Course Fees		9 0 0 00	(c) 6 0 0 00		14
15	Mortgage Payable		8 0 0 0 00			15
16	C. L. Frederickson, Capital		146 5 7 4 00			16
17	C. L. Frederickson, Drawing	19 2 0 0 00				17
18	Sales		176 1 8 0 00			18
19	Sales Returns and Allowances	8 4 0 00				19
20	Sales Discount	1 8 8 0 00				20
21	Interest Income		1 2 0 00			21
22	Purchases	85 6 0 0 00				22
23	Purchases Returns and Allowances		8 3 2 00			23
24	Purchases Discount		1 2 4 8 00			24
25	Wages Expense	45 8 0 0 00		(h)1 2 2 0 00		25
26	Taxes Expense	1 9 6 0 00				26
27	Interest Expense	9 2 00				27
28		421 6 5 4 00	421 6 5 4 00			28
29	Income Summary			(a)63 0 0 0 00	(b)58 8 0 0 00	29
30	Course Fees Income				(c) 6 0 0 00	30
31	Supplies Expense			(d) 1 0 2 8 00		31
32	Insurance Expense			(e) 3 2 0 00		32
33	Depreciation Expense, Equipment			(f) 4 8 0 0 00		33
34	Depreciation Expense, Building			(g) 4 0 0 0 00		34
35	Wages Payable				(h)1 2 2 0 00	35
36				133 7 6 8 00	133 7 6 8 00	36

Observe in particular the way we carry forward the figures for Merchandise Inventory and Income Summary. **Income Summary is the only account in which we don't combine the debit and credit figures;** instead we carry them into the Income Statement columns in Figure 14-3 as *two distinct figures.* As we said, the reason is that both figures appear in the income statement itself. We'll talk about this topic in greater detail in Chapter 15.

When you are developing the work sheet, complete one stage at a time:

1. Record the trial balance, and make sure that the total of the Debit column equals the total of the Credit column.
2. Record the adjustments in the Adjustments columns, and make sure that the totals are equal.
3. Complete the Income Statement and Balance Sheet columns by recording the adjusted balance of each account, as indicated by the following classification of accounts.

Income Statement		Balance Sheet	
Debit	**Credit**	**Debit**	**Credit**
Expenses	Revenues	Assets	Liabilities
+	+	+	+
Sales Returns	Purchases Returns	Drawing	Capital
and Allowances	and Allowances		+
+	+		Accumulated
Sales Discount	Purchases		Depreciation
+	Discount		
Purchases	+		
+	Income Summary		
Income Summary			

Study the following example, noting especially the way we treat these special accounts for a merchandising business:

	Location in Work Sheet			
	Income Statement		Balance Sheet	
Account Name	**Debit**	**Credit**	**Debit**	**Credit**
Merchandise Inventory			58,800 00	
Sales		176,180 00		
Sales Returns and Allowances	840 00			
Sales Discount	1,880 00			
Purchases	85,600 00			
Purchases Returns and Allowances		832 00		
Purchases Discount		1,248 00		
Income Summary	63,000 00	58,800 00		

The completed work sheet looks like Figure 14-3, below.

| | ACCOUNT NAME | TRIAL BALANCE | |
		DEBIT	CREDIT
1	Cash	21 9 2 2 00	
2	Notes Receivable	4 0 0 0 00	
3	Accounts Receivable	29 3 6 0 00	
4	Merchandise Inventory	63 0 0 0 00	
5	Supplies	1 4 4 0 00	
6	Prepaid Insurance	9 6 0 00	
7	Equipment	33 6 0 0 00	
8	Accumulated Depreciation, Equipment		16 4 0 0
9	Building	100 0 0 0 00	
10	Accumulated Depreciation, Building		32 0 0 0
11	Land	12 0 0 0 00	
12	Notes Payable		3 0 0 0
13	Accounts Payable		36 4 0 0
14	Unearned Course Fees		9 0 0
15	Mortgage Payable		8 0 0 0
16	C. L. Frederickson, Capital		146 5 7 4
17	C. L. Frederickson, Drawing	19 2 0 0 00	
18	Sales		176 1 8 0
19	Sales Returns and Allowances	8 4 0 00	
20	Sales Discount	1 8 8 0 00	
21	Interest Income		1 2 0
22	Purchases	85 6 0 0 00	
23	Purchases Returns and Allowances		8 3 2
24	Purchases Discount		1 2 4 8
25	Wages Expense	45 8 0 0 00	
26	Taxes Expense	1 9 6 0 00	
27	Interest Expense	9 2 00	
28		421 6 5 4 00	421 6 5 4
29	Income Summary		
30	Course Fees Income		
31	Supplies Expense		
32	Insurance Expense		
33	Depreciation Expense, Equipment		
34	Depreciation Expense, Building		
35	Wages Payable		
36			
37	Net Income		
38			
39			
40			
41			

Figure 14-3

| ADJUSTMENTS | | INCOME STATEMENT | | BALANCE SHEET | | |
DEBIT	CREDIT	DEBIT	CREDIT	DEBIT	CREDIT	
				21 9 2 2 00		1
				4 0 0 0 00		2
				29 3 6 0 00		3
8 0 0 00	(a)63 0 0 0 00			58 8 0 0 00		4
	(d) 1 0 2 8 00			4 1 2 00		5
	(e) 3 2 0 00			6 4 0 00		6
				33 6 0 0 00		7
	(f) 4 8 0 0 00				21 2 0 0 00	8
				100 0 0 0 00		9
	(g) 4 0 0 0 00				36 0 0 0 00	10
				12 0 0 0 00		11
					3 0 0 0 00	12
					36 4 0 0 00	13
6 0 0 00					3 0 0 00	14
					8 0 0 0 00	15
					146 5 7 4 00	16
				19 2 0 0 00		17
			176 1 8 0 00			18
		8 4 0 00				19
		1 8 8 0 00				20
			1 2 0 00			21
		85 6 0 0 00				22
			8 3 2 00			23
			1 2 4 8 00			24
2 2 0 00		47 0 2 0 00				25
		1 9 6 0 00				26
		9 2 00				27
						28
0 0 0 00	(b)58 8 0 0 00	63 0 0 0 00	58 8 0 0 00			29
	(c) 6 0 0 00		6 0 0 00			30
0 2 8 00		1 0 2 8 00				31
3 2 0 00		3 2 0 00				32
8 0 0 00		4 8 0 0 00				33
0 0 0 00		4 0 0 0 00				34
	(h) 1 2 2 0 00				1 2 2 0 00	35
7 6 8 00	133 7 6 8 00	210 5 4 0 00	237 7 8 0 00	279 9 3 4 00	252 6 9 4 00	36
		27 2 4 0 00			27 2 4 0 00	37
		237 7 8 0 00	237 7 8 0 00	279 9 3 4 00	279 9 3 4 00	38
						39
						40
						41

Figure 14-4

	DATE		DESCRIPTION	POST. REF.	DEBIT	CREDIT	
			GENERAL JOURNAL			PAGE 96	
1			*Adjusting Entries*				1
2	19– Dec.	31	Income Summary		63 0 0 0 00		2
3			Merchandise Inventory			63 0 0 0 00	3
4							4
5		31	Merchandise Inventory		58 8 0 0 00		5
6			Income Summary			58 8 0 0 00	6
7							7
8		31	Unearned Course Fees		6 0 0 00		8
9			Course Fees Income			6 0 0 00	9
10							10
11		31	Supplies Expense		1 0 2 8 00		11
12			Supplies			1 0 2 8 00	12
13							13
14		31	Insurance Expense		3 2 0 00		14
15			Prepaid Insurance			3 2 0 00	15
16							16
17		31	Depreciation Expense, Equipment		4 8 0 0 00		17
18			Accumulated Depreciation,				18
19			Equipment			4 8 0 0 00	19
20							20
21		31	Depreciation Expense, Building		4 0 0 0 00		21
22			Accumulated Depreciation,				22
23			Building			4 0 0 0 00	23
24							24
25		31	Wages Expense		1 2 2 0 00		25
26			Wages Payable			1 2 2 0 00	26
27							27

ADJUSTING ENTRIES

See above for the way the adjusting entries look when they are taken from the Adjustments columns of the work sheet and recorded in the general journal (Figure 14-4).

Objective 2

Journalize the adjusting entries for a merchandising business.

GLOSSARY

Physical inventory An actual count of the stock of goods on hand; also referred to as a *periodic inventory*.

Unearned revenue Revenue received in advance for goods or services to be delivered later; considered to be a liability until the revenue is earned.

QUESTIONS, EXERCISES, AND PROBLEMS

Discussion Questions

1. Explain the two-step process for adjusting Merchandise Inventory.
2. What is the difference between merchandise inventory and supplies?
3. What is a physical, or periodic, inventory?
4. For a firm using a system of periodic inventories, which inventory (beginning merchandise or ending merchandise) appears in the firm's unadjusted trial balance at the end of the fiscal period?
5. On the income summary line of a work sheet, $31,500 appears in the Income Statement Debit column and $29,400 appears in the Income Statement Credit column. Which figure represents the beginning merchandise inventory?
6. In which columns of the work sheet is Sales Discount recorded?
7. When a dormitory received a semester's rent in advance, an entry was made debiting Cash and crediting Unearned Rent. At the end of the calendar year, a large portion of the rent had been earned. What adjusting entry would you have made?

Exercises

Exercise 14-1 Prepare the complete entry (in the general journal) from which each of the items identified by number below was posted.

						BALANCE	
DATE	ITEM	POST. REF.	DEBIT	CREDIT	DEBIT	CREDIT	

ACCOUNT **Wages Expense**   ACCOUNT NO. **514**

	DATE	ITEM	POST. REF.	DEBIT	CREDIT	DEBIT	CREDIT	
2	19– Dec. 28	(1)	CP39	2 2 0 0 00		91 7 0 0 00		2
3	31	(2)	J42	6 0 0 00		92 3 0 0 00		3
4	31	(3)	J43		92 3 0 0 00			4

Exercise 14-2 The beginning inventory of a merchandising business was $27,000, and the ending inventory is $31,000. What entries are needed at the end of the fiscal period to adjust Merchandise Inventory?

Exercise 14-3 In the Income Statement columns of the work sheet, we record the Income Summary account as $68,000 in the Debit column and $72,000 in the Credit column. Identify the beginning and ending merchandise inventory.

Exercise 14-4 The Inquisitive Magazine credited Unearned Subscriptions for $48,000 received from subscribers to its new monthly magazine. All subscriptions were for twelve issues. The first issue was mailed during October of the present year. Make the adjusting entry on December 31 of this year.

Exercise 14-5 Determine the amount of expired insurance for the fiscal year, January 1 through December 31, from the following account.

	DATE	ITEM	POST. REF.	DEBIT	CREDIT	BALANCE DEBIT	BALANCE CREDIT	
1	19– Jan. 1	Balance						1
2		(4 months)	✓			4 2 0 00		2
3	May 1	(12 months)	CP59	1 6 8 0 00		2 1 0 0 00		3

ACCOUNT **Prepaid Insurance**   ACCOUNT NO. **118**

Exercise 14-6 From the ledger account for Supplies, prepare the complete entries (in the general journal) from which each of the items identified by journal reference was posted.

ACCOUNT **Supplies**   ACCOUNT NO. **126**

	DATE	ITEM	POST. REF.	DEBIT	CREDIT	BALANCE DEBIT	BALANCE CREDIT	
1	19– Jan. 1	Balance	✓			9 6 0 00		1
2	Apr. 16		CP51	3 2 0 00		1 2 8 0 00		2
3	Sept. 22		CP72	2 1 0 00		1 4 9 0 00		3
4	29		CR76		3 0 00	1 4 6 0 00		4
5	Dec. 31	Adjusting	J121		6 0 0 00	8 6 0 00		5
6								6
7								7

Exercise 14-7 Because of a sudden illness, McGregor Company's accountant was unable to return to the job by the close of the company's fiscal year. The accountant did not have a chance to discuss what adjusting entries would be necessary at the end of the year, December 31. Fortunately, however, he did jot down a few notes that provided some leads. Here are his notes.

a. Charge off $1,450 of expired insurance from prepaid account for the year.
b. No bill received yet from car rental agency for salespeople's cars—should be about $8,400 for the year.
c. Depreciation on furniture and equipment for the year is $6,000.
d. Two days' salaries will be unpaid at year-end; total weekly (5 days) salary is $2,400.

Instructions

Record the adjusting entries.

Exercise 14-8 Complete each horizontal line of the selected accounts in the work sheet on pages 418–419. (Equipment and Insurance Expense are given as examples.)

Problem Set A

Problem 14-1A The trial balance of Carter Company as of December 31, the end of its fiscal year, is as follows.

Carter Company
Trial Balance
December 31, 19–

ACCOUNT NAME	DEBIT	CREDIT
Cash	4 5 6 8 27	
Merchandise Inventory	31 4 2 7 41	
Store Supplies	7 3 3 42	
Prepaid Insurance	5 1 0 00	
Store Equipment	18 6 7 0 00	
Accumulated Depreciation, Store Equipment		12 4 1 8 00
Accounts Payable		7 1 4 3 48
Sales Tax Payable		1 2 3 49
L. O. Carter, Capital		27 5 2 9 92
L. O. Carter, Drawing	14 5 0 0 00	
Sales		88 9 8 3 17
Sales Returns and Allowances	7 4 6 92	
Purchases	40 7 1 8 92	
Purchases Returns and Allowances		9 2 8 91
Purchases Discount		7 5 1 82
Salary Expense	18 2 8 4 43	
Rent Expense	7 2 0 0 00	
Miscellaneous Expense	5 1 9 42	
	137 8 7 8 79	137 8 7 8 79

Here are the data for the adjustments.

a–b. Merchandise inventory at December 31, $32,874.90
  c. Store supplies inventory, $202.16
  d. Insurance expired, $368.00
  e. Salaries accrued, $293.40
  f. Depreciation of store equipment, $1,960.00

Instructions

Complete the work sheet.

	ACCOUNT NAME	TRIAL BALANCE									
		DEBIT					CREDIT				
1	Accounts Receivable	18	0	0	0	00					
2	Merchandise Inventory	60	0	0	0	00					
3	Prepaid Insurance	1	6	2	0	00					
4	Equipment	26	0	0	0	00					
5	Accumulated Depreciation, Equipment							15	2	0	0
6	Unearned Concession Income								1	8	0	0
7	Concession Income											
8	Sales							80	0	0	0
9	Sales Returns and Allowances		3	0	0	00					
10	Purchases	42	0	0	0	00					
11	Purchases Discount								1	0	5	0
12	Wages Expense	29	0	0	0	00					
13	Income Summary											
14	Wages Payable											
15	Depreciation Expense, Equipment											
16	Insurance Expense											
17												

Problem 14-2A The balances of the ledger accounts of Harris Frame Shop as of June 30, the end of its fiscal year, are as follows.

Cash	$ 9,850
Accounts Receivable	34,200
Merchandise Inventory	48,600
Supplies	980
Prepaid Insurance	720
Store Equipment	17,860
Accumulated Depreciation, Store Equipment	10,800
Office Equipment	6,400
Accumulated Depreciation, Office Equipment	3,210
Notes Payable	2,400
Accounts Payable	28,600
Salaries Payable	—
Unearned Equipment Rental	1,800
Mary C. Harris, Capital	63,560
Mary C. Harris, Drawing	16,000
Income Summary	—
Sales	311,000
Sales Returns and Allowances	2,140
Equipment Rental Income	—
Purchases	261,000
Purchases Returns and Allowances	4,780
Purchases Discount	1,520

	ADJUSTMENTS		INCOME STATEMENT		BALANCE SHEET		
	DEBIT	CREDIT	DEBIT	CREDIT	DEBIT	CREDIT	
							1
							2
							3
					26 0 0 0 00		4
							5
							6
		1 6 0 0 00					7
							8
							9
							10
							11
							12
	0 0 0 00	56 0 0 0 00					13
		2 0 0 00					14
	4 0 0 00						15
	8 2 0 00		8 2 0 00				16
							17

Salary Expense	$29,500
Depreciation Expense, Store Equipment	—
Depreciation Expense, Office Equipment	—
Insurance Expense	—
Supplies Expense	—
Interest Expense	420

Here are the data for the adjustments.

a–b. Merchandise inventory at June 30, $76,400
  c. Salaries accrued at June 30, $960
  d. Insurance expired during the year, $600
  e. Supplies inventory at June 30, $190
  f. Depreciation of store equipment, $2,500
  g. Depreciation of office equipment, $1,300
  h. Equipment rent earned, $1,500

Instructions

1. Complete the work sheet.
2. Journalize the adjusting entries.

Problem 14-3A A portion of the work sheet of Morris Dow and Company for the year ended December 31 is at the top of the next page.

ACCOUNT NAME	INCOME STATEMENT DEBIT	INCOME STATEMENT CREDIT	BALANCE SHEET DEBIT	BALANCE SHEET CREDIT
Cash			4 6 7 0 00	
Merchandise Inventory			38 4 7 0 00	
Supplies			1 2 8 00	
Prepaid Insurance			1 2 0 00	
Store Equipment			19 6 4 0 00	
Accumulated Deprecia- tion, Store Equipment				13 1 1 0 00
Accounts Payable				7 3 0 0 00
Morris Dow, Capital				34 4 7 0 00
Morris Dow, Drawing			13 8 0 0 00	
Sales		86 7 1 0 00		
Sales Returns and Allowances	7 6 0 00			
Purchases	42 1 3 0 00			
Purchases Returns and Allowances		4 7 0 00		
Purchases Discount		8 0 0 00		
Salary Expense	18 7 8 0 00			
Rent Expense	7 4 0 0 00			
Income Summary	32 8 4 0 00	38 4 7 0 00		
Depreciation Expense, Store Equipment	2 0 2 0 00			
Insurance Expense	3 8 0 00			
Supplies Expense	4 7 2 00			
Salaries Payable				2 8 0 00
	104 7 8 2 00	126 4 5 0 00	76 8 2 8 00	55 1 6 0 00

Instructions

1. Determine the entries that appeared in the Adjustments columns and present them in general journal form.
2. Determine the net income for the year and the amount of the owner's capital at the end of the year (assuming that no capital contributions were made during the year).

Problem 14-4A Here are the accounts in the ledger of Reiner's Health Foods Store, with the balances as of December 31, the end of its fiscal year.

Cash	$ 3,760	Income Summary	—
Accounts Receivable	518	Sales	$126,418
Merchandise Inventory	38,700	Sales Returns and Allowances	1,296
Store Supplies	428	Purchases	87,656
Prepaid Insurance	762	Purchases Returns and	
Store Equipment	25,830	Allowances	1,087
Accumulated Depreciation,		Purchases Discount	1,470
Store Equipment	5,720	Salary Expense	7,800
Building	26,000	Advertising Expense	642
Accumulated Depreciation,		Depreciation Expense,	
Building	9,780	Store Equipment	—
Land	5,000	Depreciation Expense,	
Accounts Payable	4,690	Building	—
Sales Tax Payable	928	Store Supplies Expense	—
Salaries Payable	—	Insurance Expense	—
Mortgage Payable	14,620	Utilities Expense	386
C. C. Reiner, Capital	50,610	Miscellaneous Expense	325
C. C. Reiner, Drawing	15,500	Interest Expense	720

Here are the data for the adjustments.

a–b. Merchandise inventory at December 31, $37,690
  c. Insurance expired during the year, $418
  d. Depreciation of store equipment (life of eight years with a trade-in value of $2,950 at the end of eight years, straight-line rate)
  e. Depreciation of building (life of seventeen years with a value of $2,200 remaining at the end of seventeen years, straight-line rate)
  f. Salaries accrued at December 31, $140
  g. Store supplies inventory at December 31, $106

Instructions

1. Complete the work sheet.
2. Journalize the adjusting entries.

Problem Set B

Problem 14-1B The trial balance of Parkhurst Company as of December 31, the end of its current fiscal year, is at the top of the next page.

Here are the data for the adjustments.

a–b. Merchandise inventory at December 31, $33,416.28
  c. Store supplies inventory, $198.20
  d. Insurance expired, $360
  e. Salaries accrued, $281.50
  f. Depreciation of store equipment, $1,940

Instructions

Complete the work sheet.

Parkhurst Company
Trial Balance
December 31, 19–

ACCOUNT NAME	DEBIT	CREDIT
Cash	4 7 8 1 96	
Merchandise Inventory	31 7 6 1 42	
Store Supplies	7 2 0 56	
Prepaid Insurance	4 8 0 00	
Store Equipment	18 7 4 0 00	
Accumulated Depreciation, Store Equipment		12 1 6 0 00
Accounts Payable		7 2 8 9 40
Sales Tax Payable		1 2 1 68
C. R. Ross, Capital		27 8 1 5 00
C. R. Ross, Drawing	14 7 2 0 00	
Sales		89 5 1 8 37
Sales Returns and Allowances	7 2 1 52	
Purchases	40 6 2 1 73	
Purchases Returns and Allowances		9 3 9 47
Purchases Discount		7 4 8 95
Salary Expense	18 3 2 9 40	
Rent Expense	7 2 0 0 00	
Miscellaneous Expense	5 1 6 28	
	138 5 9 2 87	138 5 9 2 87

Problem 14-2B The balances of the ledger accounts of Belfair Music as of December 31, the end of its fiscal year, are as follows.

Cash	$ 5,796	Income Summary	—
Accounts Receivable	21,481	Sales	$326,000
Merchandise Inventory	60,919	Sales Returns and Allowances	4,874
Supplies	785	Equipment Rental Income	—
Prepaid Insurance	814	Purchases	271,549
Store Equipment	18,462	Purchases Returns and	
Accumulated Depreciation,		Allowances	6,720
Store Equipment	14,710	Purchases Discount	3,817
Office Equipment	4,718	Wages Expense	27,600
Accumulated Depreciation,		Depreciation Expense,	
Office Equipment	860	Store Equipment	—
Notes Payable	2,000	Depreciation Expense,	
Accounts Payable	15,411	Office Equipment	—
Wages Payable	—	Supplies Expense	—
Unearned Equipment Rental	1,600	Insurance Expense	—
C. K. Hennings, Capital	60,266	Interest Expense	386
C. K. Hennings, Drawing	14,000		

Data for the adjustments are as follows.

a–b. Merchandise inventory at December 31, $50,838
  c. Wages accrued at December 31, $978
  d. Supplies inventory at December 31, $372
  e. Depreciation of store equipment, $2,934
  f. Depreciation of office equipment, $866
  g. Insurance expired during the year, $316
  h. Equipment rent earned, $1,200

Instructions

1. Complete the work sheet.
2. Journalize the adjusting entries.

Problem 14-3B Here is a portion of the work sheet of Donna Easely & Company for the year ended December 31.

ACCOUNT NAME	INCOME STATEMENT		BALANCE SHEET	
	DEBIT	CREDIT	DEBIT	CREDIT
Cash			3 8 6 8 00	
Merchandise Inventory			37 1 4 9 00	
Supplies			1 4 9 00	
Prepaid Insurance			1 2 5 00	
Store Equipment			18 9 8 0 00	
Accumulated Deprecia-				
tion, Store Equipment				14 7 2 0 00
Accounts Payable				6 8 8 0 00
Donna Easely, Capital				37 5 7 1 00
Donna Easely, Drawing			15 4 0 0 00	
Sales		85 9 0 8 00		
Sales Returns and				
Allowances	7 1 7 00			
Purchases	44 2 9 6 00			
Purchases Returns				
and Allowances		4 8 2 00		
Purchases Discount		8 1 8 00		
Salary Expense	18 9 2 6 00			
Rent Expense	7 2 0 0 00			
Income Summary	34 1 1 4 00	37 1 4 9 00		
Depreciation Expense,				
Store Equipment	2 1 8 0 00			
Insurance Expense	2 7 6 00			
Supplies Expense	4 4 2 00			
Salaries Payable				2 9 4 00
	108 1 5 1 00	124 3 5 7 00	75 6 7 1 00	59 4 6 5 00

Instructions

1. Determine the entries that appeared in the Adjustments columns and present them in general journal form.
2. Determine the net income for the year and the amount of the owner's capital at the end of the year (assuming that no capital contributions were made during the year).

Problem 14-4B The accounts in the ledger of Roberts Variety, with the balances as of December 31, the end of its fiscal year, are as follows.

Cash	$ 4,200	Income Summary	—
Accounts Receivable	680	Sales	$156,000
Merchandise Inventory	40,200	Sales Returns and Allowances	2,900
Store Supplies	540	Purchases	101,000
Prepaid Insurance	980	Purchases Returns and	
Store Equipment	18,700	Allowances	2,300
Accumulated Depreciation,		Purchases Discount	1,600
Store Equipment	4,200	Salary Expense	17,500
Building	30,000	Advertising Expense	2,050
Accumulated Depreciation,		Depreciation Expense,	
Building	12,200	Store Equipment	—
Land	6,000	Depreciation Expense,	
Notes Payable	3,600	Building	—
Accounts Payable	6,420	Store Supplies Expense	—
Sales Tax·Payable	1,980	Insurance Expense	—
Salaries Payable	—	Utilities Expense	1,870
F. T. Roberts, Capital	57,000	Miscellaneous Expense	420
F. T. Roberts, Drawing	18,000	Interest Expense	260

Data for the adjustments are as follows.

a–b. Merchandise inventory at December 31, $41,600
  c. Store supplies inventory at December 31, $180
  d. Depreciation of store equipment (life of ten years with a trade-in value of $6,700 at the end of ten years, straight-line rate)
  e. Depreciation of building (life of twenty years with a value of $2,000 remaining at the end of twenty years, straight-line rate)
  f. Salaries accrued at December 31, $550
  g. Insurance expired during the year, $760

Instructions

1. Complete the work sheet.
2. Journalize the adjusting entries.

15 Financial Statements and Closing Entries for a Merchandising Firm

Learning Objectives

After you have completed this chapter, you will be able to do the following:

1. Prepare a classified income statement for a merchandising firm.

2. Prepare a classified balance sheet for any type of business.

3. Compute working capital and current ratio.

4. Journalize the closing entries for a merchandising firm.

5. Determine which adjusting entries should be reversed.

Chapters 5 and 7 discussed at length the income statements for a service and a professional enterprise, respectively. Then, in Chapters 11 and 14, we discussed the specialized accounts and journals for merchandising enterprises; in Chapter 14 we also explained the work sheet.

This chapter will show you how to formulate financial statements directly from work sheets. We will also explain the functions of closing entries and reversing entries as means of completing the accounting cycle. In Figure 15-1 (pages 428–429) we'll reproduce part of the work sheet for C. L. Frederickson Plumbing Supply that we presented in Chapter 14. First we'll look at the financial statements in their entirety, and then we'll explain their various subdivisions.

THE INCOME STATEMENT

As you know, the work sheet is merely a tool used by accountants to prepare the financial statements. In Figure 15-1, we present the partial work sheet for C. L. Frederickson Plumbing Supply, which includes the Income Statement columns. Of course, each of the amounts that appear in the Income Statement columns of the work sheet will also be used in the income statement. Notice that the amounts for the beginning and ending Merchandise Inventory now appear separately on the Income Summary line. Figure 15-2 (page 430) shows the entire income statement. Pause for a while and look it over; then we'll break it down into its component parts.

Objective 1

Prepare a classified income statement for a merchandising firm.

The outline of the income statement follows a logical pattern that is much the same for any type of merchandising business. The ability to interpret the income statement and extract parts from it is very useful when one is gathering information for decisions. To realize the full value of an income statement, however, you need to know the skeleton outline of an income statement backward and forward; you must be able to visualize it at a moment's notice. So, let's look at the statement piece by piece.

Net Sales	$173,460
− Cost of Merchandise Sold	87,720
Gross Profit	$85,740
− Operating Expenses	59,128
Income from Operations	$26,612

To hammer home the concepts of *gross* and *net*, let's imagine a simple transaction that takes place many thousands of times a day, all over the world: selling a house.

Cynthia Jones, a few years back, bought a house and a lot for $32,000. Last week she sold the house and lot for $60,000. The real estate agent who did the actual selling got a sales commission of 7 percent. How much did Jones make as clear profit?

Sale price of property	$60,000
Less Cost of property sold	32,000
Gross Profit (or Gross Margin)	$28,000
Less Agent's commission expense	4,200
Net Income or Net Profit (gain on the sale)	$23,800

Gross profit is the profit on the sale of the property before any expense has been deducted. **Net income** or *net profit* is the final or clear profit after all the expenses have been deducted. On a single-sale situation such as this, we refer to the final outcome as the net profit. But for a business that has many sales and expenses, most accountants prefer the term *net income*. Regardless of which word one uses, *net* refers to clear profit.

Revenue from Sales

All right, now let's look at the Revenue from Sales section in the income statement of C. L. Frederickson Plumbing Supply.

Revenue from Sales:			
Sales		$ 176 1 8 0 00	
Less: Sales Returns and Allowances	$ 8 4 0 00		
Sales Discount	1 8 8 0 00	2 7 2 0 00	
Net Sales			$ 173 4 6 0 00

When we introduced Sales Returns and Allowances and Sales Discount, we treated them as deductions from Sales. You can see that in the income statement they are deducted from Sales to give us **net sales.** Note that we recorded these items in the same order in which they appear in the ledger.

Cost of Merchandise Sold

The section of the income statement that requires the greatest amount of concentration is the **Cost of Merchandise Sold.** Let us therefore repeat it in its entirety.

C. L. Frederickson Plumbing Supply
Work Sheet
For year ended December 31, 19—

	ACCOUNT NAME	TRIAL BALANCE DEBIT	TRIAL BALANCE CREDIT
1	Cash	21 9 2 2 00	
2	Notes Receivable	4 0 0 0 00	
3	Accounts Receivable	29 3 6 0 00	
4	Merchandise Inventory	63 0 0 0 00	
5	Supplies	1 4 4 0 00	
6	Prepaid Insurance	9 6 0 00	
7	Equipment	33 6 0 0 00	
8	Accum. Depreciation, Equipment		16 4 0 0
9	Building	100 0 0 0 00	
10	Accum. Depreciation, Building		32 0 0 0
11	Land	12 0 0 0 00	
12	Notes Payable		3 0 0 0
13	Accounts Payable		36 4 0 0
14	Unearned Course Fees		9 0 0
15	Mortgage Payable		8 0 0 0
16	C. L. Frederickson, Capital		146 5 7 4
17	C. L. Frederickson, Drawing	19 2 0 0 00	
18	Sales		176 1 8 0
19	Sales Returns and Allowances	8 4 0 00	
20	Sales Discount	1 8 8 0 00	
21	Interest Income		1 2 0
22	Purchases	85 6 0 0 00	
23	Purchases Returns and Allowances		8 3 2
24	Purchases Discount		1 2 4 8
25	Wages Expense	45 8 0 0 00	
26	Taxes Expense	1 9 6 0 00	
27	Interest Expense	9 2 00	
28		421 6 5 4 00	421 6 5 4
29	Income Summary		
30	Course Fees Income		
31	Supplies Expense		
32	Insurance Expense		
33	Depreciation Expense, Equipment		
34	Depreciation Expense, Building		
35	Wages Payable		
36			
37	Net Income		
38			
39			

Figure 15-1

	ADJUSTMENTS DEBIT	ADJUSTMENTS CREDIT	INCOME STATEMENT DEBIT	INCOME STATEMENT CREDIT	
					1
					2
					3
	8 0 0 00	(a) 63 0 0 0 00			4
		(d) 1 0 2 8 00			5
		(e) 3 2 0 00			6
					7
		(f) 4 8 0 0 00			8
					9
		(g) 4 0 0 0 00			10
					11
					12
					13
	6 0 0 00				14
					15
					16
					17
				176 1 8 0 00	18
			8 4 0 00		19
			1 8 8 0 00		20
				1 2 0 00	21
			85 6 0 0 00		22
				8 3 2 00	23
				1 2 4 8 00	24
	2 2 0 00		47 0 2 0 00		25
			1 9 6 0 00		26
			9 2 00		27
					28
	0 0 0 00	(b) 58 8 0 0 00	63 0 0 0 00	58 8 0 0 00	29
		(c) 6 0 0 00		6 0 0 00	30
	0 2 8 00		1 0 2 8 00		31
	3 2 0 00		3 2 0 00		32
	8 0 0 00		4 8 0 0 00		33
	0 0 0 00		4 0 0 0 00		34
		(h) 1 2 2 0 00			35
	7 6 8 00	133 7 6 8 00	210 5 4 0 00	237 7 8 0 00	36
			27 2 4 0 00		37
			237 7 8 0 00	237 7 8 0 00	38
					39

C. L. Frederickson Plumbing Supply
Income Statement
For year ended December 31, 19–

Revenue from Sales:						
Sales			$176 1 8 0 00			
Less: Sales Returns and Allowances	$ 8 4 0 00					
Sales Discount	1 8 8 0 00		2 7 2 0 00			
Net Sales					$ 173 4 6 0 00	
Cost of Merchandise Sold:						
Merchandise Inventory,						
January 1, 19–			$ 63 0 0 0 00			
Purchases	$85 6 0 0 00					
Less: Purchases Returns and						
Allowances $ 832.00						
Purchases Discount 1,248.00	2 0 8 0 00					
Net Purchases			83 5 2 0 00			
Merchandise Available for Sale			$ 146 5 2 0 00			
Less Merchandise Inventory,						
December 31, 19–			58 8 0 0 00			
Cost of Merchandise Sold					87 7 2 0 00	
Gross Profit					$ 85 7 4 0 00	
Operating Expenses:						
Wages Expense			$ 47 0 2 0 00			
Depreciation Expense, Equipment			4 8 0 0 00			
Supplies Expense			1 0 2 8 00			
Depreciation Expense, Building			4 0 0 0 00			
Taxes Expense			1 9 6 0 00			
Insurance Expense			3 2 0 00			
Total Operating Expenses					59 1 2 8 00	
Income from Operations					$ 26 6 1 2 00	
Other Income:						
Course Fees Income			$ 6 0 0 00			
Interest Income			1 2 0 00			
Total Other Income			$ 7 2 0 00			
Other Expenses:						
Interest Expense			9 2 00		6 2 8 00	
Net Income					$ 27 2 4 0 00	

Figure 15-2

Cost of Merchandise Sold:					
Merchandise Inventory,					
January 1, 19–			$ 63 0 0 0 00		
Purchases		$85 6 0 0 00			
Less: Purchases Returns					
and Allowances	$ 832.00				
Purchases Discount	1,248.00	2 0 8 0 00			
Net Purchases			83 5 2 0 00		
Merchandise Available for Sale			$ 146 5 2 0 00		
Less: Merchandise Inventory,					
December 31, 19–			58 8 0 0 00		
Cost of Merchandise Sold					87 7 2 0 00

First let's look closely at the Purchases section.

Purchases		$85 6 0 0 00	
Less: Purchases Returns			
and Allowances	$ 832.00		
Purchases Discount	1,248.00	2 0 8 0 00	
Net Purchases			83 5 2 0 00

Note the parallel to the Sales section; in order to arrive at Net Purchases, we deduct both Purchases Returns and Allowances and Purchases Discount from Purchases. We list the items in account-number order.

Now let's take in the full Cost of Merchandise Sold section. Does this seem like a reasonable summing up of the situation?

Amount we started with (beginning inventory)	$ 63,000
+ Net amount we purchased	83,520
Total amount that could have been sold (available)	$146,520
− Amount left over (ending inventory)	58,800
Cost of the merchandise that was actually sold	$ 87,720

An alternative way of presenting this information follows:

Merchandise Inventory, January 1, 19–	$ 63,000
+ Net Purchases	83,520
Merchandise Available for Sale	$146,520
− Merchandise Inventory, December 31, 19–	58,800
Cost of Merchandise Sold	$ 87,720

Remember that **net purchases** means total Purchases less both Purchases Returns and Allowances and Purchases Discount.

Operating Expenses

Operating expenses, as the name implies, are the regular expenses of doing business. They may be listed in descending order, with the largest amount first, if account numbers are unavailable. A Miscellaneous Expense account goes last regardless of its amount, however. Many accountants prefer to list the accounts and their respective balances in the order that the accounts appear in the ledger. We shall follow this order in this chapter.

Many firms may use subclassifications of operating expenses, such as the following.

1. **Selling expenses** Any expenses directly connected with the selling activity, such as these:

   - Sales Salaries Expense
   - Sales Commissions Expense
   - Advertising Expense
   - Store Supplies Expense
   - Delivery Expense
   - Depreciation Expense, Store Equipment

2. **General expenses** Any expenses related to the office or the administration, or any expense that cannot be directly connected with a selling activity:

   - Office Salaries Expense
   - Taxes Expense
   - Depreciation Expense, Office Equipment
   - Rent Expense
   - Insurance Expense
   - Office Supplies Expense

If the Cash Short and Over account has a debit balance (net shortage), the balance is added to and reported as Miscellaneous General Expense. Conversely, if the Cash Short and Over account has a credit balance (net overage), the balance is added to and reported as Miscellaneous Income, which is classified as Other Income.

In preparing the income statement, classifying expense accounts as selling expenses or general expenses is a matter of judgment. The only reason we're not using this breakdown here is that we're trying to keep the number of accounts to a minimum. In other words, getting bogged down in a large number of accounts could make it more difficult for you to understand the main concepts. We don't want you to lose sight of the forest on account of the trees.

Income from Operations

Now let's repeat the skeleton outline.

$$
\begin{array}{l}
\text{Net Sales} \\
- \underline{\text{Cost of Merchandise Sold}} \\
\text{Gross Profit} \\
- \underline{\text{Operating Expenses}} \\
\text{Income from Operations}
\end{array}
$$

If the Operating Expenses are the regular, recurring expenses of doing business, then Income from Operations should be the regular or recurring net income. When you are comparing the results of operations over a number of years, the net income from operations is the most significant figure to use each year as a basis for comparison.

Other Income

The Other Income classification, as the name implies, records any revenue account other than revenue from Sales. What we are trying to do is to isolate Sales at the top of the income statement as the major revenue account, so that the gross profit figure represents the profit made on the sale of merchandise *only*. Additional accounts that may appear under the heading of Other Income are Rent Income (the firm is subletting part of its premises), Interest Income (the firm holds an interest-bearing note or contract), Gain on Disposal of Plant and Equipment (the firm makes a profit on the sale of plant and equipment), Miscellaneous Income (the firm has an overage recorded in the Cash Short and Over account).

Other Expenses

The classification of Other Expenses records various nonoperating expenses, such as Interest Expense or Loss on Disposal of Plant and Equipment.

Skeleton Outline of the Income Statement

Net Sales
— Cost of Merchandise Sold

{
Gross Sales
— Sales Returns and Allowances
— Sales Discount
= Net Sales

{
Beginning Merchandise Inventory
+ Net Purchases

{
Gross Purchases
— Purchases Returns and Allowances
— Purchases Discount
= Net Purchases

= Merchandise Available for Sale
— Ending Merchandise Inventory
= Cost of Merchandise Sold

= Gross Profit
— Operating Expenses

{
Selling Expenses
General Expenses

= Income from Operations

+ Other Income

{
Interest Income
Rent Income
Gain on Disposal of Plant and Equipment

— Other Expenses

{
Interest Expense
Loss on Disposal of Plant and Equipment

= Net Income

THE BALANCE SHEET

Figure 15-3 (see pages 436–437) is a partial work sheet for C. L. Frederickson Plumbing Supply (again, based on the one in Chapter 14). Here again we find that every figure in the Balance Sheet columns of the work sheet is used in either the statement of owner's equity or the balance sheet. The first of these statements appears below.

C. L. Frederickson, Capital,												
January 1, 19–							$138	5	7	4	00	
Additional Investment, August 26, 19–							8	0	0	0	00	
Total Investment							$146	5	7	4	00	
Net Income for the Year	$27	2	4	0	00							
Less Withdrawals for the Year	19	2	0	0	00							
Increase in Capital							8	0	4	0	00	
C. L. Frederickson, Capital,												
December 31, 19–							$154	6	1	4	00	

C. L. Frederickson Plumbing Supply
Statement of Owner's Equity
For year ended December 31, 19–

We have already discussed the statement of owner's equity. C. L. Frederickson Plumbing Supply's statement of owner's equity shows why the balance of the Capital account has changed from the beginning of the fiscal period to the end of it. The statement shows that an additional investment was made during the period. Data relating to additional investments are available from an analysis of the Capital account, not from the work sheet. After one has added the additional investment to the beginning capital, the remainder of the statement is the same as our illustrations in Chapter 2. When there has been no additional investment, one simply records the net income, less withdrawals, and the resulting increase or decrease in capital.

Balance sheet classifications are generally uniform for all types of business enterprises. You are strongly urged to take the time to learn the following definitions of the classifications and the order of accounts within them. If you do, you will forever after have a standard routine for compiling a balance sheet, and this routine will save you a lot of grief and time. As you read, refer to Figure 15-4 on page 438.

Objective 2

Prepare a classified balance sheet for any type of business.

Current Assets

Current assets consist of cash and any other assets or resources that are expected to be realized in cash or to be sold or consumed during the normal operating cycle of the business or one year, if the normal operating cycle is less than twelve months.

ACCOUNT NAME	TRIAL BALANCE	
	DEBIT	CREDIT
Cash	21 9 2 2 00	
Notes Receivable	4 0 0 0 00	
Accounts Receivable	29 3 6 0 00	
Merchandise Inventory	63 0 0 0 00	
Supplies	1 4 4 0 00	
Prepaid Insurance	9 6 0 00	
Equipment	33 6 0 0 00	
Accum. Depreciation, Equipment		16 4 0 0
Building	100 0 0 0 00	
Accum. Depreciation, Building		32 0 0 0
Land	12 0 0 0 00	
Notes Payable		3 0 0 0
Accounts Payable		36 4 0 0
Unearned Course Fees		9 0 0
Mortgage Payable		8 0 0 0
C. L. Frederickson, Capital		146 5 7 4
C. L. Frederickson, Drawing	19 2 0 0 00	
Sales		176 1 8 0
Sales Returns and Allowances	8 4 0 00	
Sales Discount	1 8 8 0 00	
Interest Income		1 2 0
Purchases	85 6 0 0 00	
Purchases Returns and Allowances		8 3 2
Purchases Discount		1 2 4 8
Wages Expense	45 8 0 0 00	
Taxes Expense	1 9 6 0 00	
Interest Expense	9 2 00	
	421 6 5 4 00	421 6 5 4
Income Summary		
Course Fees Income		
Supplies Expense		
Insurance Expense		
Depreciation Expense, Equipment		
Depreciation Expense, Building		
Wages Payable		
Net Income		

Figure 15-3

	ADJUSTMENTS		BALANCE SHEET	
	DEBIT	CREDIT	DEBIT	CREDIT
			21 9 2 2 00	
			4 0 0 0 00	
			29 3 6 0 00	
	8 0 0 00	(a)63 0 0 0 00	58 8 0 0 00	
		(d) 1 0 2 8 00	4 1 2 00	
		(e) 3 2 0 00	6 4 0 00	
			33 6 0 0 00	
		(f) 4 8 0 0 00		21 2 0 0 00
			100 0 0 0 00	
		(g) 4 0 0 0 00		36 0 0 0 00
			12 0 0 0 00	
				3 0 0 0 00
				36 4 0 0 00
	6 0 0 00			3 0 0 00
				8 0 0 0 00
				146 5 7 4 00
			19 2 0 0 00	
	2 2 0 00			
	3 0 0 0 00	(b)58 8 0 0 00		
		(c) 6 0 0 00		
	0 2 8 00			
	3 2 0 00			
	8 0 0 00			
	0 0 0 00			
		(h) 1 2 2 0 00		1 2 2 0 00
	3 7 6 8 00	133 7 6 8 00	279 9 3 4 00	252 6 9 4 00
				27 2 4 0 00
			279 9 3 4 00	279 9 3 4 00

C. L. Frederickson Plumbing Supply
Balance Sheet
December 31, 19–

Assets				
Current Assets:				
Cash		$ 21 9 2 2 00		
Notes Receivable		4 0 0 0 00		
Accounts Receivable		29 3 6 0 00		
Merchandise Inventory		58 8 0 0 00		
Supplies		4 1 2 00		
Prepaid Insurance		6 4 0 00		
Total Current Assets			$ 115 1 3 4 00	
Plant and Equipment:				
Equipment	$ 33 6 0 0 00			
Less Accumulated Depreciation	21 2 0 0 00	$ 12 4 0 0 00		
Building	$ 100 0 0 0 00			
Less Accumulated Depreciation	36 0 0 0 00	64 0 0 0 00		
Land		12 0 0 0 00		
Total Plant and Equipment			88 4 0 0 00	
Total Assets			$ 203 5 3 4 00	
Liabilities				
Current Liabilities:				
Notes Payable		$ 3 0 0 0 00		
Mortgage Payable (current portion)		2 0 0 0 00		
Accounts Payable		36 4 0 0 00		
Wages Payable		1 2 2 0 00		
Unearned Course Fees		3 0 0 00		
Total Current Liabilities			$ 42 9 2 0 00	
Long-term Liabilities:				
Mortgage Payable			6 0 0 0 00	
Total Liabilities			$ 48 9 2 0 00	
Owner's Equity				
C. L. Frederickson, Capital			154 6 1 4 00	
Total Liabilities and Owner's Equity			$ 203 5 3 4 00	

Figure 15-4

Accountants list current assets in the order of their convertibility into cash, or, in other words, their **liquidity.** (If you've got an asset such as a car or a diamond, and you sell it quickly and turn it into cash, you are said to be turning it into a *liquid* state.) If the first four accounts under Current Assets (see Figure 15-4) are present, always record them in the same order: (1) Cash, (2) Notes Receivable, (3) Accounts Receivable, and (4) Merchandise Inventory.

CHAPTER 15

Notes receivable (current) are short-term promissory notes (promise-to-pay notes) held by the firm. (*Example:* Suppose you own a lumber yard and sell lumber to a builder who does not have enough cash to pay for the lumber but does have a ready buyer for the finished house. The builder therefore gives you a *promissory note,* stating that you will be paid within 90 days.) Notes Receivable is generally placed ahead of Accounts Receivable, because promissory notes are considered to be more liquid than Accounts Receivable. (*Reason:* The holder of the note can raise more cash by borrowing from a bank, pledging the notes as security for the loan.) Supplies and Prepaid Insurance are considered to be prepaid items that will be used up or expire within the following operating cycle or year. That's why they appear at the bottom of the Current Assets section. (There is no particular reason to list Supplies before Prepaid Insurance. Prepaid Insurance could just as easily have preceded Supplies.)

Plant and Equipment

Plant and equipment are relatively long-lived assets that are held for use in the production or sale of other assets or services; some accountants refer to them as *fixed assets.* The three types of accounts that usually appear in this category are equipment, buildings, and land (refer to Figure 15-4 once again). Note that the Equipment and Building accounts are followed by their respective Accumulated Depreciation accounts. (Remember how we spoke of Accumulated Depreciations as being deductions from assets?) Plant and equipment are sometimes listed in the order of their length of life, with the shortest-lived asset (equipment) recorded first. A firm that owns delivery equipment, for example, lists it first, because of its relatively short life. In other words, plant and equipment go in order from the least fixed to the most fixed; land is placed last in this category.

Current Liabilities

Current liabilities are debts that will become due within the normal operating cycle of the business, usually within one year; they will normally be paid, when due, from current assets. List current liabilities in the order of their expected payment. Notes Payable (current) generally precedes Accounts Payable, just as Notes Receivable precedes Accounts Receivable. The Mortgage Payable (current portion), which may precede Accounts Payable, is the payment one makes to reduce the principal of the mortgage in a given year. Wages Payable and any other accrued liabilities, such as Commissions Payable and the current portion of unearned revenue accounts, usually fall at the bottom of the list of current liabilities.

Long-term Liabilities

Long-term liabilities are debts that are payable over a comparatively long period, usually more than one year. Ordinarily Mortgage Payable is the only account in this category for a sole-proprietorship (or one-owner) type of business. One single amount in a category can be recorded in the column on the extreme right.

Working Capital and Current Ratio

Both the management and the short-term creditors of a firm are vitally interested in two questions.

1. Does the firm have a sufficient amount of capital to operate?
2. Does the firm have the ability to pay its debts?

Two measures used to answer these questions are a firm's working capital and its current ratio, and the necessary data is taken from a classified balance sheet.

Working capital is determined by subtracting current liabilities from current assets, thus

Objective 3

Compute working capital and current ratio.

Working capital = Current assets − Current liabilities

The normal operating cycle for most firms is one year. Because current assets equal cash—or items that can be converted into cash or used up within one year—and current liabilities equal the total amount that the company must pay out within one year, "working capital" is appropriately named. It is the amount of capital the company has available to use or work with. The working capital for C. L. Frederickson Plumbing Supply is as follows.

Working capital = $115,134 − $42,920 = $72,214

A firm's ability to pay its debts is revealed by the firm's **current ratio.** The current ratio is determined by dividing current assets by current liabilities.

$$\text{Current ratio} = \frac{\text{Current assets (amount coming in within one year)}}{\text{Current liabilities (amount going out within one year)}}$$

The current ratio for C. L. Frederickson Plumbing Supply is calculated like this:

$$\text{Current ratio} = \frac{\$115,134}{\$42,920} = 2.68:1$$

$$42,920\overline{)115,134.00}^{2.68}$$

In the case of C. L. Frederickson Plumbing Supply, $2.68 is available to pay every dollar currently due on December 31.

When banks are considering granting loans to merchandising firms, a minimum current ratio of 2:1 is generally required.

Chart of Accounts

In Chapter 4, when we introduced the chart of accounts and the account-number arrangement, we said that the first digit represents the classification of the accounts. A common organization is:

Assets	1__
Liabilities	2__
Owner's Equity	3__
Revenue	4__
Expenses	5__

The second digit stands for the subclassification.

Assets	1__
Current Assets	11_
Plant and Equipment	12_
Liabilities	2__
Current Liabilities	21_
Long-term Liabilities	22_
Owner's Equity	3__
Capital	31_
Revenue	4__
Revenue from Sales	41_
Other income	42_
Expenses	5__
Cost of Merchandise Sold	51_
Selling Expenses	52_
General Expenses	53_
Other Expenses	54_

	ACCOUNT NAME	TRIAL BALANCE DEBIT	TRIAL BALANCE CREDIT	INCOME STATEMENT DEBIT	INCOME STATEMENT CREDIT	
1	Cash	21 9 2 2 00				1
2	Notes Receivable	4 0 0 0 00				2
3	Accounts Receivable	29 3 6 0 00				3
4	Merchandise Inventory	63 0 0 0 00				4
5	Supplies	1 4 4 0 00				5
6	Prepaid Insurance	9 6 0 00				6
7	Equipment	33 6 0 0 00				7
8	Accum. Depreciation, Equipment		16 4 0 0 00			8
9	Building	100 0 0 0 00				9
10	Accum. Depreciation, Building		32 0 0 0 00			10
11	Land	12 0 0 0 00				11
12	Notes Payable		3 0 0 0 00			12
13	Accounts Payable		36 4 0 0 00			13
14	Unearned Course Fees		9 0 0 00			14
15	Mortgage Payable		8 0 0 0 00			15
16	C. L. Frederickson, Capital		146 5 7 4 00			16
17	C. L. Frederickson, Drawing	19 2 0 0 00				17
18	Sales		176 1 8 0 00		176 1 8 0 00	18
19	Sales Returns and Allowances	8 4 0 00		8 4 0 00		19
20	Sales Discount	1 8 8 0 00		1 8 8 0 00		20
21	Interest Income		1 2 0 00		1 2 0 00	21
22	Purchases	85 6 0 0 00		85 6 0 0 00		22
23	Purchases Returns and Allowances		8 3 2 00		8 3 2 00	23
24	Purchases Discount		1 2 4 8 00		1 2 4 8 00	24
25	Wages Expense	45 8 0 0 00		47 0 2 0 00		25
26	Taxes Expense	1 9 6 0 00		1 9 6 0 00		26
27	Interest Expense	9 2 00		9 2 00		27
28		421 6 5 4 00	421 6 5 4 00			28
29	Income Summary			63 0 0 0 00	58 8 0 0 00	29
30	Course Fees Income				6 0 0 00	30
31	Supplies Expense			1 0 2 8 00		31
32	Insurance Expense			3 2 0 00		32
33	Depreciation Expense, Equipment			4 8 0 0 00		33
34	Depreciation Expense, Building			4 0 0 0 00		34
35	Wages Payable					35
36				210 5 4 0 00	237 7 8 0 00	36
37	Net Income			27 2 4 0 00		37
38				237 7 8 0 00	237 7 8 0 00	38
39						39

Figure 15-5

The third digit indicates the placement of the account within the subclassification. As an example, account number 411 represents Sales, which is the first account listed under revenue. Account number 312 represents Drawing, which is the second account listed under owner's equity.

CLOSING ENTRIES

In Chapter 6 we discussed closing entries for a service business; now let's look at closing entries for a merchandising business. The same methods apply to both. You follow the same four steps to balance off the revenue, expense, and Drawing accounts.

At the end of a fiscal period, you close the revenue and expense accounts so that you can start the next fiscal period with a clean slate. You also close the Drawing account, because it, too, applies to one fiscal period. As you recall from our discussion in Chapter 6, these accounts are called temporary-equity accounts.

You can speed up the preparation of closing entries by balancing off each figure in the Income Statement columns of the work sheet. Figure 15-5 shows the Income Statement columns. After you have looked them over, let's take up those four steps and see how we come out.

Four Steps in the Closing Procedure

To repeat, these four steps should be followed when closing:

1. Close the revenue accounts as well as the other accounts appearing in the income statement and having credit balances. (**Debit the figures that are credited in the Income Statement column of the work sheet, except the figure on the Income Summary line.**) This entry is illustrated in Figure 15-6.

Objective 4

Journalize the closing entries for a merchandising firm.

Figure 15-6

	DATE		DESCRIPTION	POST. REF.	DEBIT		CREDIT		
1			*Closing Entries*						1
2	19– Dec.	31	Sales		176 1 8 0 00				2
3			*Purchases Returns and Allowances*		8 3 2 00				3
4			*Purchases Discount*		1 2 4 8 00				4
5			*Course Fees Income*		6 0 0 00				5
6			*Interest Income*		1 2 0 00				6
7			*Income Summary*				178 9 8 0 00		7
8									8

GENERAL JOURNAL   PAGE _97_

Figure 15-7

	DATE		DESCRIPTION	POST. REF.	DEBIT	CREDIT	
1	Dec.	31	Income Summary		147 5 4 0 00		1
2			Sales Returns and Allowances			8 4 0 00	2
3			Sales Discount			1 8 8 0 00	3
4			Purchases			85 6 0 0 00	4
5			Wages Expense			47 0 2 0 00	5
6			Taxes Expense			1 9 6 0 00	6
7			Interest Expense			9 2 00	7
8			Supplies Expense			1 0 2 8 00	8
9			Insurance Expense			3 2 0 00	9
10			Depreciation Expense, Equipment			4 8 0 0 00	10
11			Depreciation Expense, Building			4 0 0 0 00	11
12							12

2. Close the expense accounts as well as the other accounts appearing in the income statement that have debit balances. (**Credit the figures that are debited in the Income Statement column of the work sheet, except the figure on the Income Summary line.** The entry appears in Figure 15-7.)

3. Close the Income Summary account into C. L. Frederickson, Capital. (**Debit Income Summary by the amount of the net income; credit it by the amount of a net loss.**)

	DATE		DESCRIPTION	POST. REF.	DEBIT	CREDIT	
1	Dec.	31	Income Summary		27 2 4 0 00		1
2			C. L. Frederickson, Capital			27 2 4 0 00	2
3							3

Income Summary

Adjusting 63,000 (Beginning Merchandise Inventory)	Adjusting 58,800 (Ending Merchandise Inventory)
(Expenses) 147,540	(Revenue) 178,980
Clos. (Net Inc.) 27,240	

C. L. Frederickson, Capital

−	+
	Balance 146,574
	(Net Inc.) 27,240

4. Close the Drawing account into the Capital account.

	DATE		DESCRIPTION	POST. REF.	DEBIT	CREDIT	
			GENERAL JOURNAL			PAGE 98	
1	Dec.	31	*C. L. Frederickson, Capital*		19 2 0 0 00		1
2			*C. L. Frederickson, Drawing*			19 2 0 0 00	2
3							3

C. L. Frederickson, Drawing

+		−	
Balance	19,200	Closing	19,200

C. L. Frederickson, Capital

−		+	
(Drawing)	19,200	Balance	146,574
		(Net Inc.)	27,240

Note that you close Purchases Discount and Purchases Returns and Allowances in step 1 along with the revenue accounts. Note also that in step 2 you close Sales Discount and Sales Returns and Allowances along with the expense accounts. Finally, bear in mind that the Income Summary account already contains adjusting entries for merchandise inventory.

REVERSING ENTRIES

Reversing entries are general journal entries that are the exact reverse of certain adjusting entries. A reversing entry enables the accountant to record routine transactions in the usual manner, *even though* an adjusting entry affecting one of the accounts involved in the transaction has intervened. We can see this concept best by looking at an example.

Suppose there's an adjusting entry for accrued wages owed to employees at the end of the fiscal year. (We talked about this in Chapter 5.) Assume that the employees of a certain firm are paid altogether $200 per day for a five-day week, and that payday occurs every Friday throughout the year. When the employees get their checks at 5:00 P.M. on Friday, the checks include their wages for that day as well as the preceding four days. And say that one year the last day of the fiscal period happens to fall on Wednesday, December 31. A diagram of this situation would look like this.

				Dec. 26	Dec. 29	Dec. 30	Dec. 31	Jan. 1	Jan. 2
Mon	Tue	Wed	Thur	Fri	Mon	Tue	Wed	Thur	Fri
200	200	200	200	200	200	200	200	200	200

←————————Payroll period————————×————————Payroll period————————→

	Payday $1,000		Accrued $600	Payday $1,000

Each Friday during the year, the payroll has been debited to the Wages Expense account and credited to the Cash account. As a result, Wages Expense has a debit balance of $51,400. Here is the adjusting entry in T account form.

Wages Expense			Wages Payable	
+	−		−	+
Bal. 51,400				Dec. 31 Adj. 600
Dec. 31 Adj. 600				

As part of the closing process, the accountant clears the Wages Expense account, which yields a zero balance. However, the Wages Payable account continues to have a credit balance. In this case, there is only one way out. The $1,000 payroll on January 2 must be recorded as a debit of $600 to Wages Payable, a debit of $400 to Wages Expense, and a credit of $1,000 to Cash. The employee who records the payroll not only has to record this particular payroll differently from all other weekly payrolls for the year, but also has to refer back to the adjusting entry to determine what portion of the $1,000 is debited to Wages Payable and what portion is debited to Wages Expense. In many companies, however, the employee who records the payroll does not have access to the adjusting entries.

There is a solution to this problem. The need to refer to the earlier entry and divide the debit total between the two accounts is eliminated *if a reversing entry is made on the first day of the following fiscal period.* One makes an entry that is the exact reverse of the adjusting entry, as follows.

			GENERAL JOURNAL					PAGE 118	
	DATE		DESCRIPTION	POST. REF.	DEBIT		CREDIT		
1			*Reversing Entries*						1
2	19– Jan.	1	*Wages Payable*		6 0 0 00				2
3			*Wages Expense*				6 0 0 00		3
4									4

Let us now bring the T accounts up to date.

Wages Expense				Wages Payable			
+		**−**		**−**		**+**	
Bal.	51,400	Dec. 31 Clos.	52,000	Jan. 1 Rev.	600	Dec. 31 Adj.	600
Dec. 31 Adj.	600						
		Jan. 1 Rev.	600				

The reversing entry has the effect of transferring the $600 liability from Wages Payable to the credit side of Wages Expense. Wages Expense will temporarily have a credit balance until the next payroll is recorded in the routine manner. In our example this occurs on January 2, for $1,000. Here are the T accounts.

Wages Expense				Wages Payable			
+		**−**		**−**		**+**	
Bal.	51,400	Dec. 31 Clos.	52,000	Jan. 1 Rev.	600	Dec. 31 Adj.	600
Dec. 31 Adj.	600						
Jan. 2	1,000	Jan. 1 Rev.	600				

There is now a *net debit balance* of $400 in Wages Expense. To see this, look at the following ledger accounts:

ACCOUNT __Wages Expense__   ACCOUNT NO. __514__

	DATE		ITEM	POST. REF.	DEBIT	CREDIT	BALANCE DEBIT	BALANCE CREDIT	
1	19– Dec.	26		CP16	1 0 0 0 00		51 4 0 0 00		1
2		31	Adjusting	J116	6 0 0 00		52 0 0 0 00		2
3		31	Closing	J117		52 0 0 0 00	— — — — —		3
4	19– Jan.	1	Reversing	J118		6 0 0 00		6 0 0 00	4
5		2		CP17	1 0 0 0 00		4 0 0 00		5
6									6

ACCOUNT __Wages Payable__   ACCOUNT NO. __213__

	DATE		ITEM	POST. REF.	DEBIT	CREDIT	BALANCE DEBIT	BALANCE CREDIT	
1	19– Dec.	31	Adjusting	J116		6 0 0 00		6 0 0 00	1
2	19– Jan.	1	Reversing	J118	6 0 0 00		— — — —	— — — —	2
3									3

The reversing entry for accrued salaries or wages applies to service companies as well as to merchandising ones. You can see that a reversing entry simply switches around an adjusting entry. The question is, Which adjusting entries should be reversed? Here's a handy rule of thumb that will help you decide.

If an adjusting entry increases an asset account or liability account that does not have a previous balance, then reverse the adjusting entry.

With the exception of the first year of operations, Merchandise Inventory and contra accounts—such as Accumulated Depreciation—always have previous balances. Consequently, adjusting entries involving these accounts should never be reversed.

Let's apply this rule to the adjusting entries for C. L. Frederickson Plumbing Supply.

Objective 5

Determine which adjusting entries should be reversed.

Income Summary		
Adj. 63,000	

Merchandise Inventory	
+	−
Bal. 63,000	Adj. 63,000

(Do not reverse; Merchandise Inventory is an asset, but it has a previous balance.)

Merchandise Inventory	
+	−
Bal. 63,000	Adj. 63,000
Adj. 58,800	

Income Summary	
Adj. 63,000	Adj. 58,800

(Do not reverse; Merchandise Inventory is an asset, but it has a previous balance.)

Course Fees Income	
−	+
	Adj. 600

Unearned Course Fees	
−	+
Adj. 600	Bal. 900

(Do not reverse; Unearned Course Fees is a liability, but it was decreased. Also, it had a previous balance.)

Supplies Expense	
+	−
Adj. 1,028	

Supplies	
+	−
Bal. 1,440	Adj. 1,028

(Do not reverse; Supplies is an asset account, but it was decreased. Also, it had a previous balance.)

Insurance Expense				Prepaid Insurance		
+		−		+		−
Adj.	320			Bal.	960	Adj. 320

(Do not reverse; Prepaid Insurance is an asset account, but it was decreased. Also, it had a previous balance.)

Depreciation Expense, Equipment				Accumulated Depreciation, Equipment		
+		−		−		+
Adj.	4,800					Bal. 16,400
						Adj. 4,800

(Do not reverse; Accumulated Depreciation is a contra asset, and it always has a previous balance after the first year.)

Depreciation Expense, Building				Accumulated Depreciation, Building		
+		−		−		+
Adj.	4,000					Bal. 32,000
						Adj. 4,000

(Do not reverse; Accumulated Depreciation is a contra asset, and it always has a previous balance after the first year.)

Wages Expense				Wages Payable		
+		−		−		+
Bal.	45,800					Adj. 1,220
Adj.	1,220					

(Reverse; Wages Payable is a liability account. It was increased and it had no previous balance.)

Whenever we introduce additional adjusting entries, we'll make it a point to state whether they should be reversed.

OTHER WAYS OF RECORDING ADJUSTING ENTRIES

Recording Prepaid Expenses Originally as Expenses

In order to enlarge your experience in bookkeeping practices, it should be mentioned that some accountants record certain prepaid expenses (items that will be eventually used up or expire) originally as expenses. Examples are payments for supplies and insurance. Look at the following examples.

On May 2, a firm bought $265 of supplies, paying cash.

Supplies Expense		Cash	
+	−	+	−
May 2 265			May 2 265

On July 1, paid $360 as a premium on liability insurance policy for thirty-six months.

Insurance Expense		Cash	
+	−	+	−
Jul. 1 360			Jul. 1 360

By December 31, the end of the fiscal period, $130 of supplies are left over, and $300 of insurance is unexpired. Consequently, the following adjusting entries are required.

Supplies Expense		Supplies	
+	−	+	−
May 2 265	Dec. 31 Adj. 130	Dec. 31 Adj. 130	

Insurance Expense		Prepaid Insurance	
+	−	+	−
Jul. 1 360	Dec. 31 Adj. 300	Dec. 31 Adj. 300	

Since these adjusting entries open up new balance sheet accounts, reversing entries are required. However, in this text, we will follow the policy of recording prepaid expenses originally as assets. In other words, record the buying of supplies as a debit to Supplies and then adjust for the amount of supplies used up. Also, record the purchase of insurance as a debit to Prepaid Insurance and then adjust for the amount of insurance expired.

Recording Unearned Revenue Originally as Revenue

Some accountants record unearned revenue (revenue received in advance) originally as revenue. Look at the following example.

An ice skating rink sold $14,320 of season tickets in advance.

Cash			Season Ticket Sales	
+	−		−	+
Sep. 30 14,320				Sep. 30 14,320

By December 31, the end of the fiscal period, $10,080 of the season ticket sales are unearned. Consequently, the adjusting entry is

Season Ticket Sales			Unearned Season Tickets	
−	+		−	+
Dec. 31 Adj. 10,080	Sep. 30 14,320			Dec. 31 Adj. 10,080

Since the adjusting entry opens up a new balance sheet account, a reversing entry is required. Nevertheless, we will follow the policy of recording unearned revenue as a liability. In other words, record the revenue received in advance as a credit to an unearned revenue account and then adjust for the amount earned.

GLOSSARY

Cost of Merchandise Sold Merchandise Inventory at beginning of fiscal period, plus net purchases, minus Merchandise Inventory at end of fiscal period. Terms often used to describe the same thing are *cost of goods sold* and *cost of sales*.

Merchandise Inventory (beginning)
Plus Net Purchases

Merchandise Available for Sale
Less Merchandise Inventory (ending)

Cost of Merchandise Sold

Current assets Cash and any other assets or resources that are expected to be realized in cash or sold or consumed during the normal operating cycle of the business (or one year if the normal operating cycle is less than twelve months).

Current liabilities Debts that are due within the normal operating cycle of a business, usually within one year, and that are normally paid from current assets.

Current ratio A firm's current assets divided by its current liabilities. Portrays a firm's short-term-debt-paying ability.

General expenses Expenses incurred in the administration of a business, including office expenses and any expenses that are not wholly classified as Selling Expenses or Other Expenses.

Gross profit Net Sales minus Cost of Merchandise Sold, or profit before deducting expenses.

Net Sales
Less Cost of Merchandise Sold

Gross Profit

Liquidity The ability of an asset to be quickly turned into cash, either by selling it or by putting it up as security for a loan.

Long-term liabilities Debts that you don't have to pay right away; they can be paid over a comparatively long period, usually more than one year.

Net income The final figure on an income statement after all expenses have been deducted from revenues. Also called *net profit*.

Net purchases Total purchases minus both Purchases Returns and Allowances and Purchases Discount.

Purchases
Less Purchases Returns and Allowances
Less Purchases Discount

Net Purchases

Net sales Sales, minus Sales Returns and Allowances and minus Sales Discount.

Sales
Less Sales Returns and Allowances
Less Sales Discount

Net Sales

Notes receivable (current) Written promises to pay received from customers and due in a period of less than one year.

Plant and equipment Long-lived assets that are held for use in the production or sale of other assets or services. They may also be called *fixed assets*.

Reversing entries The reverse of certain adjusting entries, recorded as of the first day of the following fiscal year.

Selling expenses Expenses directly related to the sale of merchandise, such as salaries of sales staff, advertising expenses, and delivery expenses.

Temporary-equity accounts Accounts whose balances apply to one fiscal period only, such as revenues, expenses, and the Drawing account. Temporary-equity accounts are also called *nominal accounts*.

Working capital The excess of a firm's current assets over its current liabilities. Portrays the amount of capital a firm has to work with during a normal operating cycle.

QUESTIONS, EXERCISES, AND PROBLEMS

Discussion Questions

1. In the closing procedure, what happens to Purchases Discount?
2. What is the difference between current liabilities and long-term liabilities? Give an example of each.
3. In this chapter, the Adjusted Trial Balance columns of a work sheet have been omitted. Does this affect the use of the work sheet? Explain.
4. Describe how to calculate the cost of merchandise sold.
5. What is the correct order for listing accounts in the Current Assets section of the balance sheet?
6. What is the correct order for listing accounts in the Plant and Equipment section of a balance sheet?
7. What rule is used to recognize whether or not an adjusting entry should be reversed?

Exercises

Exercise 15-1 Identify each of the following as (1) a current asset, (2) plant and equipment, (3) a current liability, (4) a long-term liability, (5) an owner's equity item.

a. Land
b. Wages Payable
c. Mortgage Payable (due June 30, 1994)
d. Store Equipment
e. Notes Payable (current)
f. Accounts Receivable
g. Building
h. Darlene Foss, Capital
i. Cash
j. Mortgage Payable (current portion)

Exercise 15-2 Organize the following as they appear in the Cost of Merchandise Sold section of an income statement. Determine the cost of merchandise sold.

Purchases Returns and Allowances	$ 4,000
Ending Merchandise Inventory	63,000
Purchases Discount	3,000
Purchases	190,000
Beginning Merchandise Inventory	60,000

Exercise 15-3 On June 30, the following selected accounts and amounts appeared in the balance sheet. Determine the amount of the working capital and the current ratio.

Accounts Payable	$ 8,000	Wages Payable	$ 4,000
Store Supplies	900	Merchandise Inventory	46,000
Henry Drew, Capital	52,000	Notes Payable	10,000
Store Equipment	16,000	Accumulated Depreciation,	
Prepaid Insurance	600	Store Equipment	12,000
Cash	3,000		

Exercise 15-4 From the following T accounts, record the closing entries.

Sales	
	100,000

Salary Expense	
16,000	

Sales Returns and Allowances	
2,000	

Rent Expense	
6,000	

Purchases	
60,000	

Miscellaneous Expense	
6,300	

Purchases Returns and Allowances	
	1,500

J. Cole, Drawing	
16,000	

Purchases Discount	
	1,800

J. Cole, Capital	
	87,000

Income Summary	
22,000	26,000

Exercise 15-5 Calculate the missing items in the following.

	Sales	Sales Returns and Allowances	Net Sales	Beginning Inventory	Net Purchases	Merchandise Available	Ending Inventory	Cost of Merchandise Sold	Gross Profit
a	$62,000	$1,500		$37,000	$42,500	$ 79,500	$34,000	$45,500	
b	76,000		$ 74,000	36,000	65,000		49,000	52,000	
c		3,000	157,000	21,000		124,000	23,000		$56,000

Exercise 15-6 From the following information, present a statement of owner's equity.

D. C. Collier, Capital	
16,500	Bal. 60,000
	18,000

D. C. Collier, Drawing	
Bal. 16,500	Closing 16,500

Income Summary	
Adj. 48,000	Adj. 51,000
105,000	120,000
Closing 18,000	

Exercise 15-7 Arrange the following accounts as they would appear in the Current Assets section of the balance sheet.

Supplies	$ 410	Prepaid Insurance	$ 360
Accounts Receivable	18,000	Notes Receivable (current)	2,400
Merchandise Inventory	36,000	Prepaid Advertising	220
Cash	6,900		

Exercise 15-8 The Income Statement columns of the December 31 (year end) work sheet for the Conroy Company appear below. From the information given, prepare an income statement for the company.

ACCOUNT NAME	INCOME STATEMENT	
	DEBIT	CREDIT
Income Summary	26 0 0 0 00	22 0 0 0 00
Sales		284 0 0 0 00
Sales Returns and Allowances	11 0 0 0 00	
Sales Discount	4 2 0 0 00	
Purchases	122 9 0 0 00	
Purchases Returns and Allowances		1 8 0 0 00
Purchases Discount		2 2 0 0 00
Selling Expenses	48 5 0 0 00	
General Expenses	37 2 0 0 00	
	249 8 0 0 00	310 0 0 0 00
Net Income	60 2 0 0 00	
	310 0 0 0 00	310 0 0 0 00

Problem Set A

Problem 15-1A A partial work sheet for Sinclair Craft and Hobby Shop is presented below. The merchandise inventory at the beginning of the fiscal period is $24,792. C. A. Sinclair, the owner, withdrew $16,400 during the year.

Sinclair Craft and Hobby Shop
Work Sheet
For year ended December 31, 19–

ACCOUNT NAME	INCOME STATEMENT DEBIT	INCOME STATEMENT CREDIT
Sales		163 2 9 6 40
Sales Returns and Allowances	2 6 1 4 60	
Sales Discount	9 5 4 00	
Interest Income		1 6 2 49
Purchases	104 7 2 8 00	
Purchases Returns and Allowances		8 2 8 00
Wages Expense	19 7 6 2 00	
Rent Expense	4 6 8 0 00	
Commissions Expense	4 7 2 0 00	
Interest Expense	3 2 8 16	
Income Summary	24 7 9 2 00	21 9 8 6 00
Supplies Expense	3 1 8 60	
Insurance Expense	4 6 8 00	
Depreciation Expense, Equipment	1 6 7 0 00	
Depreciation Expense, Building	2 4 0 0 00	
	167 4 3 5 36	186 2 7 2 89
Net Income	18 8 3 7 53	
	186 2 7 2 89	186 2 7 2 89

Instructions

1. Prepare an income statement.
2. Journalize the closing entries.

Problem 15-2A   The following partial work sheet is for Randolph Fine Shoes.

Randolph Fine Shoes
Work Sheet
For year ended December 31, 19–

ACCOUNT NAME	BALANCE SHEET DEBIT	BALANCE SHEET CREDIT
Cash	6 4 8 2 00	
Notes Receivable	2 4 0 0 00	
Accounts Receivable	28 5 8 6 40	
Merchandise Inventory	37 7 9 8 00	
Supplies	3 1 6 00	
Prepaid Taxes	4 0 9 00	
Prepaid Insurance	4 2 0 00	
Delivery Equipment	3 7 1 0 00	
Accumulated Depreciation, Delivery Equipment		2 8 7 0 00
Store Equipment	4 3 8 0 00	
Accumulated Depreciation, Store Equipment		3 3 3 0 00
Office Equipment	3 6 1 6 00	
Accumulated Depreciation, Office Equipment		2 7 8 0 00
Building	42 0 0 0 00	
Accumulated Depreciation, Building		14 4 0 0 00
Land	5 6 0 0 00	
Notes Payable		3 6 2 0 00
Accounts Payable		19 7 2 7 80
Mortgage Payable (current portion)		1 8 0 0 00
Mortgage Payable		37 1 4 2 00
L. P. Randolph, Capital		43 3 7 2 60
L. P. Randolph, Drawing	16 7 9 6 00	
Wages Payable		8 5 2 00
	152 5 1 3 40	129 8 9 4 40
Net Income		22 6 1 9 00
	152 5 1 3 40	152 5 1 3 40

Instructions

1. Prepare a statement of owner's equity (no additional investment).
2. Prepare a balance sheet.
3. Determine the amount of working capital.
4. Determine the current ratio (carry to one decimal place).

Problem 15-3A The following partial work sheet covers the affairs of Padrow and Company for the year ended June 30.

Padrow and Company
Work Sheet
For year ended June 30, 19–

	ACCOUNT NAME	INCOME STATEMENT DEBIT	INCOME STATEMENT CREDIT	BALANCE SHEET DEBIT	BALANCE SHEET CREDIT	
1	Cash			16 1 9 2 17		1
2	Accounts Receivable			52 3 1 7 27		2
3	Merchandise Inventory			59 7 2 8 00		3
4	Supplies			5 1 6 00		4
5	Prepaid Insurance			6 6 0 00		5
6	Delivery Equipment			6 4 6 0 00		6
7	Accumulated Depreciation, Delivery					7
8	Equipment				3 2 4 0 00	8
9	Store Equipment			18 2 5 0 00		9
10	Accumulated Depreciation, Store					10
11	Equipment				5 1 8 0 00	11
12	Accounts Payable				33 7 1 8 67	12
13	Salaries Payable				4 2 6 00	13
14	T. L. Padrow, Capital				99 9 6 1 29	14
15	T. L. Padrow, Drawing			20 7 2 0 72		15
16	Income Summary	57 6 1 3 00	59 7 2 8 00			16
17	Sales		268 1 7 6 20			17
18	Purchases	208 6 4 0 00				18
19	Purchases Returns and Allowances		3 9 1 4 00			19
20	Purchases Discount		2 8 7 3 00			20
21	Salary Expense	25 7 0 0 00				21
22	Truck Expense	4 6 7 1 00				22
23	Supplies Expense	1 2 8 2 00				23
24	Depreciation Expense, Delivery					24
25	Equipment	1 3 5 0 00				25
26	Depreciation Expense, Store					26
27	Equipment	1 4 4 8 00				27
28	Insurance Expense	9 6 0 00				28
29	Miscellaneous Expense	7 0 9 00				29
30		302 3 7 3 00	334 6 9 1 20	174 8 4 4 16	142 5 2 5 96	30
31	Net Income	32 3 1 8 20			32 3 1 8 20	31
32		334 6 9 1 20	334 6 9 1 20	174 8 4 4 16	174 8 4 4 16	32
33						33
34						34
35						35
36						36
37						37
38						38

Instructions

1. Journalize the adjusting entries.
2. Journalize the closing entries.
3. Journalize the reversing entry.

Problem 15-4A The following accounts appear in the ledger of the Andrezi Company as of December 31, the end of this fiscal year.

Cash	$ 2,900	Sales	$148,420
Accounts Receivable	9,940	Sales Returns and Allowances	1,760
Merchandise Inventory	34,320	Purchases	97,540
Store Supplies	490	Purchases Returns and	
Prepaid Insurance	650	Allowances	2,930
Store Equipment	19,760	Purchases Discount	1,710
Accumulated Depreciation,		Wages Expense	15,400
Store Equipment	1,920	Advertising Expense	2,100
Accounts Payable	6,990	Depreciation Expense,	
Wages Payable	—	Store Equipment	—
P. A. Andrezi, Capital	48,130	Store Supplies Expense	—
P. A. Andrezi, Drawing	18,840	Rent Expense	6,400
Income Summary	—	Insurance Expense	—

The data needed for adjustments on December 31 are as follows.

a–b. Merchandise inventory, December 31, $32,160
   c. Store supplies inventory, December 31, $180
   d. Insurance expired for the year, $420
   e. Depreciation for the year, $860
   f. Accrued wages on December 31, $110

Instructions

1. Prepare a work sheet for the fiscal year ended December 31.
2. Prepare an income statement.
3. Prepare a statement of owner's equity.
4. Prepare a balance sheet.
5. Journalize the adjusting entries.
6. Journalize the closing entries.
7. Journalize the reversing entry.

PROBLEM SET B

Problem 15-1B A partial work sheet for Sturgis Garden Shop is presented below. The merchandise inventory at the beginning of the fiscal period is $26,600. R. E. Sturgis, the owner, withdrew $12,200 during the year.

Sturgis Garden Shop
Work Sheet
For year ended December 31, 19–

ACCOUNT NAME	INCOME STATEMENT DEBIT	INCOME STATEMENT CREDIT
Sales		164 0 0 0 00
Sales Returns and Allowances	2 2 4 0 00	
Sales Discount	1 8 5 4 00	
Interest Income		9 2 0 00
Purchases	106 1 2 0 00	
Purchases Returns and Allowances		1 4 9 0 00
Wages Expense	21 6 0 0 00	
Rent Expense	4 8 0 0 00	
Commissions Expense	5 1 6 0 00	
Interest Expense	4 8 2 00	
Income Summary	26 6 0 0 00	22 1 8 0 00
Supplies Expense	4 1 6 00	
Insurance Expense	5 2 0 00	
Depreciation Expense, Equipment	1 8 0 0 00	
Depreciation Expense, Building	2 4 0 0 00	
	173 9 9 2 00	188 5 9 0 00
Net Income	14 5 9 8 00	
	188 5 9 0 00	188 5 9 0 00

Instructions

1. Prepare an income statement.
2. Journalize the closing entries.

Problem 15-2B A partial work sheet for Heinrich Garden Supply appears below.

Heinrich Garden Supply
Work Sheet
For year ended December 31, 19–

| | BALANCE SHEET | |
ACCOUNT NAME	DEBIT	CREDIT
Cash	8 6 1 0 00	
Notes Receivable	4 2 0 0 00	
Accounts Receivable	22 1 8 0 00	
Merchandise Inventory	36 8 9 6 00	
Supplies	2 8 0 00	
Prepaid Taxes	4 2 0 00	
Prepaid Insurance	3 6 0 00	
Delivery Equipment	3 6 0 0 00	
Accumulated Depreciation, Delivery Equipment		2 9 8 0 00
Testing Equipment	4 8 2 0 00	
Accumulated Depreciation, Testing Equipment		3 6 1 6 00
Store Equipment	2 9 2 8 00	
Accumulated Depreciation, Store Equipment		1 1 1 6 00
Building	40 0 0 0 00	
Accumulated Depreciation, Building		12 6 0 0 00
Land	5 2 0 0 00	
Notes Payable		2 8 1 0 00
Accounts Payable		18 7 6 0 00
Mortgage Payable (current portion)		1 2 0 0 00
Mortgage Payable		36 8 0 0 00
D. L. Heinrich, Capital		44 8 7 6 00
D. L. Heinrich, Drawing	14 9 6 0 00	
Wages Payable		6 5 6 00
	144 4 5 4 00	125 4 1 4 00
Net Income		19 0 4 0 00
	144 4 5 4 00	144 4 5 4 00

Instructions

1. Prepare a statement of owner's equity (no additional investment).
2. Prepare a balance sheet.
3. Determine the amount of working capital.
4. Determine the current ratio (carry to one decimal place).

Problem 15-3B The partial work sheet for Ralston and Company for the year ended June 30 is as follows.

Ralston and Company
Work Sheet
For year ended June 30, 19–

	ACCOUNT NAME	INCOME STATEMENT DEBIT	INCOME STATEMENT CREDIT	BALANCE SHEET DEBIT	BALANCE SHEET CREDIT	
1	Cash			14 1 0 0 00		1
2	Accounts Receivable			46 0 0 0 00		2
3	Merchandise Inventory			56 2 0 0 00		3
4	Supplies			4 2 0 00		4
5	Prepaid Insurance			6 1 0 00		5
6	Delivery Equipment			6 2 0 0 00		6
7	Accumulated Depreciation, Delivery					7
8	Equipment				2 9 0 0 00	8
9	Store Equipment			16 7 0 0 00		9
10	Accumulated Depreciation, Store					10
11	Equipment				4 8 0 0 00	11
12	Accounts Payable				30 1 0 0 00	12
13	Salaries Payable				6 2 0 00	13
14	M. A. Ralston, Capital				83 9 1 0 00	14
15	M. A. Ralston, Drawing			14 0 0 0 00		15
16	Income Summary	54 6 0 0 00	56 2 0 0 00			16
17	Sales		260 0 0 0 00			17
18	Purchases	202 0 0 0 00				18
19	Purchases Returns and Allowances		3 8 0 0 00			19
20	Purchases Discount		2 4 0 0 00			20
21	Salary Expense	24 0 0 0 00				21
22	Truck Expense	4 3 0 0 00				22
23	Supplies Expense	1 1 0 0 00				23
24	Depreciation Expense, Delivery					24
25	Equipment	1 2 0 0 00				25
26	Depreciation Expense, Store					26
27	Equipment	1 4 0 0 00				27
28	Insurance Expense	9 2 0 00				28
29	Miscellaneous Expense	9 8 0 00				29
30		290 5 0 0 00	322 4 0 0 00	154 2 3 0 00	122 3 3 0 00	30
31	Net Income	31 9 0 0 00			31 9 0 0 00	31
32		322 4 0 0 00	322 4 0 0 00	154 2 3 0 00	154 2 3 0 00	32
33						33

Instructions

1. Journalize the seven adjusting entries.
2. Journalize the closing entries.
3. Journalize the reversing entry.

Problem 15-4B The following accounts appear in the ledger of the Simmons Company on December 31, the end of this fiscal year.

Cash	$ 3,600	Sales	$156,000
Accounts Receivable	9,400	Sales Returns and Allowances	2,000
Merchandise Inventory	37,000	Purchases	98,000
Store Supplies	460	Purchases Returns	
Prepaid Insurance	720	and Allowances	2,300
Store Equipment	18,600	Purchases Discount	1,600
Accumulated Depreciation,		Wages Expense	16,000
Store Equipment	1,800	Advertising Expense	2,600
Accounts Payable	7,200	Depreciation Expense,	
Wages Payable	—	Store Equipment	—
C. R. Simmons, Capital	49,080	Store Supplies Expense	—
C. R. Simmons, Drawing	24,000	Rent Expense	5,600
Income Summary	—	Insurance Expense	—

The data needed for adjustments on December 31 are as follows.

a–b. Merchandise inventory, December 31, $35,600
   c. Store supplies inventory, December 31, $260
   d. Insurance expired, $410
   e. Depreciation for the year, $930
   f. Accrued wages on December 31, $180

Instructions

1. Prepare a work sheet for the fiscal year ended December 31.
2. Prepare an income statement.
3. Prepare a statement of owner's equity.
4. Prepare a balance sheet.
5. Journalize the adjusting entries.
6. Journalize the closing entries.
7. Journalize the reversing entry.

APPENDIX C

Financial Statement Analysis

An important function of accounting is to provide tools for interpreting the financial statements or the results of operations. This appendix presents a number of percentages and ratios that are frequently used for analyzing financial statements.

Midwest Clothiers will serve as our example (see comparative income statement at top of next page).

For each year, net sales is the base (100 percent). Every other item on the income statement can be expressed as a percentage of net sales for the particular year involved. For example, let's look at the following percentages:

Midwest Clothiers
Comparative Income Statement
For years ended January 31, 19x6 and January 31, 19x5

	19x6		19x5	
	AMOUNT	PERCENT	AMOUNT	PERCENT
Revenue from Sales:				
Sales	$ 453 6 0 0 00	106	$ 420 0 0 0 00	105
Less Sales Returns and Allowances	25 6 0 0 00	6	20 0 0 0 00	5
Net Sales	$ 428 0 0 0 00	100	$ 400 0 0 0 00	100
Cost of Merchandise Sold:				
Merchandise Inventory, February 1	$ 116 0 0 0 00	27	$ 64 0 0 0 00	16
Purchases (net)	320 0 0 0 00	75	300 0 0 0 00	75
Merchandise Available for Sale	$ 436 0 0 0 00	102	$ 364 0 0 0 00	91
Less Merchandise Inventory,				
January 31	158 0 0 0 00	37	116 0 0 0 00	29
Cost of Merchandise Sold	$ 278 0 0 0 00	65	$ 248 0 0 0 00	62
Gross Profit	$ 150 0 0 0 00	35	$ 152 0 0 0 00	38
Operating Expenses:				
Sales Salary Expense	$ 63 6 0 0 00	14.86	$ 58 0 0 0 00	14.5
Rent Expense	24 0 0 0 00	5.61	24 0 0 0 00	6
Advertising Expense	21 4 0 0 00	5	16 0 0 0 00	4
Office Salary Expense	20 0 0 0 00	4.61	18 0 0 0 00	4.5
Insurance Expense	2 0 0 0 00	.46	2 0 0 0 00	.5
Store Supplies Expense	1 0 0 0 00	.23	1 0 0 0 00	.25
Miscellaneous Expense	1 0 0 0 00	.23	1 0 0 0 00	.25
Total Operating Expenses	$ 133 0 0 0 00	31	$ 120 0 0 0 00	30
Net Income	$ 17 0 0 0 00	4	$ 32 0 0 0 00	8

$$\text{Gross profit \% (19x6)} = \frac{\text{Gross profit for 19x6}}{\text{Net sales for 19x6}} = \frac{\$150{,}000}{\$428{,}000} = .35 = 35\%$$

$$\text{Gross profit \% (19x5)} = \frac{\text{Gross profit for 19x5}}{\text{Net sales for 19x5}} = \frac{\$152{,}000}{\$400{,}000} = .38 = 38\%$$

$$\text{Sales salary expense (19x6)} = \frac{\text{Sales salary expense for 19x6}}{\text{Net sales for 19x6}}$$

$$= \frac{\$63{,}600}{\$428{,}000} = .1486 = 14.86\%$$

$$\text{Sales salary expense (19x5)} = \frac{\text{Sales salary expense for 19x5}}{\text{Net sales for 19x6}}$$

$$= \frac{\$58{,}000}{\$400{,}000} = .145 = 14.5\%$$

Here's how one might interpret a few of the percentages.

19x6

- For every $100 in net sales, gross profit amounted to $35.
- For every $100 in net sales, sales salary expense amounted to $14.86.
- For every $100 in net sales, net income amounted to $4.

19x5

- For every $100 in net sales, gross profit amounted to $38.
- For every $100 in net sales, sales salary expense amounted to $14.50.
- For every $100 in net sales, net income amounted to $8.

Merchandise Inventory Turnover

Merchandise inventory turnover is the number of times a firm's average inventory is sold during a given year.

$$\text{Merchandise inventory turnover} = \frac{\text{Cost of merchandise sold}}{\text{Average merchandise inventory}}$$

Average merchandise inventory

$$= \frac{\text{Beginning merchandise inventory} + \text{Ending merchandise inventory}}{2}$$

19x6

$$\text{Average merchandise inventory} = \frac{\$116,000 + \$158,000}{2}$$

$$= \frac{\$274,000}{2} = \$137,000$$

$$\text{Merchandise inventory turnover} = \frac{\$278,000}{\$137,000} = 2.03 \text{ times per year}$$

19x5

$$\text{Average merchandise inventory} = \frac{\$64,000 + \$116,000}{2}$$

$$= \frac{\$180,000}{2} = \$90,000$$

$$\text{Merchandise inventory turnover} = \frac{\$248,000}{\$90,000} = 2.76 \text{ times per year}$$

With each turnover of merchandise, the company makes a gross profit; so the higher the turnover the better.

Accounts Receivable Turnover

Accounts receivable turnover is the number of times charge accounts are turned over (paid off) during a given year. A turnover implies a sales on account followed by payment of the debt.

Accounts receivable turnover $= \dfrac{\text{Net sales on account}}{\text{Average accounts receivable}}$

Average accounts receivable

$= \dfrac{\text{Beginning accounts receivable} + \text{Ending accounts receivable}}{2}$

Going back to Midwest Clothiers, let's assume the following information for 19x6 and 19x5:

	19x6	19x5
Net sales on account (from the sales journal)	$330,000	$302,000
Beginning accounts receivable (from Accounts Receivable account)	$39,680	$37,500
Ending accounts receivable (from Accounts Receivable account)	$45,840	$39,680

19x6

Average accounts receivable $= \dfrac{\$39{,}680 + \$45{,}840}{2} = \dfrac{\$85{,}520}{2} = \$42{,}760$

Accounts receivable turnover $= \dfrac{\$330{,}000}{\$42{,}760} = 7.72$ times per year

19x5

Average accounts receivable $= \dfrac{\$37{,}500 + \$39{,}680}{2} = \dfrac{\$77{,}180}{2} = \$38{,}590$

Accounts receivable turnover $= \dfrac{\$302{,}000}{\$38{,}590} = 7.83$ times per year

A lower turnover rate indicates greater difficulty in collecting charge accounts. In addition, more investment capital is tied up in accounts receivable.

Return on Investment (Yield)

Return on investment represents the earning power of the owner's investment in the business.

Return on investment $= \dfrac{\text{Net income for the year}}{\text{Average capital}}$

Average capital $= \dfrac{\text{Beginning capital} + \text{Ending capital}}{2}$

Getting back to Midwest Clothiers, let's assume the following information for 19x6 and 19x5:

	19x6	19x5
Beginning balance of owner's Capital account	$176,920	$181,440
Ending balance of owner's Capital account	$184,780	$176,920

19x6

$$\text{Average capital} = \frac{\$176,920 + \$184,780}{2} = \frac{\$361,700}{2} = \$180,850$$

$$\text{Return on investment} = \frac{\$17,000}{\$180,850} = .094 = 9.4\%$$

19x5

$$\text{Average capital} = \frac{\$181,440 + \$176,920}{2} = \frac{\$358,360}{2} = \$179,180$$

$$\text{Return on investment} = \frac{\$32,000}{\$179,180} = .179 = 17.9\%$$

As a result, we can state the following:

- In 19x6, for an average investment of $100, the business earned $9.40.
- In 19x5, for an average investment of $100, the business earned $17.90.

Problems

Problem C-1 Grabo Company's abbreviated comparative income statement for years 19x6 and 19x5 is as follows.

Grabo Company
Comparative Income Statement
For years ended December 31, 19x6, and December 31, 19x5

	19x6	19x5
Net Sales	$ 232 0 0 0 00	$ 220 0 0 0 00
Cost of Merchandise Sold	136 8 8 0 00	132 0 0 0 00
Gross Profit	$ 95 1 2 0 00	$ 88 0 0 0 00
Total Operating Expenses	69 6 0 0 00	61 6 0 0 00
Net Income	$ 25 5 2 0 00	$ 26 4 0 0 00

Instructions

a. For the years 19x6 and 19x5, determine gross profit as a percentage of sales.
b. For the years 19x6 and 19x5, determine net income as a percentage of sales.

Problem C-2 Grabo Company's merchandise inventory figures are:

	19x6	19x5
Beginning merchandise inventory (January 1)	$31,580	$37,894
Ending merchandise inventory (December 31)	$36,860	$31,580

Determine the merchandise inventory turnover for the years 19x6 and 19x5.

Problem C-3 N. C. Grabo, Capital account balances are as follows.

January 1, 19x5	$134,168
January 1, 19x6	$176,420
December 31, 19x6	$188,152

Determine the return on capital for the years 19x6 and 19x5.

REVIEW OF T-ACCOUNT PLACEMENT
AND REPRESENTATIVE TRANSACTIONS
CHAPTERS 11–15

Review of T-Account Placement

The following sums up the placement of T accounts covered in Chapters 11 through 15 in relation to the fundamental accounting equation. Color indicates those accounts that are treated as deductions from the related accounts above them.

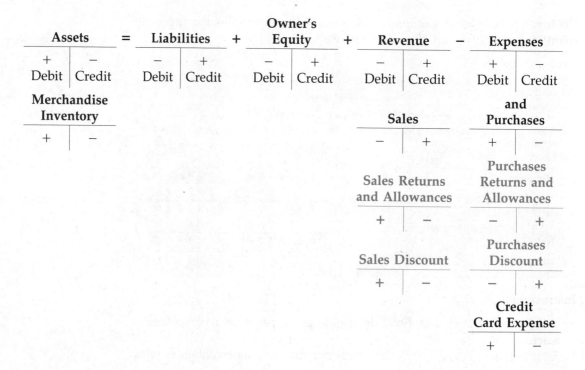

Review of Representative Transactions

The following table summarizes the recording of transactions covered in Chapters 11 through 15, along with a classification of the accounts involved.

Transaction	Accounts Involved	Class.	Increase or Decrease	Therefore Debit or Credit	Financial Statement
Sold merchandise on account	Accounts Receivable Sales	CA S	I I	Debit Credit	Bal. Sheet Inc. State.
Sold merchandise on account involving sales tax	Accounts Receivable Sales Sales Tax Payable	CA S CL	I I I	Debit Credit Credit	Bal. Sheet Inc. State. Bal. Sheet
Issued credit memo to customer for merchandise returned	Sales Returns and Allowances Accounts Receivable	S CA	I D	Debit Credit	Inc. State. Bal. Sheet
Summarizing entry for the total of sales invoices for sales on account for the month	Accounts Receivable Sales	CA S	I I	Debit Credit	Bal. Sheet Inc. State.
Bought merchandise on account	Purchases Accounts Payable	CMS CL	I I	Debit Credit	Inc. State. Bal. Sheet
Received credit memo from supplier for merchandise returned	Accounts Payable Purchases Returns and Allowances	CL CMS	D I	Debit Credit	Bal. Sheet Inc. State.
Summarizing entry for the total of purchases of all types of goods on account	Purchases Store Supplies Office Supplies Store Equipment Accounts Payable	CMS CA CA P&E CL	I I I I I	Debit Debit Debit Debit Credit	Inc. State. Bal. Sheet Bal. Sheet Bal. Sheet Bal. Sheet
Paid for transportation charges on incoming merchandise	Purchases Cash	CMS CA	I D	Debit Credit	Inc. State. Bal. Sheet

Transaction	Accounts Involved	Class.	Increase or Decrease	Therefore Debit or Credit	Financial Statement

Sold merchandise, involving sales tax, for cash	Cash
	  Sales
	  Sales Tax Payable
		CA
		S
		CL
			I
			I
			I
				Debit
				Credit
				Credit
					Bal. Sheet
					Inc. State.
					Bal. Sheet

Sold merchandise involving a sales tax and the customer used a bank charge card	Cash
	Credit Card Expense
	  Sales
	  Sales Tax Payable
		CA
		SE
		S
		CL
			I
			I
			I
			I
				Debit
				Debit
				Credit
				Credit
					Bal. Sheet
					Inc. State.
					Inc. State.
					Bal. Sheet

Charge customer paid bill within the discount period	Cash Sales Discount Accounts Receivable	CA S CA	I I D	Debit Debit Credit	Bal. Sheet Inc. State. Bal. Sheet

Paid invoice for the purchase of merchandise within the discount period	Accounts Payable
	  Cash
	  Purchases Discount
		CL
		CA
		CMS
			D
			D
			I
				Debit
				Credit
				Credit
					Bal. Sheet
					Bal. Sheet
					Inc. State.

First adjusting entry for merchandise inventory	Income Summary
	  Merchandise
	    Inventory
		—
		CA&
		CMS
			—
			D
				Debit
				Credit
					—
					Bal. Sheet &
					Inc. State.

Second adjusting entry for merchandise inventory	Merchandise
	  Inventory
	  Income Summary
		CA&
		CMS
		—
			I
			
			—
				Debit
				
				Credit
					Bal. Sheet &
					Inc. State.
					Inc. State.

Adjusting entry for rent earned (Rent Income)	Unearned Rent Rent Income	CL OI	D I	Debit Credit	Bal. Sheet Inc. State.
Reversing entry for adjustment for accrued wages	Wages Payable Wages Expense	CL SE or GE	D D	Debit Credit	Bal. Sheet Inc. State.

Index